CREATING EDUCATIONAL FUTURES:
CONTINUOUS MANKATO WILSON ALTERNATIVES

by
Don Glines

Educational Futures Projects
Sacramento, California

Published by

National Association for Year-Round Education
6401 Linda Vista Road
San Diego, California 92111

McNaughton & Gunn, Inc.
960 Woodland Drive
Saline, Michigan 48176

1995

Gratitude and Thank You

To Teresa Cantrell who spent many hours and weekends designing and revising the manuscript for *Creating Educational Futures.*

Disclaimer

BOOKS BY DON GLINES

1969   *Implementing Different and Better Schools*, Campus Publishers, D. M. Printing Co., Mankato, MN, 230 pp

1970   *Creating Humane Schools*, Campus Publishers, D. M. Printing Co., Mankato, NM, 280 pp

1973   *Creating Humane Schools*, Revised Edition, Campus Publishers, D. M. Printing Co., Mankato, MN, 400 pp

1978   *Educational Futures I: Imagining and Inventing*, Anvil Press, Millville, MN, 300 pp, 2nd Edition, 1980

1978   *Educational Futures II: Options and Alternatives*, Anvil Press, Millville, MN, 310 pp, 2nd Edition, 1980

1978   *Educational Futures III: Change and Reality*, Anvil Press, Millville, MN, 300 pp, 2nd Edition, 1980

1979   *Educational Futures IV: Updating and Overleaping*, Anvil Press, Millville, MN, 264 pp, 1st Edition

1980   *Educational Futures V: Creating and Foresighting*, Anvil Press, Millville, MN, 200 pp, 1st Edition

1988   *A Primer on Year-Round Education*, Association of California School Administrators, Sacramento, CA, 98 pp

1992   *National Association for Year-Round Education: A Historical Perspective*, with James Bingle, National Association for Year-Round Education, San Diego, CA, 48 pp

1993   *Year-Round Calendar and Enrollment Plans*, National Association for Year-Round Education, San Diego, CA, 42 pp

1995   Creating *Educational Futures: Continuous Mankato Wilson Alternatives*, National Association for Year-Round Education, San Diego, CA, 330 pp

1995   *Year-Round Education: History, Philosophy, Future*, National Association for Year-Round Education, San Diego, CA, 240 pp

1995   *The Great Lockout in America's Citizenship Plants: Past as Future*, Supplemental Edition, by William Wirt and Don Glines, National Association for Year-Round Education, San Diego, CA, 180 pp

CREATING EDUCATIONAL FUTURES:
CONTINUOUS MANKATO WILSON ALTERNATIVES

Table of Contents

PART I
IMAGINEERING LEARNING

PART II
ENVISIONING WILSON

Remembering Why

Outside Perceptions

Changing Beliefs

Understanding Spirit

PART III
IMPLEMENTING WILSON

Detailing Mechanics

<u>Ongoing Renewal</u>

PART IV
DOCUMENTING WILSON

PART V
SUMMARIZING EXPERIENCE

BIBLIOGRAPHY

INDEX

ACKNOWLEDGEMENTS

DEDICATED TO ORIGINALS
IN A WORLD FULL OF COPYCATS

Laurie Glines and Harlan Glines, who as students helped create educational futures through their involvement with the Mankato Wilson Campus School concepts, and with the Minnesota Experimental City ideas — a city without schools; their mother, Ruth Glines, who supported their participation; and current learners, Katrina Whitelaw, Samuel Maldonado, and Dylan Glines, with the fervent dream that their children will never have to attend a 1990s decade conventional school, or participate in the process of schooling — that instead they can become contributors to a truly new system emerging from the immediate transition, and eventual transformation, from schooling to learning — an environment without the century old practices, facilities, and rituals.

No child should ever be required to attend the traditional 7th grade. Hopefully those to whom this is dedicated, and parents as Polly Savage, Mark Maldonado, Teresa Cantrell, and Sharon Ray, will be able to contribute to the demise of what has long been an educational travesty.

Current K-12 schools must be replaced by far more personalized, caring climates. Buckminster Fuller stated it clearly: "We are at the dawning of a golden age — maybe — but only if we change our values, priorities, lifestyles, and institutions." His challenge, he stated, could be accomplished by individuals, who together, finally realize that they are the people, the communities, the governments, the school districts. Such an integration is an essential element toward creating a preferable 21st Century for humankind.

Laurie was a true pioneer at Mankato Wilson in breaking the traditional mold of the "middle school." Harlan entered during his "primary years." Both college graduates, they are symbols that the philosophy, concepts, and methods enabled students to achieve in their adult years. They were early volunteer educational astronauts.

The battle must yet be fought for Katrina to prevent her from being required to finish her "schooling" in a traditional secondary environment. Sam and Dylan, and future siblings, need options which allow them to avoid the self-contained elementary classroom environment of 35 students facing the chalkboard with one teacher all year. These young people, and millions of others like them throughout the United States, deserve something better than what exists. It is their individual future, as well as their potential for contribution to society, the nation, and the universe.

IN MEMORY OF
DR. J. LLOYD TRUMP

Lloyd Trump, 1908-1985, was considered one of the great all time educational leaders. An innovator, change agent, writer, project coordinator, speaker, consultant, he served as a personal mentor to many individuals, educational administrators, and college faculty. Lloyd learned the inappropriateness of 20th Century conventional education while the era of Dewey, the University of Chicago Laboratory School, the Gary, Indiana, and Nashville reforms, and the Winnetka and Dalton plans were still fresh — and perhaps more importantly, while the famous *Eight-Year Study* and its profound results became part of the education landscape.

He had the opportunity to follow the creative pioneering of Superintendent William Wirt, whose programs in Bluffton (1898-1906) and Gary (1907-1937), Indiana, had gained national recognition, especially the development of the continuous year platoon system, greatly improved school facilities, and exciting new curriculum diversity. Dr. Trump, as a principal of the renown Horace Mann School in Gary from 1941-1944, directed a program that had been open prior to World War II 50 weeks a year, 12 hours a day, six days a week, free to all youth and adults in the community; it closed for only two weeks in August. Depauw University was also instrumental in this mix, as Wirt had attended there in the 1890s, and Trump was a 1929 graduate. Both were involved, too, with the University of Chicago, where Dr. Trump received M.A. (1935) and Ph.D. (1943) degrees.

His visibility as a professor at the University of Illinois (1947-1959), where he directed the landmark staff utilization studies, and his leadership (1960-1982) as the Associate Secretary of the National Association of Secondary School Principals (NASSP) led to the famous Danforth Foundation funded Model Schools Project. Among his many publications were such titles as *Images of the Future: A New Approach to Secondary Education*; *Focus on Change: Guide to Better Schools*; *Improving Secondary School Curriculum*; and his culminating *A School for Everyone*. This later title vividly portrayed his philosophy and national concern. His 1960 film, *And No Bells Ring*, was 40 years ahead of its time.

He campaigned tirelessly with his wife, Martha, throughout the United States and Canada, and 21 other countries to help communities understand why, as Superintendent Marion Donaldson of Tucson, Arizona, put it, "Schools had to be significantly different if they were to be significantly better." His death in 1985 was a tremendous loss, professionally to those educators who counted on his leadership, and personally to those who were close friends. He and his efforts to build a new foundation for change should not be forgotten by educators of the 21st Century. The road to an ability to combine the coming technology revolution with imagineering to create new learning systems has been paved, to a great extent, by the work of this educator. Needed now is a new Dr. J. Lloyd Trump – in fact, many new versions of Dr. Trump – to provide images beyond what Lloyd could dream in the 1960s; current educators must implement transitions into, and transformations for, the coming century – and beyond.

Lloyd Trump was born in Waterford Mills, a small farm community three miles south of Goshen, Indiana, where he now lies in rest at the Violet Cemetery. He began his profession at the Jefferson Township School north of Goshen (1929-1936); was a superintendent in Marengo (1936-37), and Waukegan, Illinois (1944-47); taught at the University of Chicago School from 1937-1940; was a Fulbright Lecturer in Pakistan for 1953-1954; and was a visiting professor at six major universities. He was a pioneer wherever he was employed; it was with NASSP where he most dramatically influenced education throughout the nation.

His name became synonymous with the "Trump Plan;" he advocated that the typical high school student should spend 40 percent of the time in independent study – reading, listening, self-testing, recording, experimenting, thinking – in libraries, laboratories, shops, studios, home, and community – and through programs like Gary, Indiana, 30 years earlier, which were open late in the day, weekends, and vacations – all year.

Independent study was to be supplemented with occasional participation in large groups of 80-150 where appropriate, and in small groups of 8-15 often. Staffing emphasized team teaching and paraprofessionals. Courses gave way to areas of studies in all fields, beginning whenever the student was ready. Grouping of students was flexible, with continuous self-paced student progress in a non-graded environment a key ingredient. Students could vary the time they spent "completing" high school – not all would automatically spend four years – some more, some less.

In a presentation in 1964, long before the 90s fad of "restructuring schooling," speaking to a group of administrators, teachers, parents, and professors from five Tucson area districts and the university, Trump praised the Canyon del Oro and Walker Schools in the Amphitheater District, calling Walker the most exciting elementary in 25 years. To the audience he stated: The 60s innovations are not new; he cited his involvement three decades earlier, with team teaching, non-grading, flexible scheduling, large and small group instruction, and self-paced learning when he taught at the University of Chicago Laboratory School. He advocated that educators must provide environments for students to realize that they must develop a conscious desire to want to learn on their own, and be ready to adapt to a rapidly changing society. It is now more than 60 years — from his early experiences, to his 1964 speech — to the closing 1990s, yet schools are still trying to determine how to redesign the past, rather than to go beyond and create a new century.

In recognition of his ongoing efforts, in 1977, Lloyd was presented with an honorary Doctor of Laws by Indiana University. Following is the citation as written:

J. Lloyd Trump, Doctor of Laws

J. Lloyd Trump, internationally known educator, administrative and intellectual leader, you have provided all professional education with a new emphasis and design for instruction of our youth.

Hoosier-born and educated, you began your teaching career in your home state and returned in mid-career to give outstanding service as principal of Horace Mann High School in Gary.

Your emphasis on the responsibility of the educational community to respect and provide for the unique needs and abilities of each student came long before legal decisions for such accountability, and helped to establish a climate that demanded such commitment to individual rights and concerns.

The "Trump Plan" is synonymous with some of the most progressive and creative changes in the direction of the education of youth in this century, and your textbook, *Images of the Future*, still charts the course for innovative school programs.

Your articles in professional journals, your audio-visual productions, school surveys, and service on committees of state and national educational organizations have all brought accolades from your peers.

The Trustees of Indiana University are proud to recognize your accomplishments and your distinction by conferring upon you the degree Doctor of Laws, *honoris causa*, with all the rights and honors appertaining thereto.

SPECIAL THANKS

Wilson Campus School, Mankato State University, Minnesota

(1) To the students, parents, community volunteers, and media whose participation and support made the past 1968-1977 years possible at Wilson; (2) to the officials at Mankato State whose vision helped to design another Camelot; (3) to those faculty and student teachers who actually created and lived the dream; and, (4) to those special researchers who evaluated and documented the existence of Wilson — all of whom were part of the effort to IMAGINEER a new learning system stripped of schooling — a pre-21st Century trip to Mars. Those cited are not inclusive, but do represent a sampling of the personal dedication essential to implement another milestone toward the coming decades of educational futures.

Faculty

Mike Barkhurst
June Bayless
Dan Beebe
Gene Biewen
Tim Bothof
Gene Broughton
John Bull
Barbara Bonniwell
Edward Borchart
Perry Butler
Tom Butson
Ann Courts
Richard Coyle
Don Darling
Rosemary Doescher
Glenn Erikson
Ed Evans
Don Glines
Alan Hale
Dan Harder
Larry Herke
Lewis Holden
Helen Holmes
Darlene Janovy
Tom Jeffrey
Jerome Jekel

Orville Jensen
Iver Johnson
Olga Jondahl
Cheryl Kalakian
Arlyne Kline
Geraldine Kline
Karen Knight
JoAnn Lawson
Florence Matthees
Karen McDonald
Morris Nelson
Gail Palmer
Delores Paulson
Kathy Roth
Lynette Russ
Margaret Schmidt
Mark Schuck
Joseph Schulze
Don Sorenson
Louise Spangler
Cary Waterman
Lorna Wing
Marven Wolthuis
Sharon Woolson
Patricia Zbichorski
Laura Zeilke

University Administrators

James Nickerson, President
Kent Alm, Vice-President
Brendan McDonald, Vice-President
Merlin Duncan, Vice-President
Ben Buck, Dean
Duane Orr, Dean
Cheryl Temple, Secretary

Outside Observers

Ken Berg, Free Press Editor
Lowell Schreyer, Free Press Writer
Kathleen Long, Oregon University
Frederick Goodman, Michigan University
John Morton, National Observer
Charles Waterman, Mankato State
Jack Miller, Anvil Press Editor

PROLOGUE

Futurists, you will soon surmise, appear to be masters of unrealistic theory – until the futures they forecast begin to impact.

> - Earl Joseph, Editor
> Minnesota Futurists

It was difficult to title this manuscript. The content covers the future, past, and present. The book is practical in that it provides recipes for implementation, yet theoretical in that it envisions an eventual learning system without schools. The discussion goes far beyond the popular terms of "restructure," "reform," "redesign," "inclusion," "partnership," and "cooperation," yet addresses these topics in the course of the dialogue.

The publication features Imagineering, yet does focus on reality. It relates to holistic, alternative, positive school climate environments, yet does not limit itself to one of those agendas. The volume includes the concepts of foresighting, success, resurrecting, forecasting, excellence, caring, volunteering, transforming, transitioning, system change, research, community involvement, descriptive processes, and charter and home schooling.

The work could have focused on the public versus private debates and vouchers to illustrate that though private offerings have had the advantage, the potential for public choices to equal or exceed private has always been existent. When implemented with freedom, support, and creativity, innovators have proven a match for all but the extremely creative – those private entities which truly take advantage of their freedom from bureaucracy – or the very rich private programs – and even those have usually accepted limitations. Unfortunately, few public systems have taken advantage of their potential, and thus most have generally lagged behind the better private alternatives – they have remained "schools;" they have not evolved new learning systems.

The issues of poverty and at-risk programs versus those for the affluent environments, the multicultural diversities and minorities realities, and the inner city conditions contrasted with those in the rural farm belts are appropriate for the title, too. Societal factors as well as educational futures, and Year-Round Education as compared with nine-month calendars are considered. Individualized and personalized methods, interdependent curriculum, non-grading, accountability and assessment, the 7th grade tragedy, continuous progress learning, and the role of businesses and corporations are all addressed, as well as recommendations for successful implementation of the processes of change – and the concern for "inclusion" and "gifted" education.

Extending the school year/day as recommended in the 1994 *National Education Commission on Time and Learning* report will not improve the notion of schooling. Even if embraced, the concept is not new. Gary, Indiana, provided an excellent fifty-week, eight-hour day program in 1910. Needed now are systems for changed conditions, not more and longer of the same structure. For those especially interested in year-round education, the portrayed Mankato, Minnesota, Wilson program was a 12-month alternative, acknowledged as the most innovative public year-round school in America; its personalized continuous year calendar was the most advanced yet adopted. However, the aspirations reflected much loftier goals than mere rearrangement of attendance patterns.

The past decade, great concern has evolved regarding guns, gangs, and knives in the schools. The old problems used to be gum chewing, cigarettes, and spitballs. The chapters do not focus specifically on these issues, but indirectly address each. The described Wilson program did have students on probation with the law; many of the concepts have been used in several residential rehabilitation centers. Requiring all public school students to wear uniforms is not a solution for what needs to be done for the 21st Century.

When students select their own advisors and instructors, and create their own courses, resistance to attending school diminishes; discipline improves for they are more self-directing. Students monitor their own campus setting to help prevent drugs – accepting the fact that the use of them is an off – not on – campus option. Those in need of a Person Center are placed in a controlled environment with specially prepared instructors and appropriate structure. The focus is on the affective domain and rehabilitation, not the cognitive.

However, the reality of weapons and drugs on campus persists in many communities. Some first grade students bring knives to school and attack classmates. Such behavior cannot be accepted, but the school needs help with these youth. It becomes a community, family problem, as the "regular teachers" are not trained to handle hard core special cases or groups. It takes assistance from the police, sociologists, psychologists, and other such resources to determine the best plan to try to rehabilitate while still preserving a healthy climate.

The gang/drug/safety problems are acute and seem overwhelming. They receive great attention from the media. However – it must be remembered that the majority of schools in the U.S. are as safe a haven as they have been throughout the 20th Century – always the potential for violence, but fortunately not uncontrollable problems. Learning Centers do need to relate to and act on these dilemmas; for most school situations, the concepts described in *Creating Educational Futures* can be used – or adapted – to fit the community. The philosophy and mechanics have validity throughout America, including ethnic and language minority environments.

Though the manuscript does directly focus many pages on the Mankato Wilson Campus School, the majority of the cited topics and titles are interwoven with Wilson, addressed separately in related chapters, or alluded to in context of a given community. The book clarions calls for change, new community learning systems in the 21st Century, and moving from schooling to learning, while describing a successful program which could serve as a transition to the next decades in most every realm.

The mid-90s brought much discussion of the existing poverty problems and the effect of the conditions on students. The *Kids Count Data Book*, published by the Annie Casey Foundation, provided the statistics. A study by Greg Duncan of Michigan and Jeanne Brooks-Gunn of Columbia Universities reported that by age five, children who have always lived in poverty have had IQ scores on average of nine points below those who have never been poor – a gap not related to the education of the mother, divorce, or race. Poor children from all racial and ethnic groups were equally impaired. Nearly one-fourth of the youth in the U.S. were living below the poverty line. Society was charged with failing to see the connection between poverty, violence, and education.

During the same period, the Carnegie Corporation released a study demonstrating that the first three years of life are a dangerous time for millions of American children. Their chances for healthy development were jeopardized by lack of medical care, poverty, violence and disintegrating family. It was estimated that nearly half of the 12 million infants and toddlers in the nation confront at least one risk factor that could harm their future. The expansion of "Headstart" by Congress has helped, but the gains are not maintained over a K-12 period. "Evenstart" has not reached enough families.

As children near the school age, Rebecca Marcon, in a study of children in Washington, D.C., found that those attending preschool and kindergarten programs which push academics, as contrasted with child-centered, whole child environments, were much more likely to have low grades and exhibit poor behavior by the time they enter the fourth grade – regardless of socioeconomic background. It has long been recognized that half of intelligence development probably occurs by age four. Children learn to walk, talk, comprehend (some in two languages) all before school – or pre-school for those attending – without textbooks and curriculum frameworks. Most were not pushed; needed, instead, was an environment where they could grow naturally.

Educational innovators have recognized for decades that the K-2 school years were the most important in the state required attendance mandates – that more money should be spent on those three years than any other group of three, but traditional school districts have refused to recognize the research. The non-graded, continuous progress, child-oriented, affective domain approach has been advocated, yet not practiced on a wide scale. The value of the same philosophy pre-school programs has long been recognized, yet most districts have not lobbied for public support for the little folks.

Providing a community learning center – a beginning life center – with health, food, counseling, developmental, and child care services – is known to be a key factor – especially in poverty, low-income neighborhoods. Yet most children in these categories must "get by" until age 5 or 6 – and then be placed in a traditional reading focused school. It has made no sense. Further, "non-academic" curriculum can be academic – and lead to student success. The "basic R's" are not the answer for everyone at a given moment in time.

Mankato Wilson acknowledged these factors, and provided programs which attempted to meet each need. But it also recognized that there were affluent, or well developed, youth who did not require special food or day care services, or who were ready for reading by age 3 without any academic pushing. They created their own environment and worked at their own pace. It is important to remember that the schools are to serve all children – those in poverty, those who develop slowly, those who speak another language, and those who can move rapidly through conventional learning. Realize, too, that Wilson did not have the advantage of cyberspace technology.

Why was there a sudden surge to turn public schools over to private enterprise? The efforts in Baltimore where the private Educational Alternatives, Inc., was allowed early in its contract to operate 12 sites for 27 million dollars raised the question of why could not the Baltimore public system do the job? For the same money ($5,900 per student), why could a private company supposedly operate a better program? What was wrong with the public educators?

Why was Public Strategies, Inc., hired to run the Minneapolis Public Schools, always in previous decades perhaps the leader in urban education? What caused the demise to the extent that a non-educator was hired as superintendent? What could Public Strategies accomplish that educators and a school board could not? Even more questionable was the complete management surrender of the Hartford schools to the private Educational Alternatives, Inc. Hartford, too, at one time, was considered one of the better urban districts.

What were the Sylvan Learning Centers able to do to "beat" the public schools in remedial education? What did a 28 year old non-college graduate millionaire know that enabled him to apparently do a better job than the public schools? What will the Edison Project Schools of the Whittle Corporation be able to accomplish that, again, the public schools could not muster? Why should such private ventures be so far ahead of public educators in preparing for the coming Electronics Revolution?

And why can such as the Hyde School in Bath, Maine, (at $18,000 a year – early 90s prices) find success with troubled youngsters, and then slowly move into the public sector? Why could not educators adapt the Hyde School principles at public school costs to create success for youth? It has been a shame that private alternatives, in general – the Montessori, Waldorf, church schools, Hyde, Summerhill – not to mention the elite Andovers and Exeters – have been overall more successful than the public – especially for those ("gifted," "average," or "slow") who did not fit the traditional required for all school system. Sudbury Valley School, Framingham, Massachusetts, has verified this too.

Why has state after state seen the same headlines of the 90s as in a 1994 San Francisco Chronicle article which proclaimed: "Why California Fails On School Reform – No One Can Agree On Problems Or Solutions." Why nationally was the concept of educational alternatives for all ignored? Why did it become alternative education for at-risk, and why were those programs more successful with "problem youth" – or was it really "problem schools?"

Educational innovators have long known that creating massive upheaval quickly is a better way than to piecemeal parts. The Mankato Wilson Campus School made 69 changes at once. Most schools are willing to try only one to five at one time – and then they wonder why they are not successful. Even the prestigious *School Restructuring Report* from the National Association of Secondary School Principals found that it was relatively easy to achieve success with individual reforms, such as block scheduling, but stated that "not one school was able to completely implement all elements of a previously accepted model, and that even some well researched individual elements, as the continuous progress ideal, were achieved by only a few schools."

The partial answer to this dilemma in some states was the passage of "Charter Schools." Why was this necessary? Why could not schools-within-schools and other forms of educational alternatives allow optional patterns without special laws? Will Charter Schools be the answer for overcoming the inability of "school restructuring" to offer positive environments for all? And why a new round of schools? Why not concentrate on creating new learning systems – not redesigning schools? Why should Charters have to beg to organize, and then be forced to explain to parents waiting lists and lotteries for enrollment? Why could districts not offer multiple plans without the bureaucracy of "proposals?" Why not allow the "imagineering" of exciting descriptions?

Educational change agents have continually stated that public schools can equal or exceed private alternatives if they are allowed several keys to successful IMAGINEERING – imagining, inventing, implementing:

1. Freedom to create, to become NASA space centers for education – to innovate, to imagineer. Needed are volunteer astronauts – teachers, students, parents. There must ideally be open enrollment with choices of styles and district transportation – or schools-within-schools – or paired centers, everywhere. Required are creative persons, <u>distinct differences in programs</u>, exemption from all traditional requirements except those related to health and safety, and the option to be able to imagine a society without schools, or at least significantly different schools – in an effort to be significantly better.

2. Opportunities to implement fundamental subject programs with everything available, except for sectarian religion, that a private academic school could offer – or a "non-academic" special focus learning center – for those who want to remain longer in the 20th Century.

3. Choices of Summerhill – of student-directed, open, individual curriculum programs for those who do not want to be an astronaut and create for 2020, but who instead want a form of alternative right now for all levels – "gifted," "average," and "at-risk" – labels which need to be eliminated.

4. Support from the community, superintendent, board, central office to experiment. The *Eight-Year Study* proved that experimentation can help eliminate non-essential rituals and design new learning systems for the future. The obsolescent concept of a 4-3 yes or no voting procedure must be replaced by creative judgement.

The Mankato Wilson Campus School, among many other pioneers, proved that successful change can occur in a public school – that the public results can equal the private – even with a restricted budget – that it can be done with a community cross section of students – and that such issues as early childhood, poverty, private control, football, vouchers, dropout prevention, accelerated opportunities, fundamental options, Summerhills, and transitions into the 21st Century – can all be achieved, if only imaginative educators decide to break with uniform, group-paced instruction for all – break with tradition – and provide on a wide, wide scale – diverse, year-round, holistic, open-ended learning opportunities through transitional schools, transforming non-schools, and imagineered community learning centers for the future.

Wilson represents a breakthrough – past as future – but now current pre-schoolers will be alive in 2100 – not only 2000. The biological, and the technological revolutions are both evolving. Lloyd Trump wrote in 1977, that for the present, while schools still exist and are transitioning toward community centers, needed in addressing current realities are <u>Schools For Everyone</u> – not just uniform for all traditional patterns decreed by those currently in charge of the majority vote. Beyond schooling is learning – and new systems designed for a different society for the emerging decades of the 21st Century – led by those who volunteer as EDUCATION ASTRONAUTS – individuals and groups dedicated to flying the Mars learning capsule into the future!

PART I

IMAGINEERING

LEARNING

FUTURES

The focus is on the future – on new learning systems for the emerging decades of the next century. The concern is with the 64 global dilemmas and the changes that are essential if people are to create a sustainable society and a preferable universe.

Learning – not education or schooling – must lead the transformation away from the old Industrial Age paradigms to those of the coming decades of the 21st Century – a period of time given over 80 descriptive names by a variety of writers – one being the Compassionate Era suggested by Robert Theobold in *Turning the Century*. The historical Mankato Wilson Campus School of Mankato State University, Minnesota, though a 20th Century invention, portrays a possible prototype for the transition stages of moving away from schooling, through education, and ultimately to learning in an Opportunity Society – another of the positive interpretations for the future. Wilson, more than any other public school in the last half of the current century, deviated most from conventional schooling in setting an example of what other communities could do, if they decide to become an equivalent of the NASA space explorers for education.

Many descriptions of transitions toward future learning will seemingly dwell on the past. The exemplary Wilson School is portrayed in depth partly to archive it for history, but more importantly to assist educational futurists in using the past to launch new visions. The programs need to be interpolated in the perspective of creating dreams and implementing realities during the remainder of the decade. Approaching 2000, most secondary schools still have period 1-2-3 schedules; the elementary sites primarily feature self-contained classrooms; and the middle years continue yet with 7th grade core requirements – the same patterns that have existed in the great majority of districts for the past 75 years. Normed percentile tests automatically classify those scoring under 50% as "below average" – or worse. The Mankato effort offers documentation that such formats can be broken, and new approaches invented. Wilson is the past as future; Wilson is IMAGINEERING. Educational foresighting by futurists concludes that communities must seek far beyond the establishment Education 2000 rhetoric, and instead envision very different learning and living futures.

Turning the Century is a theme that clearly reflects this is not the time to restructure existing schools and patterns of schooling – concepts which are failing to address the potential of the great majority of youth. Rather it is one of the few rare lifetime opportunities to contribute to a transformation, moving beyond restructuring toward creating new learning systems. Realistically envisioned is a day when the present notion of school will only be history. Currently, imagination is more important than knowledge.

If technologically the space program can place astronauts on Mars by 2015-2020, then certainly in the next two decades educators can explore more appropriate learning vehicles on Earth. Moving toward interdependent curricula and related brain-compatible learning patterns are major elements in implementing significantly better designs.

Continuation of core subjects, departmentalization, and separated curriculum frameworks does not blend with going beyond – or even with – true restructuring – and that concept is moving in the wrong direction. Grade level proficiencies in reading, writing, mathematics — and the other 11 plus elementary school subjects — do not create preferable futures. Segmented semester courses are not the best teaching organization. It has long been known that many "important" classes — such as algebra — are obsolete. Two years of foreign language, five days a week, 50 minutes a day, 36 weeks a year, times two years — is a formula for illiteracy; yet to enter numerous universities, the student must become illiterate. High standards are false, for successful completion of high school in some communities is allowed with one year of a D- in art or Spanish or drama (meeting the "fine arts" requirement). A futures perspective does not vision such "restructuring" as viable.

Traditional educators believe opposition views are too critical, radical, and unrealistic. With all the national budget cuts, and negative reactions from parents and school boards, can substantive change really occur in American education? Futurists respond that it is now time to do the impossible, for the possible is no longer working. They call for Imagineering — imagining, inventing, implementing — and joining Figment and Dreamfinder at an Educational Epcot Center in guiding exciting visions on a Journey into Imagination.

Imagineering realities can become dreams; the proposed Minnesota Experimental City — a community designed for 250,000 people, partly covered with a geodesic dome, waterless toilets, no automobiles, community commons, and the latest in electronic technology — was planned with no schools. The city was the living learning laboratory. Everyone was a teacher, everyone a learner. Learning had finally become a lifelong process and no longer a cliché — and this was in 1973 — a city already with no schools.

To help people comprehend such futures, a key component was the DOR Center — disorientation, orientation, reorientation — for in accepting different ways of thinking, it is important to first unlearn the old before attempting to learn the new. Educators have known how to refocus schooling for decades; the problem has been use of the knowledge. The Designing Education for the Future Project in the 1960s published five volumes on internalizing educational innovation. In the 60s and 70s, acknowledged reform and evaluation researchers such as Matthew Miles, Everett Rogers, Kenneth Benne, Donald Michael, Gordon Lippitt, Egon Guba, Daniel Stufflebeam, and Robert Stake wrote extensively on the process.

Noted by all was that significant school change must be systemic. Part of successfully creating new programs lies in reallocating resources and a "do, then plan," not a "plan, then do" design. Too many districts spend years planning, but never achieve even piecemeal implementation. The battle of Midway beautifully illustrates the reversal of the traditionally accepted norm, for the Japanese made extensive plans, but failed in their objective, while the Americans adopted the "do, then plan" response, and won the engagement — and as a result, the war.

A form of "do" restructuring has occurred in some states through alternative education. Though the developed programs have helped many youth, and teachers have been sincere, the philosophy has been in the wrong direction. The original concept was educational alternatives (in the plural) for all, not alternative school (in the singular) for at-risk or non-conforming students. Uniform curriculum requirements and learning styles methods do not address the diversities even among gifted students. Where the few educational alternatives for all have been made available, there have been "waiting lists" and "lotteries." Can 21st Century leaders truly accept waiting lists for learning? If the programs are that successful, should they not be replicated? Systemic educational alternatives can create significant reform. At-risk projects and lotteries maintain the status quo.

Year-round education has been another positive breakaway from the industrial age in education, but unfortunately too many districts have sold the concept for space, financial, and achievement score potentials, rather than on continuous learning. Schools – like hospitals – as helping institutions, should always be open. Implementing ideas is not that difficult. In the March, 1992, *Kappan*, Glines and Long describe 32 proven historical improvements that could have been adopted in that year by any district "Transitioning Toward Educational Futures." However, communities looking at 2000, were still not willing to adopt even these old/new patterns on a large scale.

The research and development data has long been available to bring "futures perspectives and theories" into everyday classroom practice, as demonstrated by the Wilson Campus School, a non-graded pre-K-12/college site for 600 students. From 1968-77, it was considered the most experimental public school in America, operating on a normal budget, with a cross-section of youth in a conservative southern Minnesota community.

There were no required classes for anyone, K-12, and no mandated courses for graduation. There were no ABC report cards, homework assignments, grade-level tests, bells, textbooks, or schedules. Students developed their own personalized and individualized learning plans on a year-round basis. The 57 varieties of animals housed at Wilson were important in instruction. Students selected their own teacher facilitators and advisors. Kindergarten students had the same freedoms as high schoolers and studied with them in the same suites and centers. Though Wilson is now closed, the outcomes were further documented in a 1992 dissertation, and 1992 and 1994 videotapes. These pieces confirmed once more the findings of the famous *Eight-Year Study* of the 1930s, and validated the exciting period of the 1960s as moving in the right direction; it was not an era of fads and ideas that lowered test scores and destroyed standards, as depicted by those trying to defend conventional education practices.

But now, the more important questions address how even better results can be achieved moving toward and beyond 2000. The simple but honest response is again, as at Midway, "do, then plan." At the elementary level, one effective, quick method is the school-within-a-school. In a facility of 550 with 17 teachers, seven in Program A can teach conventional grades K-1-2-3-4-5-6; six in Program B can modify tradition by utilizing non-grading, year-round, team teaching, and continuous progress curriculum; and four in Program C can create their version of the Wilson School, including ideas from the Experimental City – their vision of the future. Further, they can achieve success by next year – or even the current year, if given commitment from the "system."

This does not require changing neighborhood boundaries, bus routes, or budgets at first. Ultimately "catch up" money is important for missing resources, but initially the program can be undertaken as at Wilson – with commitment, excitement, and options. Students, parents, and teachers select their learning style preference. Though not new in idea, if almost all elementary schools in the nation created similar choices, campfires would soon explode into forest fires creating an awesome systemic impact on education.

Obsolete restructuring practices of the 90s era would lead into imagineering future learning systems for the next decade.

At the high school, the elimination of departmentalization, department chairpersons, separate isolated courses, period 1-2-3 schedules, and ABC report cards could move mountains toward creating teams of professionals developing interdependent curriculum. If a big school is afraid to move together, school-within-school teams can pilot changes. At the middle school level, the elimination of the required syndrome of English, history, math, science, physical education, and "one other" would be one of the most exciting events in educational history. These current subjects and their topics of study, taught in classrooms of 35, are totally out of sync with most 12 year olds. The Wilson practices of the past prove the need to overleap reform proposals, and instead, dream of potential learning systems.

There are already more than 36 different methods of organizing for future pilot experimentation as the research and development arms of a district: paired schools, magnets, off-campus centers, district lab schools, cluster choices, schools-within-schools, and programs-within-programs to name but a few. All are realistic immediately within current budgets and politics, though these are only practices which have evolved during the 60s, 70s, 80s, 90s — not in the 21st Century. Yes, rooms need repainting and buildings are desperate for repair in many current districts; however, such realities are an excuse to leave most youth in self-contained and departmentalized classes with desks facing the chalkboard, and textbooks and homework for everyone — even for the most gifted. The Wilson program and methods — which will be described in detail — though not designed for 2020, serve to encourage educators that they can transition away from the past into the future. Even more and better educational alternatives are essential; new visions of what could be are required. Astronaut-style educational space centers should be provided for those who volunteer, even if the start is with those school-within-a-school four elementary teachers in Program C with a very limited budget. Flexibility and reordered clock patterns can be very important as a beginning. It is time to "revisit restructuring with a futures perspective," rather than redesign schooling.

When all seems impossible, the Wright brothers provide the beacon of hope: two bicycle shop proprietors who, without a high school diploma, changed transportation; they revolutionized the world! Surely the Wright brothers and sisters in the existing school communities can unite to help create a more preferable future for learning. Though in the coming sections and chapters, the focus appears to be on Wilson, the reflected vision is on the coming years; it is on EDUCATION FUTURES. Experiencing Mankato Wilson concepts documents that the practices are valid. More importantly, though, the intent is to conjure images of what learning could be in the next century.

In the following Part II, *Envisioning Wilson*, the first section, "Remembering Why," provides an overview of the program. The second, "Outside Perceptions," presents objective views from four evaluators who studied the school. "Changing Beliefs," offers the philosophy and commitments upon which Wilson was based; and "Understanding Spirit," describes the resolve that created the magic.

In Part III, *Implementing Wilson*, section one, "Detailing Mechanics," does just that by describing how the various components of the system functioned. Section two, "Ongoing

Renewal," in an introspective posture, relates the continuous reconsiderations that were part of the improvement process at the school – essential in looking into the 21st Century.

Part IV, *Documenting Wilson*, provides previous research and experimentation upon which Wilson was partially based, offers studies of the laboratory school success, and concludes with older references which were part of the Wilson vision, and the newer ones which form part of the futurists efforts to envision and help create significantly better learning opportunities for the 21st Century.

Part V, *Summarizing Experience*, ties the parts into a whole and provides a synopsis for review.

The manuscript has six purposes: to (1) envision the creation of entirely new learning systems; (2) eliminate the concept of required schooling in favor of lifelong learning; (3) offer transitional steps toward a complete transformation of education; (4) provide concrete examples of changes that can be made immediately and in the future; (5) document that the proposed structures are valid and are supported by research and experimental history; and (6) archive the existence of a school of the future in the 1960s which successfully implemented innovations not yet commonly accepted.

The proposals reflect perspectives for the future. They are drawn from early immigrant, big city, rural farm, and suburban professional communities, schools, and programs. Though Wilson was created in Small Town, America, the concepts have proven valid for current school and societal problems: violence, drugs, AIDS, poverty, demographics, and parenting. They shine, too, for gifted college prep, special education, famous "average" students, and wholesome learning and family environments. Implementation adjustments may be necessary, depending upon the locale, but the philosophies and methods are for Anywhere, U.S.A.

Envisioning educational futures, by transitioning through and beyond Wilson concepts, offers hope that eventually society will finally move from schooling to learning. Meanwhile, students need to be concerned with their present; they deserve significantly better learning opportunities and options NOW. Documentation that immediate success can be achieved, and for a far greater majority of the enrolled youth, is *possible when districts offer continuous learning alternatives.*

A semi-companion book, *Year-Round Education: History, Philosophy, Future*, expands the historical innovations of the past – especially in such pioneering districts as Gary, IN; Nashville, TN; and Aliquippa, PA – and highlights further visions of learning futures. Together they provide the challenge – to make tomorrow better than yesterday. A third publication *The Great Lockout in America's Citizenship Plants*, reinforces that commitment creates change.

A societal perspective of the dilemma is clearly stated in *Global-2000 Updated*: "If present beliefs and policies continue, the world will become . . . more vulnerable to violent disruption. . . Over the coming years, people must accept the death of 20th Century ways of thinking and being, and must prepare for the potential opportunities of new conditions in the 21st Century."

TRANSFORMATION

The past can be a prologue to an exciting future for learning, for there once was a site which for one brief shining moment was known as another Camelot, in education. The Wilson Campus School of Mankato State University, Minnesota, from 1968 through 1977, lived with the knights of the realm. The students, faculty, and parents, like that wonderful Willie Wonka, were "dreamers of dreams;" they made "realities out of dreams, and dreams out of realities."

Wilson was a beautiful story – another *Eight-Year Study* which needs to be recorded for future educational historians. It was one of the few truly significant laboratory settings, ranking perhaps with those at the University of Chicago under Dewey, and the Ohio State University in the 1930s, which involved so many of the then existing and future leaders in education. Wilson closed when the Minnesota Legislature eliminated campus schools in 1977.

In reflecting on Wilson, the model was never proposed as the wave of the FAR future, for 2020 and beyond, for even as far back as 1973, the plans for the proposed Minnesota Experimental City created an entirely new learning system with no schools. The staff believed that somewhere, sooner than later, in the early decades of the 21st Century, schools and schooling, as existed in the mid-70s, would become distant history. Looking ahead they knew that the projected technology – with so much written in the literature, but with yet so little effect on the structure of delivering opportunities – would, if nothing else, force communities to finally grasp the need to deschool the existing self-contained teacher classrooms. More important, though, then and currently were and are the human and environmental concerns; many people throughout the planet are suffering not only from poverty and changing conditions, but from the outmoded 20th Century concept of schooling.

If any of the 11 mid-90s grants provided by the New American Schools Development Corporation reach the promise of their visions, the breakup of the traditional school structure could move more rapidly than anticipated. Years ago, Erskine Caldwell offered hope when he closed one of his novels with "maybe tomorrow will be better."

Realizing that learning in 2015 absolutely should be different than through the modes of delivery in 2000, and knowing that the Wilson story mirrors only the capabilities of the 1960s – and must be reflected upon from that perspective – it is still an important study, for it clearly documents that for years there has been available – with supporting research – methods, structures, and prototypes of what could have been changed long ago.

Ironically, many of the Mankato concepts were borrowed from the 20s and 30s and even the turn of the last century. Unfortunately, they are yet appropriate in most school districts for transitioning into the learning systems of the next century. The program in Mankato became a completely unscheduled school; when learning is personalized and individualized, even daily master schedules, let alone traditional fixed ones, are not needed. The chapter on scheduling, which focuses on the mechanics of the daily method in the first two years of Wilson, is maintained as proof that it was accomplished, and historically to record the methods used in the infant years of development. Unfortunately, closing in on 2000, most school administrators still see it as impossible – yet that method was already obsolete at Wilson in 1970. To understand why, the mirror of Wilson returns the reflections to the era of the seventh decade of this century.

What is described is not "old hat" or "brand new." It is proof that schools can make successful, dramatic change "overnight" with the right philosophy and commitment. Wilson was far ahead of its time. When the descriptions appear as traditional, they only serve to illustrate how translations can be made for unavoidable conventional requirements. Wilson did not normally write "objectives" or translate work into "grade levels" or "marks," but where such discussion occurs, it is to assure those concerned regarding transitional periods, that traditions, if essential, can be accommodated by the experimental system. This Mankato program was developed long before the *Nation at Risk* report was produced, or the terms restructuring, at-risk, and empowerment became "educationese." Such 1990s "fad" terms as learning styles, cooperative learning, integrated learning, inclusion education, and strategic planning were never used, as such methodology was just common sense in the creation of daily learning opportunities.

In reviewing the influence of the Mankato Wilson Campus School, three periods should be envisioned. First, the future – 2000 to 2030 – where in the early decades of the 21st Century, learning would replace schooling; interdependent curriculum, volunteering, and ultimately Minnesota Experimental City designs with no schools – where the city is the life-long living learning laboratory – would be common; and where Wilson would only be witnessed as a fragile catalyst in the effort to "restructure" 30 years before the new century.

Second, those years of 1960-2000, during part of which Wilson was a reality. It was a product of the 60s, seen as too radical for the majority, but too traditional for those who envisioned the future, long before most could accept the demise of the self-contained elementary schools and the departmentalized, period scheduled secondary programs, which the "back to basics" movement of the 80s managed to further entrench. Wilson was part of the earlier era in which typewriters and ditto machines were still the "technology;" a computer terminal became available through Mankato State at the end of the 60s and made Wilson one of the first six schools in Minnesota to have such a "machine," and the first to use it for "primary grade" age learning for those who wanted to become proficient.

The third era, 1900-1960, must also be reflected upon, for Wilson "stole" many ideas from the *Eight-Year Study* of the 1930s; from the Dalton and Winnetka plans of the 1920s; from the research studies reported in the volumes of the National Society for the Study of Education; and from the year-round programs from 1904-1938 in Bluffton, Newark, Gary, Nashville, Aliquippa and other pioneering communities. Wilson was – "something borrowed, something blue; something old, something new."

The community of Mankato – the setting for the Wilson experiments – was predominately middle class white, Lutheran or Catholic, though as in most, there were the very high and very low income families and those of all religious faiths. Wilson was a cross-section of all of Mankato. There were students from the college faculty, but they were not the majority. There were traditionally labeled gifted and special education youth. There were those on probation, and teen-age pregnant girls, for in these latter two categories, the then existing Mankato High rejected them from the regular programs. The majority of Wilson youth would conventionally be labeled with B and C grades, though the cross-section also of A, D, and F labels provided a broad base for experimentation. The few ethnic minority youth came to Wilson, too, because of a comfort level of acceptance. The wheelchair students were there as the building was only one story, but the program became the retaining feature.

Though the staff did not face the extreme problems of the inner city environments, the methods, sometimes modified to provide a different structure, proved to be extremely successful where tried. The Center for the Person was one outgrowth, where those students who normally would be expelled, were given an opportunity in a "lockup" but humane rehabilitation environment. The focus was on the affective domain, human relations, self-image, and accepting positive societal responsibility. Wilson tried to pilot ideas that could be adapted for most all students, schools, and community climates.

This Mankato program was seen as wonderful to its supporters, awful to its critics. The staff often responded with quotations from well-known literature, as in the thoughts of a Wilson favorite, Don Quixote:

When life itself seems lunatic, who knows where madness lies? To surrender dreams – this may be madness – and the maddest of all, to see life as it is, and not as it should be.

PART II

ENVISIONING

WILSON

Remembering Why

chapter three

REFLECTIONS

Prior to 1968, Wilson had existed for years as a traditional model college laboratory school engaged in teacher training, dominated by the requirements and views of the controlling faculty of the College of Education, in concert with the officials of the local Mankato School District; it personified the best in conventional, traditional education. July 1, 1968, there was an immediate, massive, and dramatic flip-flop, so extensive, in fact, that within one year, a feature article in the *National Observer* newspaper called Wilson "probably the most innovative public school in America." Though Wilson was on the "cutting edge" of the 60s, as suggested, a number of the changes built into the "new" program were borrowed from the original *Eight-Year Study* of the 1930s, of which the Ohio State University School was a participant. It also replicated innovations borrowed from an even earlier era of Dewey and the laboratory school at the University of Chicago, offering additional validity to the results of previous pioneers in education. In other creations, it focused on implementing ideas for the 21st Century; 2030 was not seen as too distant.

Wilson reflected several key concepts: humane, personalize, significance, responsibility, individualize, option, alternative, choice, relevancy, quality, and evaluation. Goals related to decision making, self-direction, self-image, and responsibility were primary. "With freedom goes responsibility and courtesy," and "If schools are to be significantly better, they must be significantly different," were often used phrases. Knowing that Wilson would have changed again, had it not been closed, and that many of the illustrations from it and the *Eight-Year Study* should soon be outdated, the efforts at the Mankato Wilson Campus School serve as a practical illustration that wholesale change can occur in a school before 2000, given the desire, and an orientation to the future needs of the globe.

Wilson was publicly funded jointly by the state college board, the state department of education, and the local school district. Those enrolled ranged in age from 3 through 19 (the old nursery school through senior classifications), plus pre-birth parents, a two year old program, college students, graduates, families, and senior citizens, mixed together under one roof, along with constant influx of both preservice and inservice teachers and visitors. All of these offerings operated on the "average" cost per student for Minnesota districts, and were applicable to both public and private schools throughout the United States. The changes made could be accomplished by the majority; many of the ideas were successfully implemented in a number of other districts. There were no federal or private grants.

Wilson probably went further than most any other public program of choice in the implementation of nongrading, daily smorgasbord and non-scheduling, de-schooling, student selection of teachers and teacher-advisor-counselors, self-selection of curricular experiences, the elimination of all required courses and report cards, optional attendance, student freedom and responsibility, open choice for "elementary" age children, and social service projects.

To fully comprehend the programs, and the impact caused by the rapid transition that occurred (the same rapid transition is immediately possible in most systems with

11

volunteers, as options-within-schools, or districts), it is necessary to briefly focus on July, 1968. At that time, Wilson could best be described as a good, conventional school.

It was good in that overall student scores were "above average" on national achievement tests; a high percentage of those entering college were successful; and the parents as a whole were satisfied with the program. There was the same grouping of teachers as found in most every school: those who were rated superior, many of whom had developed excellent environments within the confines of their four walls; some who were acceptable but not outstanding; and a few who were weak in the existing structure, and probably should not have been teaching.

Wilson was conventional in that students and teachers had accepted all the necessary restrictions and rituals in effect in the majority of schools. The elementary youngsters were locked into "self-contaminated" rooms; the secondary school, which was in a separate part of the building, had a six period, fifty-five minute school bus-coordinated schedule. There were study halls, bells, hall passes, attendance notes from home, and at all levels, **the two great evils of the traditional system: group paced instruction, and group required courses**. The only opportunity to experiment was that which an individual teacher chose to do within the confines of his or her room, or in the fifty-five minute period, or in a back-to-back scheduling arrangement. Wilson operated as a public neighborhood attendance area school. Until 1968, the teachers received little help from the college, either in preservice or inservice education, because the teacher education programs, and teacher certification requirements continued to reinforce the traditional approach.

Implementation of dramatic reform was hampered by all the normal problems: no money, consultant help, or planned staff workshops – and inappropriate facilities and materials for the proposed changes. The new director came committed that Mankato Wilson either had to become one of the most innovative, experimental, exciting schools in the United States, or it had to close. Fortunately, many of the then existing college administrators and Wilson faculty felt the same. A dictatorial decision was made to attempt massive revision as rapidly as possible. All the staff had in common, among those who supported the decisions of the new director, was the commitment that schools truly must be different, if they were to be better.

The Gary, Indiana, schools of the 1910s, 20s, 30s offered one pattern to consider. They were open 50 weeks a year, six days a week, 12 hours a day. Students attended eight hours, but the majority of the time was spent in art, music, shops, physical education, play, and fun activities. The Nashville, Tennessee, efforts of the 20s, to break the "Caste Iron System of Education," also gave support to Wilson – and to the results of the later *Eight-Year Study*. These pioneer programs reinforced the belief that it was finally time for Wilson to eliminate the <u>rituals</u> of schooling.

The Wilson philosophy did relate to the 21st Century, for the primary concern was with the students – with people, with society – not mathematics and reading test scores. By the time the mid-90s had arrived, the Carnegie Foundation Report, *Country in Crisis*, revealed that one of four infants and toddlers were living in poverty; many of the mothers could not afford prenatal and infancy health care.

Reflections

Two of three pre-school children were cited as "at-risk." The report concluded that this nation could no longer tolerate children living in poverty. They needed pre-Headstart, EvenStart programs. Educationally, such early childhood dilemmas affected forever their world. Most never recovered to a pattern of success.

Though Wilson was not located in an inner city or rural poverty area, there were children who had special health and financial needs. More importantly, the Wilson philosophy was designed to address these societal concerns and recommendations; parent involvement, family leave, volunteering, and pre-birth through K-12 and adult programs were a way of life. Regardless of socioeconomic status or prior low achievement scores, Wilson was designed to relieve boredom, address the "gifted" too, and create a positive school climate which would lead an exciting completion of personalized student diplomas.

This Mankato prototype could not have solved all the poverty, preschool, and "schooling" needs of society and education, but its philosophy and implementation practices provided one model for how the nation could "take arms against a sea of troubles, and by opposing end them." The Wilson approach – the community in the school and the school in the community – was four decades ahead of the Carnegie Report, but it can be adapted by concerned citizens and educators to address the economic, family, and societal concerns bluntly stated in *Country in Crisis*. The "old" Wilson can assist in "new" positive actions for the Turn of the Century.

OVERVIEW

The initial effort in changing Wilson toward the 21st Century was to develop an ongoing program of innovation which would attempt to interrelate all the imaginative, exciting concepts in education. From the discussions came a list of 69 elements of change. The priority, human relations, became the major emphasis. In the effort to implement a potentially "more humane" school, students chose their own instructors based upon six "match" factors: personality, perception, age, gender, interest, and skill. Teacher and student images and relationships which match were often missing in most of the then existing other 1960s innovative programs which concentrated on the "mechanics" — team teaching, non-grading, and flexible scheduling; they were certainly missing in conventional programs where administrators made decisions on required courses, and students were either hand or computer assigned to classes on the basis of even-size enrollments and forced conflict-free time schedules (only conflict-free because they could not take three of the four singleton courses assigned to period one).

Positive motivation, self-image, daily success, and self-direction were more important at Wilson than the study of subject matter. Students selected their own teacher-advisor; the school did not retain the traditional counselor assigned to 300 students. Each teacher was assisted in being a counselor-advisor to small groups of 12 to 20 students (plus or minus) who selected each other on a mutual desire basis. This effort to create a warm adult-student match was the single greatest change made at Wilson, and did more to create a humane environment and positive school climate than any of the 68 others. The personalities of the students and teachers must relate to the extent that they can discuss, argue, hug, and make up. If this relationship does not exist, positive learning is difficult. The same is true for perception. The student must feel that the teacher perceives him or her to be a "great kid;" if the teacher believes the student is a "dunce," or if the student thinks the teacher has such a understanding, all is lost. Age also makes a difference; some students do great with the "young swinger in the short skirt;" but at this moment in time, others need a "grandma."

Gender is important, too; some students need all female teachers; for others it does not matter, while there are those who need all males. Some "first grade" students need Dad, yet most primary schools provide only Moms. The interest factor identifies that the student excited about butterflies ought to be matched with a butterfly teacher, not one who cannot stand boa constrictors, monkeys, and guinea pigs in the room. Skill is included, for if the student wants to rebuild a motor, it is helpful if the adult available knows something about this topic or is willing to learn with the youth. How many schools consider all these crucial, humane factors and allow students and teachers to find those mutually beneficial human relationships?

This personal touch in the selection of teachers and counselors led to personalized programming. Hopefully each student selected — usually accompanied by discussion with the adults at school and his or her parents — a program that was relevant to that individual at that moment in time. Students planned their own studies; there were no "teacher taught and school required courses." The curricula for each child was developed through individual conferences. Students selected their own learning areas, teachers with whom they could relate, and appropriate materials. Each person is unique; biochemistry more and more validates a philosophy of individual needs, interests, abilities, and desires. These notions have been written into practically every educational textbook published in this century, but until now have only been clichés; they seldom actually have been realities in the schools and classrooms. Yet the University of Oregon/Medford public schools 15-year longitudinal child growth and development studies directed by Dr. H. Harrison Clarke conclusively validated this reality between 1958-1973.

Wilson had no required classes, even for the "primary age" children. Attendance was optional as part of an open campus policy. Students could stay or go home if nothing relevant was offered that day, or they did not feel well, or had something of special interest elsewhere. To successfully implement such concepts, a policy of window shopping was followed. Students came to school and visited the many centers of learning that were available – those traditionally known as art, music, theater arts, mathematics, and 11 others, but which at Wilson were merged into interrelated learning teams; these varied through the years, with such titles as the Creative, Expressive, System, Communication, and Environmental Centers.

Students could study in any single area, or in any combination of interdisciplinary or multidisciplinary approaches they found of interest and value. Later Wilson began the development of interdependent curricula with a futures orientation; centers and teams were eventually to be replaced by more meaningful combinations. The ultimate goal was to create one interdependent learning system, rather than a compartmentalized school of departments and subjects, or one of interrelated or multidisciplinary teams. Integrated learning was a foregone conclusion.

In window shopping, the student looked through the "shoppers guide," observed what was being pursued by others, examined materials, considered resources, and had personal interviews with the consultant-teacher. If this advisor could help suggest a program which seemed appropriate, or if the student could devise his or her own, or if a combination of student and teacher ideas seemed to fit, the individual could start to work immediately. If nothing seemed to jell, he or she could continue to window shop in that center or in any of the other areas. There were no maximum or minimum numbers of combinations of experiences an individual could take, nor was there a limit on the amount of time to pursue learning opportunities.

The student could take two planned learning experiences in depth, (experience was used rather than course, as there were no pre-defined expectations or length of time requirements), or could be selective in ten to 15 activities. One pursuit could be followed total days for an exhaustive, intensive four weeks, or only scanned for four weeks; it could be investigated for 18, 36, or 66 weeks – the student pursued the inquiry until satisfied or until time and other interests led him or her to quest elsewhere. As the school fully developed its 12-month program, there became no need for any formal registration other than an initial one – with the agreeing teacher/team. When students changed experiences, the rearrangement was handled through the teams. The staff always had a "count" on "enrollment;" the student did not register for a "course," but instead signed to work with one or more adults.

Student progress was evaluated through learning goal sheets established in conferences with the instructors, and with the parents whenever they requested information or involvement. At least once a year there was a Family Designed

Conference for youth of all ages – where the parent, student, and advisor met to review the past and project the present and future. Much of the parent insight into individual progress was gained through comments or "chats" with students at home; but when teacher perspectives were desired, they were readily accessible by merely requesting a special conference, or waiting for the written evaluations which were made available several times a year.

To be able to respond to the parents, the areas being pursued by the student were recorded by the advisor-counselor, and kept on file in the individual folders. Their studies were readily changeable; students could start or stop experiences whenever it seemed desirable – whether November or March or August. The curricula was individually self-developed on a continuous progress, self-paced approach; there were no semesters or quarters or report cards, and obviously no final exams; there were no "fourth" or "seventh" or "tenth" grades. Students of multiple ages worked together; the appropriateness of the mix was the criterion, not the number of years spent in school. Kindergartners with seniors was not unusual.

A program was individually designed by and for each student. The diagnosis/prescription elements took into account student, parent, teacher, advisor, and society inputs. Theoretically, students might take, and many did pursue, "anything they want." There were no graduation requirements other than general guidelines that they had to complete "something" over a three to five year "high school" period, but tailored to fit individual students. Often in practical operation, the choice was made and modified through parent influences, teacher and advisor suggestions, and some colleges and employers demanding a union card (transcript showing a diploma with certain courses).

If students followed traditional restrictions, it was their option. They were told of the alternatives: they could plan for a future job or college based on maturity and other involvement factors; they could go to a community college or vocational school; they could join the army or get married; or they could make other personal choices. They were told many colleges no longer care about four years of English, three years of social studies, and two years of foreign language. But they were advised that some still do, and that if they wanted to be safe, they should take all the "right courses" – even though it would be an individual or small group experience, not a "class of 30."

To graduate, though, they could major in "basket-weaving" if they so desired. Wilson received state aid, and did give regular Minnesota diplomas; the students were not handicapped in their future decisions by lack of "proper courses" on a piece of paper. Many state universities have open enrollment policies, so no student was denied the right to attend college, though the choice might sometimes have been more limited. However, over the years, the students were not disadvantaged when submitting scholarship and university applications – even to the "best" institutions.

Younger students had the same choices and followed the same programs. At all levels, if the staff felt the student was making a serious mistake, he or she could be "required" to take a certain "course." A five year old may have needed help in the area of motor development. Wilson tried to make the program so attractive that most would select it; but if a poorly coordinated individual did not choose motor development, and if the staff was fairly certain that this was an emergency (the surgeon may make a decision about an unconscious dying patient when no relatives are known), the school could step in and "operate." The first year of Wilson, several of the staff felt that some, but not all, traditional grade one students needed a portion of their week structured during the "fall quarter," with a truly balanced group diet for the first few weeks of the "year" to help them learn to make decisions and know of their available options; thus some students were so directed. However, even these "guided youth," for the majority of each week, and in the early years, had personal choice based upon individual considerations.

The same structure could occur at periodic times during their 14 years in school, if students and staff felt that desirable. Most of the participants, most all the time, had a completely open program. If the school had ever returned to requirements, it had been decided to treat all subjects as equally important. Never would the staff decide that four years of English must be taken, but no home economics. Because of the importance of child growth and development, home economics for both boys and girls would be one of the first mandated. If requirements were imposed in a traditional high school, perhaps one year of each of 12 areas might be required, but selected by the student whenever the topic might be more meaningful and relevant at a particular time in life. Optional choice patterns work quite well, but for a school wishing to start more slowly, or for one of the school-within-a-school options being developed in the better high schools in the nation, such modest approaches are appropriate.

In the elementary, in the initial year of change, placing the 6 year olds in the early childhood center as part of programs for ages 3-4-5-6, or 5-6-7-8, works well. "First grade" students can have more structure, if needed, to start, but gradually wean away as individual readiness occurs, which might be at any age. Some will need amounts of structure at age 7 and 8, while others are quite independent at age 4. Overlapping age level teams (K-3, 2-5, 3-6, 5-8 is a good way to start the breakdown of self-contained rooms.) Wilson did that in the early months of the first year before going completely non-graded, K-12. Each school must decide on its amount of openness for young folk; the basic decision may be generalized for groups, but must be decided specifically on individual needs. The same applies not only to younger students, but to older ones as well. A decision must be made whether to let the traditional non-reader fifth grader avoid reading until he or she selects it, or require it when the prescribers deem best; Wilson found the former was usually best, but again it was personalized.

In the first year and one-half, before the realization of non-scheduling, students attending Wilson selected from the daily smorgasbord schedule. It told what "foods were available on the menu for that day – what fruits were in season." Most activities on the smorgasbord were student planned; all were optional; the daily program was, in most cases, determined by the individual student. The only reason for a "schedule" at all was to let students know if any special events were being offered, if any areas were closed, if a teacher would especially like to see them, or to indicate that a group had been scheduled to meet for some specific purpose. Ten to 20 percent of the activities needed to be cited – otherwise the menu was really not required, and thus was eventually eliminated.

The first schedule was developed daily by three persons; students could assist, but usually these were teachers and paraprofessionals who served three days a month, each on a rotation basis. It normally took them one or two hours a day to construct the schedule for 600 youth – later perhaps only 20 minutes. Initially there was a part-time clerk and a part-time administrative coordinator to handle ongoing schedule problems.

17

When the non-scheduled school emerged, no daily schedule was developed; these roles were abandoned, for when students and teachers completely organized their own daily routine, the need for two hours and three persons for scheduling was eliminated. After the founding director left, the new leader organized a "flexible quarter system schedule," where planned experiences were offered as options. This had advantages for traditional educators and parents, but notably more disadvantages related to assisting students with emerging learning needs, curriculum ideas, and future developments. It was done to accommodate the time frames of student teachers coming from the college, as perceived by those staff who were trying to provide a traditional student teaching experience.

The daily schedule, and individual biochemistry, demanded that food service be available all day. The assigned lunch period at a specific time was replaced by an eat-what-you-want-when-you-want philosophy, with a heavy emphasis on nutrition in the later years of the experiment. Flexible food service is important in an open, personalized school. Breakfast, brunch, lunch, and afternoon snacks were always available on a choice basis, though some hot dishes were options only during certain hours to provide for the realities of the cooks.

Wilson featured individualized learning and phase teaching. Once a student had chosen art as part of his or her personalized program, he or she individualized the pursuits within the field of art, or through interrelationships with other fields, such as in a combination of other "subjects" within the Expressive Center. Initially perhaps 80 percent of the day the students followed their own individually chosen schedule, although this was not rigidly fixed and varied from student to student and day to day. This was only a guideline; when "non-scheduling" was perfected, this time allotment moved to 100 percent; the student was often in informal groups formed through individual needs and friendships, but never required or scheduled by the school.

The first and most important of the five phases of "instruction" at Wilson was the one-to-one tutoring or conference between student and instructor. The curricula for each student was determined in this manner too. These meetings could be scheduled by the student and teacher whenever both were free; one-to-one sessions did not appear on the "master" schedule for that day.

The second phase involved open laboratory or open studio. This simply was "active" involvement by the student in some phase of study (painting a picture) where a teacher controlling a class was not required. When such opportunities were available, which was usually 95 to 100 percent of the day, the schedule merely reflected open studio under the "Expressive Center" column – the students could go there whenever they desired. Closely related to open lab, but of less active physical involvement was the third phase, that of independent study (reading or listening to a tape in the Media Center, or reading poetry in the Creative Center). This was usually open to all students in every area most days; occasionally there may have been a conflict which would close this possibility in a given location for part of a day, but other choices were always available as alternatives.

The fourth phase, small groups, played a major role at Wilson, but were only scheduled when students or teachers felt a need for them. A small group to discuss the topic of "student unrest" could meet when background study or interest indicated that such a session might be of value for those who would choose to attend. Students often met in their own informal gatherings. No groups were automatically scheduled to meet so many times each week at some specific hour. The fifth phase, large group, was of the common thread variety – always optional to attend – and was an example of the specials on the daily schedule; perhaps a well-known artist was in town and agreed to discuss art form and demonstrate general techniques to a group of interested students for a period of time during the day. When non-scheduling arrived, students were informed by interested teachers, word-of-mouth, and announcements on certain spaces on the walls.

The smorgasbord schedule – baked ham, roast beef, lots of turkey, broiled chicken, several salads, milk and juices, various muffins, steamed vegetables – good buffet, provided varied daily selections for each student. It is rather embarrassing if no one selects the music pie designed by Mrs. Jones. It usually indicates problems; Mrs. Jones can offer herself right out of a job. Attendance remained optional; if there were no students, there was no position for her – unless she was able to revamp her program, approach, and student relationships.

To conduct such a structure, considerable team planning, and less but essential amounts of team teaching, must occur. Teachers must talk with teachers about students, or the entire program collapses. An attractive physical environment is of value, too. Wilson had carpeted some rooms, had plants and animals in some, and had brightly colored red, purple, green, orange, yellow, and blue walls in many. Suites were created by cutting arches in the walls to replace separate classrooms.

Wilson developed a modified differentiated staffing pattern – doctors, nurses, nurses aides, technicians, and candystripers. The school program was available on a volunteer 7:30 - 5:30 plan – teachers and students came and went as they desired each day; no one was required to spend that amount of time in school, although many did – and not just the athletic teams. Wilson tried to become a community school, theoretically open 24 hours a day, seven days a week. Rigidities found in the state university system and the realities of budget prevented this, but the school did operate on a 12-month basis, always open for study except for two weeks of winter, one week of spring, two weeks of summer, and traditional holidays, matching the university contract periods.

The 12-month idea was one of the most successful. Students were encouraged to attend 175 days during the year for purposes of state aid, but otherwise came and went as they pleased. They could take vacation any week or month – whether November, January, or August. There were no reasons for students to be required to attend school only from September to June. Some parents can best take their vacations in January, if they work in summer construction trades or tourist areas, or perhaps in February if they are low in job seniority, or in October or March if that is the "slack" work period. Others have special needs if they are transferred or are unemployed and maybe homeless. Some families never have a good vacation together – even if they stay home for financial or health reasons – because of the insistence of traditional schools on September to June enrollment. Wilson students had a continuous, self-paced, individualized program, so nothing was missed if they were absent; they were encouraged to go duck hunting with Dad on a "school day." They could even get "credit" for learning while on vacation, if they planned for this with their facilitators.

The foreign language opportunities had great potential. Students were encouraged to take several hours a day of Spanish and/or International Studies. Immersing in the language over a short period of time made sense. Many went to Mexico for eight weeks or more each year; Spanish was difficult to learn in Mankato, Minnesota. Individual plans were offered for similar participation in other areas of the world; more languages were available, though Spanish was the focus.

Wilson staff believed students should be outside the school walls as much as possible. Many Wilsonites took their psychology class by working three 40-hour weeks at the nearby state mental hospital; they worked in local offices; they took social studies while on vacation trips with their parents; they interned in city government offices – all these not for pay, but for "experience completion." Wilson incorporated the off-campus direction set by the Parkway School in Philadelphia. Twelve passenger vans were purchased to enhance this process. Volunteering became a key as the Wilson concepts expanded into the communities.

Research and evaluation were weak in the first year of operation. The second year, plans were implemented to develop extensive horizontal and vertical studies of both short and long range duration. A staff person initiated "inhouse," while the Mankato State Office of Institutional Research took charge of "outhouse" evaluation. A research committee for the school was formed. Graduate students completed thesis work at Wilson. Studies in the affective, psychomotor, and cognitive were undertaken, with emphasis on the first two of these three. Significant data became available as a further contribution to the changing educational scene. Other than flawed "standardized tests," research and evaluation have been extremely weak or nonexistent in most school districts for decades in the United State. Wilson committed itself to try to correct that flaw; one of the things learned was that more innovation was needed in assessment; the "old tools" did not measure the program.

The school was managed through a Support Team: the "resident consultant;" a person for research and resources; one for the Person Center (for coordinating the human aspects, advising, and relationships); and an individual for administration (budget, scheduling, and facilities). The "directors" were autonomous persons who made decisions. If a "veto" was ever needed, it was wielded by the resident consultant (traditionally the principal). These individuals made decisions in their areas, functioned as a coordinating group for the entire school, acted as a liaison with the learning centers (where the curricular focus occurred), and worked with the various learning teams in small groups. Large group faculty meetings were held to a minimum after the first two organizational years. The learning teams (usually only three, but the names often changed along with the former "subject" combinations – Creative, Expressive, System, Communication, Environment) made daily decisions at the person level related to programs. Students made individual choices regarding their studies, and group decisions through several organizations. Learning truly was integrated.

Parent, faculty, and student advisory teams complemented the entire design. Parent involvement in the school program was greatly desired; a parent resource center was ultimately implemented. But even more necessary was student input. They helped make decisions at all levels, not just about Saturday night dances; student involvement is a major key to success in changing schools. During the first two years, the administrative structure was revamped and revised many times as the need arose, and as new programs, idea development, and improved perception became available. Students found little need for committees or councils, for almost all their concerns or requests were addressed on a one-to-one or small group basis with the teacher, advisor, or administration. The faculty, too, found less need for organization, as their concerns were handled in the same manner. The format structures changed many times over nine years; the examples described existed for a period of time; they are not a model, or the final design. They do represent possible starting points for those still locked into traditional systems.

One reason for a planning, design, or directors team; the delegation of authority; parent and student involvement; faculty decision-making; and parent, student, and faculty advisory teams, was the effort at Wilson to create an organization which would provide for continuous innovation, experimentation, research, evaluation, and dissemination each year the school was in existence. Unfortunately, most of the "name" innovative schools of the 60s leveled off or reverted. They stopped too soon — they did not go far enough. They did not continue to provide leadership toward change. Some schools must continually go "off the deep edge;" as the original "change agents" leave, there must be a mechanism for continuing to develop new and better programs.

Innovation is no longer a theory, nor change just a "bandwagon" effect. Educators, with a little creativity, considerable effort, and external support, can create different learning systems. The problem has been to find enough leadership — with the proper support — willing to go beyond existing programs. When that combination has finally been achieved in a few places, the leadership has usually moved on to "greener pastures" before the project reached its full potential. More money, better positions, enticing geographical locations, potential future, or just "battle fatigue" have led to the loss of key staff members in almost every innovative school. The replacements have often come lacking the training to step in and continue the ongoing efforts; they may have maintained the status quo, but many times have lacked the same "go-power" possessed by the originators of the project. As a result, education has had to wait for another "new model" to develop.

Wilson was one of these efforts; it could have plateaued or regressed as the others did, if it had failed to capitalize on all that is known about changing schools, if the school had been further cut by legislative economy drives, or if the director and college administrative officials who supported the project left too soon and were replaced by less committed personnel. The early "change agents" were a restless breed; in many ways this was good, as they moved and helped spread the notion of better learning systems. They sought new challenges; but the innovator ranks remained thin. Fortunately Wilson was able to maintain most of the key personnel.

To keep innovation projects renewing, "place" change agents (those who stay in one spot for some length of time) are needed, as well as "career" change agents (those who move often). Some must continue to transfer, as few in America have been willing to take on the tremendous task of rapid revision. The fad of the 90s "restructuring" in most schools has remained too long in the beginning stages, or has only been surface or organizational innovations; the impact on Pete and Sally — the focus on people, human relationships, and societal crises — has not been very significant. One of the great needs is for futures oriented "change agents" with experience in innovative schools to invade the colleges to offer options in teacher education, one of which would prepare teacher-consultants for future "beyond Wilson" programs — for communities without schools and schooling.

Realizing that many educators do know more than what exists, but that many current efforts never materialize, the Support Team organization at Wilson was established in an attempt to make it a long range project. Wilson continued to be successful; if the Minnesota Legislature had not closed all campus schools, more changes were on the horizon. Even though Wilson no longer exists, it nevertheless made a tremendous contribution to education by achieving exciting, rapid, immediate success, further proving that many other approaches are possible in education — that different and better future learning delivery systems can be developed.

Most schools have looked for cookbook recipes — they have wanted the "how" before they knew the "why." Other schools have discussed the "why" so long, they never reached the "how" stage. Wilson was a blend of the "why" and the "how." There is much necessary explanation as to why multiple changes should occur, for unless a staff truly understands the commitment, all the "hows" in all the books will not be of any value. Most schools use the lack of "how" as an excuse not to involve themselves in massive retooling, when failure to comprehend the "why," self-satisfaction with the status quo, and lack of commitment are the real culprits. The mechanics of a beyond Wilson futuristic approach are easy, if there is real dissatisfaction with what exists, and an honest desire to create learning systems for the next century.

In the final analysis, if staff are going to evolve more humane learning environments, they must take suggestions from consultants and books; look at their own strengths, weaknesses, and interests; examine their facilities, materials, and financial resources; forecast possible futures; and then determine their own patterns. They must "stay home and think." There are many guidelines, but there are not foolproof mechanisms available to ensure successful educational transformations. Through Wilson efforts, however, communities can now understand that their schools can rapidly and successfully change and improve. The Wilson program offered itself as an "idea center." If enough districts attempt new approaches, if they consider the future, better ways can be found to educate youth and the community in the 21st Century.

And Wilson was achieved before the coming **Electronics Revolution** and **Cyberspace Technology** which will completely change personal living and learning futures.

chapter five

CHALLENGES

An over quoted but excellent passage from President John Kennedy does relate to Wilson. In discussing the signing of the treaty to end the testing of nuclear weapons in the atmosphere in 1963, he said as part of his address: "But history and our own conscience will judge us harshly if we do not now make every effort to test our hope by action, and this is the place to begin. According to the ancient Chinese proverb, 'a journey of a thousand miles must begin with a single step.' My fellow Americans, let us take that first step."

That challenge of John Kennedy in many ways was the theme of creating Wilson. Changing the schools of the United States is a journey of a thousand miles, but it will never occur unless more educators, parents, and students take that single step. A few have begun. But history should record that many, not just a few, at this moment in time, reaching toward the decade beyond 2000, took that first step — toward the long overdue massive reform of American education — and even more, to the creation of entirely new learning systems. The elimination of schooling is the journey.

The 60s and 70s found a minority making an effort through team teaching, nongrading, flexible scheduling, individualized learning, carpeted buildings, and open pod designs. But these did not go far enough or fast enough, nor were they joined by the majority. They struggled against tremendous odds — lack of experience, untrained teachers, students who needed a new understanding, limited budgets, lack of parent comprehension, and the failure of the educational world to support their pioneer efforts. But they did achieve the breakthrough that makes it possible for dedicated people throughout the nation to show that with true commitment, hard work, cooperation, and student and parent support, education can create new optional, relevant, and humane learning systems.

Those starting will take much abuse. Needed are sensitive but tough hides. A number of people from all walks of life have had great dreams — goals that society cannot ignore. One of those is that someday the young people in the United States can be part of the fulfillment of an educational dream.

In 1968, educators and parents said that it would be virtually impossible to create almost overnight the Wilson School in such a place called Mankato, Minnesota. But it was accomplished, using futures oriented, for that period of time, philosophies and planning. History can record that one school during the nine years of 1968-1977 took that first step; a significantly different concept was successfully operating with its 69 listed elements of change. To be sure, many of that number needed improvement or expansion in the day-by-day implementation efforts, but theory was put into practice; the elements did play viable roles in creating a more humane school.

Had Wilson, as an "innovative, upside down school," remained open, it could have become an even bolder, different, better, futuristic learning system, or it could have reverted to a more structured form, depending upon the persons who became involved in its future. Those who were displaced when the facility closed continued to advocate change, and have tried to help create future Wilson schools, much further advanced than the old form; they could be instrumental in the complete revision of teacher education. Though the experiment at Wilson came to an end, all the frustrations, efforts, and final tears of sorrow were of tremendous value for the state and nation, and for the further encouragement toward the design of learning environments for beyond 2000.

As a viable, change-oriented institution, there were "next plans" in the formative stages, aiming toward a futuristic 21st Century learning system – both in philosophy and methods. But as further mechanical transitions, several in-between steps were immediately possible, with the Imagine Learning Center as the goal. One was the formation of programs-within-the-school. Even though Wilson was very flexible, it was not open enough for some students and teachers. A possible step might have been the identification of a unit where the adults and youngsters would have even less concern with courses, enrollment, teachers of "subjects," pressures from home, school progress reports, daily schedules, or any other road blocks. These would be adults and young people living together during the day, with a "headquarters" within the program, where they could design their own interdependent learning with utilization of the building and the world as a community. Individual students and adults were operating this way, but they were hamstrung by some pressures of the existing system. They needed an open-open maxi design, more 21st Century in nature – as in the proposed Minnesota Experimental City.

Some students needed to stay in the existing open program – it was working fine for them, as they had all the options of doing what they wanted, but within an organizational structure which provided some guidance through teams, daily schedules, advisors, and progress conferences. Students could increase the amount of planning assistance they received, so it was possible that all could be given the option of determining what learning experiences best fit their current needs.

Greater expansion of the school in the community and the lighted school concept was a must. This was being slowly accomplished through the vehicle of environmental studies and social service projects. Greater staff allocation, and priority in funding were needed to support significant research and evaluation. As in most all school districts, even in those where innovation design and evaluation are included in planning and operation, they are funded at indefensible levels; bolder steps are essential in education.

One of the major messages for reform is that education must build in mechanisms for ongoing, significant change. The traditional schools have designed new facilities, written curriculum guides, and bought different books, but the general format has remained the same. Many of the innovative schools have worked over a three year period to develop "a model;" then, in the name of quality and stability, they ceased being innovative. Wilson tried to show how schools could jump dramatically ahead in quantum overleaps. If continual retooling, which provides significant improvement, is not a built-in mechanism, schools fail to remain innovative.

The important factor is not Wilson, its faculty, nor its potential plans for improvement as a truly dynamic, ongoing change program. The major consideration is that Wilson, during a nine year period, created a dramatic impact on teacher education at Mankato State, the community of Mankato, programs throughout Minnesota, and schools in numerous other states.

It provided the courage to tackle the future. Thousands of visitors came. Two North

24

Central accreditation teams, looking at Mankato State, had the highest praise for Wilson as a model for change for the college and the nation. The staff went on consulting trips throughout the United States; articles written about Wilson were published in the August 1970 *Instructor* magazine, the March 1969 *Kappan*, and the November 1970 *Educational Leadership*, among others. Outside visitors wrote about Wilson in a July 1969 *National Observer* newspaper, in the March 1970 "Earth Science Curriculum Project Newsletter," in a 1969 issue of the *Minneapolis Tribune* newspaper, in the September 1970 *Examen* (a Mexico City based journal of cultural and educational information), in many articles in the local town and college news releases, and in other national publications, in addition to the two books published about Wilson — *Implementing Different and Better Schools* (1969), and *Creating Humane Schools* (1970). Even with all this, the school was planning major changes to move beyond its stop-gap Industrial Age innovations, toward building a method to eliminate already obsolete programs, and adopt Compassionate Era/Opportunity Society directions.

The story of Wilson is not to promote one school; it is presented as evidence to support the view that change is practical. Wilson illustrates that an ever-increasing number of teachers, parents, and students are ready and anxious for dramatic reform; it is to encourage those who have not yet taken that single step, or to urge those who have to travel faster and farther along the journey of a thousand miles. The years of frustration and success were rewarding and challenging; they further prove that the efforts started by a handful of schools in the late 50s, 60s, and early 70s were not proposed panaceas, but concrete realities leading to future change that will be relevant and humane, as people become more concerned regarding societal futures and the preservation of the biosphere and humankind.

By 1977, Wilson was already well into obsolescence, for though it was probably the most open, flexible public school in the U.S., it needed to move in new directions — to continue to revitalize the approaches to learning by becoming more futures conscious; focus more on adults as humans, not as skills or art teachers; truly create interdependent curricula and eliminate artificial teams, enrollments, and experiences; and have more students in the community and more community in the school on a continuous, extensive basis. It had to be even further individualized and personalized to illustrate that schedules were not necessary, with learning experiences that were not merely self-paced camouflages of the formation of groups whenever desired. Wilson had to have students in a true partnership; the world as the community; instant technological assistance; a better understanding of freedom; cooperation rather than competition; communication related to learning growth without unnecessary pressure. Such a summary describes programs coming in the near term future. Education must move into the world of the future — one that will hopefully be significantly different, but more importantly, significantly better.

Wilson was far beyond most schools — even those of the mid-90s — in reaching toward these concepts. Though the effort had to further change to eliminate its own obsolescence, the directions were valid, as most school districts need a transition period from where they are to where they decide to step — or overleap. Practical guidelines should provide further incentive for creative educational engineers who are seeking mechanisms for changing the structural base, and helping determine the best methods for transforming their schools into futures oriented environments. If educators have doubts regarding the feasibility of such efforts, Wilson should provide reinforcement, inspiration, and challenge, as learning seeks to reach for the unreachable stars.

chapter six

FINDINGS

The Wilson Campus School, in 1968, was determined to replicate many of the *Eight-Year Study* results of the 1930s and, more importantly, to take a step beyond. By 1976, eight years of implementation, dissemination, evaluation, and research had been compiled; the data included the extension of the program to pre-birth parents, preschool children, college students, and senior citizens. The entire K-12 student body was merged with these groups under one roof, where all ages of learners shared the same teachers, rooms, and programs as appropriate. The conclusions of the Wilson study verified that the original *Eight-Year Study* was still valid 40 years later. The findings of the staff justified the following statements regarding the Wilson youth:

1. After eight years, the reading skills of the students (including primary age children) were as good or better than students from traditional schools;

2. Writing abilities were on par, though perhaps the weakest skill; however, listening and oral communication skills were significantly higher;

3. The students reflected a more positive attitude toward learning when contrasted with youth enrolled in conventional schools;

4. They were involved in many more social service projects than students from conventional programs, and they were much more at ease in conversing with adults;

5. They had great success entering college with no grades, credits, class rank, or grade point averages, and without the benefit of ritualistic required college courses such as algebra and French;

6. The discipline problems were much fewer than in traditional schools, as was vandalism; both problems were eliminated;

7. The students were interested in a wider variety of topics than students from regular programs;

8. There were basically no failures, or students who dropped out or who did not want to graduate;

9. The early childhood program for preschool ages and beyond was significant, especially in the affective and psychomotor areas;

10. The students were advanced in accepting responsibility – especially in making decisions;

11. They were focusing more on the process of learning more about learning, rather than content, when compared with students from traditional schools;

12. Attendance at classes was no problem under a complete optional attendance policy, as they wanted to be in those they had designed or selected;

13. The non-scheduled and daily scheduled school organization worked better than the traditional yearly or semester schedules;

14. The teacher-advisor system was the single most significant part of the program;

15. The pre-K through grade 12 and college age mix worked beautifully;

16. Interrelated curricula was far more effective than separate subject teaching;

17. The precise number of hours per day a student spent in school was not especially important;

18. Students made greater cognitive gains in other areas of the curriculum — science, social studies, business, and all — than in math and reading; interest was a key factor in their growth;

19. The efforts to involve most students in home economics, industrial arts, and physical education motor skills made a positive difference in the development of the psychomotor domain;

20. Students taking Mankato State University courses while enrolled at Wilson were doing exceptionally well, drawing almost always A and B marks; this was true for undergraduates at most grade levels who participated in the program, not just "seniors," and for those students who traditionally might average Cs, but who received an A in a home economics or science (special interest) class. This was a tremendous boast for self-esteem;

21. The eight years of mainstreaming special education children whenever possible paid major dividends;

22. The remodeling of the physical facilities had been well worth it, enabling the teaming and free flow of students and staff;

23. The elimination of the traditional counselor and counselor role, replaced by a caring person-oriented adult-advisor to share — an adult-to-talk-with program — created exciting dividends;

24. The research studies conducted by graduate students from the university were of significant help in evaluating and improving the program;

25. The differentiated staff concept worked very well, as did the large scale involvement of student teachers and graduate interns from the college;

26. There were emerging significant differences in the lives of many students, as a result of their Wilson experiences;

27. By far the single most significant experience of the entire eight years, for those who participated, was the Mexican exchange program; and

28. Being open year-round for continuous learning provided opportunities for students not available at the time to other students in Minnesota.

Such data was gathered from over 30 thesis studies by university students, by surveys of parents and staff, and by observation of administrators, visitors, and professional colleagues. Further, during a subjective evaluation in 1976, many staff comments recorded both exciting advantages and improvements that should be considered; these were strongly stated, as randomly reviewed by the following 12 observations:

1. A great thing about Wilson is that the budget for vehicles (for off campus trips) exceeded the budgets for books and for furniture;

2. In eight years, parent attitudes reversed from being questioning or opposed to overwhelming support;

3. The staff is outstanding in areas of human concern; they could be more creative, more scholarly, and better organized personally;

4. The students, in general, after experiencing Wilson as compared with students taught in traditional schools, are more creative, curious, responsible, justice oriented, understanding of complexities, aware of global problems, developed as to who they are, and able to set goals for themselves;

5. The most difficult things for teachers to learn are advising, interdisciplinary and interdependent integrated learnings, and working together skills;

6. The program would be better if it were a four-day week, and if the fifth day the teachers worked on developing programs for creativity and critical thinking;

7. The program has been super for youth with problems, and for those from low income families;

8. The students are natural – not up-tight; they can relate to situations;

9. The non-readers need to work through affective self-image programs; when they decide to bloom, they really blossom, as beginning reading when ready makes a great difference;

10. When the program first started, it seemed that it would completely ruin music, drama, and sports, but the reverse has been true. Music and drama excel, and the interschool sports program is the strongest in the history of the school, including the first time ever as finalists in the state basketball tournament;

11. Complacency is one problem to guard against – the failure of staff to self-renew. Every so often a teacher should teach out of his or her fields – or even close down

the entire area for a short period to revitalize – to force further integration and interdependency; and

12.   Most students are involved in 13 to 15 experiences (courses) at the same time; a number have as many as 18 goal sheets; they are traveling in many areas of the world; they are better prepared for college than students coming from traditional schools.

Wilson made no claim to have all the answers; it had problems too. But it reaffirmed the accuracy of the original *Eight-Year Study*; it proved that a school can do everything "backwards" (as measured by traditional practices), and still be exceptionally successful. The Campus School was closed after its ninth year for political expediency – for the cost of constructing a new art building for the University. During its existence, for almost all who volunteered to enroll (a cross-section of Mankato, not an elitist group), Wilson proved to be a learning system that was significantly different and better. The staff did try to consider reality, and at the same time gather data which might support or refute programs, so that future schools could benefit from the experiences, possibly eliminating the need to "reinvent the wheel."

The evaluations of Wilson offer objective comparisons with the original *Eight-Year Study* of the 1930s. The "homemade" efforts at improving the staff relate that simple, cost-free studies often are as valuable to a school as expensive, in-depth research prepared by specialists. Every effort was made to continuously improve methods of communication and report findings, and as a result enhance the relationships among people, and the quality of the learning process. As the focus of these goals, students were evaluated often and extensively.

Reflection led to the decision by the staff and students that the administration and faculty should in turn be evaluated by the students; a system acceptable to both emerged from a number of discussions. Two forms were initially used for this evaluation; others were later developed, but these two pilots present the concept. The responses were anonymously tallied through a numbering system. Each teacher then received the results of his or her evaluation, and a composite picture of the total staff. The only ones who knew the score of a person were the individual and the principal; these two reviewed the strengths and weaknesses in an effort to maximize the potential of both the instructor and the supervisor. This open-ended evaluation philosophy did much to create the spirit of trust, warmth, cooperation, and adult-youth interaction which became hallmarks of the program at Wilson; it worked well.

Students completed the evaluation during a scheduled period of time established by their teacher-advisor. The older students used Form A, while the younger ones used Form B. The only difference was that A used a five point scale (5, 4, 3, 2, 1) while B used a three point (3, 2, 1). Those who could not read were asked the questions orally by a student teacher or other adult who was not being evaluated by the students. The instructions, questions, and forms which were used as the pilots follow:

WILSON TEACHER EVALUATION

Please evaluate your instructors in the same considerate manner in which you expect them to evaluate your work. Your instructors realize that they have considerable opportunity to tell what they think about you and your accomplishments, but there is too little opportunity for you to make your thoughts known to the teachers and to administrators regarding your opinions of them.

Today you can express some of your thoughts regarding the learning opportunities you are receiving as they relate to your own education. This form is straightforward and easy to use. Please accept it in the spirit with which it was developed, with respect for the honesty of the staff. Although you will remain anonymous, consider this a personal communication to the administrators and your teachers. It is intended for their eyes only, to help evaluate the adults, and to help them form ideas of how best to contribute to improving Wilson.

INSTRUCTIONS

A. Write the name of the teacher at the top of each sheet.
B. Read each question and think how it applies to that person.
C. Then react to each statement by circling the appropriate number according to the following plan.

FORM A			FORM B	
5 = Strongly agree	YES		3 = Agree	YES
4 = Agree	yes		2 = Undecided	?
3 = Undecided	?		1 = Disagree	NO
2 = Disagree	no			
1 = Strongly disagree	NO			

_____   _____
Name of Teacher   Date

FORM A

1. This teacher willingly gives extra time to students.	5	4	3	2	1
2. This teacher is enthusiastic about what he or she teaches.	5	4	3	2	1
3. This teacher listens to and respects ideas different from his or her own.	5	4	3	2	1
4. This teacher is able to criticize or correct without threatening or embarrassing students.	5	4	3	2	1
5. This teacher makes his or her evaluation of the work of students clearly known.	5	4	3	2	1
6. This teacher treats me as though I am a very important person.	5	4	3	2	1
7. This teacher is available to students most of the time.	5	4	3	2	1
8. This teacher seems to be interested in the problems of students.	5	4	3	2	1
9. This teacher makes an effort to treat all students fairly.	5	4	3	2	1
10. This teacher has a good sense of humor.	5	4	3	2	1
11. This teacher has a thorough knowledge of the subject he or she teaches.	5	4	3	2	1

My age is: 4, 5, 6, 7, 8, 9, 10, 11, 12, 13, 14, 15, 16, 17, 18, 19

My gender is: Male - 1   Female - 2

Outside Perceptions

chapter seven

SMORGASBORD

Several "outside perceptions" of Wilson further validate its existence and its programs, and provide additional opinions by neutral observers. During the 60s and early 70s, this school and others located in almost every state, managed to achieve rapid change within the usual parameters of any public school district – costs, conservative community attitudes, traditional facilities, inherited staff and students, rigid state regulations, limited flexibilities in funding, state department and college entrance rituals, scholarship awards, and athletic eligibility – all the real and perceived impediments that have continually hampered educators.

A number of church affiliated and private, independent schools were also able to achieve dramatic success within their restrictions. Both the tuition and public innovative programs were practical, workable models which could be implemented within the conventional education systems. This past ability to develop new designs provides futurists encouragement to reach far beyond what has been accomplished. Needed are persons who will overleap the "old Wilson" and focus on transforming education and society.

Knowing that individual and national breakthroughs are possible, more creative and committed social scientists, educators, and parents can develop significant cutting edge solutions to the learning and social ills of the nation and globe. There is hope, but dreams require action. Wilson needed further revitalization, for it was still closer to a school for the Industrial Age than a learning system for the next century. It required moving from an innovative school to futures oriented societal leadership. It did, though, promote a beacon, a lighthouse, illustrating that the impossible dream is a reachable goal within possible reality.

One description documenting the Wilson effort in its second year was prepared by John Thompson, Director, Earth Science Curriculum Project, at the University of Colorado. In the spring of 1970, he brought a bus load of science teachers and graduate students from Colorado to spend a week in Mankato. His article in their project newsletter reflects on the observations the group made of the early period at Wilson.

"Smorgasbord School"
by John F. Thompson
Earth Science Curriculum Project Newsletter

Would you believe a school without any attendance requirements? Where the students have total freedom to create their own curriculum as they will learn it? Would you believe teachers whose primary purpose it is to serve as resources for students and who issue no report cards or grades? ESCP staff members visited such a site in March and were excited by what they observed at the Wilson Campus School, Mankato State College, Mankato, Minnesota. The principal is Dr. Don E. Glines, who often lists himself as "vice president for heresy," rather than as principal.

The school started with its present philosophy in July of 1968 when Glines tore up the standard schedule and decreed that the school would become innovative and creative or close its doors. Some of the staff were not ready for the drastic change, but most of the students were. Instead of taking a few innovations and implementing them gradually over several years, Glines implemented 69 innovations at one time. In reflecting on the experience, he feels that doing all of these changes together was easier and more effective in the long run than working piecemeal. This is not to say that growing pains were not felt in all quarters, but as the school progresses toward the end of its second year, the program is functioning very well.

The Wilson School includes 600 preschool through twelfth grade students with a total staff of 33. The students had not been preselected and included young people of all abilities and handicaps – among them, children previously in special education classes. Twenty-eight percent of the students are faculty children, while the rest are from the local community. Wilson operates on a 12-month basis.

A schedule for the school is developed daily. Students may request special mini-courses or help sessions, teachers may offer special lectures or events, or the room and teacher may just be open all day for an activity without predetermined structure. Several students requested a mini-course in electronics, so one is being given. One teacher decided to put on a play and advertised for students who might be interested. He expected a few senior high students to appear and was surprised when many elementary youth came also. All will be included in the production. Several students asked to go to Chicago to see "Hair." They were told that if they could raise the money, they could go; they did and they went. When they returned, they put on an adaptation of the play for the rest of the school.

Another group wanted to go to Mexico to study Spanish and Mexican culture. Again, the students raised the necessary money and went for six weeks of study there. A bus load of Mexican students will be at Wilson in April for an exchange of learning and cultural experiences.

A computer terminal is in constant use by students from "first grade" up. Wilson students, in addition to the options available at the school, have access to the entire community and college campus. Many are working on topics of interest with professors, or with the agencies in the city, when the student projects concern local community problems or proposals.

The teachers indicated that most students take the fields of learning they would normally take in a more conventional setting, but study topics of their own rather than of teacher selection. If they are not sure what to study, the teachers serve as resource persons and offer suggestions. Students with no interest in an area do not have to study it. An Environmental Center has partially eliminated science as a separate subject and combines social studies, science, and home economics in a manner relevant to students. A Creative Center includes literature, art, music, and writing.

Elementary students are taking industrial arts. Since no teacher was prepared to teach this subject to younger children, the teachers learned along with the students, developed activities that interest this age level, and obtained necessary materials and tools. The former home economics topics include outdoor cooking, which is very popular with college and non-college oriented boys as well as girls, K-12.

Perhaps one of the most impressive aspects of the school is the spirit of cooperation among the students at all levels. Not only do the teachers and students make an effort to know each other, but the older ones are generally very willing to answer the younger enrollees questions regarding their projects. This means that the effective student-teacher ratio is much higher than it would be in a conventional setting with the same number of youth and adults.

An activity we observed in the "science" facilities illustrates student cooperation and real involvement in the learning process. Each of several students was going to check out for the weekend a baby rabbit from a litter that had been born at the school three weeks before. They were asking the owner numerous questions about such things as diet and temperature for the babies. One girl asked, "Can the rabbit stay with my kitten?" The group discussed this question and determined that it would not be a good idea, so the girl immediately arranged for another student to keep her kitten for the weekend.

Several questions are often repeated to staff members. People want to know how the Wilson approach works in areas like mathematics, how it works with special education students, and what the difficulties are in securing college admission without the usual grade point average and class rank. In "mathematics" (systems center) a programmed sequence allows each student to work at his or her own speed and level. When the individual decides he or she would like to work on a math related topic, discussion follows with a teacher who helps the person begin the study. When the student completes a packet, he or she might ask for a "unit" test. If there is a problem with learning the task, center staff are available for consultation. One day some students wanted help with division, so they set up an appointment for the following day. This became easier as the curriculum was integrated.

One of the teachers who had taught special education when the school had operated more conventionally could answer the questions on her subject; she commented that at first she had feared for the survival of her students under the new program. Now they are indistinguishable from the others and participate in the same activities. Occasionally a colleague will come to her with news of the outstanding work of one of her former pupils. The teacher herself is not considered special education anymore; she participates in all phases of the program as do her colleagues and students.

Another former special education teacher related an experience with one of her students who had special problems in reading. This youth liked to be able to come whenever he wanted to and work on reading. Consequently, he spent more time on reading than he probably would have under a conventional system. The teacher said this boy showed the best progress she had ever seen in a student with his reading difficulties.

The administration of the Wilson Campus School realized that the usual grade and class rank information required by colleges of applicants for admission would not be available for their graduates. Not wishing to hurt student chances for admission, letters were sent to a random selection of colleges and universities regarding enrollment without the usual selection criteria. The response from the colleges indicated that the absence of grades would not present any difficulties, so long as sufficient information would be provided for the college to make an appropriate evaluation of the student. This necessary information comes from teacher descriptions of their diagnoses of individual student needs and the suggested prescriptions to be followed to meet deficiencies. Each student selects an advisor from among the entire staff; this adult helps the student make wise choices and evaluates his or her accomplishments in regard to interests, needs, and abilities. Students applying for admission are being accepted at the colleges of their choice. About 65 percent of the Wilson students do enter college or other post-secondary programs.

The school is the only one of its kind that we know of, but one that offers great promise as an alternative to present educational practices. If you know of any others, we would appreciate hearing about them. We believe each school district should offer a Wilson alternative; the book by Don Glines gives some practical suggestions as to how to institute their program. Preparing teachers for such a school is our task — one we eagerly look forward to — and we thought our Burbank Class (see the article by John Thompson in "ESCP Newsletter" 21) was innovative.

chapter eight

TRYING

One of the first articles to draw attention to Wilson across the country was prepared by John Morton, a writer for the National Observer, who spent two days at the school. His visit was during those early "shakedown" months when students were still trying to test the system to see if their freedom was real, and while they were still adjusting away from tradition. It is valuable in reviewing some of the problems that were overcome during the transition period.

"Nothing is Too 'Far Out' To Be Tried In The Wilson School"
by John Morton
The National Observer

At the Wilson School in Mankato, a high school student spent the first two months of his junior year in the student center drinking pop, playing cards, and listening to rock music on the juke box.

He could have attended classes in science, English, and history just down the hall. But it is the policy of Wilson School not to force a student into anything. Indeed, he even has the option on a given day of not coming to school at all.

There is no dress code – some youngsters come to school barefoot (later they changed: Wilson students dressed exceptionally well after the first few months of "testing" their freedom), no report cards, and none of the traditional grouping into grades according to age. Students from 3 to 18 share the same building and some of the same classes. Individual programs of study are decided on by the students themselves; they also help design most of the courses. With attendance optional, a teacher who fails to attract students may be asked to look for work elsewhere.

'It's different' – this may sound like student power and permissiveness run wild, but some of what occurs at Wilson School may be a harbinger of education futures. Run by Mankato State College as a laboratory school, Wilson probably is the most innovative publicly supported school in the country.

The man behind Wilson is Donald E. Glines, one of the country's foremost apostles of educational innovation, who was hired a year ago with few restraints. "I will not say Wilson School is better than a traditional one," says Dr. Glines. "I am just saying it is different. We are trying to find something better. We can do that only by trying something different."

The Wilson reputation has grown and is sure to grow more during the coming year when teachers, school board members, and administrators from around the country are permitted to study it in large numbers for the first time.

There are other experimental schools, of course. Almost every state boasts at least a handful of public schools trying out new programs of some kind. The Nova School near Fort Lauderdale, Florida, for example, a pioneer in innovation, is ungraded from grades

37

one through twelve and soon will open an elementary school housing 700 pupils in one room.

The Matzke School in a Houston suburb is using a building without interior walls for its team-teaching approach. Marshall High School in Portland, Oregon, uses a flexible schedule that includes classes of varying size, duration, and intensity. Schools in University City, Missouri, a St. Louis suburb, have variable daily schedules and give students considerable freedom and responsibility.

Most such schools, however, try from one to a half dozen new concepts; the Wilson school is trying to pull together all manner of innovations in one place. Ideas rollick around among administrators, faculty, and students so rapidly that no single month's education program is exactly like another's. The philosophical ground shifts so fast that a formal statement of it mimeographed in May was out of date by July.

The 600 students, drawn from Mankato families on a volunteer basis, don't enroll or register at Wilson — they "shop around" for one to four weeks to see which teachers and fields of study they like. The teachers will suggest programs they think the students might like, and the students add their own ideas.

If nothing the teacher suggests suits a particular student, something special will be worked out for him. A student also can devise with a teacher one or more of three or four weeks duration "mini-courses" in a particular field, for example, minority rights, or major themes of the poetry in rock songs.

"The teachers act as consultants, guides, motivators," says Dr. Glines. "They advise, they suggest, but they do not force unless it comes down to the same sort of situation a doctor faces when he has a patient who will die within the hour if he does not do something."

Even this final veto is not exercised during the high school years. Dr. Glines is fond of saying that a high school student at Wilson can take nothing but basket weaving, if he insists, and still graduate. But the youngster is kept advised of the limitations this kind of program will impose on employment or acceptance at college.

After a period of "shopping," a student is supposed to tell what he had decided to study.

Students in lower grades have less freedom. Those in the preschool program and in what would be kindergarten and the first grade in a traditional graded school follow curriculums which teachers help decide, based on individual evaluation. These youngsters, however, still are turned loose to select courses on a daily basis and associate with older students. (Later there was much less structure for the young — they were as 'free' as secondary youth in curriculum selection.)

Pupils decide on their own what they want to take; however, teachers reserve a veto power. A "second grader," for example, may be "required" to take reading if he needs it, even if he does not want to (if it was deemed a "life threatening situation"). Similarly, if he lacks gross or fine motor development, he might be "strongly encouraged" to take physical education or industrial arts. Offering industrial arts in primary grades is itself an innovation. To date, none of the students has been "required" to take a class.

These youngsters have "responsibility hours" in which they can progress on their own, visit other programs, go to the student center or just roam the halls. "In the school I used to go to you had to stay in one room all the time," confides Leo Bosard, a "fourth grader by tradition," as if describing the deprivations of reform school. "Here you get to move around a lot and go different places."

To Dr. Glines and his staff, this mix and movement among young and old is an innovation that gives younger students someone to admire and promotes tolerance and helpfulness in the older ones.

Not all of the older students seem pleased, however. "There is too much of a generation gap," says Tammy Ollrich, a senior. And Bob Een, a junior, complains: "In their responsibility time they are supposed to be studying, but instead they are running up and down the halls, jumping on the furniture, playing cowboys and Indians — Pow! Pow! Pow!" (Later this problem was eliminated; the K-12 mix worked beautifully, once the students of all ages made the adjustments.)

How well do students do at Wilson? The program is only a year old and the real measure will come as Wilson graduates attend college. Several already have taken college level courses at Mankato State as part of their high school work and have done well.

Some students, randomly sampled, say that once they became used to responsibility, they learned at least as well and probably better than they could have in a traditional schools. None of them would welcome a return to a traditional system, citing the excitement and challenge of experimentation and freedom. "It works out about the same," says one. "Those who goof off here would goof off in a traditional school."

Mrs. Jo Lawson, an English teacher, had been fearful that the broad middle band of average students might suffer without the "push" of a traditional, structured program. "I concentrated on them for a while," she said; "at first, they just muddled along, about the way they would in a traditional system, but later, after the adjustment, they did significantly better."

The significant thing about Wilson students, says Dr. Glines, is that none of them is failing, only achieving educational goals at different speeds. "How can you fail a child in the third grade?" asks Dr. Glines. "It's incredible! The teacher has failed, not the child — 99.8 percent of the problems are caused by the teachers and the schools."

Starting this summer, Wilson is operating on a 12-month school year. A student can decide to go to school in August, skip September, come back in October, or whatever other arrangement suits him and his parents. "What's so magic about going to school in January?" asks Dr. Glines. "Kids can learn just as well in August."

Having students drift in and out in this fashion would pose problems for traditionally operated schools. So would optional attendance, since a student could hardly keep up with a class marching forward together with regular attendance and allotments of study.

Such traditional classroom practices provoke a tone of disbelief in Dr. Glines' voice. "All over America you can walk into a classroom and see 25 kids on the same page, working on the same problem, as if all 25 had the same abilities, same interests, and the same goals. Whenever a school claims it's paying attention to individual differences, it is usually hogwash."

Dr. Glines often compares the typical American public school education to a hypothetical situation in which a physician prescribes flu shots for all 25 patients waiting in his office, even though they might suffer from heart disease, ulcers, and a variety of other afflictions.

He preaches flexibility, and Wilson School reflects his beliefs. Thus, erratic attendance of students poses no problems. Each student is permitted to progress at his own speed to the limit of his abilities and interest.

Each day's schedule is devised and posted the previous afternoon (later this method was eliminated in favor of a non-schedule or hidden schedule philosophy) which gives students a chance to think about what they want to do next. Seminars are common, but formal classroom situations are scheduled only when a teacher has a specific reason for wanting all of his students together. It happens rarely.

A student completes a course whenever the teacher and he agree that he has achieved the goal he has set for himself. This provides maximum flexibility – for the student who can finish a typical 36-week algebra course in six weeks, as well as the one who needs 45 weeks. As for transferring credits and grades to colleges, almost all college admissions counselors queried have agreed to accept the teachers' subjective evaluations of a student.

"The great majority of high school students will complete their studies in four years," says Dr. Glines. "But there will be some who will do it in three and others who will take five."

As for the lad who spent the first two months of his junior year dealing cards, he soon was beset by nagging fears about never getting out of high school. So he began to study.

" I am still behind," he says, "but I will continue in school this summer."

EVALUATION

There were and have been outside evaluations of Wilson – of the total program or pieces of it. They include masters, educational specialists, and doctoral studies, legislature and budget reviews, comparative studies by the local district and college, informal surveys, and state department visitations.

One major report was submitted by Dr. Frederick Goodman of the University of Michigan. He was hired by the Minnesota State University system after the fifth year of the new program to complete an objective assessment to determine whether Wilson was serving a worthwhile purpose. The underlining is that done by Dr. Goodman. The report is typical of those developed over the nine years Wilson existed as an open alternative for families in Mankato, and as a research and development school for the state in an effort to improve, expand, and create learning opportunities for youth.

Wilson Campus School Evaluation
prepared by
Frederick L. Goodman
Professor of Education
The University of Michigan
December, 1974

EXPLICIT OBJECTIVES

An examination of written statements concerning the Wilson Campus School, and a brief but intensive set of discussions with a variety of people concerned with its operations yield the following information about its explicit objectives. Wilson exists to provide a school environment which is an alternative to the environments which prevail in Mankato and throughout the state and nation. The main features of this alternative environment are its "openness" and "humaneness," words which mean different things to different people, as shall be illustrated. The alternative exists not only for its value to the students who attend, and their parents, but as an institution in which those who wish to learn more about the value of such alternatives may try to do so. Thus it is committed to being a place to educate prospective teachers, existing teachers, and anyone concerned with the development of different pedagogical environments.

The familiar language typically associated with laboratory schools is, of course, used to describe this one. Wilson is to be "innovative and experimental;" its staff should do "evaluation, research, and dissemination." In this instance these words mean that they are trying to discover what happens when approximately 600 youth between the ages of 3 and 18 are provided the opportunity to study in a friendly setting where they participate actively in decisions about what and how they study. Further, the objective is to find out what can be "exported" from this environment to other educational institutions. The exports are to take the form of specific procedures like their advising system; the form of descriptions, advice, "workshops" and answers to inquiries; or the form of people who have acquired particular skills and attitudes.

Linkages between Wilson and the rest of the educational world are to be accomplished not only through the efforts of Wilson personnel, but through other faculty members of the School of Education at Mankato State College. The linkages are not necessarily to be established through highly formalized research procedures; the present goals emphasize responsible, realistic, fairly short or perhaps mid-range assessments of whether particular objectives are being met by students, faculty, and programs.

Although the objectives noted here are paraphrased rather than quoted from Wilson literature or leadership, they are all quite explicit. One finds them echoed and seemingly understood by the College leadership; School of Education administrators and faculty; the leadership of Independent School District No. 77; the staff, students and parents involved in Wilson itself; and even by those who have visited the school from afar.

IMPLICIT OBJECTIVES

By probing the operation of the school, two clusters of implicit objectives can be identified. As noted "open" and "humane" education mean many things to many people. They are words which frequently rally hope and doctrinaire support from "liberals"; fear and doctrinaire criticism from "conservatives." A major implicit Wilson objective appears to be to find a middle ground, to establish the credibility of "openness" and "humaneness" relative to conventionally constructed school buildings, stern economic constraints, and the vast group of citizens who have experienced public schooling as disciplined exposure to subject matter.

Wilson is viewed as an alternative school, not as the alternative. The innovative thrust of Wilson is in the direction of identifying operational gradations in the middle of a scale running from "license" at one end to "dictatorship" at the other. An emerging objective seems to be the demonstration of the principle that certain elements of "openness" can take root in a school which is not devoted to the concept per se. This usually involves striving for just the right balance between some kind of institutionalized structure, and recognition of the importance of "attitude" in dealing with that structure.

The other cluster of implicit objectives is fairly subtle, but of considerable consequence relative to the decisions that must be made about the future of Wilson. There appears to be an attempt to project the Wilson concept of decision making into other parts of the Mankato State College (MSC). This extends from a short-run goal like the encouragement of development of alternative courses of instruction for MSC students, to the long-run goal of developing an appreciation, on the part of everyone involved with the College, for the merits of sharing responsibility for decisions, carefully nurturing the judgments of those affected by decisions, and other aspects of open governance. There is, however, a sense in which it might be said that Wilson at the moment symbolizes this attitude towards decision making in the community, more than it actually operationalizes it, for it does not have many mechanisms available to it for carrying out the objective.

PERFORMANCE

The Wilson performance, in terms of these explicit and implicit objectives, has varied over time; it is commonly thought throughout the community that it has especially varied in response to different leadership.

As is so often the case with very young innovative institutions, the early years seem to have been marked by the need to try to "prove itself" through formal comparisons to more traditional programs. The interim report of the evaluation project commissioned jointly by District 77 and Mankato State College in the late 1960s quotes one of its consultants, Professor Robert Stake of the University of Illinois, as having written, "We will not understand the process of education in our lifetime." This, from one of the finest practitioners of the science of evaluation, helps put perspective on a Wilson problem.

Those closest to evaluation know that learning variables are connected in very subtle ways; experimentally necessary controls are difficult to realize, and time must be given its course. Still, where controversy is real, the necessity to attempt comparisons becomes paramount. The study produced by this group concluded in roughly the same way as the enormous *Eight-Year Study* of progressive schools in the 1930s. No one seems to be able to prove conclusively that either side has anything to worry about or cheer about with respect to things that are testable. This usually is interpreted as a victory for the progressive, for they can claim that as long as there is no significant difference in things tangible, the intangibles are on their side. That is where things still seem to lie with respect to Wilson and formal evaluation of the merit of its open, humane, alternative approach.

But there are countless other ways that are used to evaluate a program, whether they should be used or not. Basically, the "word of mouth" evaluation that was made of Wilson during the three and a half year tenure of its first "open" director was such that the proponents were left hoping for the best, and the ranks of the opponents grew, as doubts about lack of structure mushroomed. In retrospect, the drama of the period probably paved the way for the lower profile, consolidation efforts of the present director who has achieved the level of credibility now associated with the school. It is likely that neither the research effort just mentioned, nor the Report of the Consultants on the Minnesota State College Laboratory Schools in 1970, which praised Wilson and called for more money for it, while questioning the viability of other lab schools within the system, did as much to bring Wilson to its present level of confidence within its various communities as has the particular combination of directors, the first very bold and aggressive, the second very accommodating, yet fully capable of assertive leadership.

From this perspective it is understandable that a top administrator in District 77 should comment on the importance of the research done under the leadership of the present Wilson director, whereas in fact the formal research that has gone on at Wilson occurred prior to the arrival of the present director. His meaning was that the rate of innovation, perceived and actual, had slowed down. Programs in existence today enjoyed the benefit of more maturation time and experience in their planning, more sustained execution, and careful, although perhaps personal and subjective, evaluation.

There still are references to people who feel that Wilson is too loose, too impractical, too much a matter of wishful thinking. Repeatedly the observation is made, however, that negative criticism heard today about Wilson is largely undeserved and is based on past reputation and past personality clashes. Whether the remaining criticism is primarily a function of present observations or past perceptions cannot be fully ascertained within the scope of this brief study; but clearly the negativism is much reduced when compared to earlier years. Wilson is doing a superlative job of establishing credibility for the general idea of an open, humane, alternative school, thus meeting its major objectives very well indeed.

The evidence for this statement is overwhelming. From the relatively new president of Mankato State College who expressed his surprise at how little criticism of a seemingly controversial school he had detected, to the formal resolution of support for the continuance of Wilson, passed by the Board of Education of District 77 which provides Wilson with all of its students, people in position of leadership praise the credibility of the institution.

The Wilson staff has, for the most part, gotten across the idea that they do not believe that their environment is the right one for all children; thus evidence of personal preference for a more structured setting is not evidence of failure of the school. As a result of this, the vast middle area of judges – faculty at the School of Education, parents, visitors, and students – seem to be accepting the idea of an "open alternative" for some, even if not for themselves. Again and again the point is made in interviews that since the school costs no more per pupil to operate, and is so valuable for those who seem to thrive in such an environment, the alternative is practical and valuable.

DISSEMINATION

As for "getting the word out," packaging its innovations, and making a difference in state and national circles, the Wilson record is impressive. One of the things to remember here is that the Wilson staff is simply too small and hard pressed to go all over the place helping others, though the original director gave speeches and workshops in 41 states and provinces and wrote two books about Wilson during his five years at Mankato. The record for receiving visitors[1] and making visits is excellent. They put on workshops that attract all the people they can handle. But if their work is to be systematically amplified under the present budget constraints, much of it must be done by the School of Education, not by Wilson itself. This now seems to be happening. The Dean of the School recounted with pride the 80-100 students the summer workshops conducted by the first director addressing the "open alternative" had attracted each of the last three summers. Regular term workshops also exist, but a special point was made by one faculty member who requested anonymity, that the observation be made that the Wilson influence was not limited to those who attended special sessions, or for that matter even to those interested in an open school. Courses in nursing, recreation, speech, and home economics all were being impacted by the existence of Wilson.

A student teacher provided the warning that one should not draw the wrong conclusion from the fact that no more than 10 to 15 percent of those doing student teaching through the School of Education do so at Wilson. Not only may Wilson nearly be saturated by the presence of that percentage of students, but also one must not lose sight of the notion, he asserted, that many more students would probably like to student teach there if they were confident that the employment world was ready for them. They and their advisors are not altogether clear on whether putting all the eggs in the "open" basket is a good idea, when jobs of any kind are scarce. Actually the employment record of students with a record of student teaching at Wilson is claimed to be stronger than the record of those who do not. There is a question as to whether this would hold if the number of people so doing went up significantly. The student making the point was emphasizing something different, however. He claimed that many more students at Mankato than those who did their student teaching at Wilson were made aware of the

---

[1]Registration records make such figures easy to obtain. The 1973-74 Annual Report claims: Mankato State College Class Visitations – 479; Other College Class Visitations – 178; Others (e.g., teachers, administrators, board members, parents, elementary and secondary students) – 324.

viability of alternatives by exposure at Wilson. Altogether Wilson lists 11,090 formal contact hours for 112 students by members of classes, and visits by Wilson personnel to college classes.

Perhaps the most dramatic evidence of the Wilson systematic outreach is the extent to which it has disseminated its advising system. In the first interview held in connection with this report, the comment was made that the most significant word here was system, not advising, the point being that there was something tangible and clear that could be exported. In the last interview held, a one-inch thick notebook was produced, documenting less than a single year of efforts to show school systems how to use the system. At both interviews and in between, however, when the question was asked, "Which is Wilson's more important contribution, a product like its advising system or the attitude towards advising that Wilson exudes?" the answer was always unanimously the latter. This is offered as evidence of their success at meeting their objective of balancing the availability of structure with the importance of attitude towards the structure.

DISTRICT 77

The success of Wilson in its relationship to District 77 deserves special attention. It is clear that Wilson now serves a valued role as provider of an option for District 77 students. Not only has the School Board resolved the point formally, the Superintendent of Schools has made the point in writing and verbally, and has been oft quoted as having done so. There may be a much more important contribution, however, for conceivably District 77 could now pick up this alternative under its own structure if something should happen to Wilson. It is thus a great consequence to note that the Wilson goal of striving to develop a continuum of alternatives is being met by the fact that District 77 is now planning another type of alternative school, a bit less free than Wilson, a bit more sequenced with respect to basic skill learning. A meeting with District 77 administrators affirmed that this would not be a viable alternative without Wilson, for the present Wilson constituency would in all likelihood demand that the style of school they know would have to receive top priority. Should Wilson close, it would have to be reproduced within District 77; it could not be a school that was further along the continuum toward the conservative end.

It seems clear that this is the most dramatic way of envisaging progress toward the creation of more alternatives. There are also many examples, especially at the elementary level, where District 77 teachers now are influenced in the conduct of their classes by the Wilson concept. In one way or another then, at least under the present District 77 leadership, it seems clear that District 77 will not only be a receiver of the Wilson influence, it will turn into an amplifier of the credibility of the Wilson idea. The most likely step will be the creation of a small "school-within-a-school" of a more conservative type than Wilson, but very much influenced by Wilson techniques and attitudes.

SIZE

Size is of great importance to the success of the Wilson idea. Everyone seems to realize that many of the other attributes of the Wilson environment are a function of its small size. To those who worry that a school as small as 500-600 may be irrelevant to the future of secondary education in Minnesota, it should be noted that roughly two-thirds of the school districts in Minnesota list enrollment in the tenth, eleventh, and twelfth grades as smaller than 600. It is obvious to all that there are many small elementary schools; it is so apparent without checking the figures that there are also many small secondary schools. Further, it would appear that about one-fifth of the districts in Minnesota are small enough to have an all-age school like Wilson without being larger than Wilson. Of course larger districts can achieve smallness through the school-within-a-school approach as contemplated in District 77.

DECISION MAKING

The second set of implicit objectives addressed the impact Wilson might be able to have on the decision making process throughout the College. This, of course, is a "chicken and egg" concern, for if Wilson is to exist at all, it probably must exist in a climate that understands and accepts its principles of governance. Thus one is never quite sure whether a particular move in the direction of "open" decision making occurs at least partially because of the presence of the same factors which brought about the move in question.

There is some evidence that Wilson provides a focus for the "open" point of view on decision making. The evolution of the Center for Experiential and Alternative Education at MSC, with its program of studies in experiential education, has clearly been developed with the assistance of Wilson personnel and ideas. There is some small evidence that there is an element of "consciousness raising" with respect to the way decisions are made at Wilson. But the decision making apparatus at Wilson itself has been a changing phenomenon; any progress on this front is fragile at best.

FAILURES

In what areas has Wilson failed? There is a sense in which its goals are so high that it has failed all along the line. But that is scarcely the point. There are still pockets of resistance to the Wilson concept of education, in the School of Education, in other parts of the College, in District 77, in the state. Some of this is the failure of many to understand the difference between the concept of an alternative, and the concept of an "open" school as the alternative to traditional education; i.e., that the school is simply not intended for every child. But that in itself may be a failure of Wilson, for this is eventually one of their goals. They are making large strides here, but they have not yet fully succeeded.

At a different level, failure to gain more than a two-year-at-a-time "lease on life," in the sense that the special legislative appropriation that makes Wilson possible in its present form must be renewed every two years, has resulted in a morale problem and a drain on the leadership of the school. They fail to do as much as they might, for they always are busy fighting for their life.

Decision making structures between staff and parents have not been clarified to an optimal degree; although there is strong evidence that parent involvement is genuine, there is the matter of some simply not "feeling involved." There has been a failure to obtain all the library resources that are necessary for a superior program, perhaps because of the need to coordinate and justify in competition with the many constituencies within Mankato State College, as contrasted to more decentralized purchasing structures, visible in District 77.

As acknowledged, and partially discussed earlier, it has also failed to document positively the worthiness of its programs with a certain kind of formal research. To some minds this may be an overwhelming failure; to others it may be entirely excusable on the

46

grounds already mentioned, or simply because it is "still too soon to say." With this point in mind, it may be well to try to set the decision to continue or close a particular laboratory school in the context of the alleged national trend towards closing lab schools.

NATIONAL TRENDS

In the latter part of the 1960s, a period which saw the close of many college and university lab schools, the U.S. Office of Education was attempting to oversee the expenditure of millions of new federal dollars made available by the Elementary and Secondary Education Act of 1965. Research dollars were available; program dollars were available; demonstration and dissemination dollars were available. In this context lab schools not only were dwarfed, they were rendered suspect by the strong social currents of the period which suggested they served elite, irrelevant portions of society. Without developing this point extensively, it should be noted that one of the proposals that was received with considerable enthusiasm at the Office of Education in those years was a proposal to create a Regional Education Laboratory in Minnesota. This was to be but part of a network of labs; it was to bring people in colleges and universities together with people in elementary and secondary schools in new ways. Theory was to be blended with practice; research was to flow into development; and practical dissemination was to follow. The Minnesota proposal was judged one of the very best.

The linkages between the Wilson School and other educational groups are exemplary; they exist with the School of Education at Mankato State; the public schools of District 77 and southern Minnesota; the parochial schools in the area; Gustavus Adolphus University; schools in Wisconsin, Iowa, Illinois, and North Dakota; and the open school in St. Paul; linkages exist between old people in the parent generated "Grandparents Program;" preschoolers in Wilson; and secondary students doing social work in the community. The dean of the prestigious School of Education at the University of Massachusetts would suggest that these are exactly the type of linkages which were hoped for in the Regional Educational Labs. There is no federally funded regional education lab in Minnesota; there is, in Wilson, something which is trying to accomplish remarkably similar purposes. It would take very doctrinaire thinking indeed to declare that because lab schools in general have been closing, this one should close. The diversity and representativeness of its student body alone differentiates it from many of the lab schools that were phased out during the period of relatively available marginal research dollars.

THE EFFECTS OF CLOSING WILSON

The particular efforts of closing the Wilson Campus School can now be summarized.

The School of Education would lose its most exciting and possibly most effective program. Its one national claim to fame would disappear.

District 77 would lose a very attractive present alternative, and the opportunity to create still another one which is clearly on the horizon. The net effect of this is to deprive everyone of an example of seeing how a fairly well articulated scheme of alternatives can be handled. This is absolutely critical to the development of the concept of multiple alternatives, which is usually the implicit meaning of "alternative school," but which is seldom made explicit. Elementary and secondary education in Minnesota would lose a very significant model of credible open education, and its best opportunity to prepare and certify people to do this work throughout the schools of the state.

Mankato State College stands to lose in a subtle but perhaps very strategic way. The point has been made that Wilson stands for a style of decision making which features sharing, mutual respect and concern for those who will be most affected by the decision. This may be more symbolic than real in terms of its actual impact on the College. <u>But one should not lose sight of its symbolic value</u>. If everyone moves from the Lower Campus to Upper Campus, in a move which is inspired partially by program concerns, but largely by strictly economic reasoning, it is likely to be perceived by those involved as entirely a matter of economics, and "top-down" insensitive economics at that. Whether Wilson stays in its building or not after the move, the spatial fit will be constricted; some relatively new buildings will have been conspicuously abandoned, people will be operating under all kinds of tighter reins, and unless something drastic happens to the economy, <u>further</u> budgeting crises are likely to appear imminent.

<u>If Wilson is converted and lost, the decision will be seen as one which was made in a spirit that is not in the least compatible with everything that Wilson stands for</u>. The process which was actually used to make the decision, a rational approach to decision making under very tight constraints, should probably have room within it to accommodate the concerns for rationality manifested by those who live the longest with that particular decision. The community feeling for Wilson is too high to allow the institution to be closed without paying a high price in morale, respect, and trust. The need for good will, in the face of a consolidation such as this, should be considered very carefully.

All of these points, including the impact on the morale and effectiveness of the College, should be seen as important <u>educational</u> effects. Basically, Wilson is well-known as a pace-setter throughout the state. To the extent that it is not well-known, it should be; for it is deservedly well-known throughout the country by knowledgeable people in "alternative" and "open" educational circles.

CLOSING

The Minnesota Legislature officially closed the laboratory schools at the state colleges, but had the former president of Mankato State not retired and his assistants not accepted new positions, Wilson almost certainly would have remained open. However, the new president had a different agenda – the merger of two campuses. The new district superintendent and newly elected board also wanted Wilson closed to add 600 students to their overbuilt facilities; the original director had left Mankato; thus, in 1977, the initiators of the Wilson experiment were no longer involved with the decisions affecting its future.

As a result of local politics, not only sadness, but bitterness arose in the Mankato community. The new president withdrew support; the board voted 4-3 not to move Wilson intact to the proposed Union School site. The article, "An Open School is Closed" in the *North Country Anvil*, written by Charles Waterman and Jack Miller, describes their views of the Wilson successes and the disbelief that a state and district would let such a noble experiment so ingloriously close. The students did everything in their power to save their school, but it was not to be, in the era of the late 70s.

"An Open School is Closed"
by Charles Waterman with Jack Miller
North Country Anvil
Millville, MN

One of the most important educational concepts of the last ten years in America is variously known as "alternative education," (preferably educational alternatives in the plural), or by some – in the headier days of the antiwar period – "the free school movement." Whatever the descriptive, the basic concepts were essentially the same, though implemented differently: an education in which both students and faculty, backed by parents, were free from the authoritarian and bureaucratic rigidities that have oppressed American public schools.

Of the thousands of places where the idea of alternatives in education has been tried, few have produced a more impressive model than the Wilson Campus School in Mankato, Minnesota. Founded in 1896 as a "lab" school for Mankato State College, it was converted to an experimental school in 1968 under the direction of Dr. Don Glines, who has a well-deserved national reputation as an educational innovator for what he did at Wilson and has done elsewhere.

Glines began by abolishing grades and compulsory attendance. He made teachers first, and most importantly, advisors for students. He made parents important.

Here are some observations about Wilson by one of the 600 students, from nursery to 12th graders, now at the school:

"One of the myths is that because Wilson has no attendance requirement you can't get them to go to school. After I'd been here a few weeks, I saw it was fun, and now my parents have trouble getting me to stay away when I'm sick . . . "You go to a traditional school and they teach you the basics. What they don't teach you are things like dirty politics that you're gonna run into and they don't teach you responsibility. They teach you how to fit into the world as it is, and not how to go out and change the world . . . 'cause the world's in a sorry state of affairs."   – Tim Vaughn

One teacher says of Wilson that "The chances for relationships are fantastic. It's kind of, to me, like an extended family, where if you don't go along with one of the members you've got lots of others to go to."

Donna Vogel, a parent, says: "To me it is the right of every young person to have this kind of an education. Open education builds creativity, is humane, gives people choices and builds responsibility."

The offerings at Wilson number in the hundreds. In addition to the usual math, science, reading, writing and physical education, you find such things as animal care; Bach, Beethoven, Brahms & Bartok; cultural differences; death; health food; insurance; coping with divorce; log cabin construction; organic farming, natural farming & living with the earth; native American arts; people's rights, personal and social development; political systems; Russian; living on your own; U.S. labor history; weather; women's history and women's rights.

Within a couple of years of Glines' dramatic turnaround of Wilson in 1968, the school began to exert a strong and quiet influence, through example, on public school education nationwide. It did this by making educators aware that something workable, and yet akin to the "open" residential school of A. S. Neill in England, could actually be applied to U.S. public education. What happened at Wilson was quiet dynamite. Even *Time* magazine noted, and understood, what was happening at Wilson.

At a time when public education – the very heart of the liberal democratic dream – was failing; when millions of students weren't learning and many educational systems were reduced practically to trying to keep the students from tearing up the schools . . . in the midst of this malaise came the message from Wilson: <u>Here is a method that works</u>. And it works not only for the educationally oriented sons and daughters of professors and professionals. It works for all kinds of kids, including the large number of officially designated juvenile delinquents who have been assigned to Wilson over the years.

Glines, a professional educational theorist teaching at Mankato State, was put in charge of the "lab" school and told to undertake experiments. Glines decided that these should not be isolated and temporary "experiments" of the kind traditionally conducted by lab schools. Plenty of experiments already had been done. Glines felt that the school instead should demonstrate <u>practical results</u> of alternatives in education theory.

So he began working on at least two planes at once, setting up, within the college, a school of educational alternatives, to prepare college students for teaching in alternatives; and, through his directorship of Wilson Campus School, establishing what he saw as a realizable alternative to the traditional structured-education, students-behind-their-desks approach, which most teacher education institutions around the country were, and still basically are, following. He wanted Wilson to be something that could be followed and realized by any public school district anywhere which wanted to create educational alternatives.

50

Importantly he did not fire old teachers and bring in new ones; he did not insist on a school building architecturally suited to the open school concept. (Many of these now dot the countryside; they are round, architecturally open buildings, but the education of children goes on pretty much as ever, and the minds of the teachers continue unaffected by the environment.) However, Glines did knock down some walls — both mental and physical.

Personally, Glines radiates energy. He is lean and angular and, not unimportantly, red-headed. He speaks somewhat like a recovered stutterer — not eloquently, and not with much apparent respect for English. But his is the sort of speaking through which thoughts shine: He uses a minimum of words, a minimum of complete sentences, to hang the thought on. That in itself makes him exceptional among the ranks of long-winded educational theorists and administrators. Concreteness and realization, not words, seem his milieu.

With this sparseness, using slang and sometimes strong vocabulary, Glines cuts through all the jargon of American educational history and seizes a few forceful words and phrases for getting some work done. If he hadn't been a thinker, he might have been an efficiency expert. He might, too, have made his living as a stand-up comedian. A 25-minute tape Glines made about Wilson is one of the funniest pieces of material I've ever seen. He simply sits behind a desk and talks about Wilson, making hash of just about all aspects of traditional education. For example, he says something like the following:

"When I came into the school, here in this little room was this class of the retarded, with their retarded teacher. Obviously, we couldn't stand this! Who wants to have retarded children in the school? What teacher wants to be retarded?" So he abolished this segregation of the retarded, and he abolished the word "retarded," though the public schools have always sent Wilson a steady supply of "Retards." Glines does not believe in, or accept, the failure implied by retardation.

When Glines took charge at Wilson, the building underwent a sudden, un-blueprinted but complete remodeling. A wall was interfering with education here . . . soon it was gone. A door was needed in the home economics room so students could drift in and get interested from both sides . . . literally . . . the next morning there was a hole in the wall.

Glines studied the school carefully while it was operating; he walked around it and through it like a prospector crawling through old mine tunnels looking for gold. Gold to him were the student-teacher and student-student relationships.

He also remodeled the school lunch programs, setting up all day food service because he knew that some students are "protein nibblers" and don't want or need, three meals a day.

Many educators, and especially school boards, sit at desks and tables and draw up plans, playing chess with the lives of students, teachers, and staff. When Glines came to Wilson, he was on the chess board along with the others.

But the central changes Glines made were these two: He abolished all grades; and he established the advisor system.

Once grades are abolished, you do away with the phoney success-failure syndrome which ruins school for so many thousands, and historically, millions of young people. Abolish grades and you've also done away with the classroom where some shine, others show off, most vegetate at their C-level, and others flunk and die mentally.

With the advisor system, the heart of the new school became the student and the teacher, not the report card, not the teacher's grades. The important thing became the interaction between the student, teacher, and parents. At Wilson, each student chooses an advisor. Certain teachers come by certain advisees naturally. At first, an unpopular teacher might have very few until the teacher realizes a need to rethink relationships. Some get too many. The advisor is the student's helper in everything – and not mainly as a "teacher" in the traditional sense, but as a person whose job it is to help fulfill the student's needs.

Suggested study topics are compiled and published in a mimeographed printout, but all students choose their own schedules; most create their own individualized studies: not one course is mandatory. And the students know that rooms are available where they can go most any time to learn most anything. There are no attendance requirements.

Another important thing about the Wilson approach is that an advisor can't <u>control</u> a student's education. The school is permeated by the belief that students come to act very, very responsibly about their own progress, about their own education. And somehow, out of all of this freedom, Wilson students learn to read, write, add, subtract and handle all of the rest of the basics.

They also do especially well in achieving "social adjustment" and at other activities, including varsity sports. It was no coincidence that Wilson, with one of the smallest enrollments of any high school in the state, sent a team to the finals of the Minnesota state high school basketball tournament, and that it there lost to Marshall University High, another relatively "open" school, in Minneapolis. The freedom to pursue excellence has led to high achievement in all fields.

From having three kids of my own at Wilson for a total of 14 years, I'm sure, like many other Wilson parents, that this system really works. It works for the "fast," for the "slow," for the "artistic," for the "athletic." As Joe Kubicek, our area juvenile detention officer, has amply and publicly testified, it works too for the "juvenile delinquent." But at Wilson there are no brands burned into students.

Wilson works for everyone <u>except</u>, Glines realized, the student who does not want it. There are at least some who <u>want</u> regimentation, control, or at least certain established securities – and perhaps need these things for their fullest development. One student came to Wilson and was frustrated by a lack of anything to rebel against. Other students tried to help her find something, but it didn't work and she returned to a traditional school, where she is said to be happier. But it is probable that most young people would love a school like Wilson, if their parents would let them go.

Teachers at Wilson are happier too. And why shouldn't they be? While students have full control of what they will study, the teachers decide democratically all matters of educational policy. My wife, Cary, has taught at Wilson for five years and many of the other teachers are among my friends. As an ex-college teacher, I couldn't help feeling the difference between the usual distance and even hatred of students that often dominate faculty coffee rooms – and by contrast the camaraderie and quiet love for students in the Wilson faculty conversations. Nor do the Wilson teachers express any fear of bosses or administrators.

This year, the Mankato State University administration found a pretext for giving Wilson the axe. The following exchange illustrates the manner in which this brilliant administrative breakthrough was made:

University administrator: I need to declare this program a declining program so I can use the building for something else.

Questioner: Why is it a declining program?

Administrator: It's a declining program because it's not going to have a building next year.

In no way is Wilson School a declining program. It has more applicants than it can take. MSU is a declining program, and its reactionary administrators and older faculty have used the cutbacks of recent years as a pretext for forcing out the youngest, brightest, most innovative and – especially – most radical of the faculty. Only this spring the college confirmed, after years of harassment, the firing of Dr. Heino Ambros, a popular professor of political science who teaches his classes much the way they do at Wilson, creating a non-authoritarian, free and open atmosphere. Hundreds of students rallied to Ambros' support, protesting and even boycotting classes. But they could not reverse the conservative machinery of the local and state college system.

The initiative for closing Wilson came from the new MSU President, Douglas Moore. After successfully putting over his bureaucratic lie ("declining program") to his state superiors, he recommended that Wilson be closed. He then recommended that the building be taken over by the college administrative offices . . . or the art department . . . or the women's phy ed . . . or by the offices of the campus janitorial service . . . all of which was, of course, false. The art department didn't want it; women's phy ed didn't want a building inferior to that of men's phy ed; and Moore and the rest of the administration have their eye on a different suite of offices.

As for the Wilson teachers, not one had been offered a job within the university at the time this was written at the end of the school year. Wilson staffers applied for a number of openings that developed on the MSU staff – but none was hired. The senior members of the Wilson staff, who have 10 to 15 years of service, will thus lose everything: insurance, retirement benefits, and, most of all, a chance to give their remaining years of teaching to the people of Minnesota – unless ultimately there is a reversal through the chancellor's office.

The Wilson community hasn't accepted the closing without a fight. On a cold and blustery day late in March, 200 Wilson students and some supporters marched to the office of the local school superintendent. They carried signs ("LET WILSON LIVE") and they carried a coffin. They wrapped the school board offices with a petition signed by people in the community asking for a separate educational alternative for the coming year.

Before the students arrived, Superintendent Stark, whose offices are in the West High School building, went on the intercom and "explained" the situation to the West students. In a gross misrepresentation of the facts, he said it would cost the local school district $600,000 in the coming year to keep Wilson open in a separate building. In fact, it appears that the figure, considering state aid and grants and other factors, might be only $125,000 – but more likely no additional expense. And for an equal number of regular students the district normally would spend no less than $225,000.

Stark took other precautions when the Wilson students came; he posted a male faculty member at each door so that no Wilson students would be able to talk with West students.

But the protests, whether students or parents, did no good. Mankato School District No. 77, by a 4-3 action of its school board, rejected an alternative to Wilson – after originally publicly indicating a 5-2 support vote.

So the people of the Wilson community have undertaken to open a new, private alternative in the fall. It will be difficult, but they are confident that they can do it.

And it appears that the building that housed one of the finest experiments in American education will be a warehouse, or will simply sit empty next year.

AFTER CLOSING
Several Wilson faculty were eventually hired by MSU; the building was divided into four segments: a warehouse, security offices, home economics department, and preschool center. The athletic fields became the parking lot for the college cars. The private Wilson alternative continued for another eight years, but financial considerations eventually caused a closure. The building was renamed Weiking Center. Wilson student alumni placed a plaque on the interior front wall: Wilson Campus School, 1959-1977. Thus ended one of the greatest educational experiments in American history.

Changing Beliefs

chapter eleven

PHILOSOPHY

Philosophy was the essence of Wilson, coupled with the caring, personal relationships. The beliefs were not those theoretical platitudes written for a college graduate class assignment, or for the front of a district policy book and then not used. The Wilson statement of philosophy, written to represent thinking in the 1968-70 era, was the basis for program and people judgments; it was continuously modified when it could be improved to further benefit the students.

The original two categories – Purposes and Beliefs – were developed early in the conversion of Wilson. The additional "14 points" which are attached to the philosophy statement became the first revision, under a third category of Policies. The staff felt a need to explain in more detail the beginning commitments before writing a new one. This stood as a daily workable model which was constantly referred to and revised. The staff left it in draft form to force an ongoing examination of their views; as illustration, the initial version is cited. Ironically, it was several weeks after the "14 points" were added that they connected the number equalled those of the Woodrow Wilson proclamation, the man after whom the school had been named when the new traditional site was constructed in 1959.

Tentative Working
STATEMENT OF WILSON PHILOSOPHY

I. Purposes:

    A.   The school serves persons and groups by helping each one to understand and respect themselves, other people, and their world, by becoming responsible, decision-making, self-directing, value-judging, self-educating individuals.

    B.   The school benefits education as a whole through innovation, experimentation, research, evaluation, and dissemination of new programs. To this end, conventional methods should continue only where they appear to be best for certain individual students; this school should be one of those probing the future.

    C.   The school provides, as part of the experimental nature of the program, a laboratory setting for preservice and inservice training of teachers and administrators in cooperation with schools of education, especially aiding new designs in teacher education.

    D.   The school concerns go beyond educational reform to include as a major purpose assisting societal transformation, and preparing students to cope with an emerging New Age. The school must be futures oriented, and focus on the preservation of the biosphere, and the preservation of humankind.

II. Beliefs:

Stated beliefs regarding the (A) student, (B) learning, (C) program, and (D) resource are based upon present knowledge and understanding of growth and process; they may change as future research improves. The staff accepts the concept of tentative truths, realizing that there is no longer finality.

A. Student:

   1. Students are different and have different capabilities, needs, and interests which change from day to day even within the same student. All youth do not have the same capabilities in the area of symbolic manipulation.

   2. Anything taught and any method used to teach it should be appropriate to the capabilities of the students and relevant to their needs and interests at the particular time, rather than be only continual preparation for the next step in their education.

   3. Every student should find some success each day; the school must utilize every person, method, and material possible to give each individual greater chance for success.

   4. Because factual knowledge changes and multiplies so rapidly, emphasis should be placed on process and inquiry rather than on product and content. The students should be encouraged to enjoy learning, to be receptive to change, and to educate themselves.

   5. The students should be encouraged to learn how to ask questions, find answers, organize their information, and draw generalizations.

   6. Each student should have the necessary freedom in which to direct his or her own behavior, make his or her own decisions, and form his or her own values. Through this freedom students can develop respect, both for their own worth and unique qualities, and the rights of others.

   7. With this freedom, the students should be assisted as they learn to accept responsibility for the results of their behavior and decisions. A situation in which students discipline themselves is most conducive to learning.

   8. The emphasis in both teaching and learning should be on human relations, shaping, coping, tolerance, and understanding rather than on content and skills, though these are also necessary. The goal of the school program is to help the students develop an inner self capable of finding solutions.

B. Learning:

   1. Students should consider themselves capable of learning and worthy of being taught.

   2. Students should be interested in what they are studying, and motivated to learn; the most effective motivation comes from within, and occurs when they see the relevance of what they are learning to their own goals.

3. Students learn best when they are trusted, when their ideas are respected, and when their learning behavior is reinforced. Negative criticism and failure lead to discouragement and further failure.

4. Creativity is encouraged when the students feel free to question everything, when divergent thinking is rewarded, and when thought and imagination are goals of factual information and memory.

C. Program:

1. Persons affected by a decision (students, parents, teachers, and administrators) should have a part in making that decision.

2. Curriculum should not be rigid, either for all students or for all time. Continuous evaluation of the curriculum should provide for continual change as individual students and situations evolve.

3. Teachers should work and plan together to personalize the program for each student, create interdependent curricula, and provide the student the benefit of multiple personalities. Time must be made available for this cooperative planning.

4. The schedule must be sufficiently flexible to allow a variety of groupings, time patterns, and uses of resources.

5. The school should, whenever possible, respond to and encourage students and teachers rather than restrict them.

D. Resource:

1. Future educational systems require wise, knowledgeable, empathetic teachers.

2. All available human resources should be utilized in the most effective way possible to expand and enrich learning for the student. To this end, specialists should delegate their nonspecialized functions to others; teachers and counselors should not be assigned clerical duties.

3. Multiple materials must be provided, or developed if they are not otherwise available, for students of all abilities and levels.

4. Multi-sensory materials should be used to reinforce learning and to provide every possible chance to reach each individual student.

5. Teachers should be aware of new technological, biological, and psychological developments which could be utilized in education, and should evaluate the results of their use.

Additional 14 Points
STATEMENTS OF SCHOOL POLICY

1. A major element of importance in the program is the teacher-student match — a student may choose any teacher (whenever possible) in an attempt to find that

match: the personality/perception/interest/gender/age/skill of the teacher-consultants make a difference; the students need to realize that it is possible to choose a teacher other than the customary one formally assigned to assist with a learning field.

2. The affective domain is most important – self-image, success, attitude toward learning; the psychomotor is second – gross motor, fine motor, visual motor, auditory discrimination. After both of these areas are in good shape, the cognitive comes easily, if the curriculum is individually paced. All areas should develop concurrently when possible, in a confluent approach, helping individuals where any difficulty may arise. The cognitive can be a key to improving the affective, but is enhanced by considering the total cognitive needs, not just subjects such as reading and arithmetic.

3. There is no such thing as a grade level. Consultant-teachers must stop referring to sixth grade math, or second grade reading. Students should be referred to only as individuals or in temporary groups – the dream reality group, the astrology group. In a nongraded continuous progress program, comparison of a student with another, or with a fictitious group norm cannot be used to equate progress; these comparisons have validity only in individual diagnosis and prescription.

4. Each teacher-consultant-facilitator must know his or her students thoroughly in relation to student progress in his or her own area. Consultants in various teams must meet frequently to discuss students.

5. Each advisor is responsible for knowing each of his or her advisees in all areas – the affective, psychomotor, and cognitive – as related to study experiences, involvement, and other phases of school life, for checking the progress of each advisee every few weeks, and for seeing that additional help is sought from counselors, psychologists, administrators, parents, other staff, and outside professional help, if a student has a need. There should be no expectation that the staff is able to solve every problem, but the advisor is responsible for ensuring that each advisee has a program for maximizing potential and talents, and overcoming his or her difficulties – realizing that the program may or may not be successful at that moment in time; continuous review is necessary.

    a. The consultant is to send each advisor a number of reports each year concerning the work of the student; the advisor is responsible for completing the yearly evaluation report for his or her advisees and for purging or updating files – following procedure recommended by the counseling team.

    b. Each advisor must communicate with the parents, normally following time patterns established by a faculty committee. In general, the parents should realize that if the school does not contact them, the student is progressing; in the meantime, the parents may contact the school, if they feel it is necessary or desirable.

6. Each learning situation is generally to operate in five phases: much one-to-one, open laboratory, independent study, small group, and large group, as needed. There should be no problem of grouping; if some students want to meet together, or some teachers see value in a group, these should be arranged, but usually on a flexible, tentative basis.

7. The best possible curricula is usually student-developed; but, if necessary, some portions of a program for an individual may be prescribed for him or her. Optional attendance is the general policy; however, a student can be required to come to a particular learning situation, if it has been agreed upon by the student, a group of teachers, parents, and advisor.

8. All former "allied" curricular activities – such as dances, clubs, athletics – are considered part of the learning activities, as well as part of the teacher contract. Plans for activities which occur outside the usual school procedures should be discussed with the associate director for student programs. All students shall be eligible for activities, unless a faculty group has reason to prescribe exceptions.

9. The Student/Parent/Faculty Advisory Councils can submit requests directly to the Board of Directors if the request seems to affect only their group. Where the requests obviously affect another segment, they must go through the Joint Council by way of the associate director responsible for community services.

10. Students must be heavily involved in the development of the school, if the program is to be successful. Faculty are requested to encourage student participation – including younger students – in formulating school improvements and policies.

11. Faculty members must learn to function as team members in practice as well as in theory. Four people working, teaching, and communicating together for a group of students can do a better job than four isolated individuals who refuse to work together – that is, to discuss curricula, student progress, and problems, and reach a mutually beneficial solution. Student interns are members of this team. There are not two industrial arts teachers and two student interns – there are four teachers; how can four help 200 students, not how can two with some assistance help 200. This means student interns must make quality efforts.

12. There are "stop signs" at school. Students do not have complete freedom – there are restrictions – but these are similar to the few imposed when one has a license to drive: speed limits, stop signs, road courtesies. Teachers should be no more restrictive than these few simple requests indicate; but they should be restrictive, as the police and courts must be, when there are serious violations.

13. Teachers need to be aware of media center/library facilities when building curricula, and be aware that some students learn better through auditory and visual methods – that electronic technology is an asset – and seek assistance from the associate for support resources.

14. This is a 12-month, year-round, continuous progress school. Students should be able to plug in, plug out, speed up, slow down, start, or stop courses and experiences at any time, and take as long as realistically desired for study or vacation.

Before writing the original tentative philosophical draft, and when constructing the additional fourteen points, the school leaned heavily on statements regarding learning from LEARNING MORE ABOUT LEARNING (ASCD, Alexandria, VA 1959):

1. Learning is a problem of the total personality.

2. Learning is the search for an individual, personal discovery of meaning.

3. To teach persons, they must be understood; this is more easily accomplished by trying to perceive them and their work as they perceive themselves.

4. Education must start with learning that is important and need-relevant to the individual.

5. Since needs, values, and attitudes are such important determiners of perception, education must seek to help students know which are important to them and to consider each fully and in relation to each other.

6. Since personal perceptions are not readily changed through the introduction of objective evidence, education must begin with the beliefs of students and relate knowledge to their particular perceptions.

7. Perceptions are most readily changed through a re-examination of needs, values, attitudes, and the possible meanings of previous experience.

8. Knowledge is but one determiner of human behavior.

9. Learners learn in response to their needs and perceptions, not those of their teachers.

10. Education must start where the child is and permit him or her to determine his or her own direction and space.

11. Not specific behavior, but adequacy of perception and openness to experience, should be the goals of education.

    This Wilson program emerged from a philosophy of learning which was opposite that of most "conventional schools."

COMMITMENT

Wilson advertised 69 elements of change, categorized under six components. These were borrowed concepts from three sources: (1) the 1930s pioneers; (2) the revisions which were occurring in the 60s, some of which still may be appropriate for the year 2000; and (3) the experimental ideas for the future conceived by the planners of the futuristic Minnesota Experimental City. It is not productive to quarrel over the descriptions or titles of these 69, or whether they should be combined with other factors, or treated as isolated efforts; each element seemed to have a role in the transition of schools from the 60s toward the new century. They should be much improved when written for the late 90s.

Staff now need to compile their own specific lists for their particular schools. As part of this process of involvement, faculty members should first develop their own individual notions, and then merge them where agreeable with total staff design. By this process of judgment, the learning community can create a glossary of changes for the program. No group should completely accept the 69 items identified at Wilson; these were valid then and most still remain of value, but they only represent areas which perhaps constitute a change of direction for some schools, when properly implemented. They have been useful in clarifying thoughts regarding the development of optimal learning systems that ought to be available now. If a school staff becomes significantly involved in the ongoing process of improvement, "lists" should soon be outdated. These commitments, though, were part of the creation of Wilson, and thus were written for that era, not the 21st Century. They are presented in 1968 vocabulary.

COMPONENT I – PHILOSOPHY

The innovative schools have a carefully prepared statement of philosophy and purpose; the convictions expressed consider the following and other elements:

ELEMENT 1. The school is committed to the concept of HUMANENESS. Schools of the past have reduced the options and alternatives through rules, regulations, and requirements, and thus for many students have become inhumane institutions. The new more humane have increased the options, alternatives, responsibilities, and self-direction opportunities. Self-selection has become an accepted concept in individualization.

ELEMENT 2. The school is committed to ONGOING INNOVATION. Significant improvement generally occurs when there is a deep philosophical commitment that schools must be better, and that often, better means developing significantly different designs. Change as a continuous process thus must be institutionalized.

ELEMENT 3. The school is committed to INDIVIDUALIZING LEARNING. No longer a cliché in college textbooks, it is now possible and desirable to individualize learning. Materials and teacher training are the major hindrances. Each student should be working on activities designed for his or her individual needs, interests, and abilities. "Required for all" courses are basically eliminated; if required courses are demanded, assignments are individualized and personalized.

ELEMENT 4. The school is committed to CONTINUOUS PROGRESS. Students should work through materials without regard to the "chapter" others are studying.

Through SELF-PACING, as soon as they complete one set of materials they move right on to the next without waiting for the class or a group test. The materials are often student developed; the length of time spent on them is usually determined by the student in consultation with the teacher.

ELEMENT 5. The school is committed to new ROLE PERCEPTIONS. Teachers are seen as motivators, guides, and facilitators primarily working with small groups and individuals. They are no longer spoon-feeders of knowledge involved in large group-paced instruction, or with classes of 30. They readily admit they do not always "know" what the adult of the early 21st Century must study.

ELEMENT 6. The school is committed to new TIME PRIORITIES. All students do not need five 55-minute periods each week in high school for each subject, or seven and one-half hours of reading and language activities per week at the elementary level. Individual time priorities are developed rather than group. "How much time does Sally need in a particular subject?" – not, "How much time does the first grade need?"

ELEMENT 7. The school is committed to the concept of STUDENT RESPONSIBILITY. Students should have at least a 50/50 relationship in making decisions about curriculum, policy, evaluations, new programs, and individual needs. Students accept responsibility when they have the right to share in the planning of school experiences. They learn that with freedom goes responsibility and courtesy.

ELEMENT 8. The school is committed to the concept of SELF-DIRECTION. The different world of the 21st Century will demand more than ever that individuals be self-directing and self-educating. They must be given opportunities to learn those skills through independent study and responsibility time, not hall passes and tardies.

ELEMENT 9. The school is committed to positive MOTIVATION AND SUCCESS. New approaches and incentives are replacing gold stars, report cards, grades, failure, and pressure. Comparisons of unequals create false values. Marking a paper "two correct" is better than marking it "eight wrong." Each child should find some measure of success each day at school. Involving the student in making decisions part of the day, as to what he or she wants to do, rather than insisting on teacher, school, or group requirements, is one way to help ensure success.

ELEMENT 10. The school is committed to EXPERIMENTATION. Most school methods are presently based on tradition, not extensive research or thoughtful philosophy (example: ringing bells in school). Experimental efforts are adding insight; magic regulations such as kindergarten entrance dates are being replaced by more logical and rational approaches.

ELEMENT 11. The school is committed to becoming a COMMUNITY CENTER. Schools must become communities investments to the extent that they are open where needed, 24 hours a day, seven days a week, 12 months a year. Closing schools at 4:00 p.m. on weekdays, all day Saturday and Sunday, and from June to September does not make sense.

ELEMENT 12. The school is committed to becoming a SCHOOL IN THE COMMUNITY. Students often learn best outside school walls. Smaller buildings should be constructed and more programs developed which find students working on farms, in automobile garages, art museums, business offices, government centers, and other such opportunities; the COMMUNITY IN THE SCHOOL concept should also be part of a two way exchange of learning.

ELEMENT 13. The school is committed to a TWELVE-MONTH PROGRAM. Learning ought to be offered on a 12-month, self-paced basis where the learning objective is the criterion, not the hours in school or the month it was learned. As an easy way to start, students should be required to be there only the state minimum number of days, such as 180 of the 365 – minus the usual illness days and holidays – and should be able to take vacation in November or January, or March, or August, or at any time it is needed, for as long as it is necessary or desirable. This is simple in a continuous progress school.

COMPONENT II – INSTRUCTION

The innovative schools are involved in projects implementing current research findings, and are further researching new developments concerning instruction and learning. A few of the elements thought essential to explore are suggested:

ELEMENT 1. The school is committed to exploring INTERACTION ANALYSIS. Research indicates that most classrooms are dominated by teacher talk and student quiet work assignments. These methods are not as productive as self-directed study, and active student interaction, all presently very limited. Interaction, and other action studies, are implemented in concerned schools.

ELEMENT 2. The school is committed to HUMAN RELATIONS. Teacher and student perceptions of each other, teacher and student personalities, and the appropriate matches are crucial. The way adults perceive children is closely related with the way a child learns. Placing the child in contact with multiple personalities in team situations seems to enhance the possibility of the appropriate match of perceptions, personalities, gender, interests, age, and skill.

ELEMENT 3. The school is committed to developing skills of INDIVIDUAL DIAGNOSIS. Individual diagnosis of each child is absolutely essential if individualized learning, continuous progress, and self-pacing methods are to be utilized. Some good diagnostic tests are emerging in the early childhood area, but much more objectivity is needed in determining needs, interests, and abilities. Much still rests on the composite compiled by a team, rather than only one teacher. Students in school must be considered as clients as in law and medicine – each must be considered individually; subjective, caring, understanding views are valid, and of priority importance.

ELEMENT 4. The school is committed to INDIVIDUAL PRESCRIPTION. Interwoven with individual diagnosis is the necessity of individually prescribing programs for and with each individual. The schools must have a pharmacy of learning experiences. Matching curricula, requirements, choices, teacher personalities, and techniques with student personalities and learning styles is essential. A few schools are experimenting with computer decision making as an aide to providing alternatives. Others are developing student led subjective prescription sheets.

ELEMENT 5. The school is committed to rethinking LEARNING OBJECTIVES. The innovative schools have concluded that general goals and objectives such as to appreciate, to understand, to know, to enjoy, are no longer adequate as measures of specific student comprehension. In some schools, teachers and students are writing performance or behavioral objectives that are measurable in clearly identifiable terms for each learning activity. A person who _____ is a person who _____; or, given _____, the student is able to _____. However, behavioral objectives are usually not necessary or desirable. Most humane schools are using agreements reached between the student and teacher which are helpful to the student, the teacher, and the task; they do not use rigidity when open ended searching appears to be the desirable learning style for a particular student, group, teacher, or goal. Wilson seldom uses behavioral objectives, except where they benefit a specific individual or group project.

ELEMENT 6. The school is committed to applying new research regarding INTELLIGENCE. Intelligence scores and readiness for learning can be affected. There are probably 120 distinct abilities for each individual, 50 of which are now known. The spread of abilities, symbolic manipulations, characteristics, interests, and achievements forces individualization of learning. Innovative schools are exploring intelligence studies.

ELEMENT 7. The school is committed to aiding EARLY CHILDHOOD EDUCATION. Research on characteristics and achievement of students gives new perception to the importance of the early childhood years. Learning experiences must be structured to ensure that certain skills and functions are developed before undertaking "first grade" programs for which he or she is not ready. Entering kindergarten children, chronologically age 5, developmentally range from 3 to 8. Innovative elementary schools are starting new 3 to 8 year old Beginning Life Centers, and secondary schools are supporting with staff and time. "First grade work" is when they are ready, not when age 6.

ELEMENT 8. The school is committed to analyzing the APPROPRIATE DOMAIN. Investigation into the cognitive, affective, and psychomotor domains draws attention to the need to carefully consider the tasks being assigned. Students with learning problems often have difficulty in the affective and psychomotor, but educators are still predominantly prescribing work in the cognitive. Schools are experimenting with combination prescriptions in the three domains, and the goal of confluency.

ELEMENT 9. The school is committed to PHASE TEACHING. There is no conclusive research to justify classes of 20 or 35 all day in each subject. The evidence now points to teaching in five phases: large group, small group, independent study, laboratory, and one-to-one conference – as being superior to traditional groupings. Innovative schools are piloting efforts to find appropriate time allotments for instruction. The answer varies with the individual, but there are some general percentages which can be used as guidelines at both "elementary" and "secondary" levels.

ELEMENT 10. The school is committed to MULTI-MEDIA LEARNING. Learning seems to improve for most individuals when multi-media approaches are used: visuals, listening tapes, records, television, videotapes, graphs, computers – see, hear, feel, taste, smell approaches. Though not a new idea, the innovative schools are increasing the use of these factors, and conducting studies to determine differences in achievement. The computer math projects where "first graders" are learning through "technological teachers" are examples. The coming electronics revolution will dramatically reorient learning approaches.

ELEMENT 11. The school is committed to BUDGETING FEEDBACK. Budgets should provide funds for planning for change. Many of the present innovations can be handled by a redeployment of existing finances while other new ideas need more money. In addition to budgeting for planning changes, and for actually developing them, funds must be available for evaluative feedback: Is the program actually worth the money invested, in terms of time, achievement, and outcome, and in comparison with previous programs or other new ones?

ELEMENT 12. The school is committed to HUMANE ACCOUNTABILITY. The accountability movement had many desirable features. Schools should know whether they are successful. However, accountability based primarily on reading, math, science, and history is wrong, as is rigid competency-based, outcome-based, evaluation. Authentic assessment has the same flaws. Each have elements which can be utilized. Humaneness calls for learning which measures affective and psychomotor development as well as cognitive, and individual rather than group goals; it also avoids standardized comparisons.

COMPONENT III – LEARNING
The innovative schools are studying learning, learning theory, and brain research and revising the entire curriculum as a result of recent knowledge and experimentation:

ELEMENT 1. The school is committed to LEARNING ABOUT LEARNING. Though there is considerable unknown about the way learning occurs, concerned schools are involved in extensive inservice sessions to increase staff knowledge of what is known. Teachers or specialists on the staff who understand learning psychology are being used as translators to help teachers build programs focusing on how learning seems to occur for various individuals. Staff are fully aware of and involved in the many research projects attempting to learn more about learning, and are keeping in touch with genetic engineering developments and BRAIN COMPATIBLE EDUCATION.

ELEMENT 2. The school is committed to RELEVANT REQUIREMENTS. There are very few things taught in a school which everyone must know. There are some things that most students probably should know; there are other concepts, skills, and knowledge that some or a few should know. Perhaps 80 percent of what is now being taught is not relevant for every individual in the society of 1995-2015, and almost that much has been irrelevant for many individuals for years. The innovative schools are attempting to solve the problem of curricula relevancy.

ELEMENT 3. The school is committed to PERSONALIZED PROGRAMS. Each day, week, month, or year, depending upon the need, diagnostic discussions are held with and without the students to attempt to determine the best learning opportunities for each child at that moment in time. Even in conventional schools, it should be assumed that a student may have two periods of individualized reading, two periods of physical education, and one hour of responsibility time prescribed for a given day, rather than the traditional hour each of English, history, math, science, physical education, and electives – or reading every day from 9:00 a.m. – 10:15 a.m. This means that such outmoded courses as seventh grade English, required of all, are a thing of the past in the emerging futures learning systems.

ELEMENT 4. The school is committed to utilizing new CURRICULAR PROJECTS. There are a great number of national projects attempting to develop better instructional materials in most subject areas. Almost all are better than the former basic and supplementary textbooks and therefore should be considered; unfortunately, most are written for group-paced instruction, and thus must be revised by teachers for continuous progress programs. Learners who develop their own objectives and media should not be forced to use any of the projects, regardless of how good they are, if the student approach is more meaningful to the individual. Students should be encouraged to write their own curricula as they find a need to learn. Further, most new projects still are not interdependent; they are designed for the traditional segmented school subjects. Staff should select only those which can best be adapted to interrelationships.

ELEMENT 5. The school is committed to INTERDEPENDENT APPROACHES. Though most new national curriculum projects are developed through the structure of a single discipline, the forward trend schools are emerging with interdependent learning, or an interdisciplinary approach, or at least a multi-disciplinary one. The innovative schools are merging the 14 former separate subjects. Ultimately the materials will all be individualized so that they can be interrelated in almost any combination or treated separately. Best is one curricula, developed by an interrelated team, or teachers and a student, or students, who select certain interdependent learning goals.

ELEMENT 6. The school is committed to ASSESSING INSTRUCTIONAL PACKETS. Before accepting new curriculum materials, the innovative schools are using various criteria to determine which one, which ones, or which parts of which ones of the many curriculum packages available should be selected. Currently the items to consider the worth of a particular program are being listed by some evaluations under the following ten steps or criteria for decision making: problem, assessment, direction, availability, learning, content, environment, practical, decision, and action. This can apply to new technological developments as well as old print materials approaches. There can be no common textbook sets ordered for all students in a given course or experience.

ELEMENT 7. The school is committed to CONCEPTS. Specific content is not particularly important in most subjects today, but concepts and themes are valid. Africa as content becomes rapidly irrelevant – Africa in 1940 versus in 2000 – but it is of value as a tool for developing basic concepts such as modernization, or in considering values, war, racial conflict, marriage, lifestyles, poverty, and peace. Technological content is ever changing and thus is presented as a lifelong learning pursuit – as, in theory, is all learning.

ELEMENT 8. The school is committed to PROCESS, INQUIRY, AND ANALYSIS. Knowing the processes of how to find an answer, how to inquire, seek information, discover answers, analyze results – process, inquiry, discovery, and analysis – are important approaches to learning. The good new curriculum projects and the good new learning centers are creating materials designed to develop these methods.

ELEMENT 9. The school is committed to MULTIPLE STUDENT RESOURCES. Students receiving either "A" or "D" grades, and spread ten years in achievement scores on standardized tests, and six years on physiological growth, should not be expected to compete in the same curriculum. Neither should they be grouped by tracks. The exciting schools, realizing the extreme variance in learning frames of reference, have eliminated the required textbook and flag football syndromes, and instead have substituted individualized materials aimed at a wide variety of abilities and interests, yet often focusing on similar themes, concepts, and physical development.

ELEMENT 10.   The school is committed to preparing SELF-INSTRUCTIONAL PACKETS. Self-instructional learning activities must be prepared by innovative teachers and students. They are not available in most fields commercially. Learning kits, Unipacs, contracts, learning activities packages, individually prescribed assignments, goal sheets, and capsules are among the techniques being used. Rigid curriculum guides are being replaced by flexible materials students can study without personal teacher instruction or presence. However, these packets should be used only when they make sense to the particular teacher-student-content mix. Entire required-for-all courses built on contract or Unipac approaches are as wrong as the single textbook. They only supplement the pharmacy – they do not serve as "the pharmacy." Now the computer and video developments are creating an entirely new potential, far beyond the old teacher-student developed Unipac.

ELEMENT 11. The school is committed to STUDENT QUEST. Instead of, or after, even in conventional programs, any basic study prepared by the student or teacher has been completed, and after the student has perhaps pursued depth concepts suggested by the instructor, then he or she should be able to continue the same topic, which has been left open-ended; the individual may decide to QUEST an entire course by never meeting in a formal class situation. Students who QUEST generally develop their own objectives, content, and methodology, and prepare their own plans, with approval/input from the staff resource person.

ELEMENT 12. The school is committed to STUDENT EXCHANGE. Students learn more out of the school building in the environment conducive to the subject being studied. When possible, in learning a foreign language, students should spend blocks of time in other countries, and foreign students should come to the United States – not just one or two, but entire classes or large groups. Depending upon community resources, students in as many fields as possible should pursue part of the learning experience outside the school building.   Living on a reservation for a period of time is generally superior to reading a book on American Indians, but combinations of all media are best. If students have no possibility of leaving the school building, then the environment should be simulated, to the extent possible, within the school, and through technological resources such as satellite viewing. VOLUNTEERING is a crucial concept. Students should engage in volunteering in nursing homes, social services, hospitals, language centers, child care – in all aspects needed by the community.

ELEMENT 13. The school is committed to GAMING AND SIMULATION. These two notions by themselves are not that crucial; however, they are symbolic representatives of attempts to find new and better patterns of learning delivery systems. The computer and robotic worlds have opened wonderful avenues of exploration.

ELEMENT 14.   The school is committed to SELF-SELECTION AND WINDOW SHOPPING. Schools providing smorgasbord scheduling and optional attendance allow students to self-select the topics they want to study that day or year, and the materials with which they prefer to work. This is practical on a K-12 basis, but is implemented a little differently at various levels of individual development. Window shopping eliminates the need for pre-registration and the old drop/add syndrome. Students search until they find the right program for a period of time. They indicate what they have decided to pursue and commit with an instructor; they do not change until they switch an entire area – from "English to Industrial Arts." This is noted on the office records. If they take "English" 12 years, they never have to drop/add or reregister, once the original enrollment has been completed. At Wilson, the only records kept were when students committed to a new teacher, or completed a learning experience.

ELEMENT 15. The school is committed to CREATIVITY. Futures programs are learning how to promote this platitude, long a lip service goal but without concrete results. In past conventional high schools, the highest dropout rate was among students who had top scores on creativity evaluations. Creativity, problem solving, foresighting, process, are keys to the future.

COMPONENT IV – STRUCTURE
The innovative schools are developing new staff patterns, schedule arrangements, and methods of interaction and relationships:

ELEMENT 1. The school is committed to DAILY SMORGASBORD SCHEDULING MENUS, and to NONSCHEDULING. Schedules should be built daily based on the instructional tasks planned by teams of teachers, by student identified needs, and by individual choices. In an open schedule, 0-20 percent of the time is planned by the teacher. The other 80-100 percent the schedule is open to approximately ten to 25 choices, depending upon the individual level of maturity. The best daily schedules find students self-selecting from a smorgasbord offering – the restaurant menu. There are now about seven methods to accomplish this, but each calls for a compromise; any of the seven are improvements over period 1-2-3 schedules, or self-contained room/recess/reading focused schedules. Dramatic breakthroughs should occur in scheduling in innovative schools with technology. Nonscheduling is an important step for many schools. It has been used very successfully by several of the most innovative programs of the 60s and early 70s. A "nonschedule" is the scheduling goal. Wilson became a non-scheduled school during its second year. Once curriculum is completely personalized and individualized, there is no need for even a daily master schedule.

ELEMENT 2. The school is committed to NON-GRADING. Approximately 15 percent of the students presently achieve at their assigned grade level. Achievement scores range from "third to grade thirteen" for typical "seventh graders." The organization should be a nongraded mix of students; the materials should be individualized to provide appropriate opportunities for the "other 85 percent" erroneously diagnosed under the graded system. The task of the teacher is to spread the range of achievement without creating competitive or caste systems. The old country schoolhouse was a great mix. K-12 schools, or overlapping "grade level" programs (K-2, 2-4, 4-6), have more to offer than K-6, 7-9, 10-12 artificial separations. If separated, K-4, 5-8, 9-12 is a better organization. At Wilson, kindergarten and senior students work together.

ELEMENT 3. The school is committed to TEAM TEACHING. Two or more teachers, and their aide(s), planning and teaching together, maximizes teacher strengths and minimizes weaknesses; it provides multiple personalities for students, and improved perceptions for teachers. Teaming eliminates the concept of the self-contained room at all levels, K-12; it is an excellent way to interrelate curricula and provide student choice as to personality, perception, age, gender, interest, and skills.

ELEMENT 4. The school is committed to TEAM PLANNING. Team planning can occur in a variety of situations, but is essential in innovative schools. The learning team can plan a daily schedule and program for a group of students; a multi-curriculum team can plan interdependent, interdisciplinary approaches; a single curricular team can plan experiences in a particular subject field; a design team can plan for the overall development of the school program. Team planning is absolutely essential to success in team teaching, and is a way to begin teaming without actually team teaching. It avoids some teacher personality conflicts; however, as a whole, team planning without the facilitator mix, while providing many of the values, does lose those gained by sharing learning. In the long haul, team planning is more important than team teaching, but always with student options.

ELEMENT 5. The school is committed to TEAM LEARNING. This is formalizing a carryover from the rural school – the concept of students teaching students – peer, cross-age, and development skill assistance. Many individuals learn parts of the curriculum better from their classmates than they do from the teacher; they learn by discussing concepts or apprenticing with their peers. Small group, quest, and lab experiences can all be structured to provide for planned team learning and tutoring.

ELEMENT 6. The school is committed to FLEXIBLE GROUPING. Homogeneous, heterogeneous, gender, interest, and sociogram groupings are all wrong if used as permanent methods of organization. All are correct if used flexibly and alternated, depending upon the instructional plan for the day. Eventually flexible grouping leads to a pooling of individual students; from the pool generate teacher requests for students, student requests for teachers, or individual choice options.

ELEMENT 7. The school is committed to the use of AUXILIARY PERSONNEL. Use of paraprofessionals (teacher aides or other noncertified adults) is essential to the development of improved programs. Some serve in the role of instructional associates and actually teach, while many fill clerical positions. Others serve in general supervisory positions (e.g., playgrounds), or serve as special aides – persons who may share as artists or audio-visual technicians. Smaller schools often must combine these functions. If aides are not available as additional budget, the professional teacher ratio should be changed so that the adult-student ratio can be increased by employing aides. In any case, the certified teachers with whom the aide will work should interview and recommend their hiring, and determine the tasks they will be assigned.

ELEMENT 8. The school is committed to DIFFERENTIATED STAFFING. The better school districts are moving to 12-month contracts and a shortening of the time actually spent in direct contact with children each day, to allow for team planning and curriculum development to occur during the day and throughout the 12-month year. Schools are staffed somewhat like hospitals: there are master teachers who diagnose and prescribe (doctors); there are staff teachers who carry out the prescription, but who are not as well qualified to perform some of the required tasks (nurses); there are paraprofessionals who relieve the professionals from the tasks not requiring as much training (nurses aides); there are specialists such as automation technicians, psychologists, artists, and others (lab technicians and hospital specialists); there are candy-stripers who volunteer (parents, seniors, or older student volunteers). Many of these individuals are hired on a 12-month basis, but some will work fewer months of the year. This means teacher training must change; the innovative schools are now working with colleges on internship programs.

ELEMENT 9. The school is committed to INTERSCHOOL COOPERATION. Smaller schools and districts cannot provide all the services and technological developments needed; neither can they individually develop enough creative ideas to improve education rapidly. Large districts, though possibly providing more services, are burdened with bureaucratic interference. But schools and districts working together can create a confederation to share financial costs, technological developments, specialized services, and innovative ideas in almost all situations. Consortiums are essential.

ELEMENT 10. The school is committed to new DISTRICT PATTERNS. New patterns of school district organization are emerging to replace the unsatisfactory 6-3 or 8-4. Though no one knows the best system, if there is one, there is evidence the 6-3-3 is not the answer. Current thinking leans toward the educational park concept K-12, at least implemented that way in program, if not in facilities. Other systems, looking toward the middle school trend, are adopting a 4-4-4 pattern. Neighborhood attendance lines are finally being eliminated in favor of matching school philosophies with individual learning styles. Innovative schools are searching for better arrangements than 6-3-3, 8-4, 6-2-4, or 5-3-4 with required neighborhood attendance lines. Many educators now believe a non-graded pre-K-14 is best, but at least in overlapping multi-age teams, if not complete integration.

ELEMENT 11. The school is committed to NEW ATTENDANCE LAWS. It is more and more apparent that requiring students ages seven through 16, or whatever ages are picked by a state, to be in school every day, especially in a predetermined neighborhood school, is not the best treatment of all youth. Optional attendance policies and more flexibility in state laws and in selection of schools are necessary. The racial and busing arguments have temporarily interrupted this reform, but it will come. Many 14-17 year olds do not belong in schools as presently organized; not all children should enter kindergarten in September – they should be able to enroll throughout the 12-month year as they mature.

COMPONENT V – TECHNOLOGY
The innovative schools are turning to automation and to new open learning facilities:

ELEMENT 1. The school is committed to STUDENT MEDIA. Innovative schools previously developed exciting media centers to house 30 to 50 percent of the student body for many individual activities. They replaced libraries, which were usually underdeveloped, and study halls, which had no other function than to police. These air conditioned, carpeted, soft furniture learning centers had absolute quiet zones, semi-quiet browsing and study areas, and noise areas, in addition to housing the listening-viewing automation facilities for the school. Wet carrels and automated systems played an important role. Print and non-print mixes became essential. Those moving beyond this concept moved toward media tracking systems, preparing for the two-day-a-week schools, and making plans for the electronics revolution. The improvement of technological assistance and the provision of multiple resources and learning approaches is now mandated. Electronics are completely changing the previous concepts of libraries, media centers, and media materials. The old concepts need to rapidly fade away.

ELEMENT 2. The school is committed to TEACHER PLANNING CENTERS. The new school plans call for teacher planning centers to replace the "classroom for each teacher" concept. In team planning there must be areas where teachers can easily communicate. These centers should have quiet individual work, group and individual conference, and relaxation areas. When possible they should be close to the media resources and learning pods; students should have access to most of the open areas; the quiet zone should be restricted, so that concentrated work can occur when essential.

ELEMENT 3. The school is committed to MODIFIED OPEN PODS. Flexible open learning areas with arrangements for large and small groups, independent study, and individual laboratory experiences should replace the classrooms designed for 25 or 35 students. Large open noise areas with no mousey quiet or extra noisy zones are wrong, too. Where partitions are used, they should be easily movable, rather than permanent construction, and usually demountable rather than folding. In the coming years, programs and functions will change; any construction should be easily remodeled for beyond 2000. Form should support function. Completely open pods, as constructed in the 60s and early 70s in some districts, do not support all functions.

ELEMENT 4. The school is committed to ACOUSTICAL FLOORING. Carpeting developments led to acoustical flooring, which not only deadened sound, but provided a greatly improved aesthetic environment. In the past, schools often had acoustical ceilings and walls, but the greatest noise problem was from the floors. Now, though, carpeting with formaldehyde backing and glues, heavily sprayed with pesticides on top to eliminate insects, should not be used. A less allergenic material is needed. Because carpeting does hold dust, some areas of the school should use hardwood, non-porous smooth ceramic tile, or porcelain. Special built-in vacuum suctions are essential. Many highly allergic students cannot tolerate carpeting and therefore should be assigned only to the hardwood/ceramic tile areas.

ELEMENT 5. The school is committed to FLEXIBLE FURNISHINGS. New developments in furnishings are finally allowing the gradual replacement of traditional large, hard to move, rigid student desks or tables, with more flexible seating possibilities. Schools should no longer order masses of the usual style desks and straight hard library tables and chairs; wet and dry carrels, without particle board, soft furniture and carpet – without the formaldehyde/polyester overload – and other improved teaching arrangement possibilities should be the standard. Animals and plants are important school furnishings, too, but not where allergic children and staff work. All science laboratories, bookcases, and shelving should have plug-ins where needed, and be on wheels for complete rearrangement, as ideas develop and programs change; electric and water outlets are best placed in the floor.

ELEMENT 6. The school is committed to COMPUTER ASSISTED LEARNING. The use of computers will soon dramatically change the role for teachers from imparters of information to resource stimulators for individuals and small groups. It will relieve teachers of clerical and repetitious drill, and provide a tremendous aid to the individualization and personalization of learning. Already complete courses can be taught by a computer. The potential revolution of these programs on a national hookup will greatly alter learning delivery systems beyond 2000.

ELEMENT 7. The school is committed to RETRIEVAL SYSTEMS. Closely allied with computers, immediate access to viewing and listening tapes within a school, retrieval of information from local and national sources, and fingertip availability to large group material on an individualized basis will further revolutionize the role of the teacher. The cost of CAI, CBI, and retrieval is rapidly diminishing. The progressive schools are making plans to install systems which are so flexible that they can provide for true individualized learning, not just mass media feedback to individuals of group-required content.

ELEMENT 8. The school is committed to TELE-COMMUNICATION. In spite of present limitations and disappointments, there is an exciting future for instructional and educational television and the newer developments in electronic media. Tele-lecture and tele-writing systems and satellites provide opportunities for resource persons and instruction to a degree of excellence never before possible; it is a special boom for many small schools. Beyond 2000, students could have much of their learning at home, perhaps only attending the "schoolhouse" two days a week.

ELEMENT 9. The school is committed to MICRO-TECHNOLOGY, MICRO-TRANSPARENCIES, MICRO-FICHE, VIDEO DISCS and continuing developments which are multiplying in the electronics revolution, and will continue to force change in education. Schools must reflect the need for these items by increasing the percentage of the budget to obtain these tools. Until more sophisticated pieces of equipment are available, the innovative school makes sure that teachers and students have access to everything currently available. Video tape recorders offered immediate potential for all around, practical school use, while waiting for video communications systems. The satellite developments have made instant world information possible. The "old" media equipment will soon be like the tri-wing airplane.

ELEMENT 10. The school is committed to preventing ENVIRONMENTAL ILLNESS. Teachers and students are asked not to use scented perfumes, colognes, and sprays during the day. The phenol and similar ingredients are toxic to those with immune system deficiencies. Strong cleaning materials are eliminated, as are sources of formaldehyde and petrochemicals. The food service offers choices devoid of wheat, corn, milk, sugar, yeast, and soy. Plants, animals, carpeting, machines, particle board are allowed only in areas not required for use by allergic individuals.

COMPONENT VI – REPORTING
The innovative schools are developing new systems of student evaluation, program evaluation, and information reporting:

ELEMENT 1. The school is committed to INDIVIDUAL PROGRESS REPORTS. The group style comparative report cards have been replaced in innovative elementary and middle schools by diagnostic, mutual agreement, and student-parent-team conferences; individually agreed upon success measurements; individual diagnostic testing – when appropriate; and subjective analysis ratings. High schools are just beginning to modify their forms, as they fight against college-based traditions and superstitions such as Carnegie units, grade point averages, ABC report cards, and class rank. The individualized reports focus on the progress of the single student, and not on a subjective comparison with a group. The evaluation is determined in a one-to-one conference with the student and reviewed with the advisor. The traditional report card system is eliminated, replaced by portfolios, team evaluations, and other, or are made optional, so that all students and families have a choice of at least five different assessment systems.

ELEMENT 2. The school is committed to planned STUDENT CONFERENCES. The school provides time, through flexible team and schedule patterns, for teachers to confer individually with students during the school day. These are planned as regular phases of the instructional program, and not only when there are emergency or special request situations. Great rewards occur from 10- to 30-minute one-to-one conferences each week or two, as opposed to no conferences, and five periods of 45- or 50-minute groups, or 25 to 30 for instruction meetings. Assessment conferences are especially helpful, but general "bull sessions" are needed to open lines of communication. Instructional tutoring conferences are an important phase too.

ELEMENT 3. The school is committed to INDIVIDUALLY PACED TESTING. Student assessment should be as individually designed as possible. Innovative courses and experiences conducted on a continuous progress, self-paced basis allow students to be evaluated whenever they are ready, not on some group schedule. Group testing of an individual diagnostic nature sometimes has a place; it can be valid when used as a summary, but the questions are general, related to the pursued area of personal study. Subjective group attitude surveys relating to student opinions are appropriate as informational devices, but the innovative schools have eliminated the practice of trying to test all students on chapter two at the same time. No one fails tests; they are merely means of assessing how much a student knows about the topic being considered at this moment in time; the student receives no A, B, D grades on the tests.

ELEMENT 4. The school is committed to COUNSELING COUNSELORS. Counselors are developing open counseling centers and listening posts, becoming parts of teaching teams, giving large and small group instruction, diagnosing and prescribing for individual students, and opening future career oriented opportunities where students find success. Heavy emphasis is placed on the elementary school level; the concern is with appropriate learning experiences for each individual, not dogmatic subjective requirements. Some counselors are preparing as psychologists. The exciting counselor is the OMBUDSPERSON – an adult-to-talk-with – who wanders the halls like a pied piper, visiting the students, or who can be found in the "listening post." Counselors are no longer glorified clerks who sit in a cubbyhole figuring requirements and averages. They work most with groups of teachers as resource consultants; then with individual teachers with problems; next with groups of students; and finally with individual students. If the school is creating success, there are fewer individual student "problems."

ELEMENT 5. The school is committed to TEACHER ADVISORS. The ratio of 1 - 300 for school counselors does not work. Students select a teacher – an adult to talk to – who serves as the counselor-advisor-defender-supporter-encourager-scolder, mother, father, best friend, caring, sharing, loving person. They provide that immediate contact. The "trained" counselor can then be used for special roles. The advisor concept is perhaps the most important change.

ELEMENT 6. The school is committed to INFORMATION FEEDBACK. Innovative schools are making numerous revisions. In many cases the actual measurable impact on the classroom has been rather negligible. Some critics are claiming that the changes are fad, not fundamental. The good experimental schools are now attempting to ensure some measurement of what is happening to students as a result of all the innovations, experiments, and research designs. This information must be accurately reported as feedback in the evaluation cycle. The good schools have statistical, subjective, and interpretive analysis of the results of new programs.

ELEMENT 7. The school is committed to using EVALUATION MODELS. In the attempt to gather information regarding programs and students, innovative schools are developing models to measure whether their programs are enabling them to meet their objectives. One current method is where context, input, process, and product evaluations are used as steps in an ongoing and revolving cycle. Evaluation models must go far beyond what is now in vogue, and certainly encompass more than a "national assessment" concept.

ELEMENT 8. The school is committed to different PUBLIC INVOLVEMENT. A new era of public relations has been opened by the demand to explain innovations to the public. The best critics and ambassadors of the programs are the students; they must be involved first in the communication plans. "Honest sessions," truly informing parents and students of the many present deficiencies in the schools, and the real successes or failures achieved with new programs, are important phases of public relations. One of the greatest boons is that of opening attendance areas. If parents are dissatisfied, they are permitted to transfer students. Much pressure on innovation has been released by such policies. These schools are attempting to develop new formats for PTAs and other parent and community organizations, as volunteers are an important part of futures oriented school programs.

ELEMENT 9. The school is committed to INFORMATION ACTION. Many staffs gather information about their programs, but seldom use it to stimulate new developments. It has been known for years the current foreign language and physical education courses in the public schools were not reaching their stated objectives for the majority of individuals. The innovative schools are attempting to develop new curriculum materials, teaching methods, and learning time patterns.

ELEMENT 10. The school is committed to CLIENT ORIENTED EVALUATION. For years schools gave students ABCDF marks, and set behavior standards. Students were not asked to do the same for the teachers. The innovative schools are developing procedures for student evaluation of teachers. Not only are students selecting their own teachers, they are marking rating scales to help identify strong and weak characteristics. Teachers are rating teachers. No longer will the principal and superintendent determine competency. Teachers are evaluating administrators. The whole process relates to client-oriented evaluation.

SUMMARY

If schools implement these 60s era changes, they will be off to a good start; more sophisticated approaches are coming in the futuristic learning systems of the 21st Century. The few schools which have implemented all of these old innovations are ready for a quantum overleap toward the future; for those which have avoided these 69, or have only implemented a portion of them, the directions identified can serve as immediate transition steps toward preparing for the important changes which are ready to influence American education.

The listed statements archive change three decades before the new century. They are preserved in that language. Learning centers need to create a new 69, written for 2000, 2005, 2010. The past can help evolve the future.

Understanding Spirit

chapter thirteen

DESCRIPTIONS

Descriptions of Wilson programs written by the staff members responsible for their development, or by university professors and community persons associated with Wilson, explain parts of the comprehensive philosophy, and project subjective evaluations of several successful student opportunities. They help educators and parents understand efforts to transition from schooling to learning during the 70s, and provide steps towards futuristic programs for the next century.

"How Wilson Serves Me"
Jan Runyan, Assistant Professor
Mankato State University

Wilson Campus School serves me in a variety of ways, but especially as an inspiration, for the relationships among the people at Wilson ("students," "teachers," and "administrators") I find to be warmer and closer, with far fewer personal distancing factors than are found in schools operating in a more traditional manner. There seems to me to be greater acceptance of people, much higher energy levels, more spontaneity, greater interpersonal sensitivity, greater self-awareness, and more self-actualization generally than I find in most other schools. Creativity and risk-taking are encouraged and are in evidence. I believe that all of these factors enhance learning, encourage higher motivation and greater retention, and prepare more realistically for the world of today and tomorrow.

I believe that competition, evaluation, manipulation, fear, failure, and control are threatening, and to the extent each is present in a school, learning is decreased. To me the important factors in learning or any human relationships, are trust, cooperation, acceptance, friendship, and communication. I see far more of the latter set of factors at Wilson than the former. Students make their own choices. They choose whether or not they will attend the school that day; while there they study subjects of their own selection. They may confer with their advisor about their goals, their disappointments, or any number of things, but these communications tend to be like two friends talking and sharing. In the manner that we select our friends, Wilson students select their advisors.

Wilson serves me because it is an available option, an alternative learning environment, which I can explore, discover, analyze, and study. This is valuable for college students and others who wish to participate in various aspects of the program, thus gaining experience that may not only enhance their own personal growth, but may provide them with skills necessary to function effectively in such learning environments.

Wilson provides me with new learning experiences. My entire educational background, including ten years of teaching in the public schools, was nearly all in very traditional settings, where the teacher was the dispenser of information; superior-subordinate relationships were the rule rather than the exception; feelings were something that had no place in the classroom. How rewarding it is to experience learning in contrasting environments, with much different use of time, space, resources, and energies. Underlying the Wilson concept is the idea that the world and life are places for sharing, as well as within the school. Students may have many activities outside of the building each day. Certain weeks or months Wilson students may be found in other towns, states, or even countries. For me, the basis of knowledge is the ability to learn by experience and through relationships, not subject content as determined by someone else, or even subject content by itself.

Not all of the Wilson plans, programs, and procedures are effective. Each year different innovations are tried; many are modified or perhaps discarded. "Mistakes" are made; the students become critical; a few move back into a more traditional learning environment. The staff has many of the same problems found wherever people gather and work together. Wilson is not for everyone. For people like me who appreciate the learning opportunities that Wilson offers, for parents who desire this style of learning for their children, and for those students who choose it for their school years, the Wilson approach is a necessary educational experience which should be available to all in most every community.

"Complete Immersion Cultural Exchange Program"
Lew Holden, Language Coordinator
Wilson School

The Mexican exchange program of the Wilson Campus School at Mankato State University with Centro Escolar in Pueblo, Mexico, might very well be the most unique cultural student-teacher exchange program that exists between American and foreign public schools. It involves complete immersion of Wilson participants into the Mexican culture and the Spanish language; the reverse is true for the Mexicans in American culture and the English language.

It evolves at Wilson at the beginning of the winter quarter with the screening of 25 out of 40 or 50 students who have applied and who have been excited about the prospects of participating in the program since early September. (The number was limited to 25 students only because of an agreement requested by the exchange school in Pueblo – not Wilson philosophy; later the number was increased to include most all who applied.) The participants are selected by a committee of administrators, teachers, and other students. They are chosen primarily based on their genuine interest and sincerity in living and learning in a foreign environment, and their ability to be good ambassadors of our own country.

After final selections are made, the chaperons who accompany the students spend an evening with the parents to discuss the program and answer questions. The travelers then begin taking three to five classes per week that cover such topics as the geography, history, government, religion, music, art, dance, and food of Mexico. There are orientation sessions on how to understand the cultural change, what clothes to take along, how to exchange dollars for pesos and spend them wisely, and how not to commit errors of courtesy and respect.

Most of the involved students agree that traveling on the Mankato State University bus (Greyhound type) is better than flying. The bus would ordinarily make an empty run to Laredo, Texas, to pick up Mankato State student teachers who have been interning at the American schools in Mexico; when the bus delivers new student teachers to Laredo weeks later, the Wilson students are ready to return, and therefore take advantage of what would normally be another empty run. Within the country of Mexico the group uses

Mexican bus lines. The fare for the total round trip transportation in the United States and Mexico is approximately $50.00 per person (the cost in 1970-75 dollars).

Traveling by bus allows time to adapt to cultural change gradually. This is an opportunity to read about Mexico, study maps, and participate in Spanish language conversation groups. Other side effects are beneficial – sharing motel rooms, eating in restaurants, learning to budget money, and, perhaps most important, building closer friendships. The growth of self-esteem through peer acceptance of these young people becomes very evident.

The first real excitement – with some hesitation and a little trepidation for those making their first exchange trip – begins with the partaking of Mexican food, usually at the self-serve cafeteria in the bus station in Monterrey, Mexico. But there is more excitement upon arriving in Mexico City, where the group stops over one night before going on to Pueblo the next day.

Arriving at the hotel in the morning allows a full day in Mexico City. On the last trip the chaperons took the group on a walking tour to some of the interesting places in the downtown area of the ten million population metropolis. They strolled down the boulevards of the Paseo de la Reforma, dodged cars crossing streets, and learned that the pedestrian does not have the right of way. They walked along Avenida Juarez that leads to the Latin American Tower and to the Museo de Bellas Artes – all the while staring and being stared at. They saw the huge Monument to the Revolution and had lunch at the well known Sanborn restaurant. That evening they dined in another famous Mexican restaurant – a splurge before going on to Pueblo to meet their Mexican brothers and sisters and live with their Mexican families.

The real immersion begins here. The Mexicans in provincial Pueblo are warm, friendly, and loving. The young people embrace their American brothers and sisters when they are introduced and walk off holding hands to introduce them to their parents and go to their homes. There the Wilson students will eat three meals a day with their Mexican families – bananas in soup, strange tasting vegetables, hot meat, tortas (a hard roll sandwich), and many other new, interesting, and strange foods.

On school days, the students of both cultures come strolling together into the building – friendly, happy, and laughing. When the Mexicans go to their classes, the Wilson students may go with them, or meet with their chaperons for an hour. Questions are answered; some problems are solved. Experiences are shared and excitement prevails. Later the Wilsonites attend more classes with their Mexican brothers and sisters, or they go in a group on one of the many trips they will make to historical and cultural places of interest.

In addition to the sites they visit with their Mexican families, they are taken in school buses to museums and cathedrals in and near Pueblo. On one such trip they go to Cholula, eight miles away, to see the largest pyramid yet discovered in Mexico, one which has been under excavation for 30 years; on the same trip they will tour the University of the Americas. On other trips they go to nearby Santa Ana to shop for handmade articles of clothing – serapes, ponchos, peasant blouses – all cheaper than anywhere else in Mexico; to Tlaxcala to see the frescoes being painted on the walls of public buildings by a famous Mexican artist, depicting Mexican history from the time the Aztecs were conquered by Cortez to the Mexican Revolution of 1910; and to Huetjotzingo on the day of "Carnival" to watch the reenactment of the kidnapping of the beautiful daughter of the city official by the legendary Mexican bandit, Agustin Lorenzo. On their trips in and around Pueblo they will pass by many of the 365 churches — some in ruins and some still in use — built by the conquering Spaniards on Aztec worship and sacrificial sites. Perhaps the most exciting tour of all is the trip by chartered bus through the mountains and quaint villages to the Pacific — to Acapulco to spend two days in the sun.

When it is all over they will return to Mankato, Minnesota, each having spent less than $200.00, and each carrying from $30.00 to $50.00 worth of gifts. When they come to school, they will not have to "make up" the work they missed; the Wilson year-round open concept — individualized in programming — plug in, plug out as needed — allows its students to be gone from "classes" any time during the 12-month year.

In May, 25 Mexican students, and three chaperons, come to Mankato and to the Wilson Campus School. Most live with the same brothers and sisters who hosted the Wilson students six weeks earlier. They immerse themselves in our culture, as we did in theirs. We take them to see a typical Minnesota farm, and arrange participation in water sports on our lakes. They eat hot dogs and hamburgers; we take them to see the Mayo Clinic and the IBM computer plant in Rochester. They will shop in a large American shopping center and see a Minnesota Twins baseball game. While they are at school they become involved in any learning activities offered or requested.

The most rewarding phenomenon of this complete program is to watch four or five Mexican and American young people sitting together in the cafeteria at Centro Escolar, or at Wilson, communicating in English and in Spanish, laughing and joking, thoroughly enjoying each others company, knowing that these friendships can last years; when the exchange program is over, they usually continue to write, using the Spanish or English they have improved. They try to learn more because they are highly motivated; in many cases, they intend to return for visits to their respective exchange countries, for they now understand and appreciate the people of another culture.

This experience hopefully helps these young people accept the value of human beings everywhere, and hence become sensitive in their future roles as adults toward creating a better world.

"People Caring About People"
Lorna Wing Bader, Counselor
Wilson School

In the open environment of the Wilson Campus School, many varied opportunities exist for caring about people. These situations occur within and outside of the counseling center, which we call "The Listening Post." The philosophy at Wilson is that caring should not be limited to one certified person: helping skills can and should be learned by everyone; they are especially important to those who come in contact with students. Counseling (i.e., caring for others) is not only for people when they have a "problem" or concern; it is a way of relating to one another, a day by day caring for people, a way of life.

Teachers have the most extensive contact with students at Wilson, so they are in the best position to meet their needs, and to help identify those who may later be referred to The Listening Post. Counseling would not be as effective, nor reach as many people, if the staff were not as involved as they are in helping and caring for students.

To encourage and continue staff development, inservice sessions are held regularly by the counselor and other qualified personnel, allowing staff to expand their basic communication and listening skills. In the process of applying these, they grow closer and become more trusting and accepting of one another.

Psychological education (learning about self and others) is now a part of the curriculum. Learning how to relate with others, and to better understand our own behavior, has become as important as cognitive learning. A large number of staff have participated as leaders of guidance during the past years, working in pairs meeting with their student groups three days a week for 30 to 45 minutes each day. Students who are interested can enroll. These groups, beginning with Kindergarten, help children to cope with the issues and concerns they face in the process of growing, and provide an opportunity for the staff and students to meet and experience each other as human beings.

The very young may be in a group with DUSO (Developing Understanding of Self and Others) materials. This program uses a puppet who tells stories involving situations that students in Kindergarten through perhaps age eight might encounter. The children relate their experiences to DUSO by talking about their feelings through the use of music, role playing, and puppets.

The middle school age student may participate in an IPC (Interpersonal Communication) group. The purpose is to help students become more aware of their feelings, and then practice expressing them. Positive growth is emphasized – experiences which foster human dignity and worth. A variety of guidance activities are used to reach the particular developmental needs of the group: The Magic Circle, Developmental Guidance Units, Values Clarification, and Environmental Educational Experiences. Materials for guidance by the classroom teacher are abundant and becoming widely used.

Peer Counseling (preparing students to counsel other students), and Career Education groups, have been held for high school age students. Opportunities for older youth to demonstrate "caring and sharing" are provided through social service; in this program they work with and help the elderly, the ill, younger or new students, community organizations, and volunteer groups.

Prior to leading sessions, staff and counselor meet to experience and learn group leadership skills; they continue to meet once a week during their involvement period to share ideas, express concerns, critique each other on video tapes, and know each other as people.

As the Wilson population becomes involved in psychological education, the gap between cognitive and affective learning lessens; a more humane environment continues to grow. When teaching cognitive concepts, a teacher becomes more aware of how students are feeling about themselves and their role. If a student develops a positive self-concept, and is aware of someone caring about him or her as a person, the learning experience becomes more meaningful for both.

A major part of caring at Wilson involves sharing. Frequently the administration, staff, counselor, and parents meet to share concerns they may have regarding students or adults within the school. Through this sharing, more opportunities for helping are discovered and applied in day-to-day living in the school.

Students, parents, and faculty may have situations arise in their personal lives outside of the school which cause distress. The Listening Post has gradually developed into and serves as a confidential and accepting sounding board for these concerns, personal as well as professional. However, Wilson has discovered that counseling no longer consists of a set of "secret" skills to be used only behind a closed door; instead, these must be taught, caught, modeled, and visibly used daily, if the school is to foster a positive learning climate for adults as well as students.

The administration and the counseling personnel at Wilson are working toward the same goal: To create a more caring and humane environment for all people within the school. When the administration gives great support in this direction, the counselor is allowed to do what counselors should do, and that is, help people.

"Junior Practicum in Special Education: Student Reactions"
by Daryll Larson, Special Education Department
Mankato State University

Wilson Campus School provides clinical experiences for students at the pre-training and graduate level in special education, ranging from volunteer, to the junior practicum, to student teaching and internships. The impact that the Wilson faculty has upon students in training is best expressed by university students participating in this program. One wrote: "Wilson is a community of varied people who work, play, and help each other; the special education students are mainstreamed or integrated within the total program and have been since 1968 when Dr. Glines became director. Many of their interrelated learning experiences include the (1) Wilson Bakery — the youngsters bake and sell their products to fellow students at cost; (2) determining the possibilities for driver training, gun safety, and snowmobile safety; (3) swimming and ice skating — using the university pool and the new Ice Palace; (4) cooking, sewing, and industrial arts at both the elementary and secondary levels; and (5) participating in schoolwide activities such as drama, music, art, tours, and field trips without being designated or labeled.

"Wilson is People!"

Another university student wrote: "It's a good experience because I am working with different students of all ages with different problems. The materials available and the way they use them are great! I feel the special education pupils learn more at Wilson than in a traditional special education classroom by their interaction with other pupils."

Further comments by other college students included: "By working there I have gained a deeper insight into myself and my own personal feelings." "At Wilson we work with students having a wide range of abilities. This is an asset because the range of experiences available to a person in training is so varied." "I have been teaching on and off since 1960 in many different schools – and have never been associated with one that has as broad an offering of opportunities for children age three through high school. It is truly a humane school."

"Wilson Social Service Program"
J. Daniel Beebe, Associate Director
Wilson School

The staff and administration feel that the school ought to be preparing students to become humane, effective citizens. With that objective, graduation is determined in part by the ability of the student to relate humanely with other children and adults through a variety of activities in school and in the community. A social service experience at Wilson is defined as "helping others with no tangible (i.e., pay) reward to the student, other than recognition that the student has helped others or the community, and has fulfilled his or her social service obligation." The program hopefully results in a significant new dimension being added to the lives of Wilson students, as well as providing valuable aid and assistance to many organizations and individuals.

The evaluation by local agencies has been overwhelmingly positive. We generally have more requests for service than we have available students. The experiences have been as diverse as the students themselves, and have been available on a group or individual basis. Activities have been held in various locations within the school building, and in the greater Mankato community. Yet all the projects have had one thing in common: they have provided an opportunity for the students and staff to give of themselves to others.

As the effort grew, and the number of students participating increased, a full time staff member was hired to coordinate the program. The responsibilities, while many and varied, included (1) contacting local nonprofit agencies to locate social service opportunities for students; (2) contacting staff members at Wilson, the university, and the local public schools to locate opportunities; (3) disseminating information to students and their advisors regarding available social service potentials; (4) previewing and approving proposed student social service projects; (5) placing students in projects according to their interests, age, and abilities; (6) arranging transportation (i.e., school vehicles, public transportation, parents) if necessary; (7) assisting with the criteria and goals for each selected project, and with the evaluation of the services provided by the student; and (8) making periodic contacts with the project supervisors to ensure that students were meeting their commitments, providing a valuable service, and participating in service which was meaningful to them.

In many cases, some of these functions may be done by a teacher or advisor, but the social service coordinator needs to stay in contact with the advisors, maintain a record of the projects, and ensure that the responsibilities are accomplished. The diverse social services include students working in Headstart, day care centers, the state mental hospital, medical hospitals, nursing homes, meals-on-wheels, community and family service centers, civil defense, law enforcement, ambulance services, language interpreting, crisis intervention centers, and the various service organizations (helping the Lions with their fundraising for eye glasses). Many students assist the elderly or the disabled by doing physical chores and tasks; they provide and receive emotional support on a one-to-one basis.

A tutoring program (students teaching other students) has been informally in operation since the transformation of Wilson. The social service program developed that concept further through training programs for tutors, and for students acting as teacher aides, especially for the younger students in the Mankato area schools.

Students give assistance in many areas of Wilson. Several help the custodian clean the lunchroom each day; at least a dozen students help prepare and serve food on a rotating basis throughout the week. Students are trained and then give tours in the building, which takes pressure off the administration, and gives the visitors a different perspective. The central office is understaffed, so several older students provide secretarial assistance during the day. A desirable result of this has been the development of close relationships between staff, administrators, and students.

The social service projects described are by no means complete, but suggest the variety of experiences that can lead to a higher level of sensitivity to the needs of others in our society. From all indications, the social service program at Wilson has had a very positive impact on staff and students; we are committed to staffing and continuing the program. We feel that our open school facilitates social service, since students can participate most any week of the year, any day of the week, and any time of the day. Conversely, we feel that the social service program facilitates the open school by providing life experiences in the real world which supplement and complement the instructional efforts in educating youth in a humane way.

"Parents are Involved"
Elizabeth Barta, Volunteer Coordinator
Family Awareness Center

Based on the concepts that total family commitment, and involvement with the community, are essential elements in education, parents at Wilson Campus School initiated programs to enhance these beliefs. The project, suggested by the Futures Committee of the Wilson Advisory Council, is called the Family Awareness Center, and is located in an office within the school; the Center is staffed during school hours by parent volunteers.

The purpose is to foster a feeling of community among parents, staff, and students. One way of promoting this is to invite families of students to the school for breakfast with the teachers. Each advisory group is invited separately. Breakfasts were chosen because they are at an hour when the majority of working parents can attend; the event is a social activity, to help them feel comfortable coming into the school. Such contacts often give teachers a different concept of the children, after meeting socially with their parents and brothers and sisters. Those parents who can stay longer are invited to remain to visit the school or participate in the learning activities.

To locate resources among the parents, a questionnaire was sent to each family asking members to designate interests, talents, and availability. Later telephone interviews were conducted; the information gathered was compiled into a booklet called "The Parent Resource Bank." Distributed to the staff, it became a visible indication of the wealth of skills and talents available among the parents. Drawing upon this resource, the Family Awareness Center has been able to provide direct services to the staff: finding volunteers to assist in metric cooking, drivers for transportation, and aides for swimming classes.

Hoping to find more creative ways of helping, five classes were offered during the past year by parents. One of the most popular, "Handwriting Analysis," was offered jointly by a mother and a father. Another for eight and nine year olds addressed human relationships. Since beginning the Family Awareness Center, volunteers have met twice weekly with the younger children in a class on "How to Tell Time." While two staff members offered materials, such as clock dials or puzzles, the volunteers have been free to develop their own games and methods for the class. This has created a feeling among the volunteers that the staff trust their judgments and rely on their efforts.

The Center has contacted various groups in an effort to find senior volunteers – foster grandparents – to work with students in the school, and contribute their special knowledge and skills to the learning programs. Students were spellbound when an 80 year old "grandmother" related her experiences to a class studying the Depression. Other volunteers made it possible for Wilson students to cooperate in a St. Paul Open School program for an urban-rural student exchange.

To broaden the concept that learning is a life-long pursuit, efforts to eliminate the distinction between school and community are explored; from this each week the Wilson Wanderers Club, a group of six and seven year olds, is taken by volunteers to places of interest, such as the Historical Museum, the university greenhouse, and the post office. Arrangements for all-day field trips have been the total responsibility of the Family Awareness Center. One such venture was to Walnut Grove to visit the site of *On the Banks of Plum Creek* by Laura Ingalls Wilder. Students were encouraged to read the Wilder series; for those children not yet able to read, arrangements were made for a volunteer to read the book to them. It was also read on tape for the participants to "hear." Ninety-six elementary age students participated in the adventure.

In a thank you note to those who have been a part of the activities of the Family Awareness Center, Don Sorensen, Associate Director of the school, wrote: "I can see the school as one place where we can bring together the parents, grandparents, neighbors, teachers, and local business people to give the students a complete picture of life as it really is . . . " The volunteers of the Family Awareness Center represent just one group working to achieve this at Wilson.

"Multi-Age Lab"
Pat Wilhelms and Marven Wolthuis, Business Coordinators
Wilson School

At Wilson Campus School, open labs are in many of the learning areas; these classrooms are organized so that the facility is open to students of all ages for most of the day.

Two such multi-age labs are the typing and the computer areas where students K-12 sit side by side working toward their goals. The age difference seems almost unnoticeable as the interaction between students is observed. They offer help to each other in many positive, caring ways: taking the time to talk with each other, helping with questions such as spelling a word, or providing a specific command to the computer;

frequently a 16 year old boy may be timed by an 8 year old girl who is sitting at the next typewriter, or a 13 year old girl typing a report may ask the 9 year old boy beside her how to spell a word. Two 10 year olds may help each other at the computer terminal. At Wilson, everyone is a teacher; everyone is a learner.

(This report was written in 1969, long before the rush to computers; Wilson was one of the first six schools in Minnesota to have a computer terminal linked to a mainframe. "First graders" could use the typewriters and terminals as well as the "seniors.")

"The Teacher as Advisor"
Don Sorensen, Associate Director
Wilson School

The Wilson Teacher-Advisor System (T-A), which was started in the fall of 1968, was an attempt to build a "caring" climate, with direct adult participation. No special preparations were made; the program arose with the arrival of Don Glines as director who was committed, as were many staff, that an advisor system should become a part of the environment. In a lab school such as Wilson, it is imperative that new and different approaches are tried, even if they may not achieve smashing successes.

From the very beginning of the T-A System, the Wilson students have been given the opportunity to select their advisors. Several choices are necessary to ensure that there can be an equalization of the advisee load, but in recent years we have been able to give approximately 75% of the students their first choice. This makes it possible for a caring relationship to be built from the beginning, since there is a mutual seeking that might not be possible if the students were assigned to their advisors.

There is a certain amount of necessary growth in a staff, if a T-A System is to be strong. A key lies with the school counselor; inservice sessions with the faculty help them grow in effectiveness, commitment, and confidence. More importantly, the staff must know that there is a person who is ready and able to assist them in serving as advisors. The role of the counselor, therefore, must be changed, once a T-A System is incorporated into a school.

We at Wilson feel we have made some very significant progress in building a T-A System over the years, and therefore have something to share with other educators. We offer assistance and encouragement in developing site programs by sharing our successes, failures, and unresolved concerns.

"How Wilson Assists the Blue Earth County Juvenile Court"
Joe Kubicek, Probation Officer
Blue Earth County

Wilson Campus School has been of incalculable value to the Blue Earth County Juvenile Court. The Probation Department has found that certain youth, largely through no fault of their own, do not fit into the conventional school program; very often they have been battered emotionally.

It is extremely difficult for a person who has been raised in a home wherein the "normal" upbringing occurs, to see and to understand the inner feelings of many of these youth. The difficult cases very often, as many social workers can attest, come from homes within which emotional turmoil reigns, resulting in varying degrees of disrupted lives.

We believe that Wilson Campus School provides the emotional, as well as the educational atmosphere, most conducive to healing as well as learning – a therapeutic climate – in addition to the conventional educational benefits. I do not know what we would do, in our efforts to assist these youth to reconstruct their futures, without this resource in our community.

"Music at Wilson"
Sharon Postma, Music Instructor
Wilson School

Most students at Wilson Campus School take some form of music, either in the early childhood center, or in the music area available to all ages of students. In recent years, three choral groups have emerged; the senior choir has performed very creative and somewhat unusual musical productions. After a performance of the jazz-rock cantata, *Joseph and His Amazing Technicolor Dreamcoat*, this group expanded to include 60 students who arranged the music and choreography, and became the first area school to perform all the music of *Godspell*. A combined music/drama production of *You're a Good Man, Charlie Brown*, was followed by a winter original interpretation of *Free to be You and Me*, inspired by the Marlo Thomas TV special; it was delightful fun, and a consciousness-raising experience for the students who participated, and for the several schools for whom it was performed.

The upper elementary and junior high age students performed the Gilbert and Sullivan MIKADO last spring, and already this year presented *Once Upon A Mattress*. The Wilson atmosphere of creativity, the flexibility in scheduling, and the help from student teachers and interns all combine to enhance these programs. *The Wizard of Oz* involved K-12 students together and all of the subject areas. It was truly an all-school production.

Individual music participation occurs in small groups, and on a one-to-one basis, in areas of voice, piano, guitar, and recorder; special interest opportunities in music theater and music appreciation are offered. Since most learning occurs when it is enjoyable and meets the needs of the students, Wilson tries to provide opportunities that encourage them to acquire music skills, and at the same time, have experiences that help them feel good about themselves and their learning programs.

"Wilson Physical Education Program"
Mark Schuck and Lynn Russ, Athletic Directors
Wilson School

The Wilson physical education program starts with our preschool swimming activities, and our gross motor emphasis. The elementary students move through individualized developmental levels with activities progressing from gross motor, low organized games, fine motor control, lead up games, and basic team and individual skills.

The older students programs are composed of elective choices of an individual and dual nature emphasizing life time sports, such as archery, badminton, bowling, swimming, downhill skiing, cross-country skiing, tennis, paddle ball, and many more. Team experiences are available through intramurals and through the interscholastic program where Wilson sponsors teams in football, basketball, volleyball, gymnastics, and track; they have been very successful over the years in league and regional competition. As with all learning at Wilson, physical education and sports are completely optional and can be individually designed. Even though voluntary, 100 percent participate all or part of their years at Wilson.

"Relationship of Wilson and S.E.A."
Orville Jensen, Program Leader
Studies in Educational Alternatives

S.E.A. is the Studies in Educational Alternatives (originally begun as part of Wilson by director Don Glines, and called the Studios for Educational Alternatives) − a fully recognized program within the College of Education at Mankato State University; it is designed to give those students in teacher education who prefer alternative methods of securing certification a way to accomplish that desire. All of the state requirements for certification, and the college requirements for graduation are met, but in an individualized way.

One of the objectives is to place the prospective teacher in classroom settings early and often − as early as the freshman year, and as often as three or four extended periods prior to student teaching. The S.E.A. program headquarters are in the Wilson Campus School. Physically it occupies two offices, from which approximately 75 to 100 undergraduate education majors are counseled each quarter.

Programmatically the relationship of the two programs (Wilson and S.E.A.) within the Center for Experiential and Alternative Education is very intricately woven. S.E.A. is the personalized, option oriented, alterative extension of the Wilson concept into the undergraduate teacher education level. Most S.E.A. interns use Wilson staff and students extensively and intensively for portions of their seminar, field, and independent study activities; Wilson students and staff are able to call on the time and expertise of S.E.A. interns to further personalize their opportunities. It has proven to be an exciting breakthrough in teacher education.

"Studies in Experiential Education"
Robert VanderWilt, Program Leader

The Studies in Experiential Education program is a 51-hour Master of Science degree within the College of Education at Mankato State University; it is included in the Center for Experiential and Alternative Education, co-directed by Don Glines, Joe Schultz, and myself. Two other programs are housed in that center: the Wilson Campus School, and the undergraduate S.E.A. program.

Being administratively in the same unit with Wilson has provided a unique opportunity for graduate students, inasmuch as they are afforded internship and practicum experiences in the Campus School which otherwise are not easily available. They have assisted in most of the offerings including social service, early childhood, music, drama, physical education, mathematics, counseling, and environmental studies.

Many graduate students and staff have participated in the planning, supplementation, and evaluation of outdoor adventure programs for the students at Wilson. Canoe and kayak, rock climbing, and hiking trips have all been a part of this joint program effort.

The Campus School has provided a realistic laboratory setting for graduate students to work, experiment, and learn; in exchange they have contributed their individual strengths, abilities, and personalities, and have had a positive impact on the Wilson programs.

"Lower Brule Sioux Exchange"
Lorna Wing Bader, Counselor
Wilson School

Wilson students in the general age range of 11 and 12 travel to South Dakota to spend a week at the Lower Brule Sioux Reservation. They live with the Native American families and attend the reservation school. During their stay they participate in classes, spend time exploring the flora and fauna of the area, study the Sioux history, learn some of the language, go on picnics with the children, ride horses, and are treated to Native American food and a Pow Wow during the high school homecoming activities.

Sioux children return with the Wilson group; they spend a week in Mankato and attend the school. Some of the children have never been off the reservation; they are amazed at such things as the number of trees, the black dirt, and the escalators in the stores. The children gain new insights into their own surroundings, as commonly accepted things are seen through the eyes of another youth; black dirt and many trees are no longer taken for granted.

The administrations at both schools feel that this is a program they want to continue. Many similar exchanges with Indian students from a number of reservations, including the Choctaw in Mississippi, and Turtle Mountain in North Dakota, have been part of the Wilson effort. This Sioux visit serves as an example of the Wilson commitment to experience other cultures.

"West Concord vs. Wilson"
Virginia Bergman, West Concord Parent

"The goal of the West Concord school system is to develop good citizens to live in a democratic society."
- from the West Concord High School Handbook for Students, 1975-76, West Concord, MN

"It is our intent that by providing students with opportunities to make decisions that have an effect upon them, they will grow into value-choosing, self-directing adults."
- from an introductory brochure on the Wilson Campus School Mankato, MN

At West Concord, there are required classes, bells, and letter grades. Absences from school must be excused. The dress code, emphasized in the handbook, suggests "good taste, decency, safety, and health." Respect for authority is the key to the structure of the traditional system of education. The handbook says: "We expect West Concord students to be respectful at all times."

Descriptions

At Wilson, the brochure directly states: "There are no dress codes, no bells, no required classes, and no letter grades; attendance is optional." The advisory system is the key to the structure of the open school; at Wilson it is the primary means by which students receive adult supervision and guidance. One responsibility of the advisor is "to develop a close, personal relationship with each advisee and her/his parents," according to the brochure.

My daughter, Jean, is a ninth grade student at West Concord. One day in October, I attended several of her classes. The following week, Jean and I visited Wilson. We felt that the West Concord curriculum compared favorably with the offerings at Wilson. Both schools provided students a variety of enrichment courses and activities. The most obvious difference between the two schools, Jean and I agreed, was the environment created by the respective approaches to learning. The following are the impressions resulting from a brief immersion in those environments.

WEST CONCORD REPORT: The structural design of the traditional school makes more visible those few, who, for whatever reason, do not conform. The handbook forbids the use of obscene language.

Jean and several girlfriends gather in their homeroom to await the first bell. I find a seat apart from the girls. A boy enters the room. As he passes slowly before the gaze of his audience, he pronounces, in a monotone, a string of obscenities. One of the girls pushes him through the opposite door. In a few minutes, he is back to repeat his performance.

The handbook states: "Public display of affection between boys and girls is not acceptable."

As the students move through the corridors, a youthful couple, on occasion, separate themselves from the crowd; and the boy, awkwardly and tentatively, places his hand on the small of the girl's back.

The handbook says nothing about loneliness: Each time I enter the restroom that day, I see the same girl standing there – alone. In a soft voice, she introduces herself, and we talk for a little while.

Between classes, as students shift to other rooms, the corridors are filled with sounds of laughter, conversation, and the slams of hastily closed locker doors. The bell rings and, then, for another hour, there is quiet throughout the building.

WILSON REPORT: The intent of the open school structure is to provide for the needs of a community of individuals. In such a setting, conformity becomes a meaningless word.

Students pass in the corridor, two or three at a time. Several boys and girls of various ages are gathered at tables in the snack bar. Another group of children seated in an open area is watching the film, "Outward Bound."

Despite the absence of dress codes, we notice no striking difference in appearance between Wilson and West Concord students.

The preschoolers are busy in their center. Some are piling huge building blocks up high and then knocking them down. Others are finger painting at a low table.

As we continue our tour through "Bach's Box," (music center), and "The Lion's Den," (English and math focus), Jean observes: "I can't believe what I'm seeing and hearing. Boys and girls are actually working and playing together without name-calling and teasing."

A friendly student leads us to a table in the snack bar. She is a 16 year old girl who has been at Wilson since fourth grade. I ask her about the advisory system.

She explains that her major areas of interest, which she would like to continue at college, are music and physical education. Her advisor, whom she had selected from members of the faculty, is a football coach at Wilson.

Remembering the brochure, I ask if "close, personal relationships" really do develop between the advisor and advisee.

"Yes," she replies, "they really do."

The other two students, a teenage boy and girl who have joined us, agree with their friend.

Jean and I pass an open door and pause to listen to a woman's voice, "The square roots you will need to know are 4, 9, 16 . . ."

There has been a steady, but moderate, level of noise throughout the day, with no bells marking units of time. Students learn without conformity.

"Open Structure"
Mary E. Kolb, Student
Mankato State University

At Wilson there are no dress codes, no mandatory attendance requirements, and no report cards. Tailor made programs to meet individual needs are available in areas such as curriculum, student-teacher relationships, and personal growth and development.

Students are offered learning experiences such as death, ecology, and early Mankato, as well as shorthand, typing, chemistry, and science, all interrelated as parts of teams or centers. In addition to "traditional typing," opportunities include social service, leisure, and enrichment activities.

Programs have been established for continuing student involvement. Community services include nursing home visits, volunteer work at St. Peter State Hospital, Headstart, or shoveling sidewalks for the elderly; school services range from work as Spanish or music tutors, serving as school guides, or caring for the rock gardens.

Students have an important role in deciding their educational program. Each student selects his or her own advisor, the person who works closely with parents and other teachers, as well as the student, in overseeing the overall school growth of the youth.

Wilson offers a place for parents in the education of their children. They meet as a voluntary group to participate or observe in the classrooms with their children or serve as a welcoming group for new parents; Wilson is a real family.

"Experiencing Wilson"
Alice Tracy, Wilson Student

It is important to realize that the student body at Wilson represents a cross-section of the Mankato community. Within the school, I had friends ranging in age from preschool to college students to the regular teaching staff. My studies included African History, Kite-Making, and Law and Ethics . . . experiences not often found in traditional high schools.

Before I came to Wilson, I had spent a very unhappy year in a traditional high school – hiding out in bathrooms to escape classes, lying to my teachers, feigning illness . . . all of the old tricks familiar to school children everywhere, except, perhaps, those fortunate few able to attend a site like Wilson for all of their school years. I was ready to give up altogether, but the Wilson experimental program, based on the principle of providing a humane and positive learning environment for each student, gave me a new interest in my own education.

"In the process of doing research for a book about Wilson, I interviewed some teachers, and found that the school was a very different place for them, too. A social studies instructor pointed out that a teacher cannot simply sit back and wait for the students to take the initiative in the learning process, even though they do all the choosing. "I found that you had to continue building relationships if you wanted the students to be interested in taking classes from you," he said. In this way, respect for student opinion is built into the system. The richness of the Wilson experience may lie most in its great variety, and in the relationships that are formed among individuals and groups.

Summary

This beautiful program met the criterion originally established for Wilson: "If schools are to be <u>significantly</u> better, they must be <u>significantly</u> different." Wilson was a different and better learning environment for the students, families, and staff who selected this option, in a town named Mankato, located 2,000 miles north of Dallas, and 40 miles east of Sleepy Eye, Minnesota.

Remember When

*   Those evenings when you and your family went to your little one-room school to do things together?

*   Your teacher was also your friend and neighbor?

*   Your little school was responsive to you <u>and</u> your family?

*   You used to learn and play with both younger and older classmates?

Descriptions

* Local control meant <u>you</u> — not a big government bureaucracy — had a say in what happened at <u>your</u> country school?

* Older students helped and cared for younger students?

* "Discipline" meant you <u>wanted</u> your school to be a good place to be?

* In days before big government, schools could be a little different because Moms and Dads wanted it that way?

chapter fourteen

CAMELOT

Mankato State University closed the doors on Wilson in June of 1977. It had nothing to do with the program or faculty, but was motivated by the desire for a building for the college and the win/lose politics of the new president. Out of the ashes grew a private alternative education program for the people of Mankato, which lasted a number of years until funding became a severe problem.

The staff compiled a film, "Corner of the Rainbow," recording the nine years as an innovative pioneer for the nation. The former director was asked to contribute an "I Remember" review to highlight the early problems, changes, and successes as Wilson moved in new directions. It is reprinted as another example of how to begin essential transitions toward futures oriented societal and educational transformations.

I remember the beginning; July 1, 1968, I arrived at the school for my first day just as the bell rang. I knew Wilson could not function with bells, so I called the custodian and asked him to disconnect them. He looked at me, unbelieving, but when I convinced him that I was serious, he did disconnect, and that was the last time that bells rang.

I remember the master schedule. Prior to my arrival, a small group had worked to develop a traditional period 1-2-3 secondary school schedule to have it ready when I arrived. They brought it to me; I looked at them and asked if this was the only copy, and the response was "Yes." I thanked them for their work, said I was sorry I needed to do this, but then proceeded to tear it in pieces, as the anger and frustration mounted within those who were watching. One of them finally asked: "But when will we build the schedule?" I answered, "The first day, after we have met the students. How do we know what they need or want until we have talked with them?" That was the end of the traditional schedule at Wilson.

I remember building our second daily schedule in September, 1968. I had built the first day very "open" with just some welcome/explanation assemblies planned. The team assigned to develop it for the second day of school came to me in such frustration that they virtually threw the scheduling materials at me and said they refused to do it. I said fine, that I would finish it up at 3:00 in the morning – the first opportunity I would have; I was honestly swamped and knew I had other work that would take until midnight. Later they came back and said: "Give us that '____' schedule; we are just as smart as you – if you can build it, so can we!

I remember the petition the first year to have me fired as director, but I especially remember all of the students and teachers at Wilson who came to my defense. The petition drive was led by College of Education faculty members who saw the new Wilson as challenging the "correct way" they were instructing their teacher education students.

I remember knocking out the walls at Wilson, repainting the entire building with "fun" colors over the objections of many who wanted to keep the traditional light greens and tans of the old schoolhouse.

I remember resigning the second year in frustration over all of the problems; that evening, while sitting on the steps of a caboose, which was standing idle on a railroad track back of Main Street, wondering what I should do, I was discovered by another Wilson staff member whose guidance and support gave me the courage to change my mind and stay.

I remember many exciting moments at Wilson, such as our first student trip to Mexico and the laughter and tears that accompanied the departure and return, and the same when the Mexican students came to Mankato. I remember the total school involvement in *The Wizard of Oz*, and the beautiful production of *Hair*.

I remember the excitement of the first book about Wilson, *Implementing Different and Better Schools*, and even more, the second one, *Creating Humane Schools*. I remember the hundreds of visitors from throughout the United States, and the multiple invitations to speak about Wilson from every region of the nation and five provinces in Canada.

I remember the excitement of seeing our pre-kindergarten and primary age children doing such a beautiful job in industrial arts and home economics, and little Nancy, a six year old, teaching one of our burly high school football seniors how to change the bobbin in the sewing machine. He was taking Bachelor Survival, and in desperation, when no teacher or high school girls were available, he asked Nancy, who was sitting at the opposite machine, if she could help him fix the problem. She said, "I think so," as she got down from her chair, climbed in his lap, and proceeded to solve the mystery.

I remember some of the funny scenes, too, such as the year I was coaching football and was rushed in changing clothes in the temporary office during remodeling. A young woman graduate student stopped in the main office to see me regarding an internship; she was sent to the room where I was located, but I had already changed and was on the football field. She came back and reported that she could not find me. Her statement to the secretary ended work for the day: "His clothes were there, but he wasn't." I also remember those cold Fall nights with the wind whistling through the college stadium as we attempted to throw 40-50 passes each game – trying to keep pace with the Minnesota Vikings.

I remember ensuring that faculty rotated and took time to occasionally have lunch at Michaels, the best restaurant in town. When the banker and other town "notables" were critical of teachers not at school, I reminded them that I was glad I did not have money transactions during the noon hour or after the martini lunch of the executive; thus ended the questioning of Wilson staff at Michaels.

I remember so many highs and lows of our first two years. One day on my desk late in the afternoon I found a note from one of the key faculty members.

It said: "I'm staying home tomorrow; this day has been hell," and he did, for he knew he could make such a decision and would not be docked or be in trouble.

A related incident found one faculty member staying home doing spring cleaning, and when she scrubbed the floor, she saw my face — and scrubbed harder and harder, for she was so angry over what proved to be her misinterpretation of my statement. She, too, knew she could stay home "without permission;" faculty were encouraged to "get away" when necessary. As teachers worked in teams, the absence could be covered as soon as team members knew of the decision.

Then there was a third faculty member who spent two hours telling me I had better not embarrass her again. I had told a group of visitors that we did not have large groups; then when taking them on a tour we came across her room with 30 students studying the same lesson — and in trying to explain to the visitors such a classroom was normally not part of Wilson, she later exploded, for she had purposely planned such a group to help a number of students one time with fractions.

There was the complaint by the faculty member whose husband came to chastise me because "His wife needed roller skates" — she had moved seven times in six months — and it (I) was raising havoc with their marriage. That first year we moved most everyone more than once, trying to establish compatible teams, suites, and centers — and learning to interrelate curriculum. Unfortunately, she did need roller skates, as she was a "victim" of every move.

Students were involved in the frustrations too. A carload tested the open campus, optional attendance philosophy. They went to one of the junior highs, ran down the halls shouting obscenities. Of course, later they were caught and had a choice — to have their parents at school the next morning or stay home and wait for the police when the other school pressed charges. They insisted we could not do it — they had "freedom." I explained, yes, you have a driver license — you can go anywhere, anytime if you obey the speed limits, road courtesies, and stop signs. When you do not, you get a warning, then a ticket, and later a "jail sentence" if you injure others. Needless to say, they lost their licenses until they proved they could accept responsibility. There was more structure in this most "unstructured" school than in a conventional program. It was a "hidden structure."

And on the fun side was one of the inspirational moments. I was noted for long faculty meetings the first year as we tried to resolve chaos. The start of the second year, the faculty arrived for that first meeting. I greeted them and said to stay with it, for we were doing the impossible. I then recited, with a piano background, the words to "The Impossible Dream," after which, with the auditorium darkened, our choral instructor sang a beautiful rendition of it. Following, I said: "Do dream even more impossibles, and then enjoy seeing them become possible." I left and in less than ten minutes, we had established the focus for the year. It was probably the most effective meeting I ever planned as a principal.

Looking back at Wilson is always special, for I also remember the going away gifts when I left Wilson, especially the granite bookends inscribed: "If schools are to be significantly better, they must be significantly different." I remember the Don Quixote that was given to me as a reminder of our Impossible Dream.

Most of all, though, I remember all of the beautiful people in Mankato who assisted our efforts: the college officials, the newspaper editor, but especially the faculty, the students, and their parents — the veteran staff who accepted me, and the new faculty who together, with the help of those wonderful students and parents, created a different Wilson. I still receive letters from a number of them.

Wilson did change the mechanics, the schedule, the facilities — the organization of schooling and formal education — but most of all, Wilson tried to assist in the transformation of people who could help create a new learning system for an emerging society. Wilson was the growth of people toward being more humane, comprehensive, creative futurists; Wilson learned not to be concerned with the reform of schools, for it was attempting to lead the transition to a compassionate era. It was learning to unfold the deck chairs that Charlie Brown had replied to Lucy he was never able to get open, when queried as to which way his chair was facing, on the cruise ship of life.

Wilson was Willie Wonka, trying to make realities out of dreams, and dreams out of realities. Wilson was a dream about an Impossible Dream — an effort to reach the unreachable star. Wilson was that fleeting whisk of glory — a spot, where for one brief, shining moment, there was another *Camelot*.

During the closing days of Wilson, a number of letters were exchanged between staff and former staff and friends. One such informal letter from a teacher to the initial director illustrates the spirit that was Wilson, and provides a personal evaluation of what happened to some of the students who chose to attend college.

April 18, 1977. (Paul Revere's ride day!)

"We really appreciate all the support you've given us, your encouraging words, and your distribution of our advertising. No one has a job for next year as far as I know, but that's at least partially because many of us are fussy about what kind of job we're going to take. I don't intend to apply to a public school. While it is possible to accomplish these things there, it's an uphill fight, and I don't have the necessary patience anymore.

"The committee is trying the suggestions you sent regarding publishing the book — collecting rejection slips. As a last resort, I suppose we'll try to publish it ourselves. The book itself is falling into shape. Based primarily on interviews, it will focus on the experiences of six families at Wilson, trying to incorporate all of the factual data into this structure unobtrusively — at least that's where it is right at the moment.

"Now we'd like one more thing from you — we'd like you to write something for us. We know all of the things in your books — the philosophy, the changes, the how-to-do-it; what we'd like from you is something more personal: what it meant to you, memorable experiences, good moments. I realize that your time is used up at least three times, as usual, and that you have a lot of writing of your own to do; but the book won't be complete without something from you in it.

"Nothing has changed since I last wrote to you; we're still closing in 39 days. You'll realize about where we are now if I tell you that I stood at my mailbox reading your last letter and burst into tears at the last line; you did, indeed, rebuild Camelot here. Actually, though, it's less gloomy than I expected it to be by this time. What we're doing is still good, and the students are, of course, great. As always, we're so caught up in the day-to-day thing that we don't have time to realize often that it's the end of it. Please be sure to stop and see us if you get anywhere close at all; we all enjoyed your visit last spring. It would be great to have you join our Friday afternoon seminar.

"My kids are all in Minneapolis; the boys are going to the U., both of them majoring in languages. The one who caused so many worried teachers here so much anxiety because he wouldn't do math or much else, has a 4.0 average studying Greek, Latin, and Sanskrit. If you ever need an example to prove that it really makes no difference what a student does in high school, he's an ideal one. The few things listed on his permanent record when he graduated were real basics like fly-tying and tap dancing. The open school obviously ruined him for life!"

From another staff member, one paragraph again illustrates what made Wilson such a unique program.

"During the first summer session I am working disbursing materials and equipment to various departments of the University. It is not a pleasant position to watch the dismantling of Wilson. Many reams of teacher-prepared materials have been thrown away; they represent hours and hours of staff work. Areas that we were accustomed to seeing busily occupied by students are being gutted and converted to offices for various aspects of University facilities. I won't elaborate any further; I am sure it would elicit some of the same emotions in you as I feel. I am glad that most of the staff members have not been back since graduation to see what is happening. It isn't the building, but what has happened in the building, that is most disturbing to see being destroyed."

A telegram sent by the former director and a staff member unable to attend the final Wilson graduation perhaps provides a key to the development of Wilson concepts which were significantly better – and thus worth recording for history as another *Eight-Year Study* in education.

"Please let the staff, students, and parents know that we were thinking of you this week as you come to the end, but hopefully only the beginning, of an historic experiment in education. Our best wishes go with you as we each move in different directions in future years. However, we hope that the bond of Wilson will always keep all of us close in spirit, as we remember that we did indeed create another Camelot."

The Mankato Wilson Campus School closed. The descriptions of it, however, do reflect a Camelot, a program that for one brief shining moment was a significantly different and better opportunity for those who chose to attend. It was a landmark educational experiment; it provided new horizons for students, parents, staff, and learning, pre-K through university.

The 69 changes listed as Wilson innovations will be so obsolescent in the 21st Century learning systems of the future. They should even be obsolescent for programs in the 90s. For the remainder of the decade, though, as a result of the tremendous steps backward taken during the back to basics era of the 80s, the Wilson philosophy, concepts, and mechanics can still shine as a lighthouse – a beacon to point the way.

If the staff were beginning a new Wilson in the mid-90s, it would be different. It would go far beyond the ventures taken in the late 60s and mid-70s. It would form the transition toward the elimination of schooling; it would focus more on urgent future studies, on human potential, and on interdependent relationships.

It would be more creative, concerned with learning about learning, a program in the community and world, more of a non-school. Its goals would focus further toward a new system for a different era, and new commitments to human values. It would be less concerned about scheduling, college entrance, and traditional criticisms.

For the remaining 90s, though, many of the Wilson "69 changes" can be used to create alternative schools-within-schools, programs within-schools, and individual classrooms of choice. Wilson can yet serve as a catalyst to encourage educators to risk the steps necessary to move learning beyond the industrial complex. The evaluations of Wilson proved the success of its many changes. The mechanics worked; the philosophy made a difference. The effect of Wilson should not be lost.

New Camelots should arise from the ashes of Wilson. Needed are more brief shining moments of glory, but this time not to be closed by politicians, but to remain open as inspirations for others to lead the transition stages, and ultimately to create the total transformation of education in the United States. The process from schooling to education to learning should be achieved by 2020 A.D.

PART III

IMPLEMENTING

WILSON

Detailing Mechanics

chapter fifteen

ADVISING

The teacher-advisor system was initiated at Wilson in the fall of 1968; it proved to be the single most important change in the program. The warm, humane, person-to-person, self-selected relationship of the advisor as a friend, daddy or mommy, counselor, facilitator, lawyer, rewarder, punisher, defender, teacher, listener, motivator, guide, catalyst, companion, messenger, accountant – but most of all, a beautiful person for that student – did more to turn Wilson around than any other factor. Close rivals would be the implementation of the concept of responsibility, and the nonscheduled/non-requirement school; but neither of these provided the linkage to personal and program transformation that occurred through the advisor system.

The description of the conception and a rationale for the system as it emerged in 1975 – including the six-year selection patterns – is followed by a restatement, results, and recommendations for the concept as it developed in the early years of the program, to illustrate transition stages. A summarizing article, though somewhat repetitious, synthesizes the parts into a whole. Much credit for the ultimate direction of the teacher-advisor system at Wilson goes to four people: Don Sorenson, Associate Director and first coordinator of the system; Larry Herke, a Team Leader who became a prime developer of the approach; Lorna Wing, Counselor, who offered fresh, creative insight into its potential; and Dan Beebe, Associate Director, who spent many hours explaining the concept to hundreds of visitors. As in any good program, the staff who acted as the advisors were the ones who ultimately created the success story, especially Gail Palmer, Orville Jensen, Glenn Erikson, June Bayless, Jo Ann Lawson, Helen Holmes, Michael Barkhurst, Karen Knight, Lynn Russ, Lew Holden, and Perry Butler – all of whom spent many long, tedious overtime hours in the initial stages to develop a pioneer system.

The accompanying short articles were written by individuals primarily responsible for the implementation of the advising concept; they explain the philosophy and mechanics of this teacher-as-advisor system.

"The Advisor at Wilson Campus School"
By Larry Herke, Team Leader

An advisor at Wilson Campus School is the most significant link to the success of students in the total program. This premise applies to any school where this person is allowed to serve students in the cognitive, affective, and psychomotor areas of growth.

A fully functioning advisor assumes several roles while assisting advisees. According to a Wilson study conducted by Lorna Wing during 1971-72, teachers who were selected more frequently as advisors were rated significantly higher in areas of genuineness, empathy, and warmth than those who were selected less frequently. These three affective qualities are closely related and together indicate the major role of the individual.

If an advisee is convinced of the genuineness, he or she is more willing to trust the advisor with frustrations and joys which may never have been vented. Students can easily spot an advisor who is insincere and not honestly concerned with the welfare of the advisee. When students realize that the concern for them is genuine, they seem to be much more willing to face problems or tough situations which normally they might try to ignore or avoid. Much of this is due to the feeling that someone else shares the load with them. Just knowing they have someone who cares enough to spend time listening provides a feeling of importance. When advisees recognize this, they seem more willing to put greater effort into the total curriculum. The process is cyclical. Without the link of a concerned advisor, students may lose confidence or just "give up" when problems arise.

Empathy is closely tied to the feeling of genuineness. An advisee is more likely to seek help when the advisor had previously demonstrated an empathetic attitude. Few situations squelch the advisor-advisee relationship more than an impatient advisor who has little or no feeling for the situation of the advisee. The adult who can listen patiently to the student gains an understanding of the total person and is in a better position to help. The advisor has a multitude of opportunities to assist in clarifying the progress of the advisee, and to reinforce positive ideas or plans which he or she may formulate. Early in the role, advisors discover they are not people who just dictate answers to advisees. Yet the past experiences of the advisor are extremely helpful in developing a feeling for what the advisee might be experiencing. These insights are valuable when cooperatively building alternative solutions for the student to examine.

Genuineness and empathy are much more effective when tempered with the third component – warmth. If advisors can communicate such a feeling to their advisees, the total relationship can develop faster and more effectively. A smile, some reassurance, a "pat on the back," and a pleasant but forthright manner serve as catalysts in constructing and maintaining a healthy and humane relationship. An adult should not be hesitant in complimenting the youth when "things are going well." Too often counselors overlook the positive strides and instead place the "spotlight" on the negative experiences. Every positive behavior which is reinforced builds the self-concept of the advisee and promotes a more fully functioning individual.

In addition to the major role of being genuine, empathetic, and warm, an advisor suggests direction, communicates success, and assists in selecting courses or experiences; budgeting time to complete goals; assessing peer relationships; finding materials; analyzing an ineffective teacher-student match; and reviewing lack of attendance or progress in a particular experience. Times do exist when advisees need to hear some "cold facts," or perhaps they need a "kick in the pants" to get going again. The advisor has a responsibility to provide this push when it is merited; the manner in which it is given depends on the approach most effective for a particular advisee.

The last advisory role to be stressed is one of a communicator. The advisor should be in communication with the family and should provide information when expected growth in learning experiences is altered – whether this is a positive or negative change. Parents have a right to know of the progress of their children; for this reason they are given the opportunity for conferences whenever they or the advisor feel it could be beneficial. Often a phone call is sufficient, but the advisor should contact the parents at least three times each year to see if a session might be needed. When meetings are held (Family Designed Conferences – minimum of once a year) the advisee is present so that communication is open between advisor, parents, and student. The advisor communicates information to the office each quarter regarding the work of the student; an end-of-the-year report is completed. Several times exist when the advisor must contact other teachers on the progress of an advisee; this is achieved through conferences, notes, or short meetings.

Other advisory roles exist, but these form the major thrusts of "what an effective advisor is all about."

"Rationale for the Wilson Advisor System"
Don Sorenson, Associate Director
and Lorna Wing, Counselor

Students at Wilson are confronted with freedom and flexibility unknown to most students in the United States. Because they must continually make decisions concerning their educational program, the advisory system was devised to offer assistance to each youth related to his or her total educational pattern.

Under this format, K-12 students select a teacher who they feel can give them guidance or assistance in planning and implementing the program they have proposed. In reality, the advisor may only be a person the student can use as a sounding board, or as a friend to talk with in time of need. Regardless of how the advisor-student relationship develops, it is a key to the success of a program such as the one at Wilson. Roles for the advisor and advisee, and selection procedures are modified for the kindergarten children, but they too eventually select their own advisor, usually from among those of the staff who previously were/are early childhood specialists.

Roles and Responsibilities of the Advisor
1. To coordinate and be responsible for the communication between parent, teacher, and student.

   a. To hold one parent-advisor-advisee (Family Designed Conference) each year — or more often if needed.
   b. To communicate information to all advisees.

2. To dedicate four hours per week minimum to advisor-advisee business. This time may be used for individual conferences, group meetings, parent conferences. (The reality is that most spend much more time on this function, as it is far more important than "teaching.")

3. To be accessible and to develop a close, personal relationship with each advisee and his/her parents.

4. To be knowledgeable regarding school programs and potential learning experiences.

5. To recommend curriculum selection by helping students to identify weaknesses they should address, referring them to appropriate teachers, and monitoring their progress.

6. To review regularly the performance and permanent record of each advisee.

7. To work with students who have problems, perhaps following steps where difficulty develops:

    a. Teacher contacts advisor.
    b. Advisor works with student.
    c. Advisor goes to parents and/or counselor.
    d. Advisor refers student to administration.
    e. Administration takes action.

8. To maintain an advisor folder on each advisee and ensure that special activities (travel, work) and recognition (athletic, community, church) are recorded in the permanent folder.

9. To provide positive feedback through periodic phone calls and letters to parents of advisees who are performing well.

10. To write a year-end summary evaluation of each advisee.

Roles and Responsibilities of the Advisee
1. To do everything possible to build a close, personal relationship with the advisor.

2. To keep advisor informed regarding activities.

3. To take responsibility for providing material and/or making arrangements for parent-advisor-advisee conferences.

4. To sign in with the advisor each day present.

5. To be aware of what is available at Wilson and read notices provided by the advisor.

6. To attend and participate in individual advisor and group advisory meetings.

7. To perform actively in the Wilson program as planned with the advisor, teachers, and parents, and fulfill the commitments of the plan, or arrange for its modification.

8. To write a year-end summary evaluation of his or her own progress.

Selections and Procedures
    The advisory selection system at Wilson for one specific year was designed to accomplish the following: (1) give the students one or more weeks to become familiar with the faculty before choosing advisors; (2) assign 75 to 100 percent of the students to their first or second choice of advisors; (3) assign all students to one of the three advisors selected; (4) assign at least two students of the same gender to an advisor; (5) allow any student or advisor to ask for a new assignment if justified reasons are given to the advisory system coordinator.

    In implementing the plan during the opening week of school, each new student (or one whose previous advisor had left) was assigned a temporary advisor for initial guidance. During the second/third weeks, students were asked to choose three faculty members they would like as advisors. In a prior survey of the faculty, advisors indicated the desirable age range for their advisees. The students were to indicate their first choice with a one, their third choice with a three, from the faculty list (student interns, custodians, secretaries were also selected, but each student needed a permanent certified staff member, too). In previous years, students were asked to rank order five choices.

All three choices of advisors by students were compiled on individual sheets designated by the name of each teacher. After the tallies were completed, the assignments of students to advisors were made in the following manner: (1) student requests for the advisor of last year were honored; (2) teachers were then assigned the remaining students who chose them as first choice – once a teacher had received 18 advisees, the list was temporarily frozen; (3) students who needed special guidance were assigned to their first or second choice; (4) the remaining unassigned students were examined carefully in terms of their choices – it was necessary at this point to assign these students to their second and third choices, depending on how many students had already been assigned to these advisors; (5) once all assignments had been made, each list of students was carefully examined in terms of improper mixes related to gender/ethnic balances and personality conflicts. Some changes were necessary at this point. The lists of students assigned to each advisor were taken individually to that person for confirmation or recommendation. After any needed changes were made, the lists of advisees were again studied and modified where deemed necessary.

In recent years, much has been heard regarding the need for placing more emphasis on "humanizing our schools." Professional people, both in and out of the field of education, are saying educators must show more concern for the affective development of children from the moment they enter school. Teachers, counselors, administrators, and parents are becoming more concerned about the attitudes and feelings that students gain during these critical years. Some schools have responded to the call for a more humane environment by instituting some form of teacher-advisor system – an adult to talk with, or as some have labeled it, the 4T program (Teacher-To-Talk-To). Others are planning to do so and have begun laying plans for starting one in the future. Quite often, the problem does not lie in the commitment to go ahead, but rather in "how to proceed."

Wilson Campus School started its teacher-advisory system in the fall of 1968. The underlying objectives were to: (1) develop closer student-adult relationships; (2) help students improve their self-concepts; and, (3) foster an environment in which children and adults are more humane and accepting of one another. Many implementation changes were made during the years, but the commitment to these objectives remained.

Additions to the Wilson teacher-advisor system since its inception were: (1) one-to-one conferences between each advisor and the school counselor on a regular basis; (2) inservice opportunities for advisors to help them build better advising skills; (3) group activities designed to improve communication and understanding; (4) refinements in the selection process when students select their advisors; and, (5) closer relationships between the home and the school through advisor contacts.

A great amount of planning and effort will be needed in the future to build and sustain teacher-advisor systems if they are to become an important ingredient in humanizing schools. The staff at Wilson learned much from the experience, and as a result became consultants to those schools where people felt they could profit from sharing the results of the efforts in Mankato, Minnesota.

Advising

An article which tries to tie the Wilson concepts of personalizing curriculum, individualizing learning, and creating humane person relationships summarizes the advising system.

"Individualizing: Some Thoughts"
Daniel Beebe, Research Director

In any successful educational environment, the personal relationship between students and adults is crucial. In a traditional setting, various student-adult matches are based on random or arbitrary assignment. In an open school setting, there is an opportunity for a different approach. Wilson Campus School offers innovative programs and alternative learning strategies for students who benefit from a more flexible approach to education, realizing that student potential is the ultimate goal. To achieve that goal, each student is expected to participate in developing his or her own curriculum and learning experiences. Teachers are available as advisors to help the students in their decision making.

As an "open school," Wilson bases much of its program on the student-adult match. A self-direction process allows the students to design their programs and learn with instructors of their choice. To be successful, a student must be responsible, committed to, and accountable for the entire educational plan. To achieve this, the student enters into a close, personal relationship with an adult who perceives the student as a worthwhile individual. This essential relationship forms the basis of the advisor system, and is the "key" to a warm environment in an "open school."

In the Wilson advisor system, students select an adult whom they feel can provide guidance or assistance in planning and operating the program they have proposed. In some cases the advisor may be a person the student can use as a sounding board, or as a friend to talk with in time of need. Part of the advisor role is to engage in activities with the student which assist the advisors in knowing and understanding their advisees better. These may include sports, social gatherings, and home visits. To enable advisors and advisees to function in an individualized open manner, yet maintain philosophical responsibilities within the advisor system, a job description has been developed. The role of advisor includes evaluation, parent-advisor-advisee conferences, communication, short and long-range planning, general counseling, and group interaction. The requirement in the job description, that the advisor set aside a minimum of four hours per week (most spend much more time) for advisor-advisee activities, is an indication of the importance given the concept by the staff and administration.

During the first week of school, each student is assigned a temporary advisor for initial guidance and announcements. Soon after, students are asked to choose three faculty members they would like as advisors. The students rank their choices 1,2,3. In previous years, students have been asked to make five choices, but Wilson refined the mechanics of the assignment process so that all students receive one of their first three choices, eliminating the need for fourth and fifth selections.

In 1975-76, 15 advisors were assigned 16 to 18 students; ten were assigned 13 to 15; five were assigned ten to 12; and three were assigned nine or fewer students. Seventy-four percent of the students received their first choice, with 13 percent each receiving their second and third choices. Fifty-six percent of the students received their first choice in 1970-71; 68 percent in 1971-72; 78 percent in 1972-73; and 75 percent in 1973-74. While this represents a leveling off in the percentage of students receiving their first, Wilson was able to assign all students to one of their three choices. By comparison, when five were requested, nine percent received their fourth or fifth choice in 1970-71, three percent in 1971-72, and four percent in 1972-73.

The adult is an extremely important factor in determining the success of an individual student. In 1970-71, after completing the selection of their advisors, the students completed a survey revealing the factors most important in determining their first choice. From the data returned, it would seem that the primary factors involved in choosing were (1) feeling at ease, and (2) personality of the advisor. Factors such as parents or a teacher suggesting the advisor, age, gender, and knowing this person would not be one of the facilitators for the student, had less influence.

A related survey was conducted during 1971-72. In it, students rated their advisors on the Truax Relationship Questionnaire. It was concluded that <u>teachers who were selected more frequently as advisors were rated significantly higher in the areas of genuineness, empathy, and warmth</u> than those teachers who were selected less frequently. When these factors are assessed by students, they do choose those teachers as advisors who emit high levels of affective qualities. Such studies, as well as more recent information, seem to indicate that a successful advisor, like a successful teacher, is a warm, empathetic, and genuine individual.

Early in the first weeks of the new Advisor System, one of the staff had an "I have to see you now" urgency from an advisee. The session began, but the staff member realized that she had a group waiting for a "class." The director happened by where he could be seen. The staff member stepped out to ask: What do I do? The director responded: Do you need to ask? The Advisor then realized that of course, she was an advisor first, a teacher second. The class could be rescheduled; the urgency could not. That was the last time a "conflict" was posed between listening and teaching. It was amazing what the students would share with their advisor – things not even discussed with their parents: self-esteem concerns; dating and sex; alcoholic father; dislike of the coach; money for college; required babysitting; vacation plans; latchkey loneliness; mean babysitters; no lunch money; – every possible topic. The personal relationships were special.

Wilson pioneered new ideas in the late 60s; many of them are appropriate for turning the century. Another *Eight-Year Study* has proven that change is in the wind for the future of education.

chapter sixteen

RESPONSIBILITY

Humaneness and relevancy may be key philosophies in creating new, open, futuristic, responsive learning systems, but the mechanics of success rest with one basic slogan: "With Freedom goes Responsibility and Courtesy." If schools are not willing to practice the concepts implied, then change to a more open system is extremely difficult, if not impossible.

Students should have considerable freedom, but must learn to accept the responsibilities that go with self-direction, and the courtesy that must be extended to others. Making decisions and value judgments are important. The skills are not learned without opportunities to exercise these goals. In the past, concepts such as student freedom, responsibility, and daily scheduling have been barriers to change in that the majority of faculty, administration, board, and parents would not approve the program; they feared that students could not accept large amounts of freedom; the adults thought they would waste time, get in trouble, and not "learn as much."

In recent years a number of schools have been successful in developing models for use of unscheduled, open, or unstructured time. They have shown that it is a program that should be available to many of the students most of the time. The trauma of turning students "loose," and the mechanics and time necessary to build daily schedules, have certainly been barriers to improvement. How does a school overcome such barriers? What models are there throughout the country for a staff to consider for adoption or modification? Student responsibility was a key to success at Wilson.

In developing for a specific school a program related to freedom, responsibility, and open scheduling, students and staff must understand the philosophy and methods. Not comprehending the change from A to Z causes resistance. Teachers and students must consider the "why" factors in creating a daily smorgasbord schedule, or non-scheduled process; they must understand that the philosophy calls for time arrangements based upon the learning task, as determined daily by teams of teachers interacting, by student requests and decisions, by the individual or combinations of each. Schedules and choices should attempt to provide for the abilities, needs, and interests of every student on a personal basis each day; the concepts of freedom and responsibility should make appropriate utilization of time, space, professional staff, and materials. Wilson students learned to schedule 100 percent of their day.

The "what" factor becomes involved in two phases: one could be defined as teacher-scheduled time, and the other as student-scheduled time. Most schools have been afraid to attempt unstructured schedules, but those who gambled have provided excellent models. The teacher-scheduled time should usually occupy no more than 20 to 30 percent of the day, and less in the future. In optional attendance schools, time is generally controlled by student choice, not teacher demand. Even in required attendance situations, where the teacher can demand small or large groups, laboratory sessions, or individual conferences, she or he may control time only to the point that in a continuous progress, self-paced, individualized arrangement, if there is a need to work with one student, the adult may request that individual. When the teacher desires a laboratory experience for the student, it can be arranged, the same as students can be scheduled for small or large group situations or community involvement projects.

The major portion of the year could be defined as student-scheduled; 70 to 100 percent of each day, most students should be allowed to determine what they need to do with their time. The student should not be controlled by the authority of the teacher all day, except in necessary cases. In a school with extreme discipline problems, it is only the offenders who need to be "locked up" all day in specially designed areas, or placed in Person Centers – a program for helping students overcome difficulties in a confined but rehabilitation environment. Even in "problem" schools there are great youth and fine students. They should not be penalized, especially when often it is the school that has been the major problem, not the student.

What can individuals do during the time that is student-controlled? They can become involved in quest study, pursuing on their own an interest that they have developed, or an in-depth study, providing more detail growing from a program partially prescribed by the teacher; studying the equivalent of assignments given them in the past in traditional schools; or working on an independent project relating to one of their classes. A student might be the only one in school taking Latin American History, and therefore may be studying independently during this time on the topic. He or she may be working with small groups, or even in a large group. If students feel a need for special assistance from a particular teacher, they can receive it, usually on the day it is desired. They might be engaging in an activity, relaxing, having a snack, working on the school newspaper, or enjoying some other area that may not be related specifically to a field being studied.

Both students and teachers must understand where the youth may be during the student-scheduled time. These areas can be classified as study, relaxing, or activity areas. Some may be involved in what adults call good learning situations, working on a class or independent project. Others may be involved in something that may not be directly related to the classroom program, but an activity that the individual student feels is of benefit. There should be from 10 to 25 different choices available to students, depending upon maturity and facilities; the concept applies to "first grade" boys and girls, as well as to "seniors." Students in a true futures oriented setting need not account for this independent time; they may decide where to be without accountability of attendance. When they must be "somewhere," accountable to attendance rolls, the concept of freedom loses much of its potential.

Students might choose as one of their 25 possible selections the media center to study; or the student center – the student union or lounge; or a faculty/student area. They may choose a laboratory where individualized reading is established, not on a remedial basis, but as part of an approach that calls for most to improve reading by participating in the program some time during the school years. The students might be involved in another classroom session; they may decide to repeat an experience that they had previously and would like further clarification. They might go to the industrial technology laboratory and work on a project, they might be in the cafeteria – or the counseling center where they can visit with the "teacher-to-talk-to," or read descriptive college or vocational selections. They might have a conference with an individual teacher; be involved as a student assistant working in the office, media center, or laboratory; or participate in an art studio activity.

An eleventh area could be an open typing or computer laboratory. Most every student of any age should be able to process technology whenever he or she has a need and the desire – until more automated-talking systems are available. The students may go to the outdoor center – a place where they can lounge, relax, or study – or to the home economics laboratory. They could work on a school project such as the newspaper or the yearbook, or work in the science laboratory independently; they could be in a committee meeting. Students needing structure could be assigned to a teacher, or an area where quiet study is occurring, or they might select the physical education laboratory. They might go to an assessment center where whenever they are ready, in their individualized self-paced program, they can participate in an evaluation on the particular day and hour they desire. They could be in the music studio. The areas are almost endless in a creative humane school; students should be able to select from a variety of options during the time they build their own schedules.

Such opportunities are not philosophical or theoretical rhetoric; there is room for these choices even in crowded buildings. It becomes very feasible when the students and teachers overcome the notion that they must meet in the room of the teacher with 30 others every day. As soon as teachers realize that they do not have "their room" and "their students," but instead are persons working as part of a total school approach, and when they work with individuals and not group-paced instruction, these activities and choices become very appropriate. They can be implemented immediately with volunteers in a modified school-within-a-school alternative – if the total staff is not yet ready.

One of the reasons for unscheduled time is to help students develop the concepts of leisure and responsibility. The future world is going to provide adults with large amounts of uncommitted periods. People will be selective from three broad choices: study, service, or recreation. Some of their free time ought to be spent studying; self-education and lifelong learning are going to be much more important in the future world. The second avenue for use of unscheduled time is that of service; more and more people are going to offer to volunteer for understaffed state and private agencies. Third, part of their time will continue to be spent in recreational activities. In schools where choices are allowed most of the day, the students gain experience, in a controlled environment, in making decisions and in wise use of time; they learn that with freedom goes responsibility and courtesy.

It is crucial that innovative, futuristic staff understand the rationale; it is applicable in suburban, urban, and rural schools, but is implemented differently. In a "problem area," schools might only give a small percentage of the students these opportunities in the beginning; the list grows. Responsibility Cards can be issued to those who have earned them. In an area less troubled with problems, all 100 percent can be released, although about 20 percent will need to eventually be structured for a period of time before they gain complete understanding of the program. Usually the "problem learners" are caused by the "problem schools;" eliminating the latter does much to remove the former. It can be a two or three year process in difficult cases or situations; sometimes no cure is discovered for or by some individuals. In "non-problem" situations, most students can handle the responsibility factor immediately – with some needing only occasional reminders.

Responsibility

Schools embarking upon innovative, exemplary programs must accept this basic concept — one which is greatly in need of correct implementation. If educators believe that a prime purpose of education should be to assist people in becoming decision-making, responsible, value judging, perceptive, self-directing, self-educating individuals, then time must be provided for them to have opportunities to develop these skills. This statement applies to both elementary and secondary schools, to "first graders" and high school "seniors." The only difference is in the degree and method of implementation.

There are two important reasons for the acceptance of the concept of freedom and responsibility. Foremost is the philosophical belief in the future goals for education; second is the fact that if a school decides to implement a truly daily variable or non-schedule, it is virtually impossible to program all enrolled 100 percent of the time. In past efforts to account for all students, the obsolete concept of a study hall was employed in the secondary school, and constant teacher-pupil contact in the elementary. Fortunately, educators began to realize that the study hall offered little value other than that of a holding center where hourly attendance could be taken, providing an accountability process for everyone almost every minute of the school day.

Students need to learn to use time as a tool. Being tightly scheduled for six periods a day or all day in one room, with few optional choices does not lend itself in aiding youth to make judgments regarding appropriate use of time. Schools of America grew to be dependent upon organizational processes that were more intent upon managing students than educating them.

Most facilities have been administered on a ninety-ten basis — ninety percent of the decisions being made by teachers and ten percent by students. What is needed is a more nearly equal relationship. This is not to imply that all buildings should be completely managed by young people; it does intend to suggest the need for joint adult-youth consideration of school programs, not in theory, but in actual practice.

Under the old secondary school concept of study hall, or assigning students to six classes, or in the elementary school of allowing children a recess (often with restrictions), the only times students could make choices independent of the teacher were at lunch; these were limited to a few areas for short periods of time. Students have wants and needs as do adults. They ought to be able to decide during part of the school day what they would like to do — what would be most meaningful to them at a given time. The administrator or teacher cannot, during the summer, or on a day-by-day basis, decide what is best for every student every hour of every day. Students need to be "turned loose" part or all of each day.

How is this idea implemented? In an elementary school most students should have a chance each day to make decisions. Smorgasbord scheduling provides almost the entire day as choice; however, in conventional schools, responsibility time should provide some opportunity for the students to decide during the day whether this moment should be spent in the media center, on the playground, in the cafeteria having a snack or talking to friends, in the art or science centers, or in the open pod or classroom working on special interest projects. First-year students may have less time than sixth-year students, although at all levels individuals may have more or less depending upon their ability to accept responsibility; some may make decisions all or a greater part of the day.

Responsibility

Schools which have followed this pattern have discovered, much to the amazement of the skeptics, that students can make wise choices, and can be away from a teacher part of the week and "somehow" learn to read, write, compute, think, analyze, observe, draw, sing, and jump. The "crowded" elementary school curriculum takes on a new dimension with the decision-making element added. Many first-year students easily learn to self-select all day long; in the initial weeks of the program, usually part of their day should be structured to provide some group orientation to each area; this provides security for those who need it in the early stages.

At the secondary level, at least 25 areas need to be identified as options for selection. Depending upon whether the scheduling is daily variable, smorgasbord, or entirely self-selection, the students may have one, two, or six hours of unscheduled or responsibility time. Many youth should have a choice of attendance. Forward-looking schools accept the concept of optional attendance for most all; those who have experimented have found that students will attend classes where teachers have developed programs that are meaningful and realistic for the goals of the learner. They shy away from classes oriented primarily to teacher goals. Self-selected curricula motivates individuals and groups.

For student-selected options, a patio, a snack bar, the cafeteria, media center, art and music rooms, the shops, home economics areas, science laboratories, physical education, typing and computing, reading and writing laboratories, counseling and testing center, appointments with a teacher, repeating experiences for further clarification, school activities (newspaper), and study spaces should all be available. In these choices there must be a mixture of quiet spots such as individual carrels in the media center; semi-quiet, such as the lobby or rooms where students may work together in small groups; and noise areas, such as closed rooms, a patio, and snack bar where students may talk in normal or loud tones.

There are some built-in brakes in such a program. The students are taught that there are only 25 areas, not 26 or 27 unless their new suggestion should be included. They receive further explanation that with freedom goes responsibility and courtesy; in a society there are necessary restrictions. An analogy may be made with driving a car, which one may freely do — as long as the gasoline holds out — if speed limits, traffic lights, and road courtesies are observed. When traffic signals are violated, perhaps nothing happens the first time. Maybe the second time a ticket is received; but tragic results might occur the third time by running down a pedestrian or hitting another car. Students must understand that in schools, climbing on the roof and hitting the teachers, are not among the possible choices. Open campuses are advocated in flexible programs, but in some situations a closed campus may be better.

Students generally group in four broad categories in their ability to function in responsibility oriented systems the first year that such opportunities are attempted: (1) the majority of students handle the concept beautifully — except in those schools where security guards are on duty; (2) some handle it well, but need occasional prodding; (3) several handle parts of it, but need to be structured into some learning for portions of the day; and (4) there are a few who need structuring all day long — at this stage of their maturity they are not able to handle much unscheduled time. After two years, most students fall into category 1 or 2 — about 98 percent in a rural or suburban school, and from 30 to 60 percent in the inner city — or higher or lower, depending upon the extent of the "problems."

Students who fall in category 4 can usually be subdivided into two types: (1) those who are good citizens, but who for one reason or another at present need a highly structured program; (2) those who are poor citizens who abuse the opportunity for freedom. For the former, assignment to a structured schedule developed each morning by the student in conjunction with the teacher-advisor will usually suffice, while he or she gradually learns to make decisions. For the students who abuse the opportunity of freedom, a tighter structure must be provided. These youth have often lost communication with adults and need to be helped to regain this essential interacting; the best way is by assignment to adults with whom they relate. A program is necessary to guide them to accept responsibility.

A planned method whereby one time they receive the "pep talk" from an administrator; another session in study skills taught by a teacher, and other times just supervision from an aide will help most. Sensitivity training has assisted some; assigning individuals to a requested teacher or aide often is best. A few students may need further community resources, and assistance from school psychologists or other specialists, and may need to spend the majority of their time in a structured program. Identification of deviant behavior and review of cases must become a part of the evaluation so that students who demonstrate a new readiness to accept responsibility can be given unscheduled time again. Attendance can be taken by carbonizing the schedules they prepare each day, enabling all teachers to receive a copy. Structuring students usually works best if treated as a counseling rather than a disciplining situation.

There must be a follow-up evaluation after the treatment; individual conferences with an adult who can relate to the student, and truly personalized programs, have proven to be among the best remedies. If students are in classes they select because they have interest and ability in those subjects, and are with a teacher they can respect and communicate, the majority will change, though for some it may take two or three years. Usually these students have problems in the affective and psychomotor domains which need to be clarified before the cognitive can be improved.

A specific example can illustrate this message. One summer the math teachers in a school spent hours and hours analyzing new math programs and textbooks, and making decisions in preparing for innovative, exciting math opportunities for seventh and eighth graders. The staff chose several different approaches, realizing that no one program was suited for all the students. School began; the students entered this wonderful math design, with all new materials, diligently planned by teachers.

Report cards had not yet been abolished in that school; at the end of the first nine weeks, in surveying the grades given the students, a number had received D's and F's in math. Realizing that it must be the fault of the individuals, for over the summer the staff had overhauled the entire math program so that it would satisfy all the students, those receiving these grades were brought together in a group and given an old-fashioned lecture on "get busy and do your work; it is your fault that you are failing math."

The second nine weeks progressed; some of these students began to appear in the office as discipline problems. At the end of the second nine-week period, the story was repeated. The same students had received D's and F's. They were again admonished by the administration. In the middle of the third nine-week period, two of the boys in the traditional eighth grade were "kicked out" of math class. They were told they could not return – they were finished; threats were voiced; the math teacher marched them to the office. They were "chewed out" by the administration; the students threatened to quit school – in fact, asked to be "kicked out;" they said they could hardly wait until the end of eighth grade when they could legally quit in that state; they only had three months to go.

What was the administrator to do? There was no value in chastising them, or especially in expelling them, because they wanted to have the latter happen. The staff had planned this wonderful math program, but the students were failing and having disciplinary problems. They had been counseled for two years; their parents had been in for conferences. Finally, in exasperation, the assistant principal asked: "Don't you think you need any math?" The response of the boys opened a whole new world. They said, "Yes, but not the kind of math we are getting." The administrator about fell out of his chair. The students were willing to study math, but not the school-planned math; fortunately, the administrator decided to listen to them.

At that point a discussion ensued with the two boys about what math they needed. A plan was worked out whereby they could spend the next six weeks developing a horse farm on paper, for the principal knew of their interest in horses. They were at first resistant to this because what did a horse farm have to do with math? When they were asked if the farm would have a workout track, the reply was yes. They were asked what would be the circumference and diameter of the track, how many board feet of lumber would be needed, what was the current price of lumber per board foot, and, finally, how much would this track cost? Next, they were asked if it would have a corral; the answer was again yes. "How many square feet of lumber will you need, what is the price per board foot, and what will be the total cost?" They were asked if the farm would have a bunk house, and again the answer was yes; what was the angle of the roof, and the dimensions of the barn? They were asked the cost of feeding 20 horses per year; they were asked the total cost of the initial construction. They were asked how the farm could stay solvent.

As the project finally emerged, these students were given six weeks to complete a mural of a horse farm. They had to go to the art teacher for help in painting the mural; they had to go to the drafting teacher to learn how to scale the drawing; and they had to go to the math teacher who had removed them from class for help in figuring the price of the project, and all the other math needed, such as circumference and square feet. During the six-week period these two boys became excited about their project; they were provided space in the media center. The teachers, working as a team, began discussing what three teachers could do to help those who have problems; at the end of the six weeks the boys had completed a beautiful piece of work. There had been team teaching and interrelated curricula through the cooperation of the art, drafting, and math teachers.

The boys then were asked what they wanted to do next, because they had completed their math requirements. One of the conditions in this project had been that if they did it well, they would be given a C in math and passed; they would not have to complete the course in terms of traditional math hours. "We want more math," they answered: "We like math, at least we like this math." Other students in the school saw this project and suddenly desired to participate in similar learning themselves.

From this small start, students developed individual math programs, many of whom were the traditional "90 IQ dropout students." It became fun because it was meaningful to them. They went on to learn more, and in the process inspired the teachers to develop a completely nongraded, team taught, individualized, stimulating math program for the entire school.

One of the outgrowths of the project was to understand that when teachers listen to students, and develop relevant programs based on their needs, rather than requirements and programs determined entirely by educators, their whole attitude toward learning changes. These two boys graduated from high school, probably something that would not have happened had they been required to sit in the traditional group-paced program where year after year they followed the conventional requirements found in most junior and senior high buildings.

A number of schools have tried to implement similar ideas, but have failed. Usually the error has been a lack of communication and understanding. Some have simply announced this policy in September, talked about it a short time in an assembly, or sent out a few bulletins during homeroom, and then expected all to "adjust overnight" after years of structured indoctrination. A carefully planned explanation must be devised to ensure success.

The first step is that of individual talks with key faculty members to help them internalize the philosophy. Then a large group presentation is made to the whole faculty as to why and how, followed by small group sessions with parts of the faculty, and individual conferences where necessary. Various communication efforts must be utilized to ensure that teachers comprehend student-scheduled time. For the students, sessions with student leaders are a beginning. Then large group presentations are needed; there the "W's" are spelled out: why do you have student-scheduled time; where may you go; and what do you do when you are there? Some basic operational policies are established. The three "W's" are the single most important phase of the planning. Students must understand them completely: "Why do I have open time? Where may I go? What do I do when I get there?" Schools with optional attendance and open campus must work hard on the guidelines the first year, but most students will soon respond; they realize that these freedoms make it worth accepting the responsibilities.

Following the large group, teachers should take time to discuss the matter in small group seminars. The few reasons for putting some students on structured time should again be stressed. Constant work in the early stages with individuals is needed. These sessions should be of a counseling nature, not punitive. Students must be helped to realize that the correction, even when critical, is not condemnation. By the second year, or at least by the end of it, the need for structured programs should be overcome in most schools for the great majority.

Faculty-student teams can be formed in the areas of curriculum, new ideas, communication, and evaluation. They should meet often to discuss ways to improve the school programs, and help to involve the student body in the mutual relationships that should exist in a school. The communication group can explain the program to their peers. The evaluation team can develop and administer student surveys to see where better understandings and improvements are needed. The idea people can suggest changes. The curriculum group can relate the new concept of teachers and students in terms of classroom assignments. These groups should definitely represent a true cross-section of the student body. <u>Involving students deeply is the key to a successful program; they should be allowed to meet on school time.</u>

It is possible that some parents may object. If they complain, saying that they do not want their children to have student-scheduled time (do not call it "free time," or "choice time" the first year), explain that it is a joint enterprise and that the teachers are standing by to consult and to guide. Ask them if Mom has a coffee break doing the housework or at her job, and if Dad visits the canteen truck at the plant or has coffee at the office. Explain that teachers have a chance to make decisions about their use of time during part of the day, including the option of eating. Some students have a need for relaxing after a difficult experience, or for a snack if they missed breakfast, or for studying for a future evaluation. Students should have opportunities to decide what is best for them at a given time; food service should be available all day.

Note to the parents that on Saturdays and Sundays their children are often without supervision and sometimes choose to have a snack. After all this, if parents object, acknowledge that Michael or Maritza can be assigned to a structured schedule if the parents feel their children cannot be trusted yet to make wise decisions. Encourage the parents to consider the development of a sense of values. Given an opportunity to choose between a quarter and a paper dollar, the young child may select the quarter because it has a place in his or her "experience bank." He or she has held one before, and he or she probably knows that it can be traded for a treat. Given the opportunity to be master of their time, when entering college or beginning a job, students may make a series of disastrous decisions, for they have not had the opportunity to determine uses of increments of time in their previous learning experiences. Most schools are organized as if it is expected that the learner is suddenly and magically endowed through commencement from high school with good judgment regarding use of the clock. The learner must have concrete experiences in accepting responsibility.

It is true that some students will make poor choices. Sometimes they will choose a doughnut when an orange or a book would be a better selection. Adults do the same. If youth are ever to learn to make judgments, they must have the opportunities; what better places than in the controlled environment of the home and the school. Boys and girls can gradually be given, from their first year to twelfth year in school, increasing amounts of freedom, responsibility, and decision-making situations.

Sites which have successfully implemented this philosophy, the first year have parents who say: "I do not understand it. I do not send my child to school to sit on the grass and eat apples, but I like it; I have never seen Johnny so excited about school." Objective evidence gathered in buildings across the nation supports the subjective evaluations. The great majority of students and teachers who have operated under the old system of rigidity, and then under a successful program of flexibility, given a choice, would never return to the conventional. One of the truly exciting and meaningful innovations is the concept of increased variability in scheduling, and the resultant dynamic philosophy of providing youth greater opportunity for freedom and responsibility.

The barriers to the Wilson model call for a solution to one problem – those students who may not be completely ready to handle most of their time as unscheduled; in addition to any structured class time requested by the teacher, they may need an additional 10,

20, 30, or 60 percent of their time structured. The most difficult cases may need 100 percent structuring, but the students should not be left structured indefinitely without any help; advisors should plan to work individually with them. A sympathetic teacher can help arrange a program for those who are having difficulty. In schools where students choose their own teacher-advisor, this person is often the one who can most help the individual.

The question of structuring some individuals raises the spectrum of the cognitive, affective, and psychomotor domains. It is quite evident that many of the students who have problems with schools have basic needs in the area of the affective or psychomotor domains, more than the cognitive, at this moment in their development. Yet "problem schools" constantly say Johnny is a 10th grader and must take 10th grade English. Johnny has failed previous work and has received D's and F's in English for nine years; he hates the subject and usually grows to dislike the teacher. Still schools force him to take it.

Some youth are much better in the areas of personal development, responsibility, decision-making, and general attitude toward school if they are taking perhaps two hours of art, two hours of individualized reading, and an hour of physical education during the day, instead of one hour each of history, English, math, science, and physical education. The entire structure has to be revised for these youth. If educators believe in personalizing programs, they must try to plan a curriculum which fits the child. Through self-directed, partially-directed, and teacher-directed experiences, students are able to pursue studies which make the old cliches become truisms — a curriculum actually geared to the needs, interests, and abilities of the individuals, not the entire 10th or 3rd grade as a group.

Students should be allowed to window shop as part of this philosophy; there is no need to force registration before school starts. They can indicate what they think they are going to take to help schools plan staff, space, and materials. When the year begins, they go to learning experiences they thought they wanted. If satisfied, they stay; if not, they try others. After a time of window shopping, students complete enrollment cards. This eliminates the need for drop-add problems. They can change learning experiences at any time after this, but face only a small amount of paperwork; the school has a record of the efforts of each person. The approach helps diagnosis, prescription, and identification of individual commitments. There is no reason to ask students to decide by the third week of school their fate for an entire semester or year. If learning is individualized, students can start or stop experiences when it seems to be appropriate. Control is possible by requiring teacher, parent, and advisor signatures, if this is felt desirable. At Wilson, students did not sign for courses or even experiences; they enrolled with people. Learning was labeled only when it was time to record it on the transcript.

Education can and must do it; the time has come for educators to treat students with more respect, faith, and trust — as individuals — and not lock them into rigid compartmentalized schools. There is no place for hall passes, required 10th grade English, and elementary rooms with 30 desks facing the chalkboard all day long — for every individual.

There is a basic belief that visions can be implemented through four ingredients: DISSATISFACTION, COMMITMENT, HARD WORK, and CREATIVITY. Principals ask: "What do you do without study periods or rigid attendance accountability?" The answer is found through these four by developing a recipe for each school. If educators believe they should not provide the same for every student, they should change the system. For those who want a step-by-step method, a simple beginning recipe for unscheduled options is student responsibility – the students have the 25 opportunities – they can choose where they want to spend their time. Freedom, responsibility, and courtesy are dramatic concepts which open the way for creating exciting humane future learning. Current flexible methods are too restrictive for some persons; the completely open school-within-a-school goes far beyond these ideas in developing freedom – but it is still a concept attached to responsibility and courtesy.

The acceptance and implementation of these beliefs is especially important in preparing for future learning systems where many student hours will be unscheduled or spent in community based experiences. Futuristic win/win opportunities need a base of trust, freedom, and responsibility. The Mankato Wilson program tried to reflect this belief by envisioning and implementing the concept of responsibility as a cornerstone of the total commitment and personal philosophy.

SCHEDULING

For many years North American high schools have followed a ritualistic pattern of scheduling students into classes on the basis of six 55-minute periods, with five-minute passing times between the bells. Occasionally schools have varied this to seven or eight period days; junior high and middle schools have often had 42 or 45 rather than 50- or 55-minute periods. In the elementary school, scheduling has been done on the basis of assigning 25 to 35 students to one teacher in the erroneously labeled self-contained rooms. Chimes have sometimes replaced bells – an innovation!

There were absolutely no reasons for these patterns other than administrative convenience – a very simple mechanical device to handle increasing numbers of students entering the schools. Traditional methods of scheduling served a purpose at one point in history, but now educators are finally beginning to realize that self-contained elementary school classrooms, and period 1, 2, 3 organized high schools with bells ringing, hall passes, and the rest of the organizational minutia that have interrupted the learning process for a number of years, no longer make sense for the schools of the future.

There is no evidence or research to support these conventional procedures. Yet year after year principals have established conflict charts and worked during the spring and summer to fit students into slots strictly based on the number of seats in a classroom, and on invalid course requirements. The assumptions upon which the traditional system has operated will not stand the scrutiny of research. All classes do not need to meet every day, yet the traditional system has assumed they should. All classes do not need an equal amount of time, such as 55 minutes for every subject; some need longer and some need shorter periods, but even if one tried to defend equal time, why not 48, or 52, or 58, or 67 minutes? That would be equally wrong, but equally defensible.

Over the past years, many schools have recognized these fallacies and have searched for alternatives. Such variations as four 70-minute periods each week, floating periods, reversing hours so that on Monday sixth period actually meets at first period time, block scheduling, assembly schedules, multiple option schedules, and other such patterns have been tried. Even 50 years ago some schools had activity times where students had one period a day unscheduled to become involved in student programs such as clubs, athletics, assemblies, free choice, and tutoring sessions.

Ironically, in the 1940s, Wilson High in Long Beach, California, under the direction of Principal Harry Moore, was a leader in pioneering some of these new scheduling concepts. Students attended classes only four days a week and had an hour free every day. It was recognized in a leading journal as one of the 25 best high schools in America. Unfortunately, when Mr. Moore left, the new principal reverted to tradition. These varied efforts did not go far enough, nor are they any more defensible than the 55-minute period, although most of them were improvements, especially in the affective domain. Even if not in measurable cognitive terms, the Long Beach Wilson School was a more humane environment.

Educators are quite familiar with the flexible scheduling developments that occurred at Stanford University in the early 60s related to their work with Marshall High in Portland,

Scheduling

Virgin Valley in Utah, and other pilot schools, to develop a computer-generated schedule partly designed by the basic GASP system written at MIT. The program became commonly known as flexible modular scheduling. Offshoots of that design, such as those developed at General Electric, McDonnell Automation Center, Indiflex at Indiana University, and similar efforts, brought variations to the patterns.

Marshall High in Portland later developed a hand-loaded system which seemed to improve the original Stanford concept. It became quite common during the late 60s and early 70s to find a number of modular-scheduled schools in each state. When observed closely, it was easy to see that most of those efforts were better classified as inflexible, flexible schedules – or at least staff operated them that way. Most were certainly better than the old 55-minute period bus schedules where principals said: "The buses arrive at 8:30 and leave at 3:30. If I have a seven period day, and assign each student one period for lunch and one for study hall, and have five minutes in between each class for passing, then I will have a good program." All such patterns – the bus and the flexible modular schedules – are obsolete as society reaches into the next century.

While Stanford University was developing its program under Robert Bush, Dwight Allen, and graduate assistants, in conjunction with principals in the field, and while additional similar approaches were being designed as branches of the Stanford pattern in various parts of the United States, two other developments of great national significance occurred. They did not receive the publicity deserved, but in the long run should have a greater impact on future scheduling at the national level. One of these was at Brookhurst Junior High in Anaheim, California, where in 1963 principal Gardner Swenson and his associates were developing the concept of the daily demand schedule. Through the use of Royal-McBee keysort cards and four staff members, Brookhurst hand generated a brand new master schedule each day, planned three days in advance; it allowed for most groups to meet without conflict, and provided individualized schedules for students.

At the same time, principals Bob Dunsheath and Don Glines at the Canyon del Oro School, and Evelyn Carswell at the Walker School, and the staffs of those schools in the Amphitheater District of Tucson, Arizona, supported by innovative Superintendent Marion Donaldson, were developing the concept of daily teacher controlled variable scheduling, built first with cardboard slips, then pegboards, and finally by teams of teachers. The Canyon del Oro-Walker programs, along with the daily demand at Brookhurst, became prototypes for the developments in daily scheduling which occurred nationally during the ensuing years.

The major deficiency at Walker and Canyon del Oro in the early stages was that students were moved more as groups than as individuals, but both programs were able to operate with the same budget and staff as those of traditional schools. These daily schedules soon proved that they took much of the boredom out of the school day. By scheduling one day in advance, as done at the Tucson schools, teachers could ask for large groups, small groups, independent study, open labs, and one-to-one conferences on the basis of daily need. Classes could be scheduled at any hour of the day; assemblies no longer became interrupters of the program; students enjoyed the variety; attendance rates improved; discipline problems decreased; learning became more fun. The early concept of "with freedom goes responsibility" blossomed in these two Tucson schools as much as it did anywhere in the nation, as related to the public school sector of North American education.

121

Scheduling

Other schools began to operate block programs where teachers were given a core of students to work with all day, or for a given period of time. Staff in these pod-type teaching arrangements, such as Ruby Thomas Elementary School in Las Vegas, and early pioneers in California and Massachusetts, further developed the concept of flexible movement. As the ideas of freedom, responsibility, and options began to be accepted, school districts like University City, Missouri, expanded open scheduling. Ridgewood High in the Chicago area worked hard on new directions for a computerized modular system. The Nova, Florida, program built in flexible blocks at the high school level. Bishop Ryan High School in Omaha developed "homemade" modular schedules, and later developed perhaps the first "nonscheduled" high school.

Though most of these mentioned are no longer pioneering innovative schedules, they and the many others too numerous to name, were the real pioneers in educational organization related to scheduling. However, almost all of the programs had flaws. Most retained required courses; the teachers planned the curricula themselves, or as members of teams. Group requirements and group-paced instruction were prevalent. The major difference became time and methodology factors; classes were scheduled to meet as large and small groups approximately 50 percent of the week; students were open for independent study about 20 percent of the schedule, while laboratories and projects occupied perhaps 30 percent of the sequence. Classes met for shorter and longer periods than 55 minutes, and often only three or four times a week rather than the five days required in conventional scheduling. Very little true individualized instruction occurred; content and requirements, though varied, remained very similar to the past.

These flexible movements occurred at both the elementary and secondary levels; teams of teachers in open pods with blocks of time began creative organizational patterns. Those great starts bogged down because parents and educators were handicapped by the traditional concept that the cognitive domain was more important than the psychomotor or the affective. They built in rigidity, again to ensure that all students had a required number of hours in the areas educators have erroneously labeled basic skills – primarily reading, writing and math. Home economics, industrial arts, physical education, art, music, and drama – the important subjects in the primary years – took a back seat, as they always have; at the secondary level, they continued as second rate citizens – as frills or dumping grounds to and from the "academic" program.

Junior highs tried some new approaches, but stayed locked into the seventh grade curricula called required English, history, math, science, physical education, and a semester of art and a semester of music. The middle school movement was the great hope of this era, but it fell back into the trap of required content and skills at each "grade level." High schools were "scared to death" of the colleges, state departments, parents, and even the shadows of their rigid department chairpersons; they either stayed on the 55-minute period, or finally consented to try the modular system. If the schedule failed, at least the computer could be blamed for conflict and mismatch of teachers and pupils, and for deficiencies in programming.

To help solve all these dilemmas, Glenn Ovard and associates at Brigham Young University, and their laboratory school, took the concept of the daily schedule from Brookhurst, Canyon del Oro, and Walker, added their own ideas, and developed a demand schedule built daily on the computer. It was by far the most innovative, creative method of scheduling yet developed at that time in the United States. The Brigham

Young program, though retaining required classes, developed systems whereby individualized instruction and small group interaction requests could be fed into the computer, resulting in a brand new master schedule every single day of the year — about 98 percent conflict free. Though their laboratory school had to close, Brigham Young educators continued to explore this approach.

In the 1970s, bold new approaches to scheduling were created. Adopting the newest national innovations, staffs such as those at Wilson, and some of the NASSP model schools developed open daily scheduling processes; a few did not even bother to build schedules at the high school level. Wilson pioneered Daily Smorgasbord Scheduling; it was built by hand in about one and a half hours for 600 kindergarten through grade twelve students at no increase in cost, except for the quantity of paper devoured, the need for a scheduling clerk, and the people power time necessary each day to compile it. Daily smorgasbord completely revolutionized the concept of school organization and led to the ability to create a more humane approach to education. This was followed by the nonscheduling process developed later at Wilson, an even superior development — beyond the daily concept.

However, most schools need to pass through a transition from rigid, to daily, to nonscheduling. Therefore, in implementing the smorgasbord variety, the first effort must be to understand the philosophy that is involved, before the mechanics; the "why" is more important than the "how." Of the "69 changes" cited by Wilson, daily (and then nonscheduling) was only one. By itself, it was not that important; but without it, many of the other changes were not able to function.

With a more humane philosophy, the mechanics of building a daily schedule are not at all complicated; the more one accepts the freedoms and responsibilities given to and expected of parents, staffs, and students, the easier the task. If a school is not willing to adopt the total smorgasbord philosophy, a daily schedule can be constructed where required courses, attendance, and other tighter structures are possible. The daily variable schedule and the daily demand, other versions of flexibility, both provided for as much rigidity as needed, whereas the nonscheduled concept offered almost complete freedom, if desired.

In daily smorgasbord scheduling, individual students can be structured all day on the basis of need by having them complete a carbonized copy of their program each morning, or the previous afternoon, which is then distributed to the instructors. One copy can be signed during the day and returned to the advisor. Attendance can be taken the same as it is in any school. In the early stages of daily scheduling, about five percent of the students do need this structured schedule; another 15 percent need modified, less-structured forms. Some of the remaining 80 percent need occasional reminders, but after a period of one to two years, this usually is no longer necessary. The young children who have only known an open program since kindergarten have very little difficulty. The students who are in a transition stage from the old to new may have some problems, but as one would expect, many do beautifully in a day or two, or a week, or a month.

As to the actual mechanics of daily scheduling, the details would take a small book. Such a recipe is not needed for the nonscheduled school other than a philosophical commitment. The basic steps confirm that the notion is practical, realistic, exciting, and operational. Cookbook recipes can be developed as models, but each need modifying

123

for the particular school situation. Common sense procedures should enable creative administrators to write their own cookbook without waiting for "the model" to be published. Following are the 1968 procedures; with computers and sophistication, these will eventually be only for historical reference, especially as schools move to nonscheduling.

1. Each teacher or teaching team and/or group of students turns into the scheduling clerk each day before 9:00 a.m. the requests from the learning centers for the following day, for the desired combinations of individual conference or tutoring time, open studio or lab time, independent study, small or large groups. These requests contain the students desired, the amount of time, special needs, the room desired, and necessary comments. Sometimes teachers have no group needs, so only a request for open studio, open lab, individual conference, closed, or some other comment is presented.

2. The scheduling clerk spends from 9:00 to 9:30 compiling an overview of schedule problems for that day.

3. At 9:30 the clerk is joined by three other adults (at least one or two teachers, a student teacher, an aide or volunteer). These four spend from 9:30 to 10:30 or 11:00 placing the requests turned in from the teams on a master menu, which will become the offerings for the next day. This schedule is developed one day in advance; the team builds the menu in the following order:

   a. special requests or hard to schedule groups;
   b. teacher conflicts and closed requests by teachers;
   c. younger children, to ensure they are as conflict free as possible;
   d. scratch schedule of room requests already scheduled to check for conflicts;
   e. scheduling for remaining classes that have been requested;
   f. completion of "open" times such as for optional lab, conferences, independent study;
   g. check final schedule for conflicts and accuracy;
   h. recopy and create a master – then reproduce copies;
   i. distribute one copy to each teacher mailbox and post copies on specified walls in the school;

4. To list all the rooms, four large sheets of paper are used, which are then posted side by side on the walls, or are clamped together for distribution to teachers. The four who form the scheduling team each have one of these four sheets to complete. The Environmental Center rooms are listed on one sheet side by side. This is true for all the centers, as the requests as scheduled need to be cross-referenced for avoidance of major conflicts for students between the offerings, knowing that some conflicts are inevitable.

5. Teachers are rotated on and off the scheduling team on a staggered basis so that never are all three of the schedulers removed at the same time. This provides for continuity, as well as sharing the task of scheduling. It is a good inservice training technique for teachers.

6. The schedule is posted for the following day by 2:00 p.m. of the day the schedule is constructed. That way teachers and students can, if they desire, check their plans for the next day before they go home.

7. For "first graders," the counselor/advisor for each student helps the child create an individual schedule. It is usually written on a narrow schedule time sheet so that the student can carry it, or pin it to a dress or shirt, as a reminder of where to go, or for ease of assistance from an older student, if lost. Centers can be color coded and colors used on the schedule for young students instead of written words or symbols. Older students who need some structuring use these sheets too. They can be required for strict attendance for those who temporarily need help in accepting responsibility and making decisions. Except for very young children, 98 percent of the students by the second year write nothing down, but just check the schedule and go when the time arrives – or skip the schedule entirely that day if they know even before coming to school that they want to spend all of their time in industrial arts. With non-scheduling, all this is eliminated, for by then, the students are able to plan their own daily schedule, including the very young children; those raised with non-scheduling are not phased, as this is the only "school" procedure they have known.

8. Most students spend 60 to 80 percent of their time in one-to-one conferences with teachers, open lab or studio, or independent study. These do not have to be listed on the daily master schedule; if they are cited, the purpose is only to help students with the decision-making process. They may then go whenever they desire and stay as long as they wish. Twenty to 40 percent of the time the student may be in small or large groups. These are scheduled at specific times, either by the scheduling team, or informally by three to six students who together decide when they and the teacher are both open; they arrange their own time.

9. There are occasional conflicts in a schedule. These can be reduced if they bother a staff the first year by having each teacher turn in a conflict match of other experiences which cause most distress. Band might list creative writing, Indian cultures, chorus, yoga, and fencing as its biggest "enemies." The scheduling team tries to avoid placing these back to back. All classes do not meet every day, or for the same amount of time; only 0 to 40 percent of the student day is in a structured group. The rest is in unstructured small groups, individual work, or spur-of-the-moment plans; thus conflicts are reduced.

Personalized schools have so many mini-courses and mini-mini-courses of four to six students for three to six weeks that it is extremely difficult to keep track of all the conflicts. In most cases conflict charts are not attempted with short mini-mini courses, but for a mini-course which is going to extend over a stretched period of time, conflict charts can be kept if desired.

There is a different philosophy about conflicts. The traditional secondary school says it has no conflicts, but in the spring it establishes that French IV, chorus, band, journalism (all singletons), will be first period. A student must choose one of the four, but cannot take all four. In open schools, the staff believes students should take what they need; the staff builds in conflicts, if necessary, on a given day. The same conflicts do not occur over and over, as there is a completely different schedule every day. In a 12-month school, open about 240 days each year, 240 brand new schedules are constructed, rather than the one built in a traditional school, or the five built in the flexible-modular schedule arrangement. In smorgasbord scheduling, if there is a conflict, it is treated the same as if the student were sick; the student may miss the class entirely. The person may later listen to a tape of the presentation or discussion, or meet with a teacher or some of the students, or even see a video tape of it, if the session was that important. Attendance should usually be optional; sometimes students would rather spend all day in the art studio, missing all their scheduled classes, even if there is no conflict.

10. Students develop much of their own curricula; most "classes" are scheduled by students and not by teachers. Students working independently avoid conflict by scheduling one-to-one conferences. Instruction should be completely individualized, as group meetings grow out of individual needs, so missing a "class" is not like missing a group-paced program. The words "class" or "course" disappear, to be replaced by "experiences." Students in open schools are involved in multiple experiences; they do not participate in the usual courses, or class required group instruction.

11. If there is a question as to whether this schedule can work without optional attendance, no report cards, choice of teachers, individualized instruction, team teaching, nongradedness, and personalized programming, the answer is a big yes. The step beyond the daily smorgasbord is the hidden schedule or non-schedule, or only listing the few group activities which might be arranged for certain days. If a school desires some structure at the beginning, it can be provided through "daily teacher controlled variable scheduling." Where seventh graders take the usual English, social studies, math, science, physical education, art, and music, the "groups" can be moved daily to each of these subjects as requested by the teachers. A group may go 45 minutes to English, 75 minutes to art, 75 minutes to physical education, 60 minutes to math, and 30 minutes to social studies on a given day, skipping science and music. This method of scheduling is easier in many ways than the smorgasbord. Students are not given as many choices, and conflicts are not as common. This is how the first daily schedule of this style was developed in 1963 at the Canyon del Oro School in Tucson, Arizona.

12. Any size school can build daily schedules, but compromises must be made depending upon logistics, available person power, student requirements, and facilities. In large schools of 800 or over, schools-within-a-school or "house plans" have proven to be the easier way. Units of 600 in a high school of 3,600, equate to four units of 900, six of 600, or three of 1,200, and make more sense than one of 3,600. Scheduling 600 provides no difficulty, but the logistics of 3,000 do present additional time problems in developing such a pattern. In small schools of 200, the logistics are quite simple, but there is less flexibility because of the small number of staff; again, non-scheduling is a big advantage and the next step, when ready.

13. Any age level can benefit from a daily schedule. Open schools have pre-kindergarten through senior students involved. The only difference is that there is more planning and structure of the 3s, 4s, 5s, and 6s, but even for them it is a very open program; as much structure as a staff desires may be built on a daily basis. Ideally, there should be no master schedule.

14. Cost is related to the amount of paper and ditto masters (before computers) used and for the hours needed to build it. Ten years of experience with daily schedules is convincing that the advantages far outweigh the disadvantages. Educators can now build a daily smorgasbord with technology and can create individual programs, as computer systems are available through big districts, colleges, intermediate school districts, cooperative intradistrict projects, cooperation with local businesses, and many

126

other such resources. A few schools are already planning pilot trials on the new generation computers. The proposal is to feed into the computer on a daily basis the various requests and have the machine print out a brand new menu each day the school is open.

15. The teacher request sheets that were used in most schools in the 70s for daily hand scheduling were similar to the model presented. Refinement occurs when sophistication develops, or when replaced by the non-scheduled concept, or new century learning systems.

Name of Team		Teacher		Date	
Experience or Group	Amount of Time	Room Request	Special Needs	Remarks	
Dream Reality					
1 - 1 Conf					
Zen					

ENVIRONMENTAL CENTER								CREATIVE CENTER				
	10A	10B	11	11A	12	13	14	15	16	16A	17	18
9:00 9:15 9:30 9:45 10:00 10:15 10:30 10:45 11:00 11:15 11:30 11:45 12:00 12:15 12:30	Open Lab	Indian Culture / C.W.P.	One to One Conf	Open / Chem / Open	Cons / Z's	I.S. / Closed	Drug Movie / Open	Animals / Planes				

16. The early final schedules appeared as portrayed, though they later became more advanced; multiple variations are possible; computer advances make most of this obsolescent, but the historical development is important to preserve and to document success.

Scheduling

Daily smorgasbord is an exciting, practical, effective, and far better way to schedule than the conventional methods. Even more effective is non-scheduling – or often called "hidden schedule" – as students do plan and make decisions regarding their daily activities. Time itself is only a tool, but without eliminating the old traditional organizations, real improvement is limited. Scheduling opens existing horizons for creative, innovative faculty and students. Successful schools may modify their daily techniques, but they would not be willing to return to the old methods. It is not unusual for a school to make multiple modifications in their first two years of using the daily scheduling concept.

Visitors constantly ask: "Is it worth all the fuss and bother? Is the schedule really that much better?" The answer is to ask them to remember that in the early 1880s Peter Cooper and his first railroad engine was beaten in a race by a horse. In the early 1900s, Billy Mitchell was court-martialed before the concept of airpower was accepted. People laughed at the Wright brothers and other early air pioneers who sometimes crashed. Eddie Rickenbacker era pilots had to fly planes of questionable quality. The Spirit of St. Louis was also a gamble. The P-38 met a need, but only for two years; it was soon replaced by jets. Now there are 747s, Apollos, and Endeavors. Educators must decide whether they want to continue to send mail by pony express and travel across country by stage coach or iron horse, or whether they prefer to send by airmail and fly cross country in jets and rockets, assuming the pollution and energy crises can be overcome.

Daily smorgasbord scheduling is now beyond the Peter Cooper and Wright brothers stages. It is, however, probably no further along than the Spirit of St. Louis; but one day smorgasbord and hidden/non-scheduled schools will be space rockets for education. Educators should be encouraged enough by the early successes to help develop the philosophy and mechanics to a point where nationally educational scheduling will at least soon be in the advance jet era. Schedules will not be needed in the emerging learning systems for the 21st Century. The descriptions here are truly only temporary stop gaps.

For staffs not yet ready to try daily smorgasbord scheduling, or preferably non-scheduling, further explanation of the rationale behind major schedule changes is needed, along with investigations of other possible alternatives. The key concern here is not what "model" a particular staff buys, but that the school moves out of the 55-minute period, or flexible-modular, or self-contained elementary classroom approaches. Educational leaders must be committed to the notion of developing more sophisticated scheduling or no recipe will work. The principal must be willing to become involved in the extra work and frustration that accompany massive developments; he or she must be willing to break traditions.

In planning a new era, the leadership must ask whether to involve all staff or just part the first year. In a facility recently constructed for innovation, generally the entire school should adopt flexible scheduling. If the new school is not an open attendance area, part of the staff could remain more structured; if it is a large school, designed for a house plan, one "house" could remain more traditional, while the others could be "open" in varying degrees. If it is an old school with established faculty and clientele, the principal probably should work the first year to involve only 30 percent of the more flexible staff in variable scheduling, through use of the school-within-a-school concept. The middle-of-the-road group can watch and become involved slowly, while the resistors can remain in traditional scheduling patterns. In the development of commitment, administrators cannot do it alone. They must surround themselves with a portion of the staff who are committed to the implementation of innovations.

For those on the staff who need convincing, the leadership group must communicate a rationale which mandates that the schools of the future must arrange for organizations and schedules with entirely different assumptions:

1. Not all teaching jobs need be the same.
2. All classes in all subjects need not meet every day.
3. All classes need not meet the same number of periods per week or the same amount of time each day.
4. Students are capable of assuming responsibilities.
5. Learning is more important than teaching; learning can occur without the teacher.
6. Substantial improvement must occur in the instructional program; the teacher has an obligation to try to invent and experiment with ways to improve learning opportunities and experiences.

If a core of the staff becomes committed to the possibilities of variable scheduling, that nucleus should read much of the available literature related to flexibility. During this reading they should try to answer basic questions: "Why have daily teacher-controlled variable scheduling? Should we adopt smorgasbord scheduling instead? Are we ready to overleap to non-scheduling? Why would these approaches be better than what we are doing now?" What scheduling will be needed for next decade learning systems?

Most schools do currently operate on a bus schedule. The central office determines when the buses arrive and when they leave. The principal divides the day into six periods and lunch, based upon bus times. Then he or she says to Mrs. Jones, as she returns to school in the fall: "Mrs Jones, you have the most wonderful schedule; you are going to have World Literature first period this year; you will have 30 students, five days a week, 55 minutes each day for 36 weeks. You cannot have more than 30 because the schedule will not permit it. You cannot have less than 30 because we do not have any place to send them. You cannot have any more than 55 minutes because that would interrupt second period; you cannot have any less than 55 minutes because that means we would have too many students uncontrolled during the day. You just enjoy yourself and have a good time with these 30 every day." The teacher then goes into the room and says: "Isn't it wonderful, boys and girls" This year the 30 of us are going to be together for 55 minutes each morning for 36 weeks. We are going to have a wonderful time studying World Literature. Won't our schedule be exciting?"

As she prepares her course, her basic thought is focused on one question: "What can I do tomorrow for 55 minutes to occupy the 30 students?" She should be asking: "How may I help students learn tomorrow? What is the best size group for the experience? What length of time would be best? Would it make any difference whether held in the morning or in the afternoon? What room would be appropriate? How could we evaluate the program?" The teachers and students should be completely free to determine whether they want to meet at all that day, whether five or 150 students would be appropriate, and whether the time should be an hour and a half or only 30 minutes, in either a large group, laboratory, or seminar room.

These decisions should be determined by the learning situation and the various teams on a daily basis. They should not be determined by the teacher or administrator in the spring or summer preceding the school year. In conventional scheduling the administrators claim that they can predict what an individual student needs the following April; yet they make this prediction the previous April or, at the latest, during the summer. They determine then that nine months later, the student should be meeting 55 minutes from 8:30 a.m. until 9:25 a.m.; the great sadness is that in the case of a transfer student, they have prescribed a remedy before they have ever met the patient. There is no defensible position for this soothsaying rationale. A staff considering a flexible schedule must read the literature, examine the possibilities, and comprehend the philosophies underlying the concept.

They must consider the old programs originated at Stanford, Indiana, McDonnell, and Westinghouse, among others, and then consider the new potentials with the advanced computer technology. They should ask: "What is wrong with the flexible modular program?" The answer is that nothing is wrong with that program if it is compared only with the traditional six period bus schedule. The flexible modular programs are so much better than the traditional that everyone should be using the system, if that is the best step that can immediately be achieved in a given district. The flexible modular has various flaws; it is really an inflexible-flexible schedule, but it has been a way for many schools to start. The problem with the modular schedule in most schools is that there are only five master schedules. If teachers look at their schedule one day in April, they often say: "Why last April did we ever request this arrangement? Look, we have large group tomorrow, lab on Wednesday, and small group on Thursday. We wish we could change it." With a daily teacher-controlled variable schedule, or daily smorgasbord, or a non- or hidden-schedule mechanism, it is possible to change immediately. Locked into a bus schedule, or an inflexible-flexible schedule, it is almost impossible to make wholesale alterations easily each day.

Developing a philosophy is a step which is absolutely necessary when making provisions for flexible scheduling. The teachers and administrators in the particular school must study carefully the advantages and disadvantages, and then determine whether or not they agree with the basic concepts. Do they understand how variable scheduling provides daily flexibility in that the schedule can be changed to suit any particular need on any given day? Do they comprehend how variable scheduling relieves boredom? An outgrowth of daily scheduling, which was not necessarily one of the original reasons it was developed, is that students and teachers have said that school is much more interesting, "Because I do not have to sit in that World Literature class from 8:30 a.m. to 9:25 a.m. Monday through Friday." One day the student may have World Literature at 8:30, one day at 2:30, one day when he or she chooses, and one day not at all. Variable scheduling does relieve monotony, as students daily self-select their attendance and study patterns.

VARIABLE SCHEDULING MAKES TIME A TOOL; EDUCATION MUST LEARN TO USE TIME WISELY. Students and teachers are no longer locked into a 55-minute period, or a self-contained room schedule which requires reading every day, or music always from 2:00 to 2:30 MWF; they enter a situation where they can control their own time. The teacher may ask for only 30 minutes; the student may have a choice between eating for 30 minutes or studying. Both adults and youngsters must begin to learn to use school hours as a tool in providing better learning opportunities.

Variable scheduling provides opportunities for planning. Team teaching, time to dream, and interaction among professional staff are important in a flexibly scheduled school. Teachers need to share interests, abilities, and knowledge; they must maximize strengths and minimize weaknesses; flexible scheduling leads to the elimination of rigid requirements and self-contained rooms. If educators believe in the concept of individually prescribing learning within a big barn philosophy, there is absolutely no rationale that justifies departments in secondary, or self-containedness in elementary schools.

During this study, staffs need to create dissatisfaction. One of the areas that administrators and teachers have overlooked in planning to implement variable scheduling is that students must be involved; they make or break an innovative school. If the students understand the why, what, and where, as related to the process of scheduling, if they become dissatisfied with the old structure, and if they agree with the new philosophy, the attempt will be successful; they are sold on it themselves. FOR CHANGE TO OCCUR, PEOPLE MUST BE DISSATISFIED WITH THE PRESENT; THEY MUST BE COMMITTED TO TRY TO FIND A WAY TO IMPROVE. One of the possible philosophical and mechanical improvements is the adoption of the concept of variable time. Another major dissatisfaction has been the inability to truly individualize learning, and personalize student programs. If staffs become frustrated with group-paced instruction, it is not too hard to implement forms of individualized, continuous progress, self-paced approaches which force new scheduling procedures.

Alternatives ought to be considered. Each site can develop its own model. With the 90s electronic capabilities, there is "no limit" to the possibilities. The older hand forms are described for historical purposes; for smaller schools where the person built formats are still appropriate; or for districts yet without access to the latest sophisticated electronics.

Several methods of constructing a matrix have been developed over the past 30 years. One is to use a computer program based on modifications of the original flexible modular scheduling. Requests are put into the computer; basically five master schedules are derived for the year. It is time for a revival of this approach as a transition step in many schools toward scheduling developments into the next century.

A second is with the use of purchased keysort cards, particularly like those originally developed as the Royal-McBee Company Keysort System. A scheduling coordinator and scheduling clerk are needed for this approach; student schedules are placed on keysort cards. The schedule can be built daily, weekly, or on a semester basis. The computer can now speed this process, though in a small school it still works very well by this hand-card system.

A third approach is with a schedule board, identification tags, and a clerk. A schedule request sheet job order is turned in each day whereby the teachers tell the clerk the amount of time they desire for that particular day for the group that they want, including any special requests they may have, such as the room arrangements and audio-visual materials. The clerk takes the requests from the teachers and builds a schedule. This works well for schools still moving students as groups rather than as individuals – and for smaller schools-within-schools.

A fourth technique is to form scheduling teams. They may organize in a number of ways, but this usually involves a large block of time during the day. The teams can be formed on an interdisciplinary or disciplinary approach. They can be on a grade or nongraded level arrangement, but the general plan is that a number of teachers with their aides are given a number of students and a large block of time; within this block they build a flexible schedule. Four teachers with 120 students for four solid hours is one example of this approach; this style was very popular in the 60s.

A fifth way is involvement with the latest technological developments. The effort that led the way for awhile was the one developed at Brigham Young University (BYU) where their laboratory school was the first in the United States to have a daily teacher controlled flexible schedule built with a computer. The BYU step was the breakthrough toward the new technological yet even more individualized, scheduling systems.

A sixth is a combination of the methods of the previous five. One school may have part of its schedule built daily by the computer; another through the block of time arrangement, where teachers build it themselves by hand; and a third built in a more rigid fashion by a computer as an offshoot of the old bus schedule built by hand to accommodate those teachers who insist on rigid, constant time patterns. There are many possibilities in building multiple creative schedules.

A seventh is the daily variable, one which usually leads to the adoption of the daily smorgasbord approach, which then leads to no schedule, or the "hidden schedule." One of the secrets in making this work is to have very few "must" classes. Teachers should not request the same students five days a week. There should be very few large group classes (band is an example, but the entire band does not need to meet daily.) A guideline is that one large group a week is too many in the majority of classes (the fewer to none makes the best continuum.) This does not mean that students are not expected to see the teachers more often; when an adult determines there is a need for a specific group on a specific day, he or she should be able to request it. Asking for open lab causes no conflict in the schedule, nor do individual conferences. The teacher may leave students open for independent study, or ask for small groups; they normally can be easily scheduled. Part of the key to this scheduling is to request "classes" of no more than five or six students, and all with optional attendance; "must attend" classes should be eliminated — or almost.

From this framework comes the smorgasbord; the offerings include several meats, rice and potatoes, salads, vegetables, rolls, and desserts. In terms of educational subjects, what happens is that the few large group requests are scheduled throughout the day. The rest of the time the teachers merely indicate what is available to the students at that particular hour. Under one column may be listed an open lab, then individual conferences, then open lab again, and then a small group discussion, with some closed time in between. Each teacher-facilitator has similar offerings throughout the day. There is little conflict; the students go to these areas as they desire on an optional basis.

Open scheduling is a philosophical belief, but it certainly is not theoretical; it is a practical, successful way of developing programs for students. Once learning is individualized and personalized, and once the students have learned how to participate in the concepts of freedom and responsibility, open classes, and open campuses, the schedule becomes an exciting tool. It enables students to choose each day the activities that make sense to them. On a given day a student may spend the entire time in the art lab, industrial arts, or media center; he or she may divide the opportunities and spend two hours in home economics, half an hour in English, an hour and half in math, and other similar combinations. The key is that the students do the selecting. Even the large groups are optional. This works on a k through 12 basis. The only difference is that there may be a little more structure offered in the lower years; sometimes they may not have an open campus, especially if they are in heavy traffic areas. The pilot programs with daily smorgasbord scheduling have been tremendously exciting and hold great promise for the future.

The suspect is great that non-scheduled schools will be emerging as more develop open, student-selected curricular experiences. Alternative eight, then, is a school without a schedule; only special events are listed, and even those are not always necessary. Already some of the daily scheduled schools do not list independent study and open laboratory times. Some have tried no schedule on Wednesday as a way to pilot the concept – or only list special events.

As these programs develop further, free from pressure of parents, colleges, and subjects, the schedule will disappear too. In non-scheduling, students make their own one-to-one appointments; small groups of six or eight set their own times to meet. The rest of the day is open lab, independent study, and an occasional optional common thread large group. There is no need for a master or daily schedule, as the small groups and individuals schedule themselves; the other activities need no schedule. Even the few large groups (band, chorus) can schedule themselves; creative music instructors have learned they do not need the entire group at the same time every day. The band is the perfect example of only needing daily large groups for limited periods – not all year. The key to a successful non-scheduled, or hidden-scheduled school, is to truly personalize and individualize learning. Groups are still an integral part of the process; the difference is that there is no need for a permanent master time pattern.

In changing to new scheduling procedures, or any of the other innovations, the question of money always arises. Schools do need more funds; but the present problem is to use the finances available more creatively; educators must reallocate resources. If last year a school spent $150,000 on textbooks, two teachers, chalkboards, and paint for the walls, this year they may spend the same $150,000 on video viewers and computers, one teacher, three aides, and remodeling walls. Schools can create flexible schedules within their current budgets. What they must understand is that the money that is spent by the district must be reallocated, and deployed differently than in the past. Such proposals are not impossible financial arrangements; too many schools already have the proof. In considering budgets and the eight or more alternative means of scheduling, educators should realize that all are practical and immediately possible illustrations. The arrangements are reasonable; schools can begin, even if they must start schedule breakthroughs in a rather conservative manner.

One limited method to achieve a first step – the block of time – can be illustrated as follows: six teachers – two English, two social science, and two science – and two aides, are given 210 students for a three hour block of time – the equivalent of periods one, two, and three. The rest of the school can continue traditionally; the 210 students, and their teachers, are completely free to organize a program as they desire. At a given moment, all 210 may be studying individually, or some may be listening in a large group with one teacher, or all may be interacting in small groups; some may be involved independently, in laboratory situations, in off-campus volunteering, or in informal groups. Whatever they are doing has been determined daily by students and teachers who are responsible for their own time. The schedule on a given day may call for some students to be scheduled for one hour with a teacher; the other two hours may provide opportunities for them to determine the work best suited for their immediate needs. Their choices may be related to English, social science, or science. They may choose not to do any work in these particular subjects, but instead to go to the student center, to the art room, or to the physical education building for a workout. Adults and students have complete flexibility during this team arrangement to build the program that they desire. If the physical education teacher will not cooperate, then one of the options is just not available until that department is convinced to be more open.

Another arrangement might be combinations of alternatives. One team may have four hours, or 16 modules, if the schedule is built on a 15-minute module base. This provides a large block of time similar to that just described. Opposite this block might be teachers who have back-to-back schedules for horizontal, but not vertical, flexibility; they may not have four hours and 120 students with four teachers, but there may be two or three teachers working together for an hour, or 75 minutes, or other time arrangement. Three math teachers may have a group of 90 students for an hour third period, or from 10:30 until 11:30 at the elementary level. They can have horizontal flexibility, working as a team, with options for large and small groups, independent study, and other similar arrangements.

At the same time that some are involved in the four-hour block, and others are involved in horizontal arrangements, a third group may be on a conventional schedule. To illustrate to this latter group that there are other ways of teaching besides 55 minutes, or to provide longer and shorter periods of time for subjects that may demand them, the former first period for those on a conventional schedule may be 60 minutes one day, 75 on two days, and 45 minutes on the two remaining days; the conventional schedule can be varied too.

At the elementary and middle or junior high levels, there is absolutely no excuse for not having a daily variable schedule, at least for those who volunteer, or as a magnet or optional program for those who select it. As soon as educators eliminate departmentalization in middle and junior highs, and self-contained compartmentalized rooms in the elementary, there should be plans for daily movement of students to retain the desired flexibility. The easiest way in the elementary school is to form teaching teams which can function within large blocks of time, building daily schedules themselves. Four teachers and three aides may be given 150 students all day long; these seven would instruct all or some of the subjects; one teacher could teach eight subjects in the elementary school, though not recommended, or preferably only teach two or three or interrelate curriculum in their areas of strength. There may be eight or more teachers in the school; each one could be a specialist; students would move from teacher to teacher, not on a departmentalized junior high basis, but evolving from the team plans as lead specialists working together in an interrelated approach to help individual students. Though none of these approaches is heralded as the best way, each does illustrate how small, practical starts at more flexibility can be made overnight with the same budget; growth can occur toward interdependency and personalization.

Education will arrive at a transitional period where in most of the larger schools, computers will build the high school and middle school schedules on a daily basis, and where some schools-within-a-school will operate with no schedules. Smaller schools and most smaller elementary schools may continue longer on a block of time, teacher constructed approach, which is a simpler arrangement for building flexible schedules in small schools and poor districts. Daily flexible scheduling is just as easy as building a traditional schedule, if there is a commitment to the philosophy and to nongrade and individualize. The coming of daily smorgasbord scheduling and "non-scheduling" is already revamping the forward looking daily variable schedules. A society without schooling – and certainly without rigid time arrangements every day – is on the horizon – coupled with interdependent learning.

To significantly change the organization of time, requirements must change. As soon as the teachers adopt an open philosophy with very few demands for groups, it is easy to create imaginative schedules. If the art teacher has primarily open labs, perhaps only occasionally requiring a group; if the typing, computer, and industrial arts staff basically do the same; and if the social studies teacher demands no more than one large group every two weeks and perhaps two small groups a week, the schedule is relatively free. The math teacher can work primarily on an independent and tutoring basis and, therefore, have almost no demand for large groups of students. When this becomes the method of developing curriculum, teaching, and learning, the schedule becomes a relatively simple matter. Presently the reason for the computer schedules is that education is so locked into group-paced instruction, and is so often seeking to meet the group of 30, or is still teaching small groups as if there were 30, that people miss the many possibilities for exciting educational benefits.

In building daily schedules, whether variable or smorgasbord style, the students rarely, if ever, have the same pattern. They have 175 or 240, or one for each day they attend each year. The teacher-consultants in this particular mode may find themselves "teaching" on Monday. Thursday they may find that they have a "day off to dream." Team teaching and flexible scheduling allow schools to release at least 25 percent of the faculty on any given day; some teachers are usually scheduled out. Part of the reasoning for daily scheduling is to provide renewal potential for the staff.

The best way to learn the daily variable method is to have people begin building the schedule; it takes most schools an entire quarter to orient all the teachers; even then all do not understand it well. After one year, a schedule for 600 can be built each day in about an hour, unless unusual problems arise. The first efforts in most schools, though, usually take two or three hours; after one year, staff still can expect mechanical and philosophical disagreements – until they focus on 21st Century learning – and the elimination of schedules and separate subjects.

Some educators continue to ask: "Where are we in this process of scheduling?" Some have thought they should not adopt flexible scheduling because it did not do for them what they wanted it to do; they have been looking for a panacea, a Shangri-La. Education is not at that level of development in daily scheduling, individualizing learning, or providing for student freedom and responsibility. Strides have been made the past few years; there is renewed energy toward implementing these changes before the next century.

Returning to the airplane and train analogies, schools have a choice of staying in the pre-airplane stage – they can be content with the horse and buggy or the old iron horse – or they can choose to try to fly. Some have not been content with the old iron horse, in terms of organization; they have attempted to play with scheduling, just as earlier pioneers did with the notion that an airplane would fly. Those first efforts were not very successful; neither were the early attempts at flexible scheduling; but at least the attempt was made. Now that the pioneers have arrived at the Spirit of St. Louis stage – or some even at the beginning jet era – just as the air industry was forced to do, it looks as if education must now struggle through the educational counterparts of such propeller driven fighter planes as the P-38; people were excited during World War II when they learned that the P-38 flew 400 miles an hour.

Two years later the arrival of the initial jets put the propeller fighter plane into obsolescence. In the 60s society developed the present jets; in the 70s there were the supersonic airliners; in the 80s and 90s, except for the Challenger, space flights almost became common. Pioneers have even been flirting with parachuting planes safely to the ground. Where is the aircraft – or rocket – industry going after the year 2000? Once schools have a supersonic method of scheduling, before the year 2000, educators can ask the same question: "Where are we going?" There is no doubt that most all educators working with forms of variable scheduling are apprehensively optimistic.

If schools or districts do develop more humane approaches during the remaining 90s, it is a safe bet that the more futures oriented programs will be operating without schedules. More and more open concept sites will move from a modular scheduling approach to the daily smorgasbord. Almost all schools could be involved in some scheduling they regard as "flexible." During the late 90s the good high schools will eliminate the six or seven period day. Technological advances with the computer, philosophical acceptance of futures learning, and humane approaches toward curriculum and persons, should lead to exciting new concepts in the area now referred to as scheduling. The word schedule may become one of the extinct words – eliminated from the educational vocabulary.

Most schools in the early 90s were still in rigid departmentalized models with very structured time patterns. They will be forced to proceed through transition stages; this should be a rapid process. The few futures oriented and alternative open programs have shown there are better ways. As the society of the new century faces the global crises and opportunities, as the electronics revolution evolves, as values and priorities change, education will witness dramatic restructuring. Learning will be interdependent; it will be more community based; it will interface with technology; it will become more humane; it will provide flexible time arrangements. Technology will eliminate the five-day week school building. Scheduling will be seen as rearranging the deck chairs on the Titanic. Educational futures will make smorgasbord scheduling of only historical interest.

REQUIREMENTS

In open concept schools, with no graduation requirements, how do students know when they can graduate? Will colleges accept students without credits? How are diplomas awarded if the school does not follow state mandates? What happens when students transfer from an open philosophy to a rigidly structured school before they graduate? Are there any sacred courses — surely students need English to live in the United States? What if they do not learn to read in the primary years? How does the staff complete forms for insurance companies and scholarships that require class rank?

Nationally a number of schools have operated under an open philosophy regarding requirements; students have not been handicapped in graduation from other high schools, transfers to graded elementary schools, entrance to college, or future vocational advancement. Futures oriented systems do not place great emphasis on "graduation" or diplomas, for they believe that learning is a continuous, life-long process, and that generally more "education" goes on outside the school building than within it. Continuing to expand learning how to learn is more important than the knowledge that has been acquired in a specific area. Individual self-image, and the achievement of success in many affective and psychomotor areas, are more important than those in the cognitive or content knowledge.

The present society in the United States places great emphasis on competition; the measure of success is often a paper received after completing arbitrary standards. As part of contemporary North America, educators have been obligated to provide guidelines for completion of what is now referred to as high school. Requirements in open schools, and the information which must be given the students are different. Most educators already know of alternative procedures, but continue to follow the old patterns. Discussion should lead to the creation of more flexible options for youth.

Under the present varying state laws requiring attendance, usually from age seven through 16, unless a student is excused by the state from this obligation, he or she is in school during the years covering the traditional grades 1 through 8; most start in kindergarten. For the nine years, K-8, or the ten or eleven if a student begins at age three or four, in truly open schools there are no "graduation" or "promotion" requirements. The youth must be "in school" approximately 175-180 days per year, as required by most state regulations (a year-round program signifies within a 12-month period, not a nine-month session), and progress in the affective, psychomotor, and cognitive domains. The effort is commitment for each student to receive personalized programming according to his or her relevant needs, interests, and abilities on a continuous self-paced basis. Learning is considered an eleven year flow of individual growth and development.

Starting with the 12th year (assuming enrollment at age three), or the 11th, 10th, or 9th year of "formal education," depending upon whether the student begins school at age four, five, or six, if not three, slightly more rigid requirements are imposed to receive a "high school diploma" which will enhance the individual when applying for certain jobs or colleges. Most of the conventional requirements of the past have been based upon invalid stumbling blocks originating from unresearched national decisions. At present, it can be anticipated that the great majority of students will stay the traditional four years beyond the eight to eleven years already completed; for most this means starting the final four years at approximately age 14 or 15. Since "time" spent in school is not a valid assessment related to achievement, students should be able to speed up or slow down their work. They may attend more than 175 days per year, may achieve significant growth at a rapid pace in less than 175, or may have more pressing needs or opportunities elsewhere, and thus should "graduate" in less than four years. By the same rationale, they should be able to stay longer than usually enrolled, if the student and staff deem it profitable, or in programs where furloughs are involved. In all cases, four years is only a guideline base from which to make judgments.

A student should be entitled to a diploma in this timeframe whether actually studying most of the hours within the building, in the local community, or in some other area of the world. The school and the parents may expect the student to make progress in the affective, psychomotor, and cognitive domains through the areas of study selected; the goals and achievements of this progress are determined by conferences held between the students, teachers, and advisors. The final awarding of the diploma remains the authority of the staff, if there are conflicting views. The four year syndrome and state laws will eventually be revised to provide more meaningful options for those who are not able to benefit from additional time in a high school. Futures learning systems will ultimately eliminate current graduation mentality – and the concept of "four years."

If a student wishes to leave in less than traditional time, the request is made through the person responsible for enrollment procedures. A conference is held with the student, parents, and some of the staff to determine if this seems to be in the best interest of the youth. A student desiring to leave early should plan with his or her advisors and the administration in advance so that decisions related to expectations can be made and goals established. In all cases, the school should reserve the right to make final judgment; however, increasing numbers of young people should either graduate early, or delay by participating in a furlough program. Often the varying degrees of physical maturity lead to resentment, compulsion, boredom, and inactivity, or excitement and eagerness. Standards should be individualized.

Open oriented schools do not give credits or Carnegie Units or other such standard badges of completion. There are no formal classes established and required; the "courses" pursued must be determined on an individual basis. The work the student completes can be recorded on the transcript of record in areas of study identified by the "title" given to the experience pursued. The school is more interested in "learning experiences" than in the completion of arbitrary requirements.

Students should be forewarned and aware of the regulations imposed in most schools and colleges throughout the United States. Though personalized high schools are not concerned with credits and required courses, most are very conventional. If students contemplate possible transfer, in making decisions about learning opportunities they should be clearly told that the majority require the following: Four credits or four nine-month years of English; three credits or three nine-month years of social studies; one or two credits or one or two nine-month years of both math and science; two years of physical education, but often without the reward of credits; and one to three courses each year or one to three credits, usually totaling five to seven, of "elective" courses. These can be additional ones in the required areas, or can be in drama, business, art, music, industrial arts, home economics, or foreign language. Schools housing the traditional grades 9 through 12 generally expect students to enroll in five courses per year, earning at least four "credits" as determined by the teachers of each course, or 16 credits plus two years of physical education; requirements do vary from state to state and district to district; they were raised above these in the early 80s in states that jumped on the false bandwagon which said that more required basic "core" courses would solve the ills of the nation.

Humane programs believe these requirements are irrelevant for most; there is no research to support them. The belief is that if there are requirements, they should be more balanced: art, music, home economics, and the other subjects should be included. Certainly four years of English, no art, and only two year of physical education is not the best requirement for ALL students. Some schools have a series of prerequisites – a course which must be completed before another course can be taken: Algebra before Geometry, Art I before Art II. Flexible schools try to avoid all such mandates, but students should realize that most traditional schools will have them.

Open schools would rather have students work in interrelated areas such as humanities, environment, and human relations, rather than subject areas such as math, science, and music. Knowledge is interrelated; as much as possible, students should create "course titles" with broad interrelated, interdependent possibilities and experiences, as indicated as essential by the futurists; knowledge is not segmented. It is possible for students to concentrate in only one field, but they are encouraged to select, over their years in school, a balance in the diet; the philosophical recommendation is that youth should take some work in all areas related to the old subject disciplines. Home economics, industrial arts, art, music, physical education, business, foreign language, English, social studies, theater arts, science, math, and other fields should receive attention from most, but in a futures, interdependent approach. Futures curriculum can start in four areas: Urgent Studies (air, food, water); Human Potential (caring, volunteering); Interdependent Competencies (science/math/industry/technology); and Interrelated Interests (personal growth and enjoyment). These four should also be interwoven (technology – which creates food, feeds people, and provides gardening hobbies).

If a student takes work approved at his or her home school, but which might not be accepted by another, and an unexpected transfer of the father or mother would imperil high school graduation from the new building, flexible schools should act in benefit of the student and give "traditional credit and course titles" on the transcript to be forwarded. This translation can be achieved by the counselor with the approval of the student, advisor, and administrator; the final decision is that of the school, in case of conflicting views. The counselor cannot translate "nothing into something"; the students should be reminded that they are expected to pursue learning opportunities. These are, however, very flexible and varied, and if approved by the student, advisor, and parent, the choice is generally accepted as appropriate for transfer and graduation requirements. It is easy to translate work in astrology into English or social studies or science, depending upon the focus of study. Broader titles, such as Creativity, Expression, Environment, Systems, Communication, Urgent Studies, and Human Potential can also be interpreted.

The final decision and responsibility for selection of studies lies with the students and parents. The school should offer advice or counseling when desired; if a student decides not to take English the "junior and senior years," it is acceptable to the open program, but the student should realize that some high schools (in case of transfer) and some colleges require four years of English. The open school might suggest less than four years of English to provide more time for art, music, and other subjects, but the student should thoroughly understand that art is not as important as English in most schools — only in humane programs and in art schools. In futures oriented learning, "Literature" and art can be merged into a broad interdependent approach.

For those anticipating entering college or university, technical-vocational schools, or business or fine arts institutions, their general and specific catalogs are still consulted, but not treated as absolutes. Students should clearly understand that though most college entrance requirements follow the pattern of four years of English, two of social studies, two of math, two of science, physical education, and elective courses — particularly in the areas of the foreign languages — that individually they do differ. The students are cognizant that a number of institutions want heavy concentrations in math and science; others prefer work in the humanities. The youth know that an engineering student is expected to pursue more math than one interested in being an English teacher, and that many colleges, particularly two-year public community colleges, and smaller state institutions, have an open enrollment policy — anyone may enter with only a high school diploma or its equivalency. They know that certain private schools have very rigid requirements, while vocational, technical, business, and fine arts schools usually have flexible enrollment policies. These latter categories prefer high school work in the area in which the student expects to specialize; some require work in the specialization area before entering, but others require none. If students want to become foreign language interpreters, they can enroll in most foreign language institutes as beginners, though the majority would wish for some indication of a prior level of competency. Educators have this information; the students in an open school must have the same knowledge, and must understand that usually requirements are negotiable.

Credits, such as one in English, are not given in futures oriented schools. Credit can be discussed in terms of recording the progress made toward a goal the student is trying to achieve. It is to his or her "credit" if the person has learned to count in Spanish. If students are concerned about a Carnegie Unit "one credit," or "five units" for an English course, they can consult with their facilitator to verify that they are doing approximately the same work that would be one unit in a traditional school, related to transferring or college entrance; but they should not expect them from a futures program. No "credit" should be recorded on transcripts of students; only in cases where he/she would be prevented from pursuing other work because of the lack of "a paper record of such credits" would the curriculum need to be translated by the office.

Open schools are often experimental; students who make the decision to enroll should be ready to accept the risks that go with being astronauts; they must have the courage of EDUCATIONAL PIONEERS, prepared to accept the possible benefits and consequences of such programs.

Athletic eligibility is considered under the same philosophy. All students enrolled should be eligible up to the age cutoff date or total years of competition. The only reason to honor these regulations is to prevent "professional high school players," but they should be flexible. No attention should be given to those requirements based on grades in subjects and passing credits. Football may be the single most important subject for Pete, in the affective, psychomotor, and cognitive domains. As long as football is part of the curriculum and paid for by the school, Pete should play football under the same criteria that are required for enrollment in mathball. Within this philosophy, the entire notion of prerequisites is obsolete, except in very limited circumstances. He fumbled the football; he cannot take mathball!

The school should function with an open, voluntary attendance policy. Anyone presently living within the confines of the district should be eligible to attend. If space is limited, enrollment policies may be established, but most facilities can be increased by year-round education and school in the community concepts; if the program is that popular, it should be replicated. The school should reserve the right to accept or reject students, not on the basis of race, religion, or economic status, but on the maximum year-round capacity of the school. If the facility has room, almost everyone should be accepted. When the school is overcrowded with waiting lists, some students must be temporarily rejected, but then the program must be expanded to another site as soon as possible; if there is a demand, the district has a responsibility to provide for community needs. WAITING LISTS AND LOTTERIES FOR LEARNING ARE UNFATHOMABLE AND IRRESPONSIBLE. Factors such as "mutually beneficial" to both school and student, diagnostic needs of a particular youth, support by the parent of an open program, balanced economic and racial percentages, location of the home, transportation considerations, the percentage of college degree families, and balanced percentages of age and gender enrollments for experimental purposes and program development are among those to consider when accepting applicants.

The majority of students in the district will fall in the age range of five through 18, the old kindergarten through 12th grade. There must be at least limited efforts to develop three and four year old programs. Birthdate should make little difference; as long as there is room and the student is near, at, or over age three, he or she should enroll at any time – not just in September. Pre-birth and birth through three programs should be offered too; community volunteers, high school classes, and business grants can help to staff even a limited effort. These are crucial years. Laws and reality provide handicaps; because the demand is usually so great and staffs so small, limitations are necessary. Though the age cutoff dates in most states as now written are absurd, when enrollment decisions are made, birth date may be considered. If the child could be sure of staying in the open district, no problem would be encountered. If the youngster would transfer before completing the traditional first grade, the child could be denied entrance in another district because of age; early enrollment could be a potential disservice to that child. In all cases, every effort should be made to accept everyone and to consider individual differences whenever possible; practical realizations of time, space, staff, budget, and laws must be faced. Public free schools now receive minimal, if any, financial support for the three, four, and full-day five year old early childhood programs; private free schools can charge limited tuition. The idea of setting an absolute cutoff date for entrance, such as September 30, is one of the huge errors made in American education. The future for a child is determined by one minute on a clock!

Open schools should be connected to college programs more closely, as many high school students should take courses. Some of the teacher education majors should receive part of their learning experiences in open schools. The start may occur by an eventual merger of a formal or informal consortium of experimental colleges and teacher education centers within the universities. The goal is to eventually have open futures oriented learning systems available for precollege, general college, and undergraduate and graduate teacher education students. Under a confederation, school districts and nearby universities could establish three interrelated divisions: precollege, general college, and teacher education. This could ensure that students from age three through graduate school could attend open schools with flexible entrance, transfer, and graduation policies. In all these fluid arrangements, open staff must realize their obligations in regard to limitations imposed by society at present. Much of the program depends heavily upon discussion, counseling, guidance, and decision making with each student. "Talking" technology, distance learning, and other creative developments will enhance these practical concepts.

Parent input is important, if they have specific concerns. Even though the school does not make math mandatory, Mom or Dad can counsel the student into that area if he or she feels strongly about it. Sometimes students can be led to an area through "guile and cunning." The child who wants to learn to make biscuits must read the recipe. Suddenly stir, blend, mix, tablespoonful become meaningful in the vocabulary; reading becomes important. Math enters the picture – two-thirds of a cup. Diagnostic teams of teachers should met to discuss possible prescriptions for motivating the student toward an area of perceived need. Parents and staff should refrain from pressure tactics unless that approach seems best – remembering that it seldom is the answer.

The school should reserve the right to "require something" if it is felt absolutely crucial. If a driver in an auto accident is badly hurt and unconscious, and cannot sign the permission slip, nor can any next of kin be located, the surgeons will decide to operate, assuming that the patient wants to live rather than die. The fact that the patient would rather die is not known to the doctor, or perhaps would be rejected as a reaction from shock, if the patient did awaken; surgery would normally proceed. The staff should not try to "force" a student to take subjects, but should reserve the right in what they determine as a "life or death" unconscious situation to make such a final decision – though it should rarely be used. What becomes the focal point is the question of what seems essential for the intellectual and emotional development of each patient. The biochemists can say that protein, oxygen, and other such basics in specific amounts and forms are essential for life; they can be fairly accurate. But what can educators say for certain, especially related to curricular decisions? Many educators have opinions; most might say reading is essential, but is it really – in the present and developing age of technology?

What subjects would be mandatory? Is art essential for intellectual and emotional health? Is the study of the War of 1812 essential? If so, to what depth should it be pursued? When is it essential – at age 8, or 12, or 17, or every year? Why is it so important? Is it important for all, or just a few, or maybe many? Curricular decisions force the schools to accept tremendous challenges and responsibilities; the staff assumes they can make valid judgments which could have profound effects on the future of young people, especially if the new century brings the anticipated rapid changes in society.

The ultimate answers relate to humaneness and relevance. If each individual has a program designed as early as possible, interweaving factors found in society, and if the person has great input into those decisions, so that motivation and retention are considered, then credits, graduation requirements, entrance ages, and all other group prescribed solutions have relatively little value in the education of youth and adults. If the biochemists are correct, that each individual is so different in so many ways, the only plausible answer for educators is to treat problems of entrance, graduation, and adult vocational preparation on an individual basis. Schools should reject the notion of credits and the imposition of unresearched state requirements designed for the masses, not for the individual.

One of the questions constantly posed to staffs of open schools relates to the acceptance of a more flexible curriculum policy by the colleges. The general concern is that graduates of open schools could not be accepted at the leading universities. This has not been proven to be true. Surveys show just the opposite; college communities throughout the United States will accept a variety of portfolios.

As just one small piece of evidence, a letter was sent to a random selection of universities throughout North America regarding entrance without grade point averages, Carnegie Units, class rank, and traditional grades. It is essential that graduates of open concept programs be admitted by other criteria, for these schools believe very strongly that traditional rankings are a distinct form of discrimination. They do not separate the Catholics from the Lutherans, the blacks from the whites, or the rich from the poor; therefore, they refuse to partake in a system which calls for discrimination between the "smarties" and the "dummies," and that is all that grade point and class rank accomplish. The case will probably have to be heard by the Supreme Court one day, but there is great confidence in the ultimate verdict; more educators and parents are agreeing with this position of revolt against discrimination.

The response from colleges agreeing with more flexible admission policies was overwhelmingly favorable. All were willing to consider students on the basis of different evaluations; without class ranks and grade point averages, applicants from open schools have not been rejected for admission by the college of their choice as a result of lack of either convention. Some do not make their first choice on the basis of keen competition, SAT scores, or other personal factors, but all eventually are accepted by a college satisfactory to the individual.

The students who have graduated "early" — those who leave in fewer than four years — have most often found that the opportunities which developed proved to be sound judgments on their part, and a humane policy by the schools. They have been able to solve personal problems, enter colleges in winter and spring terms, enroll in vocational opportunities, start full time jobs which eased financial difficulties, and in many additional ways capitalize on the decision. Others have found that the best policy for them has been to remain four or more years in "high school." Successful open schools can help to break the lockstep graduation criteria; they can make a significant contribution to education in the United States.

The letter sent to admissions directors in the early phase of the Wilson program confirms, by the excerpts from the answers received from the colleges, what every high school can achieve. The admission directors were most willing, on an individual basis, to consider acceptance of students who presented personalized applications for enrollment.

Requirements

LETTER TO COLLEGE AND UNIVERSITY ADMISSIONS OFFICES, DECEMBER, 1968

Dear Director:

The Wilson Campus School is a laboratory arm of the School of Education at Mankato State College, funded by the state legislature for the primary purpose of research and experimentation in education. Wilson has decided to attempt vast revision this year. In the past, this school operated a good conventional program. Until July, 1968, we had self-contained classrooms, a regular seven period schedule, study halls, ABC report cards, honor rolls, and the other usual patterns found in traditional settings. Because we were doing very little different than the public schools in the state, the possibility of closing the laboratory facility was given much consideration. After deliberation, it was decided to keep the site in operation, but to transform it into an open, evaluation-oriented endeavor.

We are enclosing a brief summary of the efforts we have undertaken since July, 1968. We have started the three, four, and five year old programs as indicated. We are building the entire schedule, K-12, on a daily basis. We have developed team teaching; instruction is primarily through small group and individual approaches. We have students taking self-directed and partially-directed classes. We allow them a great deal of freedom and are working with the students to assume the same amount of responsibility.

We do not believe in failing students; generally a failure is the fault of the school for not providing a program which would be of value. Many times these youth have problems in the affective domain which need to be corrected before the cognitive areas can be improved. The students are not given credit for the completion of the experience until they have accomplished it to the satisfaction of the teacher. Therefore, they do not fail – they just do not complete it; nor do they make the honor roll, as we do not have one. We are interested in individual growth, not group comparison.

One of the many changes is an attempt to improve the evaluation of students by providing something better than the traditional ABC report cards, K-12. The system involves many individual conferences between the teacher and the student, and the student and the advisor. These culminate with individual parent conferences. The entire effort is based on a personalized philosophy, individualized learning, and self-paced, continuous progress programs. We feel that this is the best plan for the majority; grade point averages, class rank, and ABC grades have little place in the evaluation of individual students. "Grades" only had success as long as we were concerned with group structure and group prescription.

The effort at evaluation is based on an initial diagnosis of the individual needs, interests, and abilities. Based on the diagnosis, we help each student build a personalized program. Every few weeks we evaluate progress, and on the basis of that, continue the original program, or recommend a new one, as determined by the success achieved in the preceding studies. We feel that if we are going to accomplish our goals, we must truly be student oriented; youth should not be forced to fit an adult-designed curriculum offering little relevance to them. For students who are planning to go to a specific college, we suggest that they take the courses that fit the demands of that school.

Whether we are successful or not remains to be tested. This is the purpose, as we see it, of a laboratory school in the state; no matter how good we may think current educational programs are, we feel that Wilson should be different. The role should be to pioneer new approaches to education; we are not going to know if the idea may be a better way unless someone makes an effort to try.

It is easy to evaluate K-8 children; we keep folders on each student; the teachers and parents are continually informed of the progress. At the high school level, in addition to completing the same evaluation as we do K-8, we are attempting to design a format which will satisfy the requests from employers and college admission officers for a record of the success of the student in high school, and indicate a forecast for potential. At the present time we have not created a final design, but generally see it first as a description of the past studies by the student, and second, as an expression of the expectations and aspirations for the future. We expect to be able to state the objectives the student attained; we probably will include any standardized test results and subjective teacher evaluations as well. We see this as a much more meaningful description of the student than a grade point average and class rank.

Our purpose in communicating with you at this time is to request your reaction to these questions:

1. We are a laboratory school for the state; would you be willing to accept students on the basis of an evaluation which would not include conventional requirements such as class rank, ABC marks, and grade point average?

2. We are attempting to pattern a concept through which we might find a more meaningful way of admitting students to college, and at the same time relieve the high school program from being restricted by entrance regulations. We do not want to hurt the chance of any student enrolling in college, but we do sincerely feel that grade point averages have no place in individualized education. Would you be interested in joining with Wilson and other colleges and universities to develop a meaningful format?

Because we are a small school, we are not sure if there will be students applying for admission at your institution this year. However, we are desirous of corresponding with a cross-section of people representing a variety of institutions throughout the United States so that what we develop would be applicable anywhere. Since the changes in direction here, many students are interested in going to college wherever they might have an opportunity to participate in a learning environment similar to that which we hope we are developing at Wilson.

We look forward to your reply to these proposals, and would enjoy working with you in an attempt to improve the evaluation procedures for individual high school students.

Sincerely,

Director
Wilson Campus School

Requirements

RESPONSES FROM COLLEGES AND UNIVERSITIES (A Sampling)

* * * * *

"Suffice it to say, however, that you can rest assured, as far as _____ is concerned, that the absence of the usual badges such as rank and grade average will not work against your students – we lean heavily on other evaluations anyway, so that your own recommendations, and those of your staff, CEEB scores, and particularly achievement tests, can help to provide many of the answers we normally seek in the usual fumbling of the admission process.

"I think we would be interested in joining with you and other colleges to pattern some kind of program; certainly if we cannot do this institutionally, I can work with you personally, for I am much interested in the directions in which you are moving (indeed, your letter did much to destroy some stereotypes I had about places like Mankato, Minnesota!)"

* * * * *

"Please know that this institution would give every consideration to graduates of the Wilson Campus School who might seek admission to the University of _____.

"We realize you would not be furnishing us with grades or class ranks in the usual sense.

"We would have to know the specific pattern of subject matter the student has completed. We, of course, would have to have test data (we require the ACT). They key thing we would have to know is whether or not this student is recommended to us. In other words, do you believe he would be successful in his academic endeavors at the University of _____? We would insist that you give us such a statement, in the absence of grades and class rank which we have been using as predictors for success here."

* * * * *

"Thank you for your letter of December 12 in which you have described your efforts to revitalize the experimental nature of the Wilson Campus School. I assure you of our enthusiastic support for your activity and our willingness to cooperate in any way possible.

"Specifically, we would be more than willing to consider applicants for admission to _____ from your school even though they might not present the traditional credentials. I assume you would be able to provide us with sufficient information concerning such candidates and their academic achievement so that we might make appropriate evaluations of their eligibility for admission. We would continue to require them to complete the Scholastic Aptitude Test and three achievement tests of the College Entrance Examination Board.

"We would be willing to consider joining you and others in the development of a program leading to more meaningful ways of college admission. I hope you will keep us informed of your progress from time to time."

146

Requirements

* * * * *

"Many of the points you have raised in your letter have also been discussed by the faculty and administration at _____ concerning educational programs for young men and women entering college; therefore, I think that there should be no problem in working with you in having your students accepted at _____ based upon your recommendation. We are attempting at _____ to de-emphasize the grades similar to your program; therefore, we do not figure a grade point average on any of our students here at _____."

* * * * *

"There would not be any difficulty in _____ accepting Wilson students on the basis of an evaluation presented by the school supplemented by the student SAT scores and an interview by an admissions staff member. We would also be interested in joining other colleges in an attempt to improve the admissions process."

* * * * *

"Thank you for your information concerning the program at Wilson. You have prepared a very interesting and provocative statement of your plans and procedures. _____. too, is an institution interested in innovative and experimental procedures. We therefore look with a great deal of favor on your type of program, and would be happy to work with you on college admissions that do not include conventional requirements.

"I would be happy to further explore the problems and possibilities of your program as a college admissions concern. Frankly, if we have a reasonable description of the type and amount of work attempted by the student, plus your own evaluation and anecdotal records, plus the CEEB, SAT, or other standardized test score, I think that a decision that is fair to all concerned can be made.

"I am certain that our Committee on Admissions would be most willing to consider your students on the basis of an evaluation which would not include the conventional class rank and grade point average. In lieu thereof, I am sure that we will find much additional data to assist us in evaluating these students.

"I am certain that we would be very interested in at least discussing the possibility of joining with you in an effort to pattern a program which may lead toward different and more meaningful ways of admitting students to college."

* * * * *

"I was most interested in your recent letter telling us about the Wilson Campus School. The program sounds exciting and I feel sure that the youngsters going on with their education from your institution will have benefitted greatly from their experience there. _____ is attempting to put into practice on a somewhat larger scale what you are attempting to do in your laboratory school. I am taking this opportunity of inviting you to visit the _____ for I am sure we can both grow through the exchange of ideas."

147

Requirements

* * * * *

"Any university will take an anecdotal record in lieu of As, Bs, and Cs. The *Eight-Year Study* (the Harvard Report) indicated this many years ago. All a university would like is an accurate description of the student accomplishment performance levels."

* * * * *

"In our admissions program, we are not inflexible regarding secondary school transcript requirements, and over the years we have had a considerable amount of experience with so-called unconventional secondary schools that follow a system of written evaluations rather than grades and no ranking procedures whatsoever. We can work with this kind of unorthodox reporting system quite satisfactorily, and the candidate in question is not in any way handicapped as a result. I might add in passing that _____ has moved away from a conventional grading system this year, and we are now operating entirely on a credit-no credit plan."

* * * * *

"Thank you for your truly enjoyable letter. Even though your students have not applied at _____, we would be happy to accept them. I only wish that more educators would try some of the things you people are doing. Keep up the good work.

REPORTING

There are no magic solutions for those considering changing to an open, futures oriented approach to learning. Predictably, often the most posed questions are those relating to student progress. People ask: "In schools where grades, class rank, and report cards are not given, how do you evaluate and report what the student has or has not achieved? Do not give us theory, or what might be done. We know there are many theoretical solutions; right now we need a workable method that we might adopt, or blend with our own ideas.

Consensus for one procedure for appraising and reporting student progress, with possible alternatives, is a way to begin. Instead of spending hours, weeks, and months of planning and discussing, trying to develop a perfect system, it is better to quickly agree upon an acceptable method of eliminating report cards, to allow the new program to function. Schools have tried required parent conferences, "blank check" parent information requests, and many different written forms. None have been 100 percent satisfactory, but all have usually been better than the inhumane A, B, C marking system.

The suggestions are not the ultimate, but only practical examples of a staff preparing for change. In this process, the first decision that must be made is to abandon the traditional reporting system. Several experimental efforts are necessary before a staff finally is somewhat satisfied with the results. Within a year or two, if not sooner, the staff finds their system obsolete, or in need of further revision. Communities adopting open patterns must continually consider new methods of student evaluation; they need concrete suggestions, and then they must wrestle with their own format.

The Wilson form, the "Experience Record," should become past history as soon as schools are able to eliminate most all references to traditional subjects and team arrangements. Currently, curriculum terminologies such as expressive, creative, system, environment, and communication can cause colleges confusion, and can require a tremendous amount of clerical work and interpretation. As a compromise, during the transition, it is easier to use the traditional subject listings, accompanied by an interrelated report. The combinations described are not necessarily desirable in all schools; they may happen to fit a particular development in one program at a given moment in its history. They do provide a method to record "course titles" without reference to A, B, C marks, credits, grade in school, or even length in time, such as weeks spent in an experience, or whether it was a mini-involvement, a midi-effort, or a maxi-in depth study.

A local version of an Experience Record satisfies many needs, as it does give future employers a perspective of the areas of interest, and the balance of the diet selected by a student while enrolled. There is a continuing need to describe philosophies and methods which have been used in pioneering schools; these should act as catalysts for a creative staff to help develop approaches toward future evaluation in the effort to overcome tradition and keep pace with new demands for comprehensively prepared individuals.

Reporting

The most negative factor in staying with the traditional labels is that they perpetuate the continuance of segmented knowledge. Instead of being thought of as an individual person with interdependent competencies, Mr. X is known as the art teacher who teaches the art courses; there are better ways. People – adults and youngsters – should develop relevant interdependent curricular experiences by pursuing common interests without regard to labels for courses or teachers; that day is coming. Methods of recording experiences now are not what educators ought to be doing; they are only bowing to the reality that as schools move toward the end of the century, only a minority of students, faculty, and parents are ready to accept such "bold," long overdue, conservative steps. Therefore, forms are required which are immediately acceptable as transition steps for those who need to move through evolutionary strategies.

The plan suggested calls for two to four formal periods for appraising and reporting student progress each calendar year. Other informal evaluation sessions should be conducted related to growth and progress. Theoretically, each day students should appraise and report, at least to themselves, or with the teacher, advisor, or parent, and progress toward goals. From a practical point of view, this does not happen; however, as much assessment as possible and desirable is encouraged.

On selected dates – perhaps September 10 and March 10 or March 10, June 10, September 10, and December 10 of each calendar year – or any dates desired – student progress reports may be mailed home to the students and their parents. Two or three are preferable, four maximum, unless essential. These evaluations are carbonized in quintuplicate; the blue (or any color) copy goes to the parent; the buff to the file of the advisor selected by the student; and the yellow to the student file in each team center. The fourth green copy is the school record. It is maintained in the planning center until course information is copied on the permanent record or placed in the computer for reference for parent or administrator conferences. They can be discarded at periodic times and replaced by later reports, but preferably are kept to assist in compiling records for students transferring to traditional schools. The fifth (white) copy is a preliminary form which goes to the advisor soon after the decision to become involved in new programs during each reporting period – or whenever a student selects other experiences; this provides the advisor information on student goals set or experiences desired, and gives assurance that all staff members are consulting with each student regarding selected learning opportunities.

The final report during each period of time is completed through individual conferences held between the student and teacher prior to the chosen dates. The advisor keeps the advisor copies for the four "high school" years. This becomes a bulky but extremely valuable package of student progress, and forms a basis for evaluations for the future. For "elementary" students, the forms are kept for a year and gradually replaced by the new reports of the following year. Most schools have now adopted computers to ease the storage of student progress, but privacy must be ensured.

The exact report months chosen are not especially important. A set date has been found to be helpful to assure an appraisal that may otherwise be neglected; it does aid in communication between various team members, advisors, students and parents. As more 12-month school calendars emerge, four seasonal dates might be selected: spring, summer, fall, and winter. Student interns at present are usually available from colleges for one quarter only, and teacher contracts in most districts are issued on a fiscal year basis; therefore, it is sometimes desirable to have the evaluations near the end of each college quarter so there is time for any desired parent conferences or comments related to student work with a college intern. If only one or two such reports are developed, information may be accumulated through comments left in the folder of the student.

The formal evaluation form consists of four parts. At the time the student determines, in conjunction with the teacher-consultant or team of teacher-consultants, what he or she desires to pursue, the general goals, aspirations, or objectives in very abbreviated form are listed for the affective, psychomotor, and cognitive domains (they do not need to be identified as such, but the staff should be aware of progress in all areas and discuss them with the students). These are short descriptions; they can be in behavioral terms, or only in descriptive notes which might merely say "still exploring possibilities," but at least the advisor has some information on the advisee. There should not be excessive pressure on the student to start, but there is a need for communication and commitment. The total summary is only one page. Toward the evaluation date, the student and teacher discuss whether the original goals have been exceeded, reached, or not attained. This progress is then noted in the second section of the report.

During or after the conference with the student, there is a third section where the teacher can make additional remarks from his or her point of view. The form is then sent to the advisor. In this way the counselor-advisor receives copies from all the learning teams or teachers with whom the student is engaged. The "subject" teacher-consultants may only know what the child is doing in depth in the specific team; the advisor may have two, eight, or even 13 or more reports, depending upon the involvement of each student.

The fourth section is completed by the advisor-counselor during the conference held with each advisee. Time is taken from specific days to provide an opportunity for these sessions to occur. The reports are then forwarded to the planning center where the buff, blue, yellow, and green sections are separated. The white has already been torn off after the first weeks of the experience and forwarded to the advisor as the preliminary commitment. The blue is made available to mail home; the buff is returned to the counselor-advisor. The yellow is returned to the team center, while the green is maintained in the planning center to record any pertinent information in each permanent record folder.

At the bottom of the one page Progress Report is a space for teachers to record "titles" of any "experiences" taken during the period and to mark them "completed," "continuing," or "discontinued." The completed experiences are placed on the Experience Record. There is a note at the bottom of the page to encourage parent comments – by a letter from home, or by personal meeting.

Teachers are encouraged to hold conferences more often and most do. Some students are involved often with one-to-one evaluation sessions, while others have less need. Sometimes the conferences are informal, and no record – or at least no formal record – is kept, other than perhaps notes in the student folder. The teachers fill in with the student the formal four section report, and together complete the preliminary copy. This can be done once a week if desirable. It can be routed to the counselor and parent. From a practical view, this informal report is usually completed for only the first three sections; it is not sent to the counselor, office, and home, except for the preliminary page, and is usually done on a less expensive copy machine form, rather than the more expensive carbonized edition.

It has appeared best for most to set some formal periods for evaluations, rather than let them happen whenever the student and teacher feel it is time. Several teachers/selected advisors may fail to communicate often enough. The two, three, or four formal evaluations on specific dates ensure that appraisals are completed; the "do it when it seems best" philosophy is maintained by providing for other assessments to occur as needed. These can be very informal, semi-formal, or a formal carbonized report, depending upon the perceptions of the student and teacher. In the completely open "free school," formal reports are not necessary, and certainly not at a specific date, or certain period of time. Schools which can escape the formality should be encouraged to follow the informal approach, but most open staff yet believe they need a reporting structure.

Parent conferences are used as a supplement. If they desire to know more, they may make an appointment with a teacher, advisor, team of facilitators, or most any combination of school and student personnel which may seem desirable. The school administration or an individual teacher, working through the advisor, may likewise initiate the request for a conference with the parents, either at school or in the home, with or without the student, depending on the circumstances.

In no case, in appraising and reporting student progress, are A, B, C, percentage, or numerical grades used, nor is any grade point average, class rank, or other comparative analysis made. As a student progresses through work in math (speaking traditionally), the teacher may suggest a ten question "test" over the material. The teacher may even mark four correct, but certainly not six wrong. The consultant and the student can then analyze why the four were correct and the six not. If the six errors are important, the student receives help on how to overcome the deficiency. The student does not fail in terms of an "F" grade, but he or she may have "failed" at that moment to reach the goals set and/or obligations contracted, though "contracts" are not the recommended method, except in certain instances for specific individuals. The student may need to review the work again or set new goals; the individual should continue the learning process until it is determined that the additional effort is not of that much value. The purpose of evaluation is not to determine grades for report cards.

Students sometimes ask for an analysis of how they are doing compared to others; typing/keyboarding is an easy illustration. The teacher may say that the approximate mean of students who type at this school is 45 words per minute with two errors; the student can check to see how his or her skill is progressing as compared with other students.

Informal conferences, from which plans develop that seem important enough to record, or information helpful in further discussions, can be jotted in the "subject" or team file; parent comments can go directly to one teacher, a team, the advisor, or eventually to the administration – depending upon their content and value as related to the individual or the general school program, but the advisor is kept informed of all pertinent information. Parent conference summaries receive the same treatment.

For students in what used to be the traditional K-8 years, there is no concern over "passing" or "credits;" schools should just be continuous progress opportunities.

Reporting

"Courses" – experiences – are recorded on the Experience Record kept in the permanent file for that purpose, along with information such as test scores and subjective evaluations. Other records remain in the team and advisor folders. For the subjective Advisor Evaluation, the same process is followed except that a short yearly written summary statement is made by each advisor for the permanent office record so that there is a composite profile for each student by the time he or she graduates. This summary should indicate growth and development in the affective, psychomotor, and cognitive domains, and the perceived potential for future learning opportunities.

The advisors and the students, during the traditional "junior" year, compile a four-year summary of the high school program, so that those applying for college admittance in the fall of their "senior" year, or for early graduation, or for jobs, have a profile to submit; this needs to be updated upon graduation. It is not as complicated as it may seem. High school students develop during the first year, a short separate summary of their progress; this is repeated the second year. The information of the third year is combined with the two previous reports; one sheet then forms a composite profile. The fourth year, additional information is added to the previous three-year sketch; a "picture" of the individual is thus easily available with minimal advisor effort.

Each year the experiences that a student has completed are recorded in his or her folder maintained in the planning center (office). The easiest way now to satisfy the colleges is to list the experiences under a traditional subject column. Each time a student completes a "course" or "experience," whether the person spent four weeks, 14 weeks, or 40 weeks studying the subject in depth, or only giving it surface coverage, it is cited under the most appropriate column; completion is based upon meeting the commitments agreed to with the instructor. A student may have long lists of experiences under industrial arts, art, home economics, and mathematics, but may have a blank under Spanish, and minimal under social science; such a format shows anyone the interest and involvement of each pupil.

A college would receive two items: (1) a summary Advisor Evaluation, the one page subjective opinion statement of the student as seen by the teacher/advisor, including the probability of success in future school work; and, (2) a list of the experiences pursued during the four years (the Experience Record), including a section for "test scores;" student activities are listed under the most appropriate subject column. These pages of information replace the discriminatory grade point average, class rank, and A, B, C, D, F marks. The college is requested to send for any other specific information they need, such as portfolios. The same information can be sent to prospective employers, vocational schools, interest programs, or any other "beyond high school" use the student might develop; it serves as the placement file for the students until they establish one through further work or school experiences.

For students in the traditional pre-high school years, they will have subjective evaluations in the team and the advisor folders – the Experience Record, the Quarterly Records – the same as the high school student; the difference is that in the last four years, the annual summary is prepared more carefully related to college or employer criteria. If students transfer in the pre-high school years, their Experience Record list is completed and the Advisor Evaluation is prepared. If the student is going to an open concept, nongraded school, that is all that is needed. If transferring to a traditional program, a "grade placement" recommendation is sent to that school, as determined by the advisor, or in consultation with other teachers, if it is not for the "normal" yearly growth promotion to the next traditional grade level.

The flexible high school is satisfied with this reporting system, as is the flexible college.   There are many rigid school administrators and counselors who are upset if standard information is not received.   Open schools should refuse to send grades, class rank, and other, but if essential, should fill out a standard transcript for the individual.   To help the student in an emergency, the school interprets and transcribes so that a mini-course in Zen, a midi-course in astrology , and one in humanities, and a maxi-course in Dream Reality may be converted to English II, worth one credit.   This way the person who is forced to transfer at the end of the "junior" year to a traditional school can have a transcript prepared that shows conventional credits in English, social studies, math, and other requirements, but this is only considered if absolutely necessary.   There are no prerequisites or even basic requirements for all students in a given year, but for the schools that claim there are, open programs can adjust and complete a transcript to help the student.

Rarely is this approach needed for colleges, but it can be done to not penalize the applicant.   The same applies to eligibility rules and scholarships.   All students enrolled are eligible; the forms are completed accordingly.   The same can be applied to the unethical practice of signing insurance forms to set insurance rates, which is not the business of the school.   When a scholarship is involved, schools can create a class rank that is a subjectively accurate evaluation and amounts to the same placement as one devised by any percentage system.   It is done by a composite of subjective teacher evaluations at the time it is needed.   Seldom will a grade point average be essential, but it can be arrived at through test scores and ratings of the staff.   The students are protected from worry regarding conventions if they continue work in a flexible, caring organization with genuine concerns for the individual.

Several samples of the goal sheets and transcripts as they emerged over the years illustrate the need to find a system that fits with an individualized program.   It is wrong to accept standard, uniform report cards mandated for use with all youth.   Some traditions are worth preserving, but one of those is not A, B, C, D, F report cards.

ADVISOR EVALUATION

Wilson Campus School
Manakato State University
Mankato, MN   56001
(507) 389-1122

Cumulative Yearly
Summary

Date _____

_____
Student

_____
Advisor

(*Note: Use reproducible pen, pencil, or typewriter)

This is a subjective evaluation prepared by a teacher-advisor in conference with the student whom he or she has counseled during the past year; it is cumulative in that it includes a summary of previous evaluations by advisors.

(1) **Growth and Development in the Affective Domain**: (Examples: self-image, responsibility, self-direction, motivation, creativity, person relationships, critical thinking.)

(2) **Growth and Development in the Psychomotor Domain**: (Examples: physical maturity, handicaps, fine and gross motor coordination and skills, strength, athletic ability.)

(3) **Progress and Achievement in the Cognitive Domain**: Examples: (knowledge, interest, skill in curriculum areas.)

(4) **Growth in Interdependent Thinking**: (Examples: comprehending the whole; the primary, secondary, and tertiary factors — fields within fields within fields.)

(5) **Observations Regarding Future Interests and Goals**: (Examples: work, volunteer service, fine arts school, large university, small college, financial factors, marriage.)

155

EXPERIENCE RECORD

Wilson School
Mankato State University
Minnesota

Name _____
Date sent _____

Instructions: List experience and year completed. Example: Painting — 76

Art	Business	English	Foreign Language	Home Economics	Industrial Arts	Music	Math	Health	Physical Education	Science	Social Studies	Theater Arts	Other

156

Test Results

WILSON CAMPUS STUDENT PROGRESS AND EVALUATION REPORT

Name of Student _____ Team Center _____
                 Last Name   First Name

Advisor _____ Option 1 2 3 4 / F W Sp Su _____
                                                                                       Year

Instructor(s) _____

A. Goals, adjustments, accomplishments and comments as viewed by the student and teacher

(This is a sample copy of the five part, color-coded (white, yellow, buff, green, and blue), carbon form used in evaluating and reporting student progress. When initial goals are established between the teachers and the student, the blue copy is sent to the advisor. When the student is evaluated, the remaining copies are distributed in the following manner:

white copy	—	to the parents
yellow copy	—	to the instructor(s)
buff copy	—	to the advisor
green copy	—	to the permanent folder

At periodic intervals, the information on the **Student Progress and Evaluation Report** is summarized on the **Experience Record** which is kept in the permanent folder. In addition, the advisor completes an **Advisor Evaluation** once a year for inclusion in the permanent folder.)

B. Advisor Comments
   Date

C. The following, if any at this time, should be recorded on the student Experience Record.

    1. Listing of experience(s) completed:

    2. Student and teacher opinions of effort put forth regarding the experience(s):

Note to Parents: If you wish to hold a conference with the above-named advisor or instructors regarding this report, please call the school with your request. You may wish to respond with a written statement

WILSON CAMPUS SCHOOL
PROGRESS REPORT

Name of Student _____ Subject/Team Center _____
                (Last Name)   (First Name)

Advisor _____ F W Sp Su _____ Instructor(s) _____
                              (Year)
                                                  _____

A. Goals set by student and teacher   Date _____

B. Adjustment/accomplishments toward goals as viewed   Date _____
   by student and teacher

C. Additional comments by teacher

D. Advisor comments

E. Disposition of the experience: Completed   Continuing   Discontinued
    Experience titles   1. _____   _____   _____   _____
                     2. _____   _____   _____   _____
                     3. _____   _____   _____   _____

Comments: _____
_____
_____

NOTE TO PARENTS: If you wish to hold a conference with the above-named advisor
                         or instructor(s) regarding this report, please call the school with
                         your request. If you prefer, you may respond with a written
                         statement.

WILSON CAMPUS STUDENT PROGRESS AND EVALUATION REPORT

Name of Student _____ Field/Center _____

Last Name   First Name

Advisor _____ Option   1   2   3   4   /   F   W   Sp   Su   _____

Year

Instructor(s) _____ Approval Signatures _____

_____   _____

Dates	Goals, methods, adjustments, and comments as viewed by the student and teacher

Dates	Accomplishments as agreed upon by student and instructor

Dates	Advisor comments

Dates	The following should be recorded on the **Experience Record**
	_____
	signature

Note to Parents: If you wish to hold a conference with the above-named advisor or instructor(s) regarding this report, please call the school with your request. If you prefer, you may respond with a written statement.

Copy   1 office   2 transfer or college   3 parent   4 advisor   5 team   6 preliminary

Studios for Educational Alternatives - Wilson Open College Studio
Mankato State University, MN

TEACHER EDUCATION EXPERIENCE AGREEMENT

F   W   Sp   Su

_____   _____   _____
Last name   first name   middle name   Date requested   Enrollment per year

_____   _____   _____
Title of experience requested   SEA course number assigned   Credits

_____   _____   _____   _____
Approval of advisor   Approval of student   App. consultant   App. SEA office

_____
Briefly state why you desire this experience:

_____
Indicate briefly, but specifically, what you hope to learn or experience:

_____
Explain how you expect to complete and then evaluate your experience:

_____
Evaluate the completed experience with your consultant:

Transcript recommendation   P   N   I   A   B   C   D   NC   _____
                                                              Consultant signature

Return consultant copy to SEA office for recording of credit

Date _____

1. Consultant copy   2. Advisory copy   3. Student copy   4. SEA copy   5. Other copy

160

chapter twenty

CALENDAR

In July, 1969, the Wilson Campus School adopted a year-round calendar labeled the Personalized Continuous Year. It was designed as a voluntary single track (non-space saving) drop-in, drop-out, speed up, slow down, vacation when desired implementation of the Wilson philosophy. It was created to also serve multiple-track (space saving) purposes if the need existed.

One of the first in the country in the revival of year-round education (YRE) – earlier programs were inaugurated in Bluffton, Indiana (1904) and numerous other communities, all of which were disrupted by a variety of factors, including World War II – Wilson was close behind the specialized 200-day, 50-15 calendar piloted in Hayward, California, in 1968 under the leadership of Bernard Moura at the Park Elementary School.

At Wilson continuous learning was available for K-12. It was handicapped by the faculty college contracts and vacation schedules, budget considerations, lack of air conditioning, and moderate understanding among the staff and community – it was a pioneer program. In spite of these and other factors, YRE did exist and benefit many students.

Wilson wanted people to be able to take advantage of learning opportunities continuously, with interruptions only when preferred. The staff felt schools, like hospitals, should never close. They are both helping institutions, and education, like health, should be available 24 hours a day, seven days a week, 12 months a year – as modeled by the Nevada casinos.

Traditional schools are usually closed June, July, and August. If there is a summer session, it is short. The summer curriculum is, by and large, discontinuous from the September to June curriculum, whereas YRE intersessions offer continuous learning. Too often little 2nd grade Billy gets all excited in July about the bugs he found in the nearby field or in his yard or alley. He "captures them" and runs into his house to ask Mom to help. Mom hollers, "Bugs, get them out of here – I can't stand them – and besides I cannot teach you anything about the creatures."

Undaunted, Billy has a plan. He will go to his school for certainly his teacher will help. Upon arrival, though, he finds a big sign – CLOSED – you cannot learn about bugs in July; come back in September.   Still not discouraged, he keeps his bugs and excitement alive and arrives with them at school in the fall, only to find that bugs are not in the curriculum guide until April and besides, his second grade teacher hates bugs (science) – that is why she chooses to teach second year. First and third grade staff must be amenable to science, for the former science-oriented youth like "animals" and the latter are smart enough to want to ask questions about rockets. But in between the transition, the middle teacher can avoid most science, except for the textbook variety.

Then, too, construction workers, among many others, in states such as Minnesota, have minimal work in January and February when the snow is piled high and the temperature is -20. The obvious time for their family "summer vacation" is in the winter, when they can "escape" to Florida for little Sally to see the Atlantic Ocean, go to Disney

World, get a suntan, learn to swim, see the alligators, have Daddy spend time with her, and then return to learn in August rather than January. Moving van drivers, baseball players, those low on union or work seniority lists, tourist resort employees, farmers, and many others cannot be away during the summer. Skiers do not want to go to Colorado in July.

Ironically, the majority of people cannot take or do not want a summer vacation most years; in much of California and similar geographical states, it is too hot, expensive, and crowded in August, but September-October, and April-May bring precious weather – or February for snow enthusiasts – while in the warm "off-months" the beaches and parks are relatively empty, the prices are down, and the crowds are reduced.

Learning opportunities were always available at Wilson. Many youth earned "credit" (traditional concept) when on vacation. They might rappel in the Colorado Rockies, explore science at the Kennedy Space Center, or study American Indian cultures and history in Montana – including visiting the battlefields where Custer met his match. They could read books about the topics, keep a diary, interview on tape persons with knowledge of the subject, take pictures, create a videotape, prepare a "term paper," write a book of their experiences – multiple ways to document their "learning" off-campus without a teacher present in a stuffy classroom sitting at a desk. Such activities could occur year-round.

To enhance the process, staff wanted to create a Wilson program which would be, as much as possible, available round-the-clock. One of the parts was the Personalized Continuous Year timeframe. In year-round education terms, it was a "single track;" all students had the flexibility of the same options without saving space. However, if essential, the plan could be mandated in a manner to ensure the same program remained, by scheduling the students to attend or vacation certain months on a self-selected basis to achieve space. The multiple-track rotation was individualized through a mandatory – with options method, where families were "required" to alter their patterns, but could select what for them were the best weeks of the year, related to their lifestyle preferences and employment realities.

For the most part, Wilson was a "voluntary single track," for with all the off-campus learning programs and optional attendance, space was seldom an issue – except, as in all facilities, where special environments could always be enhanced by expansion.

The calendar at Wilson was simple. In theory, the school was open 365 days a year, 24 hours a day. In facility/staff reality, it was open approximately 240 days from 7 a.m. to 5 p.m., the result of the faculty contracts with the college and the usual budget restraints. The mechanics were an easy formula: students "owed" the school about 170 days (Minnesota requirement for financial support), minus illness and special consideration absences. They could attend any 170 of the 240 days the facility was open – or all 240 – or gain "credit" through approved off campus ventures beyond the maximum.

When the curriculum was completely personalized and individualized, students had total flexibility. Staff had the same optional attendance choices. There was no coverage problem, as faculty worked in teams of teachers with whatever combination of aides, volunteers, and student interns was available at a given moment or budget year. If 600 students were enrolled, it was assumed that perhaps 500 would attend each day, and that three to five teachers might be absent. Therefore, balance was not a problem. Families/students/staff could vacation whenever they desired year-round – for a day, week, month, months – or even furlough for a year.

They did not need to request permission – except for long periods (as in furloughs). Most students informed their teachers and/or advisor, but if Dad could take two days off during hunting season, or had an opportunity to take the family on a business trip, or if he was fired from his factory job and wanted to talk with the family – or if Mom wanted the kids to stay home for a day, or go to "grandmothers," that was great. Staff had the same options. The year-round calendar day schedules were completely optional and voluntary. Wilson did not believe in rigid mandatory "vacation days" for the different single or multiple track plans – such as in the 60-20 calendar.

For overcrowded schools which must create additional space and be more accountable to parents/community/state – then the Personalized Continuous Year – though it can be mandated – more preferably is humanely implemented on a mandatory-with-options plan. Assuming 600 students in a school built for 450, families and staff request by 1st, 2nd, 3rd choice the weeks they prefer their vacation days. They are told that most all (exceptions can be granted) must take some time off in the "winter" and be in school sometime during the "summer." Then the scheduling process selects individuals according to their preferences to ensure that always 450 students and appropriate staff are in the building, and 150 youth and perhaps five faculty are on vacation for that week/month. Deviations from the "norm" are permissible, as it does not usually matter whether the count is 140 or 160 youth and four or seven teachers out, as long as an approximate balance is maintained. An "Appeals Board" can be established to consider situations where the parent/student/staff feel mistreated.

Subject/grade level "matches" are not a problem as all staff "teach" K-12 students; they all function in a 2nd or 3rd "subject" as part of the interrelated curriculum, and all work as members of teams. The only key is to ensure that at least one teacher is in the building who knows "science" well – or at least one who can 'hug' "kindergarten" children. The mandatory-with-options system is not theory – it works; it is not time consuming after the first year when the mechanical "bugs" are eliminated. The personalized YRE calendar is an exciting transition toward the future.

Year-round education as currently perceived is not a panacea. However, it is an essential part of developing a philosophy of continuously available life-long learning. The article by Lowell Schreyer of the *Mankato Free Press* expresses how Wilson was successful in interweaving the concept of YRE with all its other programs as early as 1969 – after the first year of the "new program." It added another dimension toward converting Wilson from 20th Century schooling to 21st Century learning.

MANKATO FREE PRESS – AUGUST 13, 1969
"Wilson goes to 12-month School Year"
by Lowell Schreyer, Feature Editor

School boards sometimes talk about the 12-month school year. The public often eyes it as a way of getting more out of its school construction dollar. But still the nine-to-ten month school year continues. Except at Wilson Campus School, which initiated the much-discussed but seldom-tried 12-month school year this term. Wilson will be open around the year except for a two-week Christmas vacation, one-week spring break and two-week fall break. "There is absolutely no reason for having schools open only from September to June," said Dr. Don E. Glines, director of the school. He pointed out there is no research to indicate that children can't learn in summer. The growth of summer school programs proves it can be done. In addition, some occupations are geared to summer employment and the only time feasible for a family vacation may be winter. The whole thing ties in with Wilson's emphasis on personalized programs as each student moves forward at his own pace. "You want the student to be able to progress at his own rate of growth, as fast or as slow as the student needs," he said. "As they go through they don't have to wait for anybody to catch up."

This individualizing of programs is ideal for the 12-month school concept. Glines doesn't care when students take their vacations – summer, winter, fall or spring. It's all the same to him. "When the students return, they commence where they were when they left. If dad wants to take the kids duck hunting, great! We encourage it. There's not enough of this."

Wilson Campus School, which gained a national reputation as an education idea mill in only one year, will also be concentrating on quality instead of quantity this coming year, according to Glines. The quantity in the past year has been in the innovations put into motion as the laboratory school was revamped from an essentially traditional school to what *The National Observer* termed as probably "the most innovative publicly supported school in the country."

"The first year the emphasis was on developing a different school," said Glines. "The second year it will be on developing a better school." Not that there won't be more innovations in addition to the 12-month year. For one thing, there will be "smorgasbord" scheduling providing even more choice for students to design their own programs. Old curriculum materials will be discarded in most major areas and new materials brought in.

A lot has happened to the 580-student school during Glines' first year there. "It was a traditional egg crate last July," he said. "You look at now and it's entirely different." As during the past school year, school bells will be out. So will be grade designation, required attendance and grades. The famous doughnuts will be in.

School will be open for instruction from 7:30 a.m. to 5:30 p.m. Students won't be required to be there those hours. Optional group classes will be offered from 8:45 a.m. to 3:15 p.m.; the rest of the time will be available for lab work and counseling.

"Students can look over the opportunities and decide, 'What do I want today? How much cake? How much meat?'" explained Glines.

Wilson students, incidentally, are on their own some 85 percent of most days and in class meetings the rest of the time. Glines sees no need of calling a group meeting unless some students have a common interest they want to discuss. "They can read and go to the resource center on their own," he said.

A few students last year never went to class, but they still learned by meeting with teachers periodically while working on individual projects. The Wilson system doesn't leave students as free of adult supervision as it might at first appear. Some direction comes in the form of guidance from teacher counselors which the students select themselves. Students also take "tests" periodically – but not for grades, only to let them know if they are ready to go on to new material.

Individual conferences indicate to students and parents how the student is doing. Glines considers this of much more value than letter grades. In the event a student appears to be skipping something he should have, the teacher-counselors point this out to him. "If this is obvious, then we'll step in and say, 'You took seven experiences, but you left one out,'" said Glines.

School authorities also have a veto power if a student is going too far off base in his yearly selections. "Last year we didn't have to use it once. We hope we won't have to invoke it, but if there is an obvious lack we'll tell them."

In explaining the philosophical approach of Wilson school, Glines often uses the analogy that students, like patients in a doctor's office, should have individual diagnosis and prescription. "The trouble with education in the United States today is group prescription," he said. "The first 30 patients that walk in get flu shots – in spite of the fact one might have a broken leg, another an ear infection. The tragedy is staff haven't even met the students but their programs are already set." Wilson attempts to determine where each student is and prescribe on an individual basis from that point on, he added.

Glines believes the traditional system perpetuates failure. He explained that one can predict with almost 100 per cent accuracy that an entering 7th grader, for instance, who has made a poor academic showing throughout elementary school will have D's and F's again in the coming year. "These kids with problems shouldn't have more reading and math," he said. "The real problem is their self-image. If they like themselves and school – they need to take something they're interested in – then the whole attitude changes."

Under the self-selection policy at Wilson, such a student could decide to take only fields such as shop, art and physical education – areas in which he does well. He could also choose classes where he gets along well with the teacher. On top of that, attendance is not compulsory.

"There is no longer a discipline problem," said Glines. "If he gets mad at the teacher, he can leave. He finds success in school – he likes the teacher – he likes school. That's the turning point. The next year you can ask, 'Hey Pete, don't you think you need some math?'" said Glines.

Not too far from the old time country school in some ways, Wilson will drop all boundaries between various age levels. A student of sixth grade age may find himself sitting next to one of first grade age. "As long as he has an individual program, it doesn't make any difference," he said. "If you have a first grader, a fifth grader and a 12th grader at home, do you make them eat at different tables?

"Kids help kids," he added; "if a young one gets stuck, the older ones help." There will be more team teaching at Wilson this coming school year. "Where there is one teacher, it's okay if there's an obvious skill the kid needs," said Glines. "But what if a student comes along and the teacher doesn't know what's wrong or if she does know but doesn't have the skill to remedy it?"

Some children, he pointed out, need a "tender loving care" teacher while others need the staccato type teacher – "Sit down and stop jumping around the room!" The youngster has a better chance to get the skills and matching personality from a teacher team rather than from one, according to Glines.

Curriculum changes will mean an overhaul in almost every core area to get materials with more relevance to today's youngsters. That means Tom, Dick and Jane readers are out.

"Kid's don't balk at learning but at the irrelevant things we ask them to pursue," said Glines.

The youngsters at the lower end of the age range will have more opportunity to take industrial arts and home economics – almost unheard of at that level, related the wiry, exuberant educator who sometimes skips along as he describes kindergarten children.

An overseas program will be in store for Wilson this coming year. The school has been contacted about the possibility of entering into an exchange program with Spain. Wilson students already have a background in a Spanish-speaking country through their exchange program with Mexico.

Physical changes coming at Wilson include some non-traditional paint schemes. "We're going to wild colors," he said. "We don't like walls, so we are trying to camouflage them." Glines is an "anti-wall" man and is presently punching holes in a few at Wilson.

Space needs change from year to year, Glines explained. That's why he feels a school interior should never be limited in how the area is divided up. "Folding doors are a waste of time," he said. "Then you have a traditional classroom."

Glines is often criticized but never ignored for his forward looking ideas. He has been called in as a consultant to the school systems in and out of state and has just returned from an advice–giving trip to Fort Lauderdale, Fla., which is putting up a large building, hollow as a barn, for 1,200 middle school students. In October, he makes a similar jaunt to Fresno, California.

Visitors have come to Wilson from as far as both coasts. Of 50 Minnesota districts that looked at the Wilson program, 30 percent are anxious to start it, 40 percent aren't sure and 30 percent "think it's awful." In Minnesota, Bloomington is trying the most Wilson-type program. Other suburban districts piloting some Wilson ideas are Burnsville, Hopkins, Minnetonka and White Bear.

Glines favors a more pleasant atmosphere in a classroom. One elementary room at Wilson has carpeting and pillows in one corner for a reading area. One third of the school will be carpeted this coming year. "Carpeting deadens sound," he said. "Where does all the noise come from? The floor. School boards put in acoustical ceilings. Why not acoustical floors?" – but always mindful of the effect old or dusty or formaldehyde backed carpets can have on allergic youth.

"Kids also like to lie on the floor when they study," he continued. "Look at the home. You don't sit in the most uncomfortable chair when you want to read a book." His hand

166

gave a wave of disgust at a few stiff-looking desks in another room. "I'd like to get rid of them if I could, but who'd take them?"

Looking back at his first year at Wilson, Glines reported that although children had the opportunity to take only so-called "snap" courses, more took English and social studies than ever before. Some took as many as nine classes rather than the usual five. There were also fewer discipline problems.

"On the negative side," said Glines, in this first year, "we still had some kids who were turned off. In a traditional system they would have gotten Ds and Fs. There were some kids who did nothing but drink cokes and visit. They did improve socially, but we still need more changes to enable us to completely reach those youth."

While results of the Wilson system cannot be evaluated fully after only one year, Glines believes his youngsters are doing at least as well as they would in an academic school. Some high school level students have even been taking college work at the parent Mankato State College.

He has never claimed Wilson was better, only different. But Glines thinks Wilson is fulfilling its laboratory role of innovation, experimentation, research and evaluation – in short, exploring for a better school.

chapter twenty-one

ROUTINES

There were key concepts which made the Wilson program significant, but there were "nuts and bolts" mechanics which enabled the structure to function; in the early days, mundane, conventional topics had to be faced. These "routines" should be questioned by some, will be controversial for many, and may seem to conflict with previous statements made about innovation and flexibility. As more and more persons became interested in the process of beginning programs similar to Wilson, educators constantly raised questions that are minor problems, but ironically do cause friction during the change-over process in most schools. Often principals would say: "We now think we understand how to individualize learning, but what can we do about communication systems related to such topics as assemblies, attendance, announcements, and new students?"

The easy answer is that each school must work out the solutions to the satisfaction of the specific staff. However, there is no need to reinvent every wheel. Seven items illustrate difficulties which arise at the practical everyday level; the Wilson staff temporarily resolved these areas of conflict until more permanent agreements could be reached. Seldom have any of these minor areas stopped the total innovation effort, but they have caused emotional arguments. Even after two years, many faculty members were not happy with the solutions reached as of that date, but at least the school was able to develop a base from which to operate.

The first topic considers the orientation of groups, especially following long vacations in traditional nine-month schools. The others address homerooms, group names for scheduling purposes, assemblies, visitation policies, parent communication regarding requirements, and student selection of advisors. These are only suggestions related to immediately converting a traditional school to a Wilson style program. They are not the answers which are emerging toward and into the next century.

GROUP ORIENTATION: The first two weeks of a given school year find changes of staff and students (even year-round schools confront a problem from transfers in July or late arrivals in the August-September period, for YRE programs are in the minority nationwide). A simple way to organize is to place students in temporary "advisories" by age level to assist the mechanics for new staff and students, and to explain the major changes in the program. In true year-round education, this is usually a very short introduction, or may only be geared to persons new to the school.

It is helpful to schedule students into "must" orientation assemblies the first three days, where each of the various teams has a chance to introduce staff members and discuss with, or present to the students, the "shoppers guides" of the possible experiences, and the policies of the team or center. This way the staff is assured that most students are at least exposed to the potential of each area, and that the individual has been encouraged to visit the various centers and consider learning experiences with many teachers. Thus, every pupil has an opportunity to meet or hear from all staff.

Other than these group assemblies, the students window shop on their own during the first week, and follow the optional choice program. During the second week, they request their new advisors, and later record their chosen instructors/facilitators, and sometimes their chosen fields of study. These can be changed at any time, but an initial selection helps most everyone off to a good start.

Though this may seem rigid, remember the calendar should be considered a 12-month year – the student can continue straight through until August, even if in only a separate summer program, and then in September continue the same experience with the same advisor with no interruption, other than vacation – except where a staff member has resigned. The two week "group period" is merely a concession that in reality, until there is complete differentiated staffing and true year-round education, most districts are locked into group teacher contracts, parent transfers, and "summer vacations;" this practice allows any necessary retooling of staff and program. The assembly line in the auto plant stops for a period of time to convert to the new models; the short interruption is merely a retooling process to allow the latest designs to roll into high speed production.

These group orientations are especially helpful for young students; the traditional K-1 persons should usually have some of these sessions periodically throughout the year until most of the individuals are able to be pretty much self-directing. They should be allowed great amounts of freedom during these years, and should choose their own teachers and classes. Most schools find it best – especially if they do not have three and four year olds, and full day five year old programs, as at Wilson – to group structure about half of each week of the "grade 1" age level students into each area of study on a balanced diet of equal amounts of time, so that the youngsters have a chance to receive basic orientation in all the various centers. Having multi-age grouping dramatically reduces the problems, as the older, "veteran" 2nd and 3rd "graders" can orient the younger folks.

During these shopping weeks, terms such as seventh grade and homeroom can be used when external or internal forces deem this best, but they are only for expediency. On the district census cards which help determine state aid, most mandate recording of a "grade level," for the funds are often a different amount for various grades. As more schools become involved in all aspects of year-round education, nongrading, and individualization, these "old practices," even on a temporary basis, will not be as necessary; at the moment they sometimes are forced upon innovators. The program must operate within the confines of reality; the total flexibility concept for which education should be striving will eventually be possible throughout North America.

ADVISORY: On a temporary basis, a period of time, such as 8:45- 9:00, may be referred to as Advisory. Attendance of all students should be encouraged: the Advisory is a means of school communication; an opportunity to receive messages; make individual appointments with the advisor; establish group counseling sessions; share information regarding school programs; process the "official" attendance; discuss improvements in the school; conduct group seminars related to relevant interests; and encourage student involvement in areas of concern. This should not be confused with the 1930s innovation of mandatory, assigned "homeroom."

Students who do not come to school in time for Advisory check with their advisor during the day to mark off attendance so that state aid can be claimed; students should be encouraged to see their advisor for at least a minute so that they can determine if there are messages or appointments. Even though under this system Advisory is optional, the same as all other classes, students and teachers should be encouraged not to wander the halls from 8:45-9:00. Teachers should be in the centers available to students, not in the coffee room. Students should be in individual or group sessions during this time, or planning their day. Where there is no Advisory period, subjectively the opinion is strong that there is a definite communication gap. At least during these few minutes there is a chance to say hello and help students plan their daily schedules; the success of the entire effort is communication between the advisor and the advisee (often called the 4-T program for very young folks – teacher-to-talk-to).

Unless there is a very special reason, the intercom should not be used at any time. As there is seldom justification, except for emergencies, the "Do not open until Xmas" sign is a good way to put this policy into effect, renewable each Xmas. There is little call for a daily bulletin; a weekly, or on a need basis, is usually ample, and then it should be held to a half-page. Both the intercom and bulletin goals can be attained if students communicate with their Advisory each day. Messages for individuals and small groups of students should be sent to their advisor, not advertised through a bulletin. Notices about new experience offerings can be announced on team bulletin boards or other such arrangements.

Responsibility and involvement are the keys. The advisor should stress the importance of communication; an advisor should see that the time is profitably spent. The students will not come unless they are required, if all that happens is the taking of attendance. Advisory should not be required as being contrary to general philosophy. Some students need to sleep late, or may have out of the building programs early in the morning; others may have no group classes scheduled and would rather spend the time at home doing independent study. They are not required to stay until 3:15 p.m.; therefore, they should not be required to be in school at 8:45 a.m.

Advisors should make it clear to their advisees that attendance is important in terms of state aid; even more important, each day school should be of value. Whether they come to Advisory or arrive later, they must understand why they are asked to check with their advisor who should communicate well enough with his or her advisees that they will want to visit with the adult they have selected; over 80 percent of the students usually get their first or second choice of advisor. For those students who never report for attendance or communication, the advisor must call them for a conference. Lack of verification decreases the financial reimbursements, and raises questions about the advisor-student relationship.

Schools do have to face realities regarding state aid. If the student does not report by noon, in many states attendance cannot be claimed. The students and staff must understand that yearly the school receives, depending upon the state, several thousand dollars for each student. Though this is not the major criteria for measuring success, schools do need enrollment figures and money if they are to stay open under existing state regulations; each individual must understand that there are two major reasons for one attendance check per day: state aid, and all-school, or one-to-one, communication.

GROUP NAMING: Schools should not use traditional labels such as "second grade" or "tenth grade." There is no such person in the program, nor is there any content that relates to such a name. Substitutes such as the graduation year – "97s, 99s" – are merely stop-gap efforts. They are almost as out of step as the "second grade." Every effort should be made not to use the words "special education," "early childhood," "gifted," or "at-risk."

The program calls for work with individuals; there is seldom reason for group names to be applied randomly. The interaction should discuss Sally or Billy, not the "seventh graders." There are few external and rarely, but possible, internal situations which demand a label. In almost every case, these have nothing to do with the program; there are times when, because of the "outside society," grade level names will be necessary. State census cards and high school athletic teams are potential transitional exceptions. Occasionally the Gray-Y will want to send information to the "fifth and sixth grades." Comparative research studies (to be avoided whenever possible) with other districts now and then demand "third graders."

Advisors should explain to their advisees that they need to know that if they transferred to a traditional school, they would be in the seventh grade, or that sometimes there will be a call for "seventh graders" as a class, but only for reasons related to living in the community. Regarding the school program, these terms should not be used by students and teachers – not for scheduling, identification of subject content progress (there is no sixth grade science curricula), or other such requests or discussions. Educators must learn to talk about individuals. The traditional middle school "academic" achievement spread can range ten years; the physiological spread can cover at least six years. How can educators pretend there is a seventh grade for English or a sixth grade group for softball?

Learning experiences for students are based on interest and need, and in most cases are automatically nongraded; there is very little true scope and sequence. For what "grade level" is the Indian cultures experience designed? Use of names such as Instrumental Ensemble (which is already nongraded), Astrology, Zen A, Zen B, Fractions, Vikings, or whatever, to identify ad hoc groups of students who may want to meet together from time to time for discussion or instruction, but have no relationship to grade levels, is within the philosophy.

Terminology can be developed for the particular group involved. If it is important that a similar age level of students meet, perhaps because they desire common sessions, the age classification can be used – all the students who closely fit the 11-12 year old title can be requested as 11-12 year olds, not sixth and seventh graders. It is necessary to put theory into practice. Work with individuals; work with nongraded groups; work with age mixtures. When traditional groups are desired for some very specific purpose, use the ninth grade tag, but use it sparingly. How can schools truly individualize if they continue to call for the "senior class" day after day? Once in a while, yes; consistently, no.

ASSEMBLIES AND LARGE GROUPS: Assemblies and large groups should be kept to a minimum, but there are good reasons for having them, most always on an optional basis, but occasionally required for important communication. A film on pollution of lakes in the United Sates should be of interest to almost all citizens and could be shown in a large group. The police captain speaking on drugs could be another large group appropriate for almost all to hear. Assemblies relating to college could be of interest to a wide variety of age levels, not just "twelfth graders." *The Wizard of Oz* performance is another example of the large group common thread class or assembly, as would be the announcement of new school policies, or motivational or inspirational gatherings. Large groups related to class work can be scheduled by including the name(s) of the experience(s). Large groups open to all can be called by the title or topic; meetings can thus be labelled too.

When it is desirable or necessary to limit the assembly — the entire student body is desired, but there is a need for split groups for lack of seating, or for appropriate presentation of topics — the assemblies should be labelled overlapping and suggestive. A presentation on drugs could be labelled Drugs 10s-19s, and the other, Drugs 3s-12s. The overlap leaves the flexible choice to the student. It means that the middle student can choose to go to either one, but tells that the presentation in the 10-19 assembly will be in language aimed at older students and the 3-12 to the younger. It does not force a magic cutoff, but tells the 9-10-11-12-13s that they can attend whichever they prefer. They should understand that the drug conference for 3s to perhaps 12s, and then 12s to 19s is the way the speaker has probably organized his or her vocabulary; some 11s are 14 in the knowledge of drugs, and some 14s are only 11, and thus could attend whichever session would be appropriate to their level of interest, knowledge, and maturity. An 11 year old might attend the younger session on drugs, but the older assembly on Indian cultures.

Related to groupings, IQs should not be considered. As outlined, research by Guilford indicated that there may be 50 known IQs for each individual; the total may rise to as many as 120. Gardner has talked of the seven basic intelligences. All the old IQ did was confuse and label, though it is generally true that all things being equal, the student in the traditional system with a 140 IQ can do better work in the basal reader than the student with a 90. With technology, drugs, and environmental changes, researchers suggest that the United States may soon have the scientific capacity to give most everyone a minimum IQ score of 120. Studies show that a student in math may have a low IQ in abstract reasoning, but an adequate one in the numerical and computing areas. Biochemistry has proven to be of great support toward individualization. People are different physically; the research is now being applied to intellectual and emotional development. Seldom should student assemblies or large or small groupings consider the prior IQ formula.

VISITATION POLICIES: The letter sent could be an indication to the staff of plans for visitors for a given year, as well as information for guests. Though visitations are a tremendous burden, outstanding innovative schools are swamped. The staff should see this as a compliment to the program, as an opportunity for an exchange of ideas from other school districts, for evaluative comments from outsiders, and for a chance to disseminate innovations or good programs. However, too many visitors mean there is no time to develop new creations or work with individual students; there must be an effort to control the numbers. Comments and suggestions as to visitation policies should be welcomed, as should help with and for the student guides and special guests who might be with the school several days.

One sample letter sent to visitors is presented for illustrative purposes.

Dear Visitors:

The school will be pleased to have you visit on (Day) _____ (Date) _____. To coordinate the day, we must request that you be here by 9:00 a.m. so that we can gather all the visiting groups together by 9:15. We realize this means that some of you coming from a distance must be up with the robins – or polar bears. We are sorry if this inconveniences you, but it is important that you be here for the beginning. When you arrive, please report to the Planning Center where you can register and leave your coats. If you arrive early, nutrition is available in the snack bar. At 9:15 you should be in Room 7 for a 30-minute orientation. From 9:45 to 10:30 student guides will take you on a tour of the building and program. From 10:30 until 3:00 you are "on your own," to visit those areas which most interest you, talk with the students, and interact with the faculty. We encourage you to make several trips around the building during these hours, as the program changes so often you may miss an important part of it if you stay in one spot or make only one tour. We strongly recommend a question-answer-evaluation period before you leave; please let us know your plans so that we may organize a session for 3:00 p.m.

Unless special arrangements have been made, we expect that you will be here all day, as we find an hour or two-hour visit, or even a half day, just leaves many "outsiders" confused. After your first visit here, you are welcome to come again even for short periods, but still by appointment. We generally restrict visits to Tuesday and Thursday, with occasional out-of-state exceptions for Friday or Monday to utilize weekend travel time. We try to avoid any visitors on Wednesdays and preferably not on Mondays or Fridays, as we have found that we cannot find time to improve the program if we are constantly engaged in visitations. We are sorry to be so inflexible – it does not seem to fit with a school that advertises itself as flexible – but we have learned that until visitors understand the program, the orientation period is essential.

We do not have extra staff assigned for visitations, so that it is almost impossible to handle one group at 9:00, another at 9:20, another at 9:45, and another at 10:15 throughout five days of the week. We have tried letting people just drop in and wander through the building, but this caused many public relations problems. We have had 500 visitors in a month; unless there has been some formal orientation the first time, we have been unable to date to provide a satisfactory experience. Perhaps with growing technology we will be able to provide more flexibility.

On days we have small groups, you may purchase the usual school hot lunch sometime between 11:00 and 1:00 for a modest price. The facilities are not great; you may prefer to eat at other hours from the snack bar, as food service is available all day, or you might wish to eat lunch downtown, or even skip lunch. In case this is your first trip, we have enclosed a map of the town to help you find the building. You may park anywhere on the streets near school except in the yellow zones. Please be sure each member of your group receives the information in this letter. If we do not hear from you, we will assume that you will be here on the cited date. If for some reason you are unable to come, please let us know so that someone else wishing to visit may use the time. We look forward to seeing you and hope you enjoy your trip to Mankato Wilson.

Sincerely,

PARENT COMMUNICATION: One of the problems which innovative schools always have is how to inform parents of the changes, and how to encourage them to understand the new efforts. The usual large and small group and individual parent conferences should be continued, as well as newsletters and open house policies for visitations. One way to keep them informed of philosophies and programs is to send home whenever the time seems relevant a communique related to the topic at hand. A sample that could be mailed to reinforce activities confirms that if students and parents understand the philosophy, there still may be opposition, but not a revolt. It is when they do not understand well enough to at least accept the possible risk that the school is in trouble. Described is one such effort related to experience selection.

TO: Parents and Students:

Attached is a sheet for students to indicate what experiences or 'courses' they wish to participate in and with what consultants they prefer to study at the present time. Theoretically, we should not be enrolling for classes or making any abrupt changes at the moment, as with the 12-month concept students should continue at their own pace. As they complete various goals and experiences, they should begin new ones at the moment that is most appropriate. However, we are handicapped by the fact that though the school is open continuously, teacher contracts are on the nine-month and three-month systems. This means we have new staff to work with, as well as returning teachers. We have transfers attending for the first time along with those who are returning, if they took a long vacation.

Students can continue the same program they had in June, August, or October before vacation interrupted, and often with the same instructor; many will register for exactly what they have been doing. As we further implement the 12-month concept, we will not "reregister" each year. Being realistic for now, we are taking the first week for group orientation, followed by an enrollment period. Before registration occurs for the coming year, we believe it will be to the benefit of both student and parent to read the reconfirmation of the school philosophy regarding requirements:

1. There are no required courses for any age level, or for graduation. The responsibility for the decision as to areas of study rests with the student and parent. The school will offer counsel wherever it is desired, but we do not know what is the best combination for every individual. Students should consult their parents regarding their choices, as parents must sign the registration form. They should consult with their advisors, as the advisors confirm the selection. The school does reserve the right to require participation in an experience, if staff determine it is in the best interest of the student, but we try not to use this authority.

2. We believe in a balanced diet, preferring that all students take some art, music, industrial arts, home economics, physical education, theater arts, math, science, English, social studies, environment and ecology, Spanish, business, and other such studies. We feel that these should be interrelated as much as possible for knowledge is not segmented; we do not believe in separate departments or "subjects." An interdependent art, music, and literature program under a humanities approach makes more sense than to take separate courses in music, art, and literature. Trying to take 14 different subjects at one time is rather difficult. By interrelating there is much more opportunity, but if a student sticks to the traditional subject areas, rather than take all 14 at once, we prefer one, three, five, or seven at a time, if they are in depth. Ten or more are fine, if some are only

partial involvement; students may change studies several times during the school year so that they can eventually become involved in all the areas. The research is quite clear that students learn best those things that are relevant and meaningful at this moment in time. The drop-in philosophy is encouraged in all areas for students who just want periodic experiences without the pressure of registering.

3. For younger children, self-image, success, peer relationships, and motor development are much more important than reading and math. When the affective and psychomotor areas are functioning well, students seldom have difficulty with the knowledge, content, and skill areas in the old concept of "reading," "math," and "science." Not all the "first grade" children should take reading and math every day; some should not take them at all, while others should have heavy doses. The child needs individual diagnosis and prescription for learning, such as the M.D. completes related to health problems. Reading and math are learned best when they are part of an interdependent curriculum; stir, blend, 1/4 cup make a fine reading/math/home economics learning experience.

4. At the high school level we award a regular state diploma if the students spend four years progressing in the experiences they have chosen. They can leave in less than four years or stay more than four by arrangement. Though we believe that the state requirements and those of most colleges are wrong, parents and students should be forewarned in case of transfer that most high schools require four years of English, three year of social studies, two years of physical education, one year of math, one year of science, and seven additional elective courses. If there is any possibility of transfer, it would be wise if students took these classes. If they stay here, they can select those which are relevant.

5. Entrance to college, vocational school, fine arts school, and other special institutions is governed by them individually. Students should consult catalogs of the programs where they think they might be interested in attending. Many colleges have an open enrollment policy; all that is needed is a high school diploma or its equivalent. Some colleges still require certain courses for admission. As a general rule of thumb, most colleges want on the transcript three or four years of English, two or three years of social studies, two years of math, two years of science, two years of physical education, and preferably some foreign language. In making decisions about the future, everyone should be aware that we believe home economics, art, music, business, and industrial arts are just as important as the traditional requirements; we would recommend that students take less English and some art, or take interrelated courses where English and art can be combined. If families are worried about college admissions, the safe bet is to take work – preferably interrelated – in the areas previously thought to be most important – English, social studies, math, and science.

6. We have just completed a six-page document describing graduation requirements and philosophy. Students confused about what to take can seek help from the school. We hope this statement makes it clear that we believe students should take an interdependent balance of all the fields; no one area is more important than another. However, many schools will follow the rigid state requirements, and some colleges do have very tight entrance procedures. In deciding what to take while here, parents should work with their children on an individual basis and urge

involvement in all areas; but if there is concern regarding what other schools require, they should consider the traditional outline as a base.

EARLY CHILDHOOD: In 1968, the Wilson staff stated: "At long last, educators are finally beginning to focus national resources on the problems and opportunities associated with learning experiences at young ages. Many books have been written; psychologists, including Piaget, have contributed immensely; and Operation Head Start has given hope. There is now exciting research in this area; diagnostic tests and prescriptive materials are available to educators." Studies completed, such as one by Kirschner and Associates from Albuquerque, which surveyed 58 communities from July 1968 to January 1970, reported multiple changes in local education and health institutions "consistent with the Head Start goal of assisting poor children and their families to develop their capabilities more fully." These efforts are bringing to the nation fresh insights in understanding children ages birth through eight. Educators are learning that the early childhood years are probably the most crucial in the development of an individual.

Studies of *Sesame Street* by the Educational Testing Service gave excellent support to the effort to upgrade the learning of disadvantaged children. Among the many evaluation results were the following findings: children who watched the program showed greater gains in learning than those who did not; this was true for disadvantaged inner-city, advantaged suburban, isolated rural, and children whose first language was not English. Children who watched the show most gained most; three year old children made greater gains than older children; those who watched the programs with their mothers and then discussed it gained more than those who did not. One of the conclusions stated that the television program is "one of the most remarkable educational experiments ever undertaken."

Yet during the 60s and 70s, there were some states without publicly supported kindergartens, and many districts without optional full-day programs for five year olds. Practically no communities have publicly supported learning for the three and four year olds. The five year olds are usually limited to two and one-half to three hours; then the six year olds are stuffed into a rigid graded classroom all day where they are divided into groups and where many receive the wrong prescription. In the next years, school districts throughout the United States should give great attention to the needs and interests of children ages three, four, and five. Philosophies should be dramatically overhauled. If money is short, the senior class funding should be reduced before the kindergarten. These trends are developing; in the meantime, what can be done immediately?

A few schools do have all day programs for the five year olds at public expense. They have done it by a reorganization of the structure; by eliminating self-contained rooms, they have freed space to be used more flexibly. They have been able to create industrial arts and home economics areas. The staff is better utilized. Physical education and industrial arts specialists, science areas, and all other important programs for elementary children can be developed by the same staff in the same building with the same budget, although additional money should be sought to continue to improve the opportunities.

By reallocating staff, more adults can work with young children; many should be men. "Daddy" is badly needed in the kindergarten. Motor subjects like physical education take priority, along with the affective. In the all day kindergarten, reading and math skills can be taught; many children are ready sometime during the year; but some are not ready for reading until the "3rd or 4th grade." By using parent volunteers, and by hiring paraprofessionals, the adult-youngster ratio can be reduced to 1-10, which is about maximum.

Programs for three and four year olds can be started by having older students help. This is especially true when schools can arrange, as some have, programs where junior and senior high students, both boys and girls, as part of their home economics, family living, psychology or sociology classes, meet many of their goals by working weekly with the young students. Babysitting, child care, and child growth and development experiences provide excellent year-round help. The more the secondary program features independent study and individualized approaches, the more feasible this becomes; obviously location near the junior or senior high helps, but this problem is solved with flexible busing arrangements. Wilson purchased 12-passenger vans to take students to projects as part of the school-in-the-community concept; the early childhood program can be one of the opportunities.

Through such arrangements, public schools are actually conducting part-day three and four year old programs and full days for five year olds at no extra cost for the district. By the use of parent and community volunteers, student help from class projects, paraprofessionals, and student teachers where available, and by reallocating some money and positions from the high school budget, exciting beginnings are possible. The imaginative districts with commitment are developing exciting programs for young children.

Considerable freedom is being allowed early childhood students; they are learning to be more self-directing. They go by themselves throughout the building, and into most programs. They select industrial arts and home economics; they learn to sew on machines, and use the simple power tools in shop. They decide when they want to go for a snack. There are programs in operation – not theoretical, but practical examples – where young children select teachers and have more freedom than high school students in many of the traditional districts; Wilson reflects this practice in an interrelated manner.

What schools are finding as they work with these youngsters is that individually they are so different that they, more than any others, need personalized programs; they develop in such different stages. Some are ready to read at age four while others are better off to wait until age seven or nine. Some are big and strong and have excellent motor development, while others are two years "behind" general expectations in physical and fine and gross motor development. Some handle freedom and responsibility beautifully; they can be "turned loose" most of the day and fairly well self-direct their activities, while others need considerable supervision, structure, and direction.

The mechanics of such a program are in flux in a number of districts. In some they move from room to room; in others they operate from a home base, but move during the day to various centers; others are kept in one general area but with many alternatives within the center. More districts are now turning to the possibility of six and seven year olds staying in the early childhood center as headquarters and roaming from there. Much has to do with the physical layout of the building as well as staff attitudes. Group structure is needed in the first months, but periods of freedom are built in to give the youngsters opportunities to learn to make choices.

Routines

There are no recommendations which fit every student and all districts. Obviously three and four year olds generally need more supervision and guidance than five and six year olds. Assuming that districts will attempt to start pre-kindergarten programs in the near future, and realizing that many of the present "kindergarten" and "first grade" experiences are appropriate, the following suggestions for beginning limited four, expanded five, and modified six and seven year old programs are offered.

1. There should be a headquarters or home for early childhood where the students can spend the day, be taught certain skills, play, return to when lost, hang their coats, or generally seek security or feel at ease. Some students will only report there to check in at the start of school, check out at the end, and perhaps return for some activities; many may spend the majority of a day in the shop, science, home economics, physical education, and math areas, rather than the early childhood center. Depending upon staff, many of the activities can be available in the center, but most early childhood areas do not have space or adults for extensive industrial arts, music, art, home economics, and physical education involvement.

2. The former first and second graders can become part of the early childhood program, or they can be left outside it. Again, the cliche; it depends. Some are ready to self-direct almost immediately. For others, it may be better to keep them in an early childhood "pool" temporarily, and then move them into self-direction programs as individuals; thus, some would leave at age five, some at age six, and others at age four or seven or even eight. This approach begins to provide for individual differences. Those who read early and are responsible can walk down to the shop by themselves with no difficulty; those who are shy, or irresponsible, who cannot read, who need security, can stay in the suite of rooms (the Beginning Life Center) as many hours or years as desirable; they can be taken to other areas of the building in groups. For schools not utilizing four year old, and full day five programs, the Beginning Life Center can involve K-3; in non-grading, if the school is not completely non-graded, there should be overlapping teams so the split would be K-3, 1-4, 2-5, 3-6, giving less or more mature youth a choice of multi-age levels.

3. Generally the four, five, and six year olds should be moved in small groups part of the time until near Christmas in the nine-month year. The four year olds need more group movement to home economics when they are first learning to function there. The fives need less of this, but during the kindergarten year they usually should be moved in small groups so that they experience activities in all the areas. This gives them a chance to discover where the (in traditionally identified "subjects") art, industrial arts, home economics, physical education, science, math, and other rooms, materials, and teachers are located. Many of these activities should be supplemented by, or substituted for, experiences in the special areas. Learning to accept freedom of choice, and the responsibility that goes with it, should be a major goal in the early years – as well as interrelationships.

4. Some six year olds may need modified group movement in the fall, depending upon the individual. Some know how to read, they know the teachers, and they know what they want to learn. The first day they are off and running like strong "third graders." Some are not yet completely comfortable and seem to fit better into the shelter of the Early Childhood Center. Most are in between; therefore, whether they operate from an advisor they have chosen as they do in some schools, or from a "homeroom"

base, or from the Beginning Life headquarters, they can be given (or select) daily schedules where during the week about half of their time is scheduled into equal amounts in all the traditional subject areas — some art, reading, math, science, home economics — and then the other half of the week, they can choose when and where they want to go and for how long. By Christmas, most are ready for a complete self-selection program.

It is amazing how well five and six year olds can accept responsibility and be self-directing. All they need are opportunities to develop and demonstrate their capabilities. Some are ready at age four and some are not at age eight, but the pattern is that most can handle greater amounts of freedom within the Beginning Life Center, and lesser amounts in wandering the building; most become quite self-directing during the early part of the old "first grade;" they do not need constant supervision and direction. Some nine year olds still need tight structure, whereas many six year olds are quite independent. Plan the program for the individual — not for kindergarten or first grade or third grade groups. For the district just beginning to give freedom to five, six, and sevens, keeping the sixes and often the sevens as part of the early childhood program, moving them out first as groups, and then giving them freedom as individuals seems to work well.

5. The Early Childhood Center should be about two-thirds carpeted so that many floor activities are possible. About one-third should be left with easily cleaned floors for extremely messy activities, and for programs where wood or tile or other is a more appropriate surface. Part of the Center should have bright multi-colored walls, and lots of interesting live plants and animals. Guinea pigs are just excellent pets; many should be available for those students who enjoy a furry friend. However, for those students with allergies (about 25 percent), they should primarily learn in areas free of carpeting (dust, formaldehyde, pesticides); free from plants (molds); animals (danders); and paints (hydrocarbons). Therefore, one room of the Center may need to be reasonably barren, with student projects and non-toxic displays brightening the room.

The suggestions are not earthshaking, nor in detail; the major message is merely to convey the need for two, three, and four year olds, and pre-birth publicly supported programs, and for voluntary full day five year old offerings. Most sixes can be treated with great amount of freedom and responsibility, and can function with amazing self-direction; many sevens and eights, though, benefit yet from attachment to the Beginning Life Center. These "open" early childhood programs are now available in a few school systems, but in the coming years they will be quite common. The real tragedy is where there are only traditionally planned group half-day kindergartens, and self-contained first and second grades, with no alternatives or options for students or parents other than private schools. Each district is obligated to look anew at their efforts for these early age youngsters.

RESEARCH: Practically all of the conventional programs exist without adequate research support; districts are doing very little to change the picture. Education must develop a research and evaluation stance that is beyond the Iowa Basic Skills Tests. Innovation truly is needed in evaluation; staff and money must be channeled in that direction. Reliance must be placed on subjective analysis; more concern must be given to the affective and psychomotor domains.

Why do schools compile a class rank? It is another form of discrimination. Most schools do not separate the Protestants from the Jews; they try not to separate based upon place of residence; they do not separate the minorities. If people believe in nondiscriminatory practices, then how can they justify separating the "smarties from the dummies" – and that is all class rank and grades accomplish. Court cases will eventually resolve this failure of educators – unless there is a change of direction. Is there any research to validate grades in a humane school! The answer is no; the response is the same in examining almost any of the practices of the public schools.

Educators can immediately do three things to increase their evaluation potential. Depending upon the size of the district, one or more persons with research ability, along with clerical aides, should be hired. It can be done within the current budget, but it again does mean a reallocation of allotments. This job, or these positions, are responsible for "inhouse" studies. Surveys, testing, report writing, and resource contracts can be part of the job descriptions. It is amazing what one, or several individuals with clerical aides can do. This inhouse data provides immediate feedback related to many concerns – and it does not mean reliance on standardized tests.

A second step is for the district to set aside a small amount of money the first year, gradually increasing the total, until a first class evaluation effort is built in as part of the essentials. A third effort can be made by contacting nearby universities, offering master and doctoral candidates the students and problems to be researched. College classes can gather data; professors can analyze small parts of the program to gather information for a book for their classes; contracts can be signed with colleges to provide "outhouse" evaluation. Some systems are putting large sums into accountability and assessment packages. This is fine that they want evaluation of their programs, but almost all stress tests which study group comparisons in reading and math skills; much is being overlooked. What about evaluating whether the students like school, are learning more about learning, or accept more responsibility than the year before. What effect do the current programs, policies, and staffs have on these factors?

Only a limited number of universities have taken the lead in providing research and evaluation centers in education, especially in the affective and psychomotor domains. But even more, what have the public districts done to evaluate at the day-by-day grass roots levels in the schools? A handful of big districts have research offices, usually pitifully understaffed; they are charged with cognitive results and demographics. Several districts have placed evaluation directors in specific schools. But in most systems, very limited money and staff have been provided for research/evaluation/development. The "D" part is almost the key – developing new approaches through the "R" and "E" phases. The allocation of both staff positions and budget monies clearly indicates this deficiency in education.

Schools can start research, development, and evaluation programs if the commitment is there. They may be small efforts in the first years, but if educators believe that the functions are important, they must be programmed into the budget by re-allocating resources.

EDUCATIONAL REVIEW COMMITTEES: At Wilson, the Educational Review Committees developed from a concern for increasing the amount of feedback the older youth received related to their program selections. Goal sheets, regular advisor-advisee-parent conferences, and written reports from teachers continued to serve as the basis for evaluation. The Educational Review Committee was composed of teachers and administrators whose task was to review and analyze the performance of each individual and make specific recommendations in a conference with the student. In an open, individualized school, it is imperative that students receive continuous evaluation through an ongoing recycling process. The group consisted of two faculty members chosen by the student, one faculty member chosen by the faculty, and one administrator or other representative appointed by the director.

Each member reviewed the permanent folder independently and responded in writing to nine criteria, such as involvement and balance. The folder included records from previous schools, copies of all goal sheets, and the personal written evaluations by the advisor. The members could gather firsthand information from the students, parents, teachers, and advisor. Once the information was completed, the Committee met with the individual and the advisor to share impressions, highlights, or concerns and offer recommendations. For those few about whom they had serious reservations, the director was responsible for meeting regularly with the student and advisor during the following year.

The work of the Committee was very time-consuming, but one which was worthwhile. Benefits included a critique for students, an additional and often much-needed pat on the back for some, an increase in staff and administrative knowledge of what the students were accomplishing, and a reinforcement for the advisor working with the individual. There was no intention or inclination to prescribe requirements, but rather to assist each in an ongoing process of self-reflection and analysis related to present and future aspirations.

NEW STUDENT ORIENTATION: In any school environment, new students usually benefit from assistance in adjusting to unfamiliar programs, procedures, staff, and classmates. At Wilson, the student was required to act independently and responsibly to a degree not found in most schools. To be successful, the new enrollee had to assume this role quickly. As adults who wanted youth to be self-directing and responsible, the staff therefore needed to participate in assisting the growth of these characteristics in new students. They organized a systematic procedure for orientation.

As a first step, the family was asked to complete a regular application form and, in most cases, have a personal conference with a member of the administration. Once accepted, students, particularly the young and those who had been in nine-month rather than 12-month schools, were encouraged to participate in one of the workshops which were 12 days in length; the students worked in a group with a team of staff members. This provided a transition stage from a traditional school to an open philosophy with a futures orientation. The staff found that the degree to which the parents understood the program could be a determining factor in student success, or lack of, at Wilson. To address this concern, parents were encouraged to attend one or more of the group orientation sessions, at which time the program was discussed in detail. They were encouraged to participate in various aspects of Wilson throughout the year. The student was assisted in the following ways: 1) each participated in a large group meeting with an advisor and the administration; 2) met in a small group with either an advisor, counselor, or one of the administrators; 3) had an individual planning conference with either an advisor or one of the administrators; 4) took part in special group interaction and orientation sessions held by the counselor and advisors; 5) selected a personal advisor in the opening weeks; 6) met with the advisor and his or her parents early in the year; and 7) spent time with "veteran" Wilson students.

This latter assistance by peer students was a vital part of the adjustment. Each new person chose or was assigned a peer helper who was responsible for giving day-by-day help in learning about programs and procedures, and meeting staff and other students. These peer students, who received Social Service "credit," were called Walkie Talkies (younger students) and Peer Counselors or Student Advisors (older students). The school counselor worked closely with both groups in developing skills and understandings related to providing a welcome to new families.

The New Student Review occurred after their first three months at Wilson. This Committee consisted of teachers and administrators who met with the student and advisor to evaluate progress, and to offer direction in planning a balanced program of studies. This approach represented the integration of many past efforts to assist students. It was based on three aspects: 1) a sincere desire that students be successful and happy in their Wilson activities; 2) the need to house students in the most effective educational climate possible; and 3) a response to students, parents, student teachers, and teachers who felt that all youth should be given a chance in the Wilson philosophy if the environment was appropriate for them.

BUDGET: 1973-74

Classified salaries (support personnel)	9,513
Unclassified salaries (staff)	390,442
Student help	1,040
Rent of data processing equipment	2,835
Other purchased services	465
Subscriptions and memberships	147
Laundry	500
Repairs	697
Telephone	1,874
Postal service	725
State car mileage	1,000
Duplicating	750
Xerox	50
Supply room	2,500
In-state travel	500
Out-of-state travel	1,050
Educational materials	13,727
Educational equipment (including furniture)	3,325
SUBTOTAL	431,140
Food (hot lunch program)	6,079
TOTAL	437,219

Routines

Based on the data available June 28, 1974, the per pupil cost for Wilson students was determined as follows:

Salaries and supplies	$431,140.00
Maintenance costs	$37,764.87
	$486,904.87
Total number of students	629
Cost per pupil ($468,904.87/629) =	$745.47

This summary of the items of the budget at Wilson does try to illustrate that it was just a typical school with no special funding. The $745.47 was less than other schools in the local district; their average cost per pupil for the same expenditures listed was approximately $796. The Wilson figure was lower than the state average, and much lower than expenditures per pupil in some of the rich suburbs of Minneapolis which were expending over $900, or $200 more than Wilson.

SUMMARY: Reviewing "Routines" illustrates that even the most innovative schools have to struggle to overcome the "nuts and bolts" that sometimes interfere with the creative futuristic efforts to improve curriculum and help people. It indicates that in reality situations, major, significant changes can occur in American education. The school map diagrams that Wilson was just another traditional building. The program flourished, not because of special facilities, but rather from a spirit, an attitude. People at Wilson wanted to change, if that change would assist the transformation of persons and society. They wanted to help create a preferable future for humankind.

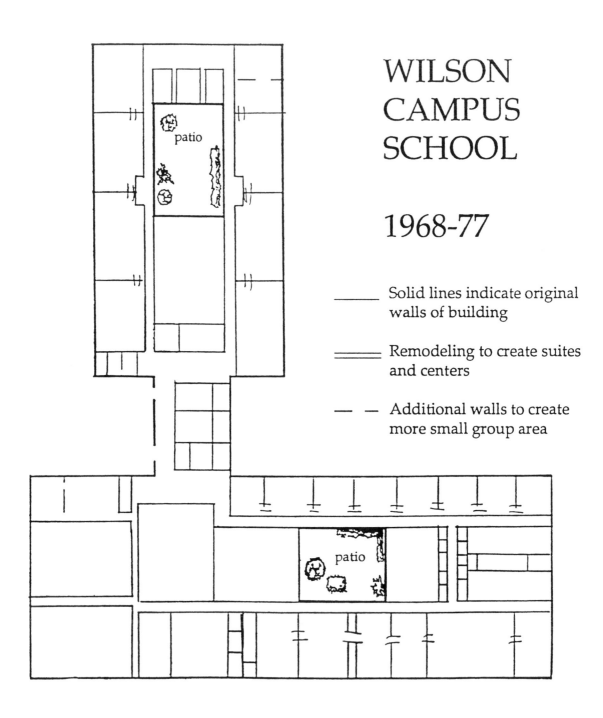

WILSON
CAMPUS
SCHOOL

1968-77

_____ Solid lines indicate original
walls of building

======= Remodeling to create suites
and centers

— — Additional walls to create
more small group area

Ongoing Renewal

chapter twenty-two

REVISITING

Most of the Wilson formats that have been described were the ones originally established. But programs and staffs need continuous self-renewal. The changes that evolved the second and third years illustrate the need for ongoing growth. Rather than viewing it as later Wilson developments, the revisions should cause reflection upon the present patterns in the schools close to the frame of reference of each individual. Assuming that the effort being made in each is good – a sincere desire to do the right thing – and that overall program quality may be very good, it is, nevertheless, often time for exhaustive reexamination. The more Wilson worked at the change process, the more the staff realized that the outstanding organization is the one which continuously considers renewal.

The faculty found that the first year of major revisions was a period of chaos, but everyone expected it, so the effort survived. The second year was one of frustration – people thought the program should be working well – but the major focus instead became correcting the mistakes of the first year. The third was the stability time – the change process slowed – people needed to rest, to catch their breath, to see that the concepts were working; the programs had improved and people were feeling good about their accomplishments. The fourth year was one of quality – there were almost no parent complaints, no discipline problems, little student unrest.

In the midst of the fourth, the staff realized it was time to reexamine the program; even the most innovative designs need self-renewal. They discovered curriculum techniques, processes, and ways of working with people that would have been helpful to know the first year; they realized that they could not live on their glorious past. The fifth year was a period of considerable retooling. Wilson was great for the 70s – a leader, and innovator. But if it had stopped where it was then, it would have become just another school – no longer a viable institution, an innovation leader focusing on improving programs or seeking new ways to further help people. Wilson had to be continuously concerned about its evolving future.

One of the outstanding international education critics, a true advocate of deschooling society, visited Wilson during this renewal effort. He commented: "If students have to be in school, this is as good, if not the best, place that I have seen." The farsighted futures leaders of today are saying that the restructuring of schools is not enough – that the real issue is the transformation of the entire society. They see the eventual elimination of schools as they are now constituted, in favor of new lifelong living/learning systems. They believe those working in present institutions should do two things: first, cause immediate revision of many of the current traditional efforts, regardless of how good they seem to be, or have been in the past, for since their original implementation, better ideas have developed; and second, prepare students and teachers for the essential renewal of society which must come in the near future, and which is already slowly underway.

A summary of some of the self-renewal steps the faculty faced illustrates that they knew they must change Wilson. Many of the original concepts were no longer innovative – a new invention had improved a given technique. Areas needed a fresh look – a different approach in exploring possible better ways. But more than anything, the focus on individuals and society, as great as it had been over the first four years at the school, needed new direction. Described are some of the possibilities the staff discussed in the early efforts to rethink – a starting point, not just toward a better Wilson, but rather toward the renewal of humankind – a broader global perspective. They are presented as the result of brainstorming and imagineering sessions, in no order or priority; instead, they provide a listing of possible suggestions in four general categories: (1) concepts to be achieved; (2) organizational changes to accomplish the goals; (3) methods of planning for these revisions; and (4) mechanisms for change. These reflections were 1970s thinking, not those of the late 90s. The process, if not the programs, is still relevant in designing learning for the next century.

CONCEPT GOALS

1. Students and staff – persons – must focus more than ever upon problems, improvements, and solutions for individuals and for society.

2. Programs more than ever must focus on person-to-person relationships and topics of interest and need – and true concern over global survival.

3. The curriculum interrelationships must be expanded, with teams organized in regard to people, societal, and human concerns, not subject oriented disciplines; learning must become interdependent.

4. Even more, the emphasis on cognitive development and subjects must be eliminated as the focus of the general growth period; they are only relevant related to specialization.

5. People, as warm, open humans concerned with such as racism and pollution, must become involved in studying broad human and ecological fields; later they focus on narrow topics as current science and social studies – chemistry and history.

6. There must be more complete commitment, dedication, and willingness to try new designs from the less dedicated faculty; they must leave neutrality – or transfer.

7. New approaches to student involvement must be person-centered: advisory groupings, topics of interest, analysis seminars.

8. Personalized, interrelated topics must overlap beyond present methods of individualization.

9. Person-centered leadership is needed constantly in the building; part-time organization involvement is effective only if a daily personal approach is available for students.

10. The program must expand further into the community, and the community into the school.

11. The triangle of spirit, mind, and body must evolve toward confluency in seeking the full human potential of everyone involved with Wilson.

ORGANIZATIONAL CHANGES

1. The commitment must move from a voluntary 12-month to a mandatory-with-options year-round education, continuous learning philosophy.

2. Learning cannot "close" in September for two weeks, as it destroys continuity; teacher contracts must be issued throughout the fiscal year as needed.

3. The enrollment must be raised, the college program incorporated, and busing provided for the fringe enrollment areas in town.

4. The large media center library must be eliminated in favor of a relevant mobile system.

5. The unseen schedule is working, but the philosophy of it must be followed by all staff.

6. Three interrelated houses, with one of the houses containing three interrelated studios, must improve the focus: Wilson needs an expanded Happy House, a Future House, and a Contemporary House, with studios centered on persons, survival, communication, and leisure.

7. Camouflaged math and English, as separated physical skill centers, must be eliminated; they must be more interdependent, and interrelated with persons, activities, interests.

8. The available program options must be expanded, as well as the option system of learning styles.

PLANNING FOR REVISIONS

In attempting quantum overleap, and exciting self-renewal, a proposal was made to further incorporate Wilson completely with the developing innovative teacher programs as was originally planned. The effort would feature person education rather than teacher education; it would maintain close ties with the Minnesota Experimental City concepts, liaison with the flexible professors in the College of Arts and Sciences, and with community consultants. The college age portion of the pre-kindergarten through graduate program would include four studios: Future, Person, Transition, and Logistic. The Future Studio would be centered on the work of the Compassionate Era thinkers; the Person Studio would focus on human relations and interpersonal communication; the Transition Studio would feature interdisciplinary studies, learned in a fashion compatible with the open school philosophy, so that future "teachers" would know how to adapt traditional content to the new approaches; the Logistic Studio would be an opportunity to learn how to adapt to the different organizations, facilities, scheduling, and methods of instruction.

The pre-college (Wilson School) program would develop a Happy House where mostly two and three year olds would headquarter in a large, open, flexible, infant school center, still using the entire building, but utilizing Happy House as a base of operation until approximately two-thirds of the learning programs for the child were in the Future or Contemporary House. He or she could be weaned as early as desirable – at age three, four, five, six, seven, or later – depending upon maturity and similar factors.

Revisiting

The Future House would occupy one wing of the school with volunteer teachers and students; traditional content would be put in the background, as the focus would be on the new era, with this as a transition stage to the community-based living/learning system of the Minnesota Experimental City. The Contemporary House would be in another wing and would continue to change from 1970, to 1980, to 1990 to 21st Century models more slowly than those in the Future House, which would attempt quantum overleap – major changes each year. The Contemporary House teams: Persons and Survival (old science, social studies, home economics, health, and industrial arts); Persons and Communication (old English, math, Spanish, media, and business); and Persons and Leisure (old art, music, drama, literature, and physical education), would remain innovative arms, but with a different perspective than those in the Future House.

All of the staff would be provided release time to rejuvenate in the Renewal Center – perhaps ten to fifteen percent per quarter, or retooling once every three years – all on the present budget. Research, technology, and community coordinators would assist both the college and pre-college programs. The staff would "teach" kindergarten through graduate "experiences." Teacher self-renewal would be a must, if such changes were to significantly materialize.

College Arts and Sciences must assist in the creation of an innovative teacher education program, as that group controls three of the four years of undergraduate work. Therefore, a further plan would merge cooperative staffing and direction with "on loan" persons from the traditional schools in the college.

Though not all these designs evolved, each idea was given serious consideration; many were implemented. The concepts are an illustration of why ongoing renewal of both public school and teacher education programs is needed. A pre-kindergarten through graduate design, with a Center for the Study of the Future, and a Center for the Person, cooperatively established between Education and Arts and Sciences, would be a tremendous breakthrough in the reform of schools and universities.

MECHANISMS FOR CHANGE
1. The school should make extensive use of marathons (days to focus on nothing but change).

2. The school should develop student and teacher improvement centers. Not all teachers should teach every day, every week. As in a war, the good general always has some troops in reserve. They are not all on the first line battlefield, as school staffs are usually mandated. The United States would never win a war if the armed forces were organized like educational institutions.

3. Seekouts should be organized by students to locate new student learning directions; guest consultants, and outside resource stimulus should be sought.

4. The entire learning community should focus on the future – a study of societal directions and what people must do to achieve a preferable next century – and act for the present.

5. Renewal should involve as keys, teacher and student reexamination of themselves and programs, time to refresh the spirit, and Centers for the Future and the Person.

Revisiting

During the fourth and fifth years, increasing numbers of requests came for information regarding the revisions made at Wilson related to scheduling, counseling, studios, and the option system; for a more thorough summary of the problems Wilson faced over the first several years; and for the continuing evaluation results. The summary of these early efforts at renewal, which were the results of grappling with ideals, were ideas which evolved from serious reexamination.

The elimination of the daily schedule worked. Wilson went beyond the originally planned revisions. When a school truly individualizes and personalizes its program, the master schedule, as educators have known it in the past, is no longer needed. The five phases fade: (1) the one-to-one conferences held between staff and student do not need a group, all-school schedule; they are made by individual appointments; (2) the formal small groups meet at times they schedule themselves; next, they say: "Do we need to meet again? If so, when? For how long — thirty minutes or three hours?" Finally, they decide to meet next Thursday at 11:00 a.m. No all-school schedule is needed; (3) there is a minimum of large groups in a personalized school; when there are common thread sessions, speakers are announced by word of mouth, by posters, and through the announcement board, but again no schedule is needed, other than the reservation of the auditorium or other large group facility, if required. The informal small groups are arranged by the students among themselves; (4) the open, active, individualized lab opportunities (arts, sciences, physical action, movement) are always available and do not need scheduling; and (5) the passive, independent activities are self-directed.

Wilson operated an unseen schedule; students individually planned themselves. They knew if there was something they wanted to do that day, or whether they had individual or small group appointments. The concept was extremely successful; the only initial difficulty was among those staff and students who sought to revert to tradition by arranging to meet groups through the unseen schedule every Monday-Wednesday-Friday at 11:00 a.m. for the next six months. Mechanically, it can work, unless every teacher tries to do it. Philosophically, though, it is not valid, and does interfere with flexibility. Fortunately, the majority of students and teachers (and eventually all of them) played the game straight, so that personalized scheduling on a daily basis did occur without the interference, staff time, and expense of a daily all-school central office schedule.

The counseling situation worked without an all-school counselor. The teachers-as-advisors system was beautiful. Wilson did find the need for a warm, human, real counselor who could help as a resource to the teachers — counseling them and individuals whom the advisor could not seem to help and seeking community resources — truly counseling and not clerking. Such a person was therefore hired, after the traditional ones had been released or transferred. The school operated three years without a "counselor," proving the conventional roles were not needed.

The 1, 2, 3, 4 option system which evolved on a trial basis the third year worked very well as a counseling tool. Students signed to work with the adults they chose, indicating what degree of structure they preferred with that adult — one being a very free school oriented option, two an open school approach, three a modified flexible approach, and four, considerable structure. As there was no registration for courses or subjects, the students selected the amount of guidance that fit their style related to working with adults in whatever learning endeavor being assisted. Communities can use the option system to design schools-within-a-school, but Wilson stayed with the option program as a counseling and guidance arrangement.

After moving to the studio plan for curricular teams, the program was definitely more person-centered, problem of society oriented, interrelated. The teachers in the Studios for Emerging Environments (old social studies, science, health, home economics, and physical education – one of the names and combinations used for a period of time to create interrelationships) moved toward becoming environmental staff (not science teachers or health teachers), concerned with solutions for people and society. Therefore, identifications such as home economics were eliminated; two men and two women who previously staffed this nongraded K-12 center joined with other studio members for an even broader perspective on human considerations. Sewing and cooking were taught, especially to the primary children to assist with psychomotor development, but the priority focus was on people and the environment.

Even the short-term enrollment Prescription Center, developed by the Studios for Evolving Persons, interrelated skill tools so that students could drop in for brief periods of concentration to overcome a deficiency they discovered in some other phase of the school program. Such efforts were only steps; as part of the self-renewal project, Wilson still needed a huge overleap.

The original systematic evaluation at Wilson was sporadic, but followed three definite approaches: individual students, total school evaluation, and national accountability. Through these efforts the staff was satisfied that meaningful learning and worthwhile student experiences were being obtained through the program. There was no doubt that discipline problems, as commonly described in most schools, were almost entirely eliminated. Problems did occasionally occur, but they were minimal after the first years. An acceptance of responsibility in an open school, close personal staff-student relationships, and the nongraded mix of age levels were apparently the major ingredients for eliminating most of the usual disciplinary situations.

Wilson participated in studies to compare students in the open program with those in more conventional settings. Wilson did not believe in group comparison use of such tests as the IQ, the Iowa Basic Skills, or the various other achievement batteries. However, the school cooperated in research studies in an effort to reach some conclusions based upon more conventional ratings. In the area of the cognitive domain, Wilson held its own. Test scores were above the average of schools using more conventional approaches to learning. Those tests did not measure many of the cognitive knowledges felt important. In the affective domain, Wilson students scored significantly better in surveys of self-image and attitude toward school. Their norm indicated that generally they liked themselves and liked their school better than the norms achieved by students in more conventional programs. In the psychomotor areas, the test results and comparative studies were not as conclusive, although analysis was very positive toward the Wilson approach, especially for young children.

As far as national accountability efforts, Wilson was more concerned first with self-direction, responsibility, decision-making, self-image, success – the affective domain. Second, the program was aimed at the important motor skills. The staff challenged the "experts" to help develop measurements for these areas. If they ever had accepted the challenge, Wilson would have been happy to be very "accountable," even in the cognitive, but such cognitive evaluation had to include knowledge in all areas, not just language arts, math, science, and social studies. Content in industrial arts – recognizing different wood – was just as important as math for many students.

It had been said that innovators were not evaluators, but this was no longer true. Wilson was one of the few schools with a research coordinator. Dozens of studies at the master thesis and educational specialist levels were conducted as integral parts of the philosophy. More effort was going into the evaluation of Wilson than most public schools. Conclusive "proof" was not available after five years, but from what evidence there was, and from subjective staff evaluation, after five years there was no indication that the school was headed in the wrong direction; most guidelines pointed to continued innovations within the same general philosophic stance, which then became the reality for another four years. There was no doubt that the students liked Wilson; attendance was far superior in comparison with traditional schools. Wilson students were successful.

PROBLEM AREAS

Most of the comments regarding Wilson were extremely favorable, confirming the conclusion that overall the program was a success. There was no doubt that the positive by far overcame the negative. However, no attempt was ever intended to hide the fact that there were problems. The greatest difficulty, and one which remained, was that of quality staff. Wherever there are excellent teachers, there are excellent programs. The great adult at Wilson was the one who was that warm, empathetic person, who used the indirect approach, and who had a good interrelated cognitive background. But the real key was that wonderful, lovable, hug-argue-kiss-makeup relationship with youth; youngsters flocked to those areas with such persons. The experience with students selecting their own "teachers," "advisors," and "courses" was convincing that tenure laws must be changed to provide easier dismissal of those who do not fit – or at least ease the transfer policies to schools and programs which match their styles. The need was for "Pied Piper" teachers.

Wilson had to take the existing staff, building, student body, and budget, with no inservice training, and no consultants, and in two months during the summer of 1968, create a complete about face. In the succeeding three years, the outstanding teachers became great; the middle improved; even the weaker teachers improved, but settled further toward the bottom in comparison with the greats. Unfortunately, some personality conflicts existed between staff members. Teacher A could work with Teachers B and C, so it would seem A, B, and C would make a beautiful team, but B and C tangled. Progress was slow in this area, even after "human relations" sessions, but measurable improvement was described.

Another problem came from a small portion of the community – namely from a minority group of the college faculty, and the former local neighborhood "leaders" who had lost control of "their" school, both groups of whom generally opposed the director on basic personality and philosophy differences. Closing the first year, a petition was circulated to have the director removed and the school returned to "sanity." This was met head-on by a group of "for" parents and students who developed a counter petition greater than the "against." Then an open meeting was held for four hours one evening in a combination of large and small groups to air concerns. It was made clear by the administration that there would be at least one educational alternative in Mankato, and that those not liking the Wilson design could transfer to a more structured school in the city. The director remained and the program flourished.

Finance and maintenance areas, as in most places, were problems. The school operated just below the 50th percentile of the cost of education in Minnesota. During the second year of the first five years of the program, a special "catch up" fund was provided to buy badly needed library books, tapes, carrels, carpet, and multiple classroom materials, in all former "subjects." The other years, the school operated on the conventional budget. The fourth year, a 25 percent cut occurred because of a drop in college enrollments. Wilson had less money for its fourth year for daily operation than in its last year as a traditional program, 1967-68.

All funds were state tax dollars. There were no federal grants or other special reimbursements. The key was not more money, but reallocating resources. Schools must take their current budgets and use them differently. That is how Wilson provided more financial flexibility on the same budget allocations as those for a conventional facility. Staff was increased at no additional total cost through differentiated staffing, combined with student teachers and non-paid volunteers.

Care of equipment is always a problem; students were exceptionally good in using materials that were left on open shelves for them. However, over the five years the school lost several cassettes, "wasted" some art supplies, and had some damage to equipment by the usual "few," so that as a result, Wilson moved from a very liberal help yourself policy on supplies to a middle-of-the-road approach. In teaming, too, it became necessary to assign teams to care for certain areas of the building; some rooms, such as the auditorium, became "nobody's room," and thus lack of care occurred. Later, each of the studios had responsibility for a portion of the building.

A last unusual beginning problem was the lack of student and parent involvement groups. They seemed to be so content with the personalized approach to learning, and their ability to have immediate person contact with those with whom, or when, or where there appeared to be a problem, that student and parent advisory groups, councils, and other similar efforts never flourished. It was difficult to know how a "group" felt, as there were no representative groups; through individuals became the method of determining group judgment. Wilson was not able to convince students to seriously protest and go on strike until they decided to fight the closing of their school. The fifth year "working plan" was through ad hoc student-faculty-parent committees on topics of interest and need, but formal, continuous involvement groups had not succeeded during the initial years. Later a Parent Resource Group was established; it successfully provided instructional support to the staff, and reinforcement for families.

As an overall evaluation, there appeared to be little doubt regarding the future value of flexible, open, personalized programs for the school districts of America. The Wilson pilot was just one small but extremely meaningful experience to help indicate the future direction of education. If the United States is built upon such concepts as freedom, responsibility, democracy, tolerance, justice, and humaneness, then a key value in the society is one of the major concepts that school districts have failed to accept — the meaning of alternatives — of choices of learning styles.

Revisiting

Current schools cannot solve all of the societal dilemmas. Those students involved in gangs, drugs, and weapons need to be in a structured Person Center; they need rehabilitation. However, the Wilson philosophy of assisting others and gradually increasing responsibility can be a cornerstone for new approaches; the old structure of schooling does not work for these youth; though they may need a "lockup" model temporarily, there are many other students in the same neighborhoods who can slowly — or rapidly — depending upon their values and priorities — benefit from being in a localized version of Mankato Wilson. The underlying premises were based on people — not outmoded notions of required curriculum, uniformity, scope and sequence, regimentation assignments, and the inertia of institutions.

chapter twenty-three

DESIGNS

To arrive at a point where all staff were ready for the later efforts at major renewal, ongoing reform was necessary during the early years. The designs pursued were not forward looking, futuristic, or creative 21st Century versions, but are included as a history of the change process at Wilson, and to assist with the understanding of the transitions that are part of the procedures of trying to futurize, or at least make more innovative, a school long wedded to tradition. The proposals are essentially those that were first offered to the Wilson faculty for their consideration. Most of the items were adopted and became part of the renewal effort; others were slowly adopted or modified, while a few were not implemented, or were rejected; after further discussion, some of the ideas were ultimately discarded.

It is crucial to continually make every effort to rethink, and to increasingly provide additional alternatives. During the first three years of grinding innovation, the existing structure was modified continuously. Such constant movement was essential if Wilson was not to be another victim of the innovative school dropout syndrome; a recycling process is mandatory. On paper, the new directions and mechanics may not seem like great changes, but in practice, they may be the beginning of a tremendous impact. Person-to-person emphasis, real interrelationships of curricular approaches, and roving staff members began to transform Wilson into a better school. Month-by-month revisions of varieties of structures do and must occur in any viable educational endeavor. There were areas where the Wilson faculty soon saw a need to improve before further long periods of time were allowed to elapse.

TEAM RESTRUCTURING
During the renewal period, evaluation by the Wilson staff indicated agreement that they must focus more on persons, and students as persons, not on "kids to be taught." They had been doing well in this area; they just felt they needed to do even more. It was agreed that there should be further organizational restructuring to enable them to more easily plan and communicate their efforts to help individuals learn. After much deliberation as to whether to stay in four teams, or reorganize into two, or even merge into one (the ultimate goal), three became the magic number.

Those selected in this agreement were the Studios for Emerging Environments, the Studios for Evolving Persons, and the Studios for Future Media. The underlying theme was that the teams must be concerned with people as individuals – as groups – as humans – as persons; they must be concerned with the physical and human environments in which people live; and they must be concerned with the changing means of communication and technology.

Discussion reemphasized that learning and instructional styles must include more than the one-to-one conferences, small group discussions, large group presentations and open labs of the past. Variations of these styles of involvement continued to be the heart of the people-to-people contact, but there was little doubt that as society approached the next century, other communication systems would supplement or replace many of the current methods. There would be no de-emphasis on close personal relationships; these should improve in quality and quantity; the opportunities should be enhanced by the revolutions coming in the technological world. The studios concept, within the three broad teams, became just another stepping stone toward improving communications between, and interrelationships of, the variously labelled previous disciplines.

The Studios for Emerging Environments included the old subject areas of science, social studies, home economics, health, and physical education. There was debate as to whether it would be better to break these into sub-teams such as the Survival Studio, Activity Studio, Community Studio, and other, corresponding somewhat to simple mergers of two or three of the old disciplines, but it was decided this would defeat the purpose of attempting true interrelationships. It was realized that people in these common areas would work together in their "disciplines;" this was encouraged as far as person and program development related to science only, but the plan was that the real effort would be toward interrelating each of the disciplines within the combined team, as well as with subject areas or studios from the other two teams.

The second grouping, Studios for Evolving Persons, drew the old subjects of English, early childhood, special education, music, and theater arts. As before, there was debate whether to put music and theater arts together in the Creativity Studio, and the others into separations as the Expressive Studio, but again the decision was that this would tend to divorce rather than marry disciplines. It was realized that English people would join to discuss English; there was no objection to this; encouraged also was the Creative Studio approach – music and theater arts – to operate as one subgroup in their planning and sharing of facilities and ideas. But there was a desire not to separate them from the English, early childhood, and special education areas; therefore this became one team instead of three separate studios. In the subgroupings which occurred during this transition stage, and because of facilities, the Creativity Studio concept (music and theater together) was followed rather than music as music, and theater arts as theater arts.

In the Studios for Evolutionary Design were the old areas of math, business, industrial arts, art, Spanish, and the Media Center. Math and business needed to expand beyond the old System Team; they could interrelate quite well with industrial arts through math concepts, distributive education, and technological developments. Art, industrial arts, and math had no difficulty in interrelating geometric patterns. Spanish and the Media Center worked side by side, not only because they were physically part of the same complex, but because of the conviction that most of the foreign language program could be taught through media rather than the group of 30, or the one-to-one conference; records, tapes, film strips, books and other materials were utilized on an individual basis. This did not eliminate the one-to-one and small group approach in Spanish, but it did mean that the media and Spanish fields would explore all possible avenues of increasing the technological output in the teaching of foreign language. Mathematics and Spanish started working together through the computer; art, Spanish, and media were naturals. Business, in terms of personal keyboarding and creative writing, matches better with English; but business as related to computer development, electronic dictating machines, personal computers, and computer science fits better with math and media. If there had been a larger business staff, perhaps their functions and teams may have been different. Typing and shorthand were forms of 1960s media; the Wilson staff knew these would be replaced in the coming years with computerized approaches, even at the home level, through dial access retrieval systems, talking typewriters, video phones, and instantaneous voice recording and printing machines – with translations into multiple languages. Wilson was among the first in Minnesota with computer terminal access, but it was still late 60s technology.

METHODS OF INTERRELATING

One lesson that had been learned in all the prior teaming was that to effectively interrelate curriculum, the old "academic" subjects had to be merged with the "non-academic." It overcame the notion that the non-academic were not important. Everything was equal at Wilson. If the "non-core" were separated, they remained less valued.

Wilson wanted the three newly created teams and groups of studios to interrelate as much as possible – to become interdependent learning. Social studies, as part of the Environmental Center, continued to work with English of the Person Center as a "splinter studio" effort; math of the Media Center teamed with science of the Environmental Center; art joined with theater arts; all other such combinations occurred. The design created three broad studio groupings which would fill the need for a structure that could take Wilson another step toward further focus on individuals and on interdependent programs for them. These expanded theme studios seemed to be the best action at the moment. Within these teams, rather than students signing for subject matter such as science, home economics, social studies, biology, cooking, or the Civil War, they merely selected the person or persons with whom they wished to learn in the Environmental, Person, or Design Centers.

The selection of a person to learn with, rather than the selection of content, was a tremendously significant step forward in the implementation of a Person Philosophy, rather than a Knowledge Philosophy. The staff at Wilson could teach anything they felt capable of teaching without regard to certification. An adult who may have majored in English, but who had a strong art skill, could teach art. The same person may have assisted with and learned with the student in music. She or he may have said, "I'm sorry, but – I'll help you find assistance" – if a youth asked that adult to be his or her "teacher" for the molecular theory. In all these endeavors, efforts to personalize and interrelate continued to be tantamount.

By the same token, the staff at Wilson taught all age levels. The good "teacher" can teach any age; separate elementary and secondary certification is counterproductive. Some staff prefer certain ages, and some do better with certain age groupings, but like the good parents who follow their children through many consecutive years, the outstanding adult members of the school eagerly welcome the opportunity to work with a cross section of ages and abilities in diversified learning experiences.

The Wilson registration records indicated that Billy Smith was working with staff members X, Y, and Z. Those persons, as adults, working with an individual formerly labeled student or youngster, on a person-to-person relationship, planned a meaningful program with the youth, or with the group of students involved. The experience was given a label whenever the adults and youngsters so desired for communication purposes, but as far as the office was concerned, there was no record of what an individual student was studying with staff members X and Y until after the experience was completed.

In the practical application of this system, the person formerly labeled "student" said to the person previously labeled "history teacher X": "Could we learn together?" "Sure," Mr. X said, "I would enjoy learning with you." Some of the learning which occurred might be in the former area of economics as a single discipline, in which Mr. X served as the primary or only resource person. Another of the interests of the student might have been in the area of the theater; Mr. X, in the role of the facilitator, helped the student seek a theater arts person to plan a coordinated program with the learner, perhaps in the area of theater history. The student may have discovered that Mr. X had talents in math, too; therefore, Mr. X may have "taught" he or she math that year. Suddenly, Mr. X was no longer a "teacher" of "social studies," but instead was a person who related with another human; they both discovered areas where they would like to learn and study together. Mr. X became a facilitator in social studies, theater arts, and math for that individual, or might have become part of a team of adults helping the participant. Other students may have joined in a similar pattern; Mr. X may have found himself studying with a small group in economics; he may also have tutored several individuals in math.

The system by which this was accomplished was similar to previous methods. The "student" and the "instructor" together prepared the goal sheets or plans for the coming weeks. As it became apparent that at this moment in time the student wanted to pursue only a small aspect of what had been known as one particular discipline, such as some phase of economics, the study may not have been interrelated, other than what the student learned in the subject, as it related to common fields; but later Mr. X may have said: "Now, how can we use this knowledge of economics?" Such a question led to learning concepts in different disciplines.

With this philosophy, if the individual selects Latin American History as a topic, it may become immediately apparent that he or she should interrelate the geography, art, foods, music, and languages of Latin America, along with the pursuit of its general history. Before Mr. X approves the final agreement with the student, he encourages and helps the learner plan interrelationships with other studios. Mr. X may decide he can only do the pure history part; he has the student go to Ms. Y in art, Mr. Z in music, Mrs. A in home economics, and Mrs. B in Spanish; these persons meet with the individual, or a group of individuals if more than one want to study together, and add suggestions related to their Latin American backgrounds. On one goal sheet, five teachers may contribute comments, or all five can develop separate sheets related to their special concerns or abilities, but each interwoven with the Latin American interest of the individual, or the group of individuals.

As these begin to accumulate with the advisor or advisor team, the adult further discusses with the student the total interrelationships; it is the responsibility of the advisor to make every effort to ensure that as much learning as possible is interdependent. If the advisor finds that the student has suddenly developed an interest in industrial arts, but this was not part of the previous agreement with the Latin American interrelationship, he or she should have the student visit with Mr. C to discuss how he could help introduce the technological developments of Latin America into the total study.

This is not as complicated as it may sound, as the comments to be written on the goal sheets are only those needed by the various persons involved. The advisor has continual conferences with the student; the learner does the leg work between staff in the effort to interweave the program. There may be a time when the five or six staff working with the person studying Latin America need to have a meeting with the individual to coordinate all the learning activities; or instead, a note in the mailbox may be mandatory, or "a glass of juice environment" conference might be essential. The interrelated program can exist as long as all are informed, know the intent of the experience, and understand the total relationship that the individual has determined with all the staff persons.

Interdependent curricular efforts become easier as teams begin to function effectively. The work of the individual within the various studios can be reviewed at the team meetings when "staff" discuss "students." The progress reports (goal sheets) must not be used as threats; they must not be exclusively cognitive, or final demands that must be met; they must stress affective and psychomotor growth as well. The outcomes can be very closed (Juanita is going to finish the following three novels in the next six weeks); or they can be very open (Pete plans to drop in and out from time to time to explore areas and pursue interests as they develop). Each sheet must be individually tailored — personalized for each child. Educators have often turned many students away from an area because they were not ready to be pinned to specific goals that must be accomplished in a set period of time. For some, all that is needed is to show a spark of interest in possibly doing something in the field; for others the best decision during a conference might be a very structured set of immediate objectives. Educators have too often forgotten the affective, in the zeal for cognitive growth. They, in general, have also ignored the research on brain compatible learning.

The advisors must insist that the goal sheets be done correctly for each individual. It is important to eliminate the vagueness that means nothing; it is vital not to be so specific that the student cannot escape, or, just as wrong, describe the proposal in teacher terms. The plans for the student must be personally oriented and written so that he or she, the parents, and the advisors can clearly understand the intent. Advisors reject and send back to the "teacher" any progress reports that do not communicate. The concept of giving the same goal to large numbers of students must cease, unless there is specific defense for doing this in a particular situation (understanding what causes AIDS might be a rationale). The Advisory Team must ensure that their advisees are receiving personalized attention.

To assist with the goals of personalizing and interrelating, the Wilson staff increased their efforts to expand such areas as theater arts, industrial arts (technology), health education, and the media center, through additional interns and staff; the traditional areas continued to be adequately staffed. To help balance loads and further interrelate, Mrs. A taught more than math; she helped with drafting, as industrial arts and math became part of the same team; teachers did not think of math as math, and industrial technology as technology, but instead concentrated on how best to help the person.

As staffs become teams, they plan for close relationships within the teams. Mrs. D, Mrs. E, Mr. F and Ms. H may have a prime responsibility for what formerly was called early childhood; their major role may be in that focus, as they work as a team to develop the affective, cognitive, and psychomotor areas for young children. They are joined by other adults who help them, particularly those from the Studios for Evolving Persons. Such an approach was no great change from the past, other than reemphasis; as the transition to new programs occurred, Wilson faculty knew that certain areas had to be staffed related to traditional programs that existed in the past, but that the emphasis must be on evolving persons, not on early childhood as a separate entity. It meant that the group that could be labeled the Creative Studio would be heavily involved with early childhood, as these younger children need music and theater arts as much or more than the older students. It meant those with physical education backgrounds must be involved with gross motor development, while the technology oriented must help the young with fine motor control. The entire focus must be on the growing individual, and programs designed for and with that individual, or for and with groups or persons needing or desiring similar learning activities.

The three theme teams representing the various studios were used as the vehicle for interrelating curriculum, future program development, discussions on the progress of individuals, and the success of the current team efforts. Illustrating how one student created interdependent learning with a number of adults on a person-to-person level led to many creative examples within the various teams. At Wilson, "Curriculum Was What The Student Was Learning At That Moment In Time." The individual was in the spotlight; the program branched from his or her interests and abilities, and input from staff, parents, and friends as the learning commitments evolved. The emphasis was not on developing programs first, then placing students in them. Some persons needed more structured offerings, while others needed more flexibility. Wilson was dedicated to planning individualized, personalized, learning opportunities with students at all age levels.

ADVISORY TEAMS

The emphasis through the three groups of studios on the person, and on interdependent programs, could not but help force the members of the Emerging Environments Studios to discuss the student as an individual. However, there was a need for even further focus on persons. This additional thrust was through the mechanism of the Advisory Teams. Approximately four regular Wilson staff members (balancing the veterans) were placed together on Advisory Teams with their advisees. They were usually assisted by two interns, and undergraduate candidates. Thus seven teams of four regular, plus two master intern teachers, or six or more adults, worked with approximately 80 to 100 students. Each had his or her own personal advisor, but when the selected person was not available, the student worked with one of the other three staff members or the interns. The latter became full-fledged advisors as soon as they felt comfortable with the assignment and had formed solid personal relationships with individuals. Students could, at their request and acceptance by the receiving adult, be transferred to another advisor or Advisory Team.

By having a group immediately on call if the regular advisor was not available, such as during a vacation, a scheduling conflict, or the desire for advice from more than one adult, the student had access to additional communication. The group made every effort to know all the advisees so they could help and support everyone. As staff talked about those on their advisory teams, the focus was on the student, the adult or adults best suited for the individual, and the need for and amount of guidance or structure that may be desirable for each person.

The Advisory Team also consisted of people from different disciplines and degrees of experience. They had diversified, yet compatible personalities as members, including a mixture of male and female, youth and experience. Interns were assigned to the teams as assistants. As soon as they learned advisory techniques and were familiar with the students, they were given their own advisees — students who selected them. Interns participated as full-time members of the Advisory Team, carrying a heavier load than that of an assistant. However, the Wilson student remained identified with a veteran advisor on the team so there was continuity from year to year, as the interns came and went on short term arrangements. There was need for guidance of the interns as they learned the Wilson system; this organization provided for this inservice function.

There was discussion of changing the name of advisor or advisory team to facilitator or counselor or motivator or guide. The staff found a need for some name which would be a "handle" in describing a person-to-person relationship, one that indicated that the adult was not necessarily giving advice to the student, but instead was sharing with him or her the experiences in learning and growing. There were many suggestions, but no unanimous agreement as to title; there was a need for a "label" for purposes of communication.

The Advisory Team arrangement provided for a focus first on students and then on programs for them. The Curricular Studios provided a mechanism for developing interdependent opportunities for individuals and groups. This combination provided a priority, while allowing for a structure which enabled both person and program enhancement to be pursued simultaneously.

TEAM MEETINGS AND LEADERSHIP

The faculty during this period of renewal voted to continue staff meetings on Wednesday afternoons (early dismissal), but reverted to the staff "required attendance" efforts of the past, unless there was a very specific reason for a member to be absent. "Teachers" made every effort not to schedule long field trips and appointments on Wednesday, realizing there would always be exceptions. The arrangements closed school at 1:00 p.m. on Wednesday, with food service available all day. There was disagreement among staff regarding closing; several faculty believed the school should not close at all, but the majority favored this planning time in the initial stages of personal and program development. Later in the Wilson history, the Wednesday closing was eliminated.

From 1:30 to 3:30 or 4:00 – or sometimes to 5:30 on a voluntary basis – on the first and third Wednesdays, the interrelated Curriculum Studios met to discuss programs, how students were functioning in them, and the relationships of the two. On the second and fourth Wednesdays, the Advisory Teams met to discuss the advisees in their group and consider how they might further help each student. With four Wilson faculty members, plus two interns, most teams knew every student quite well; each unit usually had representatives from the Curriculum Studios. When there was a need to discuss a student, and the Advisory Team had little input or knowledge of the person in a given area, other than through their role as an advisor, they sought contributions of other staff on the curriculum team where there appeared to be difficulty; various subgroupings could come together to work with youngsters, and/or on student programs and problems.

Each of the three curriculum teams appointed a staff leader. These three people were responsible for ensuring that the first and third Wednesday meetings of each month were well planned and conducted, that studio members were there, and that tasks were accomplished. They had the title of Learning Associate, and were delegated authority through the school program leader (principal) in regard to calling meetings, organizing the team, setting agendas, allocating budgets, reaching learning decisions, and implementing programs. These associates also served on the Planning Council with the program leader and the associate program leader; the five thus formed an adult leadership group to coordinate learning directions for the school. Students were often involved in the meetings of the various teams and the Planning Council, especially when they were affected by the decisions.

As for the Advisory Teams, the people on each selected one person to act as coordinator, plan agendas, and provide leadership for the two or three hour meeting; the coordinator was responsible for ensuring there was follow-through on the discussions related to advisees who were having difficulty, or who in some way needed further interaction by or with selected adults (specific staff members, parents, agency providers, volunteers, community resource persons, college faculty, medical personnel, or any number of beyond Wilson contacts).

Both groups – the Curriculum Studios and the Advisory Teams – met at any other time that was necessary or desirable related to their needs. If the Studios for Emerging Environments desired to meet more often than two or three hours every other week, the Learning Associate of that team had the authority to call a meeting for whatever time seemed best for the entire group. The coordinator for the Advisory Team did the same, calling additional sessions to discuss areas of concern, or creating ad hoc groups of adults to spend more time on a particular student.

As far as the informal subteams, such as the Creative Studio, or the Survival Studio, or under old names like science, the people in those similar subteams usually ranged in number from three to five; Wilson did not give them identified team designations, but persons in various interest disciplines could organize their own methods of meeting when necessary. If they felt the need for an organizer, they could arrange this, but the preference was that the people with special interests in the topics previously called social studies decide among themselves that they should discuss the student learning opportunities at a mutually agreeable hour without establishing a formal structure. The staff also requested the Learning Associates to ask various subgroups of adults from the studios to meet if it seemed necessary. Solidly merging theater arts and music in the second year was a new effort; if the Learning Associate for the broad studio realized those people were floundering – not really working together – then he or she arranged for them to meet to evolve improvements; often, other staff were needed to interrelate activities.

ADDITIONAL STUDIO RESPONSIBILITIES

There were further curriculum team responsibilities related to students, programs, and interdependencies. The staff and students were heavily involved with visitors. Rather than the administrators planning for visitors, each team, on a rotating basis, was responsible for guests for a given week. The Studios for Evolving Persons might have had the responsibility for the first week in October; those staff could delegate the assignment for a given day to people in the Creative Studio, who then met with the visitors to ensure that they were well attended to during the day; they participated in the question and answer session in the afternoon and selected students to act as guides and interacters. All the office did was to coordinate the dates of visitations and prepare the assignments, though the program leader met with all guest groups the first 30 minutes for orientation, usually in person, but through a videotape if he was not available.

The teams were also asked to plan additional adult involvement, such as parent conference schedules; golden-agers or other volunteers to work in programs; members of the community to visit during the day for a short tour; informal lunch sessions with students; and assisting youth from each of the studios for extensive volunteering in the community. Students, especially the older ones, were usually not in the Wilson building every day for six hours.

The three teams were responsible for the assignment, supervision, inservice learning, and evaluation of the undergraduate and graduate student interns assigned to Wilson by the various cooperating colleges. The central administration office made the initial placement of the individuals to one of the three teams; acted as resource consultants; served as an appeals board if problems developed among student interns; and coordinated the seminars which were conducted for the preservice participants with the help of the teams. The day-by-day assignment, planning, learning, and evaluation were the role of the various studios, as well as reassignments which could be achieved internally or through the Planning Council. Generally the student interns rotated to other areas as desired. Program need and loads, as well as individual experience desires, could thus be accommodated. The Learning Associates were responsible for coordination of these efforts.

FACILITIES AND EQUIPMENT

To aid in creating interrelationships among the students, some facility and equipment reorganization was constantly necessary in the effort to improve Wilson. Though the exact room arrangements were not that important, and are meaningless in terms of specific numbers, moves during this renewal period are included to again reemphasize the need to continually assess all avenues of improvement – the notion that ongoing revision must be made in the six components of a school: philosophy, learning, curriculum, organization, facilities, and evaluation.

The former "Secondary English" people moved, as there had been too much of a gap in the continuous flow between the previous Communication Team. The split left many students caught in the middle. The Media Center concept for the entire school needed more emphasis and more space, so "English" was moved to create space. The theater arts area was merged with music and the Evolving Persons Studios; in the interrelated effort, English, music, theater arts, and other creativity efforts could be better correlated within themselves, and with other curricular experiences which were closely related.

Two rooms and the big library were cleared and made into a media complex for the entire school, with great efforts to interrelate all teams or studios into the curriculum, and all ages into the program. (Ironically, this big media center was later dismantled in favor of a tracking system for books/tapes nearer the staff and students.) The previous year some areas and some age levels never saw the library, except to pass through the hallway; exits were limited to two in the print section, eliminating the passageway, and providing for better circulation control. Another room became the production center as part of the media complex, and again made available for large group use. The doors between all media areas were opened to provide a steady flow throughout the wing, being closed only when a production with media equipment was in process, or when a scheduled large group needed the closed door environment. More use of the auditorium was made by common thread large groups, by theater arts, and music. New curtains were installed, and better control supervision of equipment housed in that facility became possible.

The new Quiet Room was made attractive and was modified through carpeting and other improvements. The square footage was less, but adequate for the demand – an

203

area with minimal noise which could be closed off without interrupting the flow through the entire wing. Additional space was provided for the graphic arts materials; an intern worked with art, industrial arts, and home economics to develop crafts and other projects related to the three interrelated disciplines. The Environmental Studios gained part of an area to compensate for the loss of the Quiet Room.

The administrators continued to encourage sharing interrelated facilities, the same as they tried to encourage interrelationships of curriculum and students, and the development of quiet and loud spaces for students. They continued to paint areas of the school with bright colors to enhance the environment, both through cleanliness and cheerfulness. They improved the control of facilities and equipment; each studio improved its methods of preventive maintenance. Too many walls were previously damaged by carelessly banging tables against them. The carpet was torn by improper lifting or failure to cover flaws until repaired. Paint was discolored or chipped by inappropriate use of masking tape. It was learned that by working together, with each studio trying hard to see that their area was not damaged, many past maintenance difficulties were solved.

In the category of supplies and equipment, each team became responsible for devising a system for supervision of the equipment. In physical education the staff agreed on methods for prevention of loss; they then had to insist that the procedure be carried through by all. The new piano could not be immediately damaged; the new tape recorders could not disappear. The administration helped to tighten oversight, but the recommendation was that the supplies appropriate to each area needed to be better supervised; the administration stepped in only if the system was completely contrary to the philosophy, but there was nothing in the Wilson philosophy that said the school should lose many dollars worth of materials each year. They believed in honesty, and knew that the tax dollar was hard to find; they did not want equipment to be destroyed or stolen or the building defaced, as a matter of school policy. Support was needed from each person to ensure that systems were devised whereby students had flexible and open access to materials, but did not take advantage of the freedom and opportunities for learning that were provided through Wilson approaches to learning.

Such growing pains illustrate the second year evolvement. These were all resolved, modified, or replaced by better and more creative arrangements. However, in transitioning from a very traditional school to 21st Century learning systems – with no schools as they existed in the Wilson era – most faculties and communities will need to evolve gradual but rapid; conventional but innovative; realistic but inventive methods of creating the eventual transformation. The key is ongoing renewal. Wilson the second year was not like the first; Wilson the third year was not like the second; Wilson the fourth year was not like the eighth. Staff must be willing to create dramatic improvements each year to reach the educational version of the Mars space capsule by 2015. The Wilson program described in 1970 must only be a page in history in 2020.

OPTIONS

The option system, which was offered in the third year, was continued during the next major "renewal period," though usually on a very informal basis. Wilsonites had a choice of selecting Option 1 − free; Option 2 − open; Option 3 − planned; Option 4 − closed. This system did not indicate that the openness at Wilson did not work. To the contrary, the great majority of students automatically followed Option 2, which was the basic organization for the first three years. But the choices enhanced the personalization and individualization process by providing under Option 1 more freedom and less structure than for those who chose Option 2, while Options 3 and 4 provided for a more defined structure. The program took another step toward meeting the needs of wide variations in learning styles. The students, parents, and faculty were very supportive of this approach. The major concern was to ensure that all understood the differences between the four options and that the student related to the option selected.

Under Free Option 1, formal evaluations occurred only once a year. The student was even more self-directing in planning the learning experiences. He or she could come and go as desired, but yet worked in cooperation with adults selected as facilitators, who felt an obligation to communicate with the student enough to follow progress, or if only to know that the individual had decided to take a three-month vacation from the studio, person, or program originally selected.

The Open Option 2 continued by choice as the major Wilson focus; the person evaluated his or her work in conjunction with staff members three times a year; there were fairly definite, but very open-ended, commitments and goals established, with the understanding that the individual could change if desirable; he or she continued optional attendance and great flexibility in planning the learning program. The student was accountable for communication with the instructor from time to time, and for the completion of evaluation sessions.

The Planned Option 3 required the student to report daily to the advisor for a session, not necessarily related to plans for the entire day, but certainly related to what he or she was going to do that day in the fields that were selected, such as when he or she was going to work with an adult in a given team, or whether a subject was to be skipped that particular day or week. Under Option 3, the student was not required to go to the curriculum activity daily, but plans for completion of work were to be ongoing.

Under Closed Option 4, the individual was "required" to complete the agreement made in the specific area, but again that agreement did not have to be a one-hour-a-day approach. The student may have agreed to come in only two hours a week, or for two 30-minute periods, or for eight hours, or once every two weeks; but at least there was an agreement that the student was to follow; if the individual did not, the facilitator-teacher sought a conference. If that did not work, the facilitator communicated to the advisor, and he or she visited with the student. If that did not work, the advisor communicated with the Associate Program Leader, and/or the parent. All this occurred within the first week, or at the latest, two, after it was discovered that the student was not performing.

ALTERNATIVE SELECTIONS

During this particular period of renewal, Wilson tried further changes. In addition to the four options, two alternatives were offered. One was the Interest Alternative Selection; the other was the Prescribed Alternative Selection. Under the Interest Alternative Selection, the student chose to participate in the same Wilson program that was available the first three years. There were few changes from the original programs or philosophy. Under the Prescribed Alternative Selection, the staff divided those students who chose it into four categories: infant, primary, middle, and high school. In the infant program through the traditional kindergarten years, the student program was more prescribed by the instructors; they built in the options and choices for the students as they saw fit. They might require that the student attend physical education activities so many times each week. In the primary – the old grades 1-4 – the student selecting the prescribed approach was required to participate in activities of each of the three teams at least the equivalent of one year of the four-year period.

Breaking this into traditional language so parents, teachers, and students understood, if the school were divided into departments, the student would be required to go to art the equivalent of one year sometime during grades 1-4; the same was true for music, industrial arts, physical education, home economics, math, theater arts, science, social studies, and other such areas; that was the intent. It was not spelled out in those subject area terms though, as this would have further divided attempts to interrelate teams; but through the advisor system, it was the responsibility of the counselor and parent to see that those experiences, whether interrelated or taught separately, were included in the four-year program. The same principle held true for the middle school and high school

This again was not a retreat which said that the open program did not work. To the contrary, the staff believed in the non-required approach, and believed that they should continue the efforts to see that the individuals selecting this program had complete choice. If staffs believe in providing alternatives and options for students, they must offer for those who need more structure an environment where they will succeed. Wilson would never have gone back to a program where they required English four years, math two years, and no art in high school; or home economics only one semester in junior high. The priority course which would have been required, and would be required in the high school under the Prescribed Alternative Selection, was Child Growth and Development; other courses needed were Social Psychology, Human Relations, Values, Urgent Studies, Self-Concept, and Health and Nutrition. Those titles relate to the most important "courses" high schools could and should consider, if they have requirements. Few students selected the "Prescribed Alternatives," but it was another one of the "experiments" to model how all schools could provide for individuals, not groups.

Later these options and alternative systems were abandoned as formal offerings, for few found a need for them. However, such individualization was always available informally for students who might benefit. These were tried on a structured basis for a period of time only to contribute to research and development in education and to determine if they might contribute to Wilson being an even more successful home base for most all youth.

If Wilson had ever returned to mandates for everyone, staff would have seen it as imperative that the topics taught under the former traditional disciplines such as home economics, art, industrial arts, Spanish, and others were treated the same as English, math, science, and history. Under the planned Prescribed Alternative Selection, staff assured that each student would spend at least the equivalent of one year every four years in a given area. The student could take more than one year in an area; he or she could take four years of home economics, three of English, and other such combinations through the choices that remained open to each individual; the equivalent of three of the four years were completely open and optional. However, instead of having one year required and three optional, staff could plan with the students to see that perhaps this year the obligations in home economics and English were completed, and another year the obligations in art and science, remembering all the time that this terminology was traditional and that the programs at Wilson were interrelated and becoming interdependent.

The 1-2-3-4 option system held true in both selection processes. The 1-2-3-4 choices operated as described in the Interest Alternative Selection, and the same under the Prescribed Alternative Selection, in all the experiences the student electively selected. The only difference was that Option 1 was not in effect during the year that the student chose to fulfill the "one-year requirement" in "home economics." Options 2, 3, 4, though, were involved in the "required" year of home economics; different arrangements were worked for individual students.

The optional system continued to provide for complete individualization; there was no return to group teaching and group requirements. Requiring a student to fulfill a year in home economics did not mean that he or she had to complete it all in one year, or with a group. The person could spread it over two years or shorten it to five months; staff and students could completely tailor the program to individual interests; the adults had the authority to say to the youngster that he or she must take a course in child growth and development as part of the selection under the Prescribed Alternative program.

What occurred, in effect, through the four option system, and through the Prescribed Alternative and Interest Alternative Selection systems, was provision for a student to: (1) continue in exactly the same Wilson program that had existed for three years; (2) be much more free than ever, if he or she chose all studies in Option 1 in the Interest Alternative Selection; or, (3) be more structured, if he or she chose Options 3 or 4 in all areas under the Prescribed Alternative Selection system. Wilson increased the alternatives and options, and furthered the efforts toward individualization, by trying to reach the interests and needs of students in a relevant manner. As an experimental research arm, such variations were essential in seeking ways to improve the program. In retrospect, almost all chose Option 2, under the Interest Alternative, the original design. This explains why these options were later formally dropped, but it was proven that they work and can be adopted by other schools.

WINDOW SHOPPING

The process of window shopping, related to students deciding what adults they would like to learn with and in what areas or topics, was continued. Ideally, students should decide what and how they want to study, and with what materials; they come to the facilitators and say: "Could you help me learn what, how, or why . . .?" Some youth have difficulty deciding their interests and needs. For them, the staff developed offerings which individuals might attempt as an approach to involvement in special or interdependent curriculum fields. Most Wilson students were somewhere in between; they planned a good share of their experiences, but needed resources and suggestions from the adults.

Options

With this in mind, each of the three Studios offered "shoppers' guides." Outside the various physical spaces within the school, lists of 40 or 50 suggested topics which students might wish to pursue were posted. The staff developed carry-home "shoppers' guides" which listed the same topics with a sentence or two of explanation, so that students and parents could discuss possibilities. Philosophically, Curriculum Became Whatever The Student Desired To Learn And Was Learning At That Period Of Time; the decision was based primarily on interest, need, and preferred methods. Staff were encouraged to suggest areas to the students so they could consider alternative selections, and have as diversified a curriculum as the creative minds of both working together could develop.

Searching for interesting teachers and learning areas is an exciting process, the same as looking for purchase of an exotic island, though it can be frustrating if the student has no concept of what might be an exotic choice. Curriculum development and window shopping were two-way processes at Wilson, where students and staff contributed ideas for experiences that should be offered. The Wilson philosophy was that the student should be able to take anything he or she could possibly dream, even if only one person in the school wanted that pursuit, as long as materials could be found, an adult resource person was available in the community, and the student was motivated to complete the specific learning goals.

The following list of experiences (this was the curriculum) is an actual example of what 600 K-12 students were involved in during one 12-week period of time in one of the nine years as a result of the window shopping process and personalization – utilizing existing budgets, staff, facilities, and community resources, but without the handicap of a requirement of 15 to 30 students for a class of 55-minutes, or for an all day room of 30 young people. Perhaps only one person was studying a listed topic.

Aztec Indians	Logic Puzzles	The Womans Role
Canoe Tripping	Make Believe	Art
Challenge Lab	Middle Choir	Math
Calculating Machines	Paper-mache Sculpture	Reading
Biology	Prices are Ridiculous	Beginning Recorder
Filing	Science Experiences	Best in the News
Driver Education	Shakespeare	Bridge
Fantasy	10,000 Grammar Mistakes	Clay Sculpture
Games	Tool Subjects	Commercial Art
Girls Woodworking	Weather Forecasting	Gardening
How the West was Saved	Wilson Bakery	Individualized French
Beginning Composition	Wilson Wanderers	Keedy Geometry
Biology in Agriculture	Spelling Skills	Taxidermy
Current Global Issues	General Science	Chemistry
Literature: Vonnegut	Swimming	Chess
Model Building	Symbolism	Children in the Olden Days
Earth Science	Things Your Mother Never	Daffy Dramatics
Everything About Eggs	Taught	Down the Mouse Hole
Language	Typing Lab	Nature Study
Pots and Plants	Uncle Gilby Stories	HEED Project
Physics	What Did I Miss	Medicine and Biology
Spelling Bee	Who Will be President	Household Chemistry

Drug Chemistry
Dream Reality
History of Ireland
World War III
The Young Decorator
Independent Business
Independent Computer
Independent Geology
Open Lab Kitchens
E x p e r i m e n t   a n d
Observation
Spanish
Geography
Future Histories
Unevens
Advanced Composition
After Wilson - What?
American Trail Blazers
Word Games
Activity Center
Concrete Poetry
Creative Hands
Industrial Arts
Environment Today
Landforms
Hungry World
Philosophy
Japanese Journey
Making of a City
Natural Foods
Probability and Chance
Visual Communication
Weaving Off-Loom
Hillbillies
Mars
After   the   American
Revolution
Death
Dickens World
Dinosaur Tracks
Dream Analysis
Environmental Concerns
Exploring II
Foods and Facts
French Writers
Grilling Out
Insurance
Field Hockey
Harmonica
Jeopardy

Palmistry
Penmanship
Sing-Along
Two for the Show
Wright Brothers
Track and Field
Consumer Math
IPC
Norse Myths
Language Arts
Swing Choir
The Bear Awakes
Advanced Algebra
Modern Poets
Music Drama
Native Americans Now
Orff and Recorder
Puppets
Perelandra
Play Reading
Prisons
Recorder
Research Paper
St. Olaf Singers
Stage Design
Women Writers
Third World Crises
Mankato Sioux
Last Picture Show
Math MIA
One-pot Meals
Peer Counseling
Personalized Spelling
Science in the News
Special Topics in Math
Speed/Accuracy Typing
Spring Plants
Typing Problems
Understanding Divorce
Values Clarification
Vocabulary
Walkie Talkies
Weight Control
Welding
Word Origins
Coed Volleyball
Keeping a Journal
National Liberation Front
Romantic Poetry
Shorthand III

Softball A
Tennis
Trees, Twigs, Terrain
Potluck
DUSO
Adaptation
Best Buys and Deals
Bicentennial Studies
Calico
Cycle Touring
Creative Hands II
Display and Exhibit
Where Are You Going
Driver Training
Edgar Allen Poe
Environment of a Rope
Fortran Programming
Grammar
Improving Cursive Writing
Its A Small World
Leisure Activities
Animal Drawing
Bible as Literature
Cheyenne Struggle
Detective Stories
Creative Writing
Energy
Golf
Metrics
Reading Magic
Springboard
Gift of Love
School newspaper
Whodunit
A Womans Place
Woodworking
Arabic
Business Law
Codes and Ciphers
Dating and Marriage
Food Power
Grammar Lab
History for Everyone
How to Tell Time
No Fun Eating Alone
Oral Language
Problems in Ecology
Reading Unlimited
Sharpen Your Wits
Writing Stories

Options

Arab World	The Source	Rock and Blues
Bicycles are Fun	Tolkein Trilogy	Sewing for Spring
Meeting the Orchestra	Film Making I	Simple Economics
Metric Cooking	Film Making II	U.S. History
Mexican Folk Dance	From the Movies	Weight Training
Old Mankato	Joseph Conrad	Yoga, Music, and Your
Peace Studies	Limnology	Science – Plants
Photography	Live Things	Tutor Time
The Beat Generation	Magic Carpet	Action Ecology
Racism and Literature	Outdoor Studies	Arabic Literature
Sex for Todays Girl	Pets in a Jar	Dracula and Friends

The focus is to realize that all these subinterest topics were part of the broader interrelated curriculum studies of each student, and that they were ongoing simultaneously in a facility for 600. Few other schools, and certainly not conventional ones, could match the individualized opportunities available for Wilson students.

PARENT COMMUNICATION

In making changes in the Wilson program, parent nights were utilized; every effort was made to encourage them to attend. In a large group one evening, descriptions were presented of the changes that had been made to improve the school. This session was followed by small groups, where the advisory teams further explained the programs and answered parent questions; that was followed within the first weeks with a parent conference to ensure that the student-parent-advisor team was in agreement (Family Designed Conference).

Program changes occurred throughout the year; students who may have been on vacation continued when they returned wherever they were the last time they attended Wilson, whether fall, winter, spring or summer; they could follow their previous programs, or begin new efforts, but the parents were informed, as well as the advisory team and the facilitators. In January, June, and October, progress reports went home. These three year-round evaluations provided the parents with a summary of progress after the summer, fall, and the winter/spring periods. They were mailed home rather than individually carried, as was the practice in the early years.

LIGHTED COMMUNITY INVOLVEMENT

Parents were very important in implementing the lighted school concept. Most of the staff volunteered to work one or two nights some weeks, from time to time, provided compensation in the form of days off, or some mornings off, was available. Through better use of student interns, utilization of the interrelated team concept, and use of the advisor system, the building was open from 3:30 to 9:00 p.m. two evenings a week, or at least 6:00 to 9:00 p.m. in selected areas.

Parents joined their children in the use of the media facilities and the gymnasium. In the instrumental music program, as well as the choir, there were opportunities for parent-student instrumental and vocal groups; this gave Dad a chance to pull his old horn out of the attic, or the old tune from the hip pocket. Theater arts, with student-parent groups rather than all students, were appropriate too. Parents also used the facilities for study, and though every room was not open every night, there were multiple opportunities for involvement. On certain evenings the science labs, shops, or home economics facilities were open; specific availability was announced in advance through the students, activity board, weekly newsletter, school paper, and various other communication media. Through staggered use of regular staff, graduate interns, parent volunteers, and student interns, the program was adequately covered.

There were many requests from both students and parents for the building to be open more in the evening and on weekends. The school-in-the-community concept had expanded to new heights. If the community-in-the-school was to grow to meet the visions, further steps were necessary. The evening lighted school was part of the effort by allowing those families who were not available during the day to participate at other times. Increased parent volunteer involvement illustrations included one father directing one-act plays for combinations of students and parents; another teaching students how to build a rocket; and another directing a musical group; many parents were learners and became involved with their own children in such activities as learning to use the computer terminals which were available some evenings.

Involving parents in the lighted school also proved to be a good way to ensure that each staff member worked in other studios, as they volunteered to assist in another learning area; the "math" teacher could be in "industrial technology," if that was a major focus on a particular evening. Parent involvement during these times was not for gripe sessions, or for extensive conferences. "School" was conducted at night the same as though it was part of the day program, with parents perhaps learning to improve their typing or art skills. The evening approach was further a way to answer part of the problem of enhancing student-parent togetherness in the program as they were excited regarding the curriculum opportunities. This learning approach partially replaced the need for a parent advisory group, and worked as a community communication network. Through teams arranging for visitors from the community, especially those who were non-Wilson parents, plus the lighted-school effort, much of the misunderstanding of the "school on the hill" was resolved.

ROVING PERSONS
For the first three years the students at Wilson had complete freedom to come and go throughout the entire building and community. They had been "rovers;" this policy continued. The staff had been more stable, having a headquarters where most spent the majority of the day. This "headquarters" approach continued in that students who wanted to learn the old "chemistry" as part of environmental interrelationships were anxious to find the "chemistry teacher" in an area where they could do laboratory experiments. "Science" oriented staff had to be available to students a majority of the day in properly equipped facilities. Some of the excellent adults became so swamped with students who chose to work with them that they found it hard to escape their center. The physical separation of facilities at Wilson, though doors were cut in walls to provide "suites" and "centers," still handicapped some of the interdependent flow because of the hallways and the L-shaped building designed around two outdoor, well-utilized courtyards.

In spite of such possible handicaps, if programs were to be truly interrelated, and if the focus on helping persons meant involvement in several learning areas, then more flexibility of staff movement was essential. Many had "wandered" to a variety of learning situations the first two years. The already in place "splinter team" curriculum organization, teacher interests, administrative suggestions, and student requests led in this direction, but needed was a more coordinated plan; many staff were heavily involved, but some had only minimally utilized the "rover" concept. It was important that all share in exchange activities. Therefore, the "roving person" approach was implemented on a more formal pattern. Each staff member arranged more planned time out of his or her center. This might have been one hour a day, one hour or one day a week, one day every two weeks, or several times each week, or continuously "in and out" for a period of time, depending upon the need related to team teaching projects, learning requests, and sharing with students and staff.

The concept can easily be described by simple illustrations using traditional subject and school terminology. A math teacher, instead of remaining each day in the math center, or in the future media studio, or in the systems suite, purposely arranged one day of a given week to be in the home economics center. Here she became a "teacher" of that subject. She knew how to cook and sew and discuss family life situations. She was seen as a fun "cooking teacher" and not as the "old hard math teacher;" home economics was no longer for "non-college" because the math team was there, too. The math teacher learned about the program in another field; she saw students in a different light; they saw her from a changed perspective. She even taught some math, such as two-thirds of a cup.

The next week she may have gone to industrial arts. Little "second grade" Johnny showed her how to cut out a turtle on the power saw; she learned to use the goggles, the sander, the varnish, and other tools. She was suddenly the learner; the student became the teacher; the entire atmosphere changed. She discovered interests of Johnny, found ways to interrelate math and industrial arts, and, therefore, better understood the problems and successes. The teacher came to know other students; some who did not come to math were in industrial arts. She was able to talk with them as persons and perhaps find ways to interest them in math. The "industrial arts" and "home economics" teachers were expected to share similar time and experiences in the "math" areas (remembering all these centers were interrelated).

Such interaction could occur in the Early Childhood Center where interlocking rooms (passages cut in the walls) were established as a modified version of the British Infant School. A young child could have most all of his or her learning experiences in those designed rooms with the assigned staff, but this did not happen. The teachers from art, home economics, Spanish, industrial arts, science, physical education, and such fields came to the center to help teach and interrelate their areas. The young children went throughout the school, the same as the high school age students – to the shops, gyms, art areas, home economics, media center, science zoo, music auditorium, and similar facilities. The entire staff became roving members of the Beginning Life Center – or "Happy House." Those who usually worked with early childhood conversely were scheduled into all the "traditional subjects" (now merged as teams, centers, suites), thus enhancing the entire roving person and interrelationship concepts.

This approach was a tremendous way to better understand the value of all programs in the school, to comprehend the efforts of various "disciplines," and accept their contributions to the student. It was a great inservice device, and a fine way to sell interrelationship of curricula. It involved staff in more than "one room;" it made the teacher a learner and the learner a teacher; it broke monotony and depression. Even more, it allowed people to know people – to meet on a person level, rather than teacher-student levels, or teacher to teacher in the lounge, at a faculty meeting, or on an advisory team.

The person approach was the key to success. Though Wilson followed this philosophically from the beginning, the renewal emphasis of the roving person concept enhanced the program further and paid tremendous dividends.

SCHEDULING REVISIONS

Everyone agreed the 55-minute period in the secondary school, or the rigid schedule in the self-contained room, were horrendous; further, flexible-modular scheduling was only a small step in the right direction. For three years Wilson worked to perfect the most advanced scheduling process; a daily smorgasbord approach. Then Wilson reached a point where staff were able to develop a nonscheduled school. This was a fantastic breakthrough in education; even if it had not been completely successful, they learned that they could reduce scheduling to a minimal effort – only listing special activities on a given day. Eventually this did become the non-scheduled school, or as some referred to it, the "hidden schedule." Students and teachers "scheduled" activities but together and independently. There was no need for a master or daily school schedule. This is easy when learning is personalized and individualized.

As a transition stage, staff developed a "special interest" calendar; they eliminated the need for a scheduling clerk, and required only minimal effort from a planning team. The basic concept was that generally all areas of learning, and most all learning activities normally available within the building, would be accessible every day. Specially planned events inside or outside the building, new functions, or resource opportunities needed to be brought to the attention of those interested, but Wilson eliminated the use of the loudspeaker and the daily bulletin. Information was spread through the weekly newsletter, the school paper, the team announcement bulletin boards, personal conferences, posters, and word of mouth. The "daily special" list became an extension of these forms.

PLANNING COUNCIL, RESEARCH, AND STAFFING

The school administration was revised and the staffing patterns altered. Rather than the "Board of Directors" as existed, a "Planning Council" was operationalized. The day-by-day all school administration was still in the hands of the Program Leader (formerly titled Director); this person was assisted by an Associate Program Leader. They were both assisted by the Administrative Coordinator and the Research Coordinator. The Program Leader put heavy emphasis on interrelating curricula and the roving person concept. The Associate had a primary concern with the emphasis on person-to-person approaches. The Administrative Coordinator handled much of the business manager activities. The Research Coordinator had an exceptionally important position in improving and developing the efforts in research and evaluation for the Wilson program, and communicating findings and methodologies in the community and nation.

Wilson did not accept the accountability movement, as it was focused on the old "basic skills" of a few cognitive areas. The concept of accountability was fine; but it must include first the affective domain – how the program is assisting in the areas of self-image, success, self-direction, responsibility, decision-making, and family and peer relationships. Second, it must assess how the program is assisting in the psychomotor area. Certainly motor skills developed in the five and six year old group are just as basic, if not more so, than measurements taken in reading and math. Finally, the cognitive must include knowledge in areas other than English, math, science, and social studies. The research and communication efforts at Wilson were designed to help with ascertaining a total picture of the individual, one with priorities, not just limited to I.Q., math, and reading scores as administered in most conventional districts.

The Planning Council consisted of the Program Leader, the Associate Program Leader, and the Learning Associates representing each of the three teams: the Studios for Evolving Persons, Emerging Environments, and Evolutionalry Designs. Their task was week-by-week assessment of the program and long-range planning. They formed a direct linkage between the planning center personnel and the staff and students. From time to time students, the research and administrative coordinators, and other staff participated in the Council meetings and activities. All were involved through the sessions that were held from day to day and week to week in the daily operational procedures of the school, and were encouraged to participate through group or individual suggestions.

Every effort was made to balance the staff, so that the former "nonacademic" subjects were treated equally with the former "academic" subjects; each was important. Slowly the staff alignments reached a point whereby the old emphasis on the "academics" was disappearing. This trend toward balance in the learning opportunities at Wilson was a healthy sign for continued improvement in the future.

These ideas were not 21st Century in design — not even into the 90s. They only illustrate that after being in operation for three years as "the most innovative school," the staff began to overhaul what they had created. Most of the proposals were minor adjustments; a few were dramatic shifts. It is important in analyzing change and reality, that if a school is to grow, if it is going to improve, continuous self-renewal of staff, students, program, parents, and community is essential.

Wilson continued for nine years. Some of the revisions worked beautifully; others were never fully implemented; several were tried and dropped, or never begun except on paper. The Wilson program had a process through which it was constantly evolving; Wilson was never "being;" it was always "becoming."

In the latter years, under a new director, further adjustments were undertaken — some adding to creativity and some taking away. On the positive side, a major expansion of the volunteering and social service emphasis occurred during the last four years. In the neutral area, more precise student records toward graduation were developed, including a review committee for graduation competencies. On the negative side, the daily variable and nonscheduled school approaches were modified to reflect variable scheduling somewhat by quarters — but only to accommodate the large number of students involved from the traditional college programs. The new director saw that as positive; the original one would not have accepted the modification.

It is necessary to develop a continuing mechanism for change. In fairness to the program, it must be noted that during the last three years before closing, the major focus was on attempted preservation. The students, staff, and parents of Wilson, and much of the community, spent hundreds of hours in efforts to prevent the new politically oriented for personal gain college administration from eliminating the campus school. Had the 1968 president remained, Wilson no doubt would yet be flourishing. But after his retirement, and the 1974 arrival of a different chancellor appointed president, the handwriting was on the wall.

The survival struggle removed much of the renewal creativity in the last two years.

214

The staff continued a beautiful school; they graduated half of the "junior class" and several "sophomores" who were ready and who requested it, along with the seniors, the final year, June 1977, to prevent them from being required to return to the traditional Mankato high schools.

The new futures oriented curricula, the attempt to implement many more of the concepts of the Minnesota Experimental City, and the dream of piloting a truly futuristic learning system for the 21st Century, never completely materialized. Thirty-three of the finest teachers in America received registered letters notifying them they had been dismissed, some after 20 years of service at Wilson. The students were dumped into traditional neighborhood schools. Humaneness had once again lost a battle with bureaucracy.

But the spirit of Wilson remained alive in the hearts and minds of those who participated in this second *Eight-Year Study*. As the 21st Century arrives, that spirit should assist the emergence of new futuristic leaders dedicated to creating their own version of the Camelot called Wilson.

CHOICES

Visitors to Wilson constantly asked for advice creating renewal and change in their own local schools and districts. Before suggesting possible beginning approaches, they were always reminded that there are a tremendous number of research, experimentation, practical application, and implementation illustrations to document beyond a doubt that the conventional education patterns are not the best learning programs for all students; they were told that these should be read first and cited in the communities. The evidence is overwhelming that the numerous variations, typified by the one developed at the Wilson Campus School, when compiled as educational choices, are far more appropriate for the majority of youth.

However, knowing that the ruling coalition in most districts, will not permit an overnight creation of multiple selections by families and staff, it was suggested to them that the best solution at that time was to possibly implement new designs with a small but critical mass — usually a 20-40 percent cross section of volunteer students and staff at no additional cost. Such efforts generated immediate success where the philosophy was well expressed, the commitment was solid, and the implementation support was tangible.

There are more than 36 ways to begin innovative opportunities, ranging from one teacher in one classroom to a total system. Related to adapting Wilson, the school-within-a-school is a common pattern, but one seldom utilized correctly. An elementary building wishing to offer Wilson, or preferably much more futuristic options, can take a staff of 20 and create perhaps three alternatives: seven teachers can teach k-6 in self-contained classrooms and follow the conventional model, but with their 21st Century focus; eight others can modify the traditional by possibly offering team teaching, flexible scheduling, continuous progress curriculum, non-graded classes, individualized instruction, futures issues, and open facilities; the remaining five staff can move to the "end of the hall or into one pod" and in their space create their version of Wilson — the Minnesota Experimental City — their dream. They are free to be visionaries. This does not cost more; the teachers, rooms, materials are already there. It does not even change the bus routes. Parents can choose Program A, B, or C. It can still be one student body, however, through cooperation and collaboration among staff, shared assemblies and lunches, all-school activities, team sports, library and media utilization, environmental recycling center, and common holiday plans.

A second, and preferred method, is to select at least one school, involve voluntary staff, students, and parents, and have the participants implement their version of the future. In larger districts, a "Wilson" can be part of a three or four school cluster, where parents desiring the conventional can remain in that format. Utilizing the "neighborhood cluster" concept, rather than isolated "neighborhood schools" gives parents a choice of programs. In a variation, all four could be entirely different, as in the Minneapolis Southeast Alternatives project where parents could select any one of four models: (1) contemporary; (2) continuous; (3) open (Wilson)/futures; or (4) free. All can create their versions toward alternative futures for education and society. A fifth choice could be a close resemblance to the futuristic experimental city model.

Choices

A third, the "paired" concept, where there is a true choice of School A or B, provides the opportunity to innovate without forcing parents to accept the experiment. In a fourth variation, a district can create its own laboratory school — its version of "Wilson Campus," sponsored by the school board rather than the college — even a form of a Charter School. A fifth method, a program-within-a-school deviation offers the chance to try new ideas part of each day or week, such as scheduling an interdependent block for 90 students three hours a day. Sixth, teachers can plan time in their own classrooms to pilot innovations, individually or as part of a team. Seventh, using intersessions in year-round calendars is another exciting, but cautious method of evaluating potential success before implementation, as "innovations' and "futures oriented" proposals can be tried in three week blocks without any loss of the "regular" 180-day year.

A glossary of 36 such methods only outlines the tip of the iceberg in exploring the many possible facets, but each suggestion does indicate an approach that offers a feasible method for creating a vision, a Wilson, or a total 21st Century learning system. Such considerations are needed now as school district personnel are experimenting with instructional, curricular, and organizational approaches in an attempt to move education toward the future. To date, progress has been slow and the steps small; no district yet appears to be a "model" for pioneering programs which may be more appropriate for the societal changes which are projected to emerge in the years ahead. On the bright side, the efforts of a number of districts have led to practical ways that schools can begin to do more to develop futures-oriented curricular and instructional options within existing budgets, laws, and politics. Most all are possible in any size school system in any location, and at any grade level, though smaller rural schools often need to implement the basic concept differently than those located in large urban or suburban settings.

None are seen as very advanced, or 21st Century in nature. They are only simple ways to begin, but important in that they have the capability of creating exciting developments which can lead in the coming years to the replacement of the neighborhood schoolhouse by lifelong learning systems. Most all have been implemented successfully somewhere. They vary in their long range potential, but each can contribute to a district commitment to identify compassionate era learning opportunities for those families ready to volunteer. The key element has been to offer choices, alternatives, options to the more conventional approaches to schooling. Great success has been possible when starting with volunteers and no increase in the budget. The districts which have not been able to develop these opportunities for students, teachers, and parents have been those that have tried to mandate programs, or those which have sought acceptance of 70-80 percent of the community before offering them. Humane districts understand that creating viable choices by teacher and parent request for a small minority is part of the American ideals of democracy, freedom, and choice as personified by the multiple church denominations.

Starting immediately with a volunteering minority of only 20-40 percent of the students has proven to be preferable to not starting at all; it has been a mistake to wait until a large majority demands that one or more of the approaches be offered in the district. A win/win spirit of cooperation and judgment has been an essential ingredient — of offering options and alternatives — replacing the win/lose competitive voting — of trying to require that all students fit into the same mold. The latter philosophy has created unnecessary conflict, and has reduced the opportunities to offer significantly different and better choices for more youth in most communities. Several of the plans may be used to provide for a variety of learning and teaching styles. Alternatives are for everyone, not just for those unfortunately labeled "at-risk." Each of the 36 cited can be utilized in a district for the development of stepping stones toward the future.

1. Futures Courses: Schools and colleges can offer one or two semester courses, usually through social studies electives, for students who wish to concentrate on a study of the future (Future Studies; Alternative Futures.)

2. Futures Units: In teaching the transportation unit in 5th grade social studies, students spend less time on the past and present modes, and more time studying possible future transportation systems.

3. Futurizing Courses: U.S. history can be taught by starting in 2025 rather than 1492. Will there be wars, money, inflation, marriages, racial conflict, churches, schools, full employment, professional sports in 2025? Historical perspective is utilized where important. Most all existing courses can be taught from a futures focus.

4. Multiple Schools-Within-a-School: Four optional programs can be offered in a high school of 2,000. Five hundred twenty-five might choose the conventional approach; 750 might prefer a modified 60s/70s effort updated to the 90s; 300 might choose the Parkway School without walls concept; 425 might select the Center for the Future — pioneering a voluntary new era learning system. A smaller elementary school may offer three options: contemporary; team; futures approaches.

5. School-Within-a-School: Instead of four or more options, students in a middle school can be offered two — the current more contemporary approach, and the pioneering futures-oriented alternative.

6. Total School: A district can create a cluster of four elementary schools; three remain contemporary, but the fourth, filled with volunteer parents, students, and teachers, implements futures-oriented curriculum, instruction, and organization.

7. Total Classroom: One elementary teacher can take 30 volunteer students and develop an all-day, all-year effort, creating futures-oriented approaches, while the other staff continue the more conventional self-contained room and basic curriculum requirements; it can be a non-graded country school, or a grade level choice.

8. One Department/Subject: Social studies courses and units can be selected as the beginning vehicle. Each offering in the subject or department is revised to create a futures-oriented curriculum.

9. Assembly Schedule: On Wednesday in a secondary school, 15 minutes are taken from each period, leaving a 90-minute block of time once a week or month where all the staff and students are free to involve themselves in futures-oriented study and activities.

10. Block of Time: Four hours a day, an English, social studies, math, and science teacher can combine for a team futures-oriented approach to their interrelated disciplines for those who volunteer. The other students may take the same subjects in the traditional mode of four separate periods.

Choices

11. Program-in-a-School: A special two-hour program on futures can be offered to students who select a concentrated futures involvement. Often science and social studies are combined to implement this concept, perhaps called Global Futures, in either elementary or secondary schools.

12. Individualized Program: Students can create their own futures-oriented learning experiences, in cooperation with a committee of teachers which approves their individualized plan. It could involve six months of practical work on a solar project, with all the related political, financial, environmental, and science research and study.

13. Stations-in-a-School: Futures-oriented teachers are identified. Students can seek these individuals as their instructors, through which they can then focus their learning activities toward the future in an interdependent mode. In a high school, if students select six, they have the flexibility of an all-day, week, or month project.

14. Theme Approach: An elementary school can arrange each month to have all classrooms devote time most days, perhaps in science-social studies blocks, to offer theme futures related topics: oceanography in September; space in October; the human condition in November; telecommunications in December; and similar topics for January through June.

15. Classroom Future Center: Each Wednesday from 1:00-2:30 p.m., those teachers who volunteer can set aside this one and one-half hours to concentrate on a futures topic (the future of water), organization, and philosophy, while maintaining the conventional curriculum the rest of the week.

16. Local Topics: Teachers can weave local futures-oriented topics into the current curriculum; the overfishing of the anchovy beds; the preservation of the redwoods; the closing of the lumber mills; the restrictions on salmon fishing; the damming of rivers; Indian fishing rights on reservation streams.

17. Portable Resource Units: Teachers can create homemade futures-oriented materials, activities, and resources that can be placed on carts or in kits and transported from room-to-room as desired.

18. Magnet Schools: Futures curriculum, organization, and/or instructional "models" can be put in place in one or more schools as an optional part of the district magnet school effort.

19. Cluster Concept: Instead of three neighborhood schools, the three can create a neighborhood cluster. One can be a contemporary program; one a modified contemporary; and one a design toward a new era learning system. Parents and students select their preference.

20. Stations in Pods: As students come to the math pod, they can select a more conventional teacher and methods; a modified contemporary instructional mode; or a futures-oriented approach to learning math within the same pod.

21. Schools in Pods: Students have a choice of a team of teachers in a pod teaching their subjects conventionally, or futures-oriented: English and French taught in one

pod can be taught traditionally, but in Pod II can be taught with a perspective toward the coming decades.

22. Ad Hoc Efforts: When time permits, teachers in the classroom can insert random futures activities to help students begin to develop a futures perspective. A futures wheel focused on "more people means" leads quickly to students identifying tertiary and beyond consequences of more people.

23. Mini-Courses: Each Thursday, or Thursday afternoon, the regular classes can be canceled; instead students and teachers engage in short, specialized futures topics of interest in the form of mini-courses.

24. Interdependent Teams: As a step toward the elimination of departmentalization, a must from a futures perspective, a beginning can be made by merging, for example, social science, science, and physical education and health into an Environmental Center. Or stepping beyond, curriculum can be organized by the interdependencies of Urgent Studies; Human Potential; Interdependent Competencies; and Interrelated Interests.

25. R and D Center: Industry creates new products through research efforts. Volunteer students, teachers, and parents can assist in creating new human learning programs by the establishment of a district R and D facility. Extensive data in the cognitive, affective, and psychomotor domains can be gathered – and often analyzed through graduate school student theses.

26. Off-Campus Centers: Futures-oriented programs create a demand for community living and learning. Some students can learn psychology – past, present, and future – by working in a mental hospital, or interning with a psychologist. They could concentrate on psychological potential in the years ahead – perhaps the efforts of conscious and unconscious learning research.

27. Futures Afternoons: Schools can create one afternoon a week or month where teachers work with their classes on futures concerns, topics, and forecasts. On Tuesday, all classes can feature curriculum related to the 64 global dilemmas.

28. Futures Week: One week a year, or semester, all scheduled courses can be suspended. Instead, students can sign for futures-oriented classes and activities. Heavy involvement of the community in the planning and teaching helps create a futures perspective beyond the schoolhouse.

29. Non-Paid Social Service: To realistically understand the have/have not gap, as one example of this approach, students can be assigned or volunteer to work in social agencies assisting the have-not people of the community and world. Focus can center on ways to narrow the gap in the future, perhaps eventually helping to preserve the biosphere and humankind.

30. Urgent Studies – Required: Rather than another year of English or science, or other traditional subjects, students can be required to take Urgent Studies – to concentrate on the 64 global dilemmas that threaten world survival – especially the threats to air, water, and food.

31. <u>One Period, Four Traditional</u>: An instructor with five classes of U.S. history or home economics, can continue to teach four in the more conventional approach. However, for one period the instructor can experiment with volunteer students in teaching the course with futures techniques, technologies, and curriculum.

32. <u>Stimulus Center</u>: Schools can interrelate this facility with the library/media complex. This program features a constantly changing stimulus of possible futures studies — activities, games, computers, films, projects, books, tapes, ideas — as a supplement to other instruction, or as a separate entity — enabling students to engage in futuring on their own or with a group.

33. <u>Infant School Corner</u>: Borrowing a page from the British Infant School, one corner of a classroom can be created as the "21st Century Space." Displays, activities, discussions, readings, games, murals, and other possibilities can be one of the rotation selections in the curriculum.

34. <u>Laboratory School</u>: In the past, there have been a few significant laboratory schools: the ones at the University of Chicago; Ohio State University; and Mankato State University were three of the best. They pioneered new directions; they affected the future of education. Designating one building as a laboratory school concept within a district enables the volunteers to experiment with new futures-oriented learning opportunities in conjunction with a futures-oriented cooperating college of education. Here the electronics and biological revolutions might be interwoven with Urgent Studies and the Human Condition as part of the pioneering.

35. <u>MXC</u>: The proposed Minnesota Experimental City — MXC — (not built) was designed to be the most experimental in the world — housing 250,000 people in an entirely 21st Century environment. The MXC was planned for construction between 1975 and 1990 with no schools or universities. The city was the living learning laboratory; learning was considered a lifelong process. Schooling was not involved. The basic ideas of the MXC can be borrowed for implementation as the basis of a district effort toward creating a new learning system for the future. Many of the concepts can be implemented now in most districts.

36. <u>Yours</u>: The best of the methods is the one which can be designed by creative individuals in schools, colleges, districts, and communities throughout the land. Such efforts are essential, according to most futures writers; they already consider the present schools obsolete, and certainly so if projected into the next decades.

As more educators develop new ways to move education toward the future, the list will expand, be better, and more creative. There will soon be some quantum overleaps. Meanwhile, these suggestions offer the opportunity for every school district in America to begin to plan for and implement programs for students more in line with the needs of youth who will be in their prime well into a projected significantly different 21st Century.

LEGACY

In 1943, Dr. Fred G. Bratton wrote *The Legacy of the Liberal Spirit*, one of the truly outstanding interpretations of freedom. It was a history of the development of Christianity, written from a different perspective. Dr. Bratton classified the volume under the category of "necessary," for in it he attempted to describe the spirit which the Allied Nations were at the moment fighting to preserve; he sought to interpret the history of freedom in its most critical stages. The United States now faces further crises — this time of a global nature that may determine the future of humankind. No longer can survival issues be avoided, for they are far more awesome than ever envisioned in *The Legacy of the Liberal Spirit* in the first half of the 20th Century.

To meet the emerging education portion of these challenges, the majority of futurists indicate that the present schoolhouse must go the way of the dinosaur; it has already proven itself to be obsolescent. To create learning systems appropriate for the times, significantly different leadership is essential. The pioneer educational spirits of the 1930s are gone. Most of the leaders of the reform efforts of the 1960s retired, are in semi-retired positions, or are only effective at the local rather than the national level. As 2000 has arrived, it is crucial to search for new vigor among present educators who would like to lead the way, and to assist them in envisioning possible methods which can be used to create the essential societal and educational programs which must come in the years ahead, if the youth of the nation are to avoid the fate of the early civilizations of Egypt, Greece, and the Roman Empire.

Past leaders of reform, as illustrated by Martin Luther King addressing societal change, and J. Lloyd Trump educational designs, had dreams. Their ideals, beliefs, visions, which were sometimes criticized, scoffed at, even made the brunt of ridicule and laughter, and which sometimes were planned or implemented incorrectly, were nonetheless great goals for the globe, for the nation, for education. These suffered a setback in the late 70s and through the 80s, but beyond 2000 holds promise, if the new leadership comes committed to turning dreams into realities.

The problems of education are minute, when contrasted with the problems of the global village, but educators must help create preferable futures, before it is too late. No longer can they content themselves with the schools which now exist, nor with the pace of change of the proverbial snail. Educators must move more rapidly through transitions toward transformations. If they can once again dream, perhaps education can contribute ever so much more to the visions of a better country, a better global society — and the preservation of Spaceship Earth — by not only imagining the future, but by beginning to implement many of the dreams now.

The 70s and 80s were rocked by retrenchment. The focus was on teacher negotiations, finance and stagflation, desegregation, core curriculum and test scores, and a return to the "Three R's." Seldom was much heard regarding different curriculum for the future; the real concerns were not for the students, but with "popular" reports. Even the alternative schools movement moved in the wrong direction, being an escape from the traditional program for those who were unhappy, rather than providing true choices of options for all. Education became politics — a power struggle. Decisions were made on political realities and personalities, not on how to move from what is to what ought to be for the nation. The Nation At Risk Report, by the Commission on Excellence, was one example of promoting trends going in the wrong direction.

The 60s saw a group of risk takers – true scholarly educational leaders who challenged tradition, the colleges, and society – they were not "non-academic flakes." It is time for their replacements to surface again with a commitment to action. It is finally time to stop petty bickering about Carnegie Units, B-minus grades, the length of the lunch period, and the route of the school bus. The hour has arrived to dramatically change the school systems by offering choices and options – by allowing those ready for a different future to launch 21st Century thinking from a "futureport."

Learning leaders should search deeply for new questions, make more significant contributions to society, and create better designs; giving students the ability to read, compute, and respond to examinations is not enough. They must transition toward being different persons, educators, and leaders. However, before the individual can make the decision to dramatically change, he or she must understand why.

Present conventional schools which do not offer true options of learning styles and school calendars, and real choices of mandated or self-selected curriculum are among the most inhumane institutions in America. They closely rival the prisons; the only difference is that after 3:00 p.m., on weekends, and during June, July and August (if they have been on good behavior), they are paroled. If one visits a prison lockup, and then goes immediately to a conventional elementary school from 9:00 to 10:15 a.m., the analogy is obvious, for it is possible to have target practice – even shoot a cannon down the halls – for no one would be hurt. The warden has ordered the guards to keep all the prisoners in their cells from 9:00 to 10:15; it is not exercise time. Everyone knows that the only valuable activity in a conventional school at 9:00 a.m. during the back-to-basics "reform" was reading. The music teacher had best not try to interrupt the class schedule; such specialists could end in solitary confinement. It is not wrong if students, teachers, and parents are in this condition by choice. The problem is that most are not there by choice; they are assigned to their "neighborhood school." The reverse picture could be painted for those assigned to some version of an open space site, or a futuristic learning system, when those parents prefer the traditional box. A small minority of schools – less than five percent – throughout the nation during the 60s and 70s attempted to create alternatives to this situation. The task now is for the majority of educators to determine how their individual efforts can help create programs of choice for each student in the public, private, and parochial sectors.

One of the biggest obstacles to creating new learning systems has been a lack of commitment to an innovation philosophy – a concept which is not theoretical. Many teachers and administrators become impatient when new designs are discussed, for they want to know "how" – they do not want the "philosophy." These educators soon are lost, for they do not have an in-depth understanding of the rationale for the changes, and thus quickly say: "We could not do that here," or "We must move more slowly." Before transitions into 21st Century systems can be successful, there truly must be that commitment, and thus, futures orientation stresses comprehension. Once educators understand why, they can turn to what changes, and then how, realizing that the how has two parts: the process and the mechanics.

Too often there is not a meld between theory and practice. There has not been time for those with personal experiences in creating new learning processes to summarize their convictions; those teachers and administrators who meet the day-to-day problems which develop when beginning massive new programs usually do not have the opportunity to write in "accepted journals." Some of the most valuable "how-to-do-it" materials are not on the market simply because those on the firing line do not have publication time and outlets. Most of the books on change currently available in the bookstores have been written by college professors who are not on the daily school production line, or by principals who developed one program, wrote about it, and then went on to other pastures, such as superintendencies, consultantships, college teaching, or private foundations. Very few of the original grass-roots "change agents" – those principals, for example, who started a program in the direction of innovation during the 60s and 70s, are still directing a public school. They left the implementation of these innovations to those who followed them. Fortunately, a few of the younger who were influenced by the accomplishments and research of the 60s are beginning to think of turning to the challenges of the late 90s and early next century.

Most of the "innovative schools" of the mid-90s merely replicated or rejected patterns developed by the innovators two to three decades earlier. A specific example was the demise of modular scheduling. One plan, co-developed by Stanford University and Marshall High in Portland in the 60s, was not necessarily the latest nor the best, but it was a good start; it was lost to the retrenchment which followed; individualized learning and smorgasbord and self-scheduling offered much greater promise. Ironically, now schools are beginning to consider modular scheduling as "new." Speeches given years ago on large and small group methodologies, open labs, unscheduled time, independent study, and open pod facilities are no longer innovative; in many communities they are far out of date. Unfortunately, the concepts are still "brand new" and valid for the great majority of schools, as a transition phase for those who are yet operating traditional programs.

The Nova, Marshall, Ridgewood, Walker, Meadowbrook, Mt. Kisco, Melbourne, Brookhurst, Abington, Evanston, Ferris, Fox Lane, Roy, Foster, Lincoln, Lakeview, University City, Thomas, Oakleaf, Matzke, Metro, Parkway, Canyon del Oro, Wilson, and all the other exploratory schools – the early, exciting 60s attempts to change American education – as good as they were – and still outstanding alternatives when contrasted with existing programs – are not the designs for the 21st Century. However, historically they are important to recognize, as these schools, their teachers, students, and parents – were real pioneers. They changed; they did not always "prove" to be better, but they did prove that educators could create different, optional ways of educating boys and girls. They were in tune then with the now emerging concept of brain compatible learning. Their efforts will not be lost; they provided the breakthrough to enable eventual development of learning systems which will be significantly – in terms of their effect on humans, not just statistically – better.

These early schools cited are no longer "models," or those districts before them in the 20s and 30s – Bluffton, Gary, Nashville, Aliquippa, Winnetka; there is need for new pioneers – to illustrate that though many of the ideas honed years ago in the original staff utilization studies are still applicable, they are only stepping stones for what must come, if education is to assist with the development of a more humane society, a preferable future. Unfortunately, those few schools which did attempt some change in the 80s adopted the empowerment, rigor, core rhetoric of the reports which focused on "past glories" to compete with the Japanese, when the efforts should have been toward the developments of "learning spaceships" for the future. Observers of the current societal scene are not advocating a return to the 1960 models. Instead, they ask questions: where is education headed beyond 2000? How accurate might the mid-60s Philco-Ford production of the movie titled *1999 A.D.*, eventually become, where it was projected that students would attend a "formal" school only two days a week? – a reality which now will not occur until into the next two decades.

Educational futurists are both encouraged and discouraged. They are encouraged by the evidence of commitment in a growing number of schools to at least try new ideas. More are adopting scheduling changes, utilizing computer technology, small group instruction, resource centers, independent study, team teaching, non-grading, teacher aides, and new curriculum materials.

Unfortunately, in most of the sites adopting some mechanical and curricular changes, Johnny and Mary are not receiving significantly better learning, at least not tangible evidence. There seems to have been little impact at the classroom level. Group-paced instruction is yet prevalent; students still get D and F grades; there is the problem of the in-school dropout; many inner city and some rural schools are reminders of failures; the suburban schools, with middle class A and B college-oriented values, are resistant. In examining individual children, teachers, and classrooms, the findings seem to indicate that in only a small percentage of the situations has there been observable improvement. There is evidence that more effort is needed in the affective domain, but the cognitive continues to dominate; the challenge is to interrelate the research related to affective and psychomotor patterns. Explorers as leaders do need to become societal and educational futurists.

The environments where improvements have occurred have provided America with a cadre of educators committed to the idea that schools can and must become learning centers, and that significantly new directions are possible. The task is to decide what changes really are an improvement, and then determine how they can best be implemented. Experimenting with those innovations of the past 40 years, or returning all schools to "fundamental" begs the question. Instead, focus should be on those which beckon in the 21st Century. Refinement of the innovations of the 60s which are still valid can be included as they are interwoven with the future.

There is now a need for maxi-education. Dr. William Alexander, then of the University of Florida, in 1970 described traditional programs as minimum and maximum: mini-eduction, the kind schools have offered for many years, covers the bare essentials, but leaves much to be desired. Midi-education, those attempts made by the team teaching, modular scheduling, open pod efforts of the 60s, cover more and leave less to be desired. Though these mid-reform efforts, which formed only a small portion of the programs in America, were generally great improvements over the mini-schools, they did not go far enough. What Bill Alexander suggested as the next step was the maxi – a school which would cover most all and leave little to be desired; maxi-education would find school programs featuring humaneness, relevancy, options, alternatives, and possible, probable, and preferable futures.

No public school in America is a maxi-school yet; a few have tried to break the lock step of the mini- and midi-restrictions. The new ideas, technology, and developments coming in the early 2000s could make most of the current efforts very obsolete. Educators should dream toward 2009, toward 2020 – and then create the programs which will help transition individuals through the present society, into the world of the 21st Century. The transitions should pave the way for the first decade ahead, for regardless of how "innovative" a school now professes to be, it already belongs in the pages of past educational history.

The coming maxi-school is possible. Educational leaders – whether they now consider themselves mini or midi – must begin further retooling, enabling learning centers to reach the present portraits of maxi-education soon; if they will truly lead, they can prepare their communities for the tremendous, fantastic, revolutionary opportunities which should descend upon education between 2000 and 2020. To launch such an effort, alternatives must be provided within the current public school system. The past three decades witnessed mixed trends: retrenchment toward the "basics;" the open space school; and emerging technological developments. The 90s end the latest 30-year cycle of change – 1900s, 1930s, 1960s – setting the stage for another round of innovations in the early years of the next century – if the optimistic view of the future prevails.

Educational leaders during the transition to a new era need to accomplish three things: (1) undergo a personal transformation – they must change their lifestyles, values, attitudes, and priorities; (2) give leadership to changes in their institutional policies, myths, and practices; and, (3) become long range futures planners.

Several films and books produced during the 70s still have meaning for educators planning ahead. One of the most interesting is *Midway*, not for its superb acting (the book was well written), but for an analysis of how the best laid plans often fail – why good planning often is a matter of "dumb luck." The Japanese had an excellent battle plan, fine leader, superior forces, and every other advantage – on paper. Yet a series of events triggered defeat. They lost sight of their original goal – becoming confused over destruction of the airfield at *Midway*, or destruction of the fleet. Indecision found them loading and unloading torpedoes. Their key leader was too far removed from the battle. They changed plans and sent their inexperienced pilots on the first bombing run over Midway. The U.S. decoded an intercepted message and sent three carriers to Midway, when the Japanese expected them to be at Pearl Harbor. Admiral Nimitz made correct judgments and firm decisions, while the Japanese hesitated. They failed to break radio silence to receive instructions which would have altered the outcome of the battle. Communications systems failed at a crucial time – the radio on the scout plane which spotted the American fleet went dead. And lady luck assisted the U.S. by coincidence, for U.S. dive bombers found three Japanese carriers without air cover; in six minutes the carriers were destroyed.

An excellent plan backfired, and led to a defeat from which the Japanese were never able to recover. Those planning educational change should see and read *Midway*, in an effort to fully understand how the factors of goals, implementation methods, pitfalls, chance, judgment, and decisions all are interwoven and can lead to successful or unsuccessful planning outcomes, as well as anticipating discontinuities: What if the radio fails or the American carriers are at *Midway*?

Futureworld, the Hollywood movie, was another good example of futures planning that can go awry. The City of Delos was planned as a fantastic failsafe human resort, where for $1,200 a day one could obtain the most exotic of all vacations. The potential of robots was well depicted; the world was to be controlled by them, "For the betterment of mankind," according to the scientists who plotted to take over through genetically created human robots. Big Brother became a reality; but the key to all that happened in Delos was not that the machine people were a potential danger out of control, but that humans were the ones who would make the decisions related to whether the world moved toward a preferable future.

A View of America from the 23rd Century was another film for those involved in futures planning. John Gardner played a 23rd Century historian. The discussion centered on how they ever let it happen — "they" being the current inhabitants of the planet who during the last quarter of the 20th Century let catastrophe strike; most of humanity was eliminated through nuclear biochemical war, famine, and other forms of destruction. The 21st Century became one of isolated populations and dictatorial control. The 22nd Century found the population increasing, people coming together, and slowly regaining their freedoms. The 23rd Century became a golden age compared to 1975-2000 A.D.

The key question was raised. Why, with all the intelligence, technology, knowledge, concerned citizens, organizations, and governments could not the people of this period in history prevent disaster, and move into the 21st Century with optimism, and a world better than ever? The message of the film could become a reality, if the wrong plans are developed, and the wrong decisions are made, in the next two decades.

Educational futures planners face many other problems as they look beyond 2000 A.D. One is the "blizzard of paper" facing people today. "Big Brother" advances when it is realized that government organizations, without a court order, can go to a bank and command the financial records of individuals for the past five years. Checks a person writes are on microfilm; there is a computerized locating system; credit card charges are kept on file; long distance phone call records are available. From these records trained analysts can almost recreate the person — describe lifestyle, values, habits. He or she becomes an open book.

The blizzard of paper does not stop there, when one considers the avalanche of forms, copies of directives, memos, advertisements that are dumped on desks daily. Many are beginning to advocate "locking up the reproduction machine." How can futures planners communicate without an overload of paper? Will electronic writing and speaking create the same "paper problem?" Arthur Clarke, writing on communications in 2276, considered the potential impact of the computer in *Imperial Earth*:

> He stared thoughtfully at that little box on the table, with its multitudinous studs and its now darkened readout panel. There lay a device of a complexity beyond all the dreams of earlier ages — a virtual microsimulacrum of human brain. Within it were billions of bits of information, stored in endless atomic arrays, awaiting to be recalled by the right signal . . .

> Duncan walked to the Console, and the screen became alive as his fingers brushed the ON pad. Now it was a miracle beyond the dreams of any poet, a charmed magic casement, opening on all seas, all lands. Through this window could flow everything that Man had ever learned about his universe, and every work of art he had saved from the dominion of Time. All the libraries and

museums that had ever existed could be funnelled through this screen and the millions like it scattered over the face of Earth. Even the least sensitive of men could be overwhelmed by the thought that one could operate a Console for a thousand lifetimes – and barely sample the knowledge stored within the memory banks that lay triplicated in their widely separated caverns.

The issues for educational leaders for the future do not stop with robots and computers. How do they cope with current values? While thousands in the U.S. are destitute, 100,000 people pour into the Super Bowl at high prices, while another 75 million watch on TV. The networks pay millions to televise the game. Companies shell out multiple thousands per minute to advertise, some of the products being of questionable value for society – soft drinks full of sugar and caffeine; beer; and automobiles, not built as safe, pollution-free, and energy-saving as possible. Television equipment valued at millions is used, not to mention the sums spent on the half time shows, and all the parties and hoopla of the prior week.

The issue here is not that a football game is wrong – seen by large crowds and televised; economically, many jobs are provided. Sports have been a healthy part of the culture in the past, but can they continue to be under the conditions of the Super Bowl? Can values allow homelessness and poverty in the U.S., while baseball and basketball players – not to mention corporation executives – are individually annually paid millions?

Educational futures planners cannot solve each ill of society. They will be plagued with the problems of planning as witnessed through the review of *Midway*; they will face the blizzard of paper – the communications/involvement syndrome; they will face the issue of personal and societal ethics and values in the coming decades.

Perhaps it will be impossible to change education in the public schools in time to make a difference. William Irwin Thompson in *Darkness and Scattered Light*, questioned possible success: "Many times it is a waste of energies to try to innovate from within, to try to reform the system. Those energies are better spent outside the system creating in a pure and free form the counterfoil institution. If we look at innovation through history, this has been the case, even of people in institutions. The innovative individuals have always been marginal personalities who somehow or other are protected by other marginal personalities from the institution itself. They generally conflict with the bureaucracy, or the theocracy of the priests who are trying to maintain the old paradigm."

Conversely, Willard Wirtz, former Secretary of Labor, stated: "I see the prospects of change coming through the educational rather than the political processes. At least in the immediate present, it is not going to be possible to change the habits of political leadership enough. So I fall back on the necessity of changing the capacities and the attitudes of the political membership. And, at that point, it becomes largely a matter of what the educators can do."

As discouraging or as encouraging as these quotations may be, if there is any hope, some educators, somewhere in the public schools, must create beginnings, if transformations are to occur. The immediate transitions will be difficult; whether the first decade of the 21st Century becomes one of crises or opportunities may partly hinge on the response of the education community. There are no guaranteed steps or solutions which ensure administrator success in the efforts — only commitment that futures planners can be catalysts by leading transitions into the 21st Century.

To accomplish this mission, needed are different patterns of curricula, school organizations, human relationships, focus on the adult-youngster, adult-adult, and youngster-youngster roles, perceptions, and relations. The adult may be "labeled" teacher, consultant, advisor, counselor. The youngster may be a student, learner, person, child, he or she. These intermixed terminologies should be no barrier, for usually a concept is learned best when it is taught; therefore the learner should be a teacher, and the teacher a learner. The key factors are learning, the enjoyment, the process, and the human relationships which are established between two or more persons who are learning together. Most important is the emergence of educational leaders who can comprehend the societal crises facing the nation, envision the implications for education, and devise the means to allow people to move toward the future in alternative ways, but with common bonds of preservation.

It will not be easy. As Benjamin Levine reminded the world in *He Who Spits Against the Wind*, the writer of *Common Sense*, the writer of the first draft of the Declaration of Independence (including a provision against slavery), the inspirational writer for much of the early spirit of the French Revolution, the man who some label a combination of St. Francis, Thoreau, King, and Ghandi — died a man without a country. Innovative leaders will often have to face the consequences of a Tom Paine, but if many become risk takers, speak out on the future, and provide a community focus on the crucial questions of the time, the fate of Paine may be avoided; a critical mass of individuals is required.

However, in becoming an educational risk taker, the individual must remember that when Tom died in New York in 1809, at the age of 72, no one came to the funeral. His landlady, a Frenchwoman whose husband Paine had befriended in France, and who was devoted to him, arranged for the transport of his body to a small farm he owned in New Rochelle, and there he was buried, while only Madame Bonneville and her two small sons stood watching, and weeping.

What had Paine done to deserve such a fate from Americans who owed him, as much as any single individual, the freedom that is now enjoyed by millions? Are current educational leaders willing to state what they believe, even if it is not politically expedient? For all Tom Paine did was state his beliefs in the *Age of Reason*:

I believe in the equality of man; and I believe that religious duties consist in doing justice, loving mercy, and endeavoring to make our fellow creature happy.

All national institutions of churches, whether Jewish, Christian, or Turkish, appear to me no other than human inventions, set up to terrify and enslave mankind . . .

I do not mean by this declaration to condemn those who believe otherwise; they have the same right to their belief as I have to mine. But it is necessary to the happiness of man, that he be mentally faithful to himself. Infidelity does not consist in believing or disbelieving; it consists in professing to believe what he does not believe!

Futurists remind that in the current world and educational conditions, "Imagination is more important than knowledge." They recommend that, "In a universe full of copycats, it is important to be an original."

In *Multiple Intelligences*, (1983), Howard Gardner related that his ideal school of the future would be based on the assumption that not all people have the same interests and not all learn the same way. The chapters on nurturing multiple intelligence are of interest, as are many of his ideas, but unfortunately, he still focused on schools as if they would be the mode in 2100.

Buckminster Fuller, in *Cosmography*, (1992), published after his death, believed that "People are powerfully imprisoned in Dark Ages simply by the terms they have been conditioned to accept." As high technology has the capability of taking care of the needs of everyone on the planet, the prerequisite of having to earn a living becomes obsolete. There are adequate resources to care for and sustain all at a higher standard of living.

People are excited about projections in such books as *Airport Cities 21: New Global Transport Centers*, (1993). Supersonic transports are well accepted, as are aircraft that carry 2,000 passengers, and a five-star categorical system of classifying airports for the future. If new "airport cities" are needed for the 21st Century, why should not educational designers create "learning centers" for the next decades.

Peter Drucker in *The Ecological Vision*, (1993), claims that he is not a futurist, but a "social ecologist," a new breed of viewers of the emerging scene whose role is to identify the changes that have already happened – to perceive and analyze those irreversible trends that have not yet had an impact and are not yet generally seen. The job is not to create knowledge but to create vision. The social ecologist must be an educator. The concept may be one of the missing components in assisting educational leaders to risk their future in "imagineering" learning for the 21st Century. This could be their legacy for those who follow in the coming decades.

Fred Bratton, a model of "by his fruits ye shall know him," was rejected as a minister by church after church because he did not profess the "required rituals;" he dared to explain the human political decisions that created the current forms of Christianity – and how, for illustration, the majority belief could easily have been Unitarian rather than Trinitarian, had the balance of voting bishops been skewed toward the Unity. But he finally found a church in West Springfield, and a college called Springfield (Massachusetts), where he could interpret religious freedom. Needed now are educational leaders who can interpret educational freedom as "essential," if there are to be created very different and very better learning systems for a new golden age for people in the coming decades of future history.

PART IV

DOCUMENTING WILSON

chapter twenty-seven

HISTORY

Historical perspectives reflecting potential alternative futures acknowledge the symbolism of those who dare to inspire and challenge. Education leaders, facing the uncertainties of beyond 2000, can gain courage from numerous literary societal idealists and visionaries.

Representing this spirit at Wilson were Don Quixote, fighting windmills and honoring chivalry; Figment – that precious purple dragon – and his friend Dreamfinder, guiding dreamers through the Epcot Journey into Imagination; Willie Wonka, offering the inventiveness of his chocolate factory and the magic of his wonderful golden wrapped bars; and Lucy and Charlie Brown, clarifying that it is finally time to determine which way the deck chairs are facing and learn how to unfold them on the cruise ship, EDUCATION. Such luminaries mirror all who envision realities out of dreams and dreams out of realities – who become the dreamers of the dreams for transitioning from schooling to learning.

Wilson was based upon Camelots of the past, but was conceived for the future; it tried to help create new systems. Wilson validated that the effort to "restructure schools" could not generate the responses needed to significantly alter educational and societal futures. The eight components of history – Disturbing Images, Startling Practices, Exciting Designs, Realistic Leadership, Delightful Research, Enjoyable Change, Preferable Futures, and Rewarding References – document this conclusion. They also offer springboards toward quantum overleaps for those willing to do the "impossible."

Disturbing Images

The national education reforms championed in the 1980s and front 1990s were obsolescent when proposed. Ironically, this condition gave guarded optimism for creating new learning futures; the difficult task became moving beyond reinventing the past. The existing studies, which provided ample evidence for eliminating many of the conventions of schooling, were reinforced by the majority of students who readily admitted that they cheated in their high school and college classes – especially in their weak and personally irrelevant required subjects – to pass, earn scholarships, or gain recognition.[1]

The traditional wisdom "innovations" suggested for "restructuring" were available throughout the entire 20th Century; even the best ones that should have been rapidly adopted were merely old wine in refurbished wineskins. It was already known that the heralded political rhetoric such as rigorous core curriculum, more homework, and site based management would not cause major improvements. The America 2000 plan announced by then President Bush in April, 1991, was but one example of the dichotomy facing communities.[2] His outline for better and more accountable schools, with emphasis on higher standards in math, science, English, history, and geography, measured by new national achievement tests, had little chance of enhancing education. It was no surprise that he was not able to become the "Education President" – his 1988 announced goal.

Further, the Clinton Goals 2000 project based on the six national goals adopted by the Governors when he chaired the project while still in Arkansas, seems doomed to the same fate. It is still based upon politics and traditional schools, though the emphasis on flexibility may yet allow for some success.

History

The Bush plan to establish academies to train teachers in five core courses; the advocacy for improving literacy, work force readiness, and adult education; and the effort toward coordinating local, state, federal, and private child and family services was noble in intent, but, as structured, would not create significant change. Expanding choice, done correctly, should have been accomplished within the public school districts long before the concept became the proverbial political football and entered the private sector. The two rays of optimism — the three to seven research programs, and the 535 models — were both dimmed by the focus on creating a new generation of schools! If, instead, the concepts had involved inventing the future toward a day when schools no longer existed, the national educational focus could have envisioned beyond the multitude of reports, articles, books, and projects promoting the restructuring and revitalizing of an airplane that should not be flying.[3,4,5,6]

Previous change efforts in education have seemingly evolved in 30-year cycles. In the 1840s, urban schools were open 250 days. In the 1870s, the vacation schools were organized. In the early 1900s, the proposals by John Dewey and Carleton Washburne and the work at the University of Chicago Laboratory School, and at Winnetka, Illinois, among others, led to individualization.[7,8] In the 1930s, change struck the education scene again, with the Ohio State University Laboratory School reflecting the *Eight-Year Study* and many of the other national experimental modes of that era.[10] The designs of the 60s led to the existing alternatives models, further reflecting dissatisfaction with the established practices.[11,12]

In prior centuries, innovative learning reforms were advocated by such writers and philosophers as Froebel, Rousseau, Pestalozzi, Emerson, and Thoreau;[13] in the recent past by such as Freire, Holt, Pearce, Kohl, Kozol, Neill, Dennison, Trump, Jennings, and Glines; and currently through organized efforts as portrayed by the holistic education, the Center for Reform in Education, and brain-based learning networks.[14] Related to the 30-year repetition in the change cycle, societal and educational futurists long projected the turn of the century as a tremendous period of societal ferment, and thus a major opportunity to not only revamp the education system, but all of society.[15,16,17] They have given hope to this era as the transition period away from the industrial age lifestyles and schooling patterns toward the ultimate transformation to a significantly better society — and learning beyond schooling.[18,19] Futurists have called for the establishment of NASA concept space centers for education — a commitment to true research and development.[20]

With such evidence already available entering the 1990s, questions surfaced: (1) How could educators continue the existing K-12 conventions, which had only tradition and minimal research to support the practices? (2) How could it be argued that restructuring schools would make a difference, when a century of experience indicated the contrary? (3) How could Congress spend another 535 million dollars on "new model schools," when schooling was already suspect? (4) Why should business contribute 300 million dollars to "beat the Japanese," when economic competition should not be the goal of learning? and, (5) Why should there be a need for a private, for-profit national school system, as proposed by several entrepreneurs? Responses would include the belief that there is not time to study and reject again ideas that have been proven, and that the true innovations of the past, if quickly implemented, would allow educational inventors to focus on entirely new lifelong living/learning systems.

Startling Practices

There are many startling practices which validate the futures position. As illustration, research favoring the graded classroom concept is scarce. The evidence that is available on school organization has supported non-graded/multi-aged teams and centers for decades. The Goodlad and Anderson classic, *The Non-graded Elementary School*, summarized the data in 1959.[21,90] The Mankato Wilson Campus School, in 1968, proved the practice by mixing pre-K through college students in the same rooms, with the same instructors and philosophy; however, school districts continued the graded pattern. Now, in another cycle, non-grading is becoming popular again as confirmed by the 1992 publication by Anderson and Pavan, *Nongradedness: Helping it to Happen.*[94] It is time to realize that multi-age groupings better conform with child growth and development at all levels, and rapidly adopt the practice. Then creative people can create the step beyond non-grading for the 21st Century.

The promotion of the junior high (grades 7-8-9) proved to be a mistake, especially since the underlying reason was to appease a housing problem in the 1930s. In the 60s, a group of inventors designed the middle school for youth chronologically approximately 10-14 (traditional Grades 5-8), knowing that achievement levels were spread from Grades 2-12.[22,23] It was to feature non-graded interdependent curriculum teams, pod-oriented facilities, individualized evaluation, daily flexible schedules, an affective domain focus, much choice and freedom, and teachers whose compassions were with that age group.

Some of the original middle schools (Mt. Kisco, N.Y.; Barrington, Ill; Indian Hills, Beechwood, and Lima, Ohio), were headed in that direction. Unfortunately, nationally the concept became a space salvation. With declining enrollments, the 9th grade was moved back to the high school; educators debated whether to include Grades 5 and 6 or just 6 (the latter usually won). They failed to implement the planned curriculum reform.[24] They did, however, proceed to change the name over the door from junior high to middle, and ruined the greatest chance in 50 years to invent an entirely new happening in education. The original plans still hold promise for improving the life of long suffering 7th graders; if the 60s concepts were rapidly adopted, educators would then be free to design the replacement for the middle school beyond 2000.

Report cards – A, B, C, D, F and O, E, S, U, NI modifications – have no place in learning. They destroy self-image, create super-egos, segregate students, and are of no value to the learning process. In the 60s, Mankato Wilson School eliminated all grades, Carnegie units, class ranks, and other badges of courage; students learned, behaved, graduated, went to college, found jobs, married.[25] The evidence was conclusive; similar experiments from the 30s were thus reinforced. There is no need to restructure report cards; instead the practice should be dropped in favor of Wilson-style evaluation methods for use during the transition, while creative people invent for the future.

Authentic assessment is not new. The open concept schools of the 60s did not give multiple choice or true false tests. Most did not test at all, but when they did it was a comprehensive written examination, oral explanation, or portfolio. The Scholastic Aptitude Test results and group basic skills tests were ignored as being irrelevant. Wilson gave no traditional tests, but instead asked students to perform, explain, process, think, clarify – but not respond to rote exams. The important aspect of education is the growth of the individual, not a comparison with others, or a system to determine entrance to college.

Phi Delta Kappa, in 1991 and 1992, sponsored two conferences on a "critical issue:" Tracking and Ability Grouping. Why would a leading education organization need to support such a summit in the 90s, when the evidence in 1925 indicated that students were not helped academically, and were hurt socially. After extensive studies from 1910 to 1920 of low income inner-city youth in Detroit, Los Angeles, and London, and more affluent students in Winnetka, Iowa City, and San Francisco, among others, the *24th Yearbook of the National Society for the Study of Education* stated: "No one at all conversant with the facts can avoid the conviction that the mass instruction of pupils and the promotion of them in large groups . . . whatever merits they may have administratively, leave much to be desired pedagogically . . . children do not fall into permanent natural ability groupings so that they may be taught in a class of homogenous ability . . . for even the best ability grouping does not fit individual differences."[26]

Schools of the 1930s and 60s which acknowledged the research eliminated forms of tracking; only ad hoc, special interest, or as needed groups were utilized. Cooperative learning and collaborative teaching were widely used, but not "named," as individualizing learning experiences through excellent teaming and differentiated staffing required five threads: one-to-one interaction, small groups of various diversities, open laboratory, independent study, and occasional common-thread large group presentations.

Mankato Wilson in the 60s was heavily involved in volunteering; students of all ages assisted in homes for the elderly, the state mental hospital, the local hospital, preschool programs – anywhere in the community where caring was a special need. Volunteering was more important than mathematics. Senior citizens were in the building continuously as volunteer aides and as learners. The staff eliminated textbook sets, and instead spent the money on purchasing 12 passenger vans to facilitate the two-way school in the community – community in the school – programs. Students took courses at Mankato State. Some graduated from Wilson with one or two years of college credit. Even elementary youth took college work; the actual credits were awarded when they entered a university – and this was three decades past. Yet, reaching into 2000, nationally most students still spend the day at a neighborhood site in traditional classrooms listening to a "teacher."

The period 1-2-3 secondary school industrial factory model schedule, and the 9:00-10:15 reading; 10:15-10:30 potty time; 10:30-11:20 math; and 11:20-11:50 lunch and bus-determined schedule for primary students, have been known to be inappropriate for many years. Yet, as early as 1968, Wilson was able to develop a K-12 daily smorgasbord schedule, and later a non-scheduled learning format, as did Bishop Ryan High School in Omaha. Prior to that, in 1963, Brookhurst Jr. High in Anaheim, and the Canyon del Oro Secondary and Walker Elementary in Tucson, developed less sophisticated daily scheduling for all students and teachers. What appeared on the surface to be very unstructured programs, were more structured than the traditional, but in a manner that provided for responsibility, choice, and self-directed learning.

The inflexible flexible weekly patterns of the Indy-Flex, GASP, and Stanford computer assisted schedules were adopted by Marshall High in Portland, Ridgewood in Chicago, Virgin Valley in Utah, University City in Missouri, Huron in South Dakota, Abington in Pennsylvania, and numerous other high schools in the 60s. Educators knew then that the 50-minute period, five-days-a-week scheduling process was wrong, yet most secondary schools continue to follow this extremely poor practice. All classes do not need to meet in the same size group, for the same amount of time each day, for 36 weeks. A foreign language cannot be learned under this arrangement. Utilizing time more wisely can be a learning experiment into the 21st Century.

To create a non-scheduled environment, curriculum must be personalized and individualized. Students develop their own learning patterns, as evidenced in *Adapting the Schools to Individual Differences*, where research from 1914 was cited: "Individualization of instruction improves efficiency through increasing the number of children who profit, and decreasing the number who fail or are adversely affected . . . the net result of individualization increased the achievement of the group as a whole." In 1921, Helen Parkhurst summarized one practical method to implementing such an approach when she described *The Dalton Laboratory Plan*.[26]

The research and experiments from these earlier efforts – and related to exploration for the future – summarizes why the K-12 Wilson made the changes described, including no required courses, group-paced classes, or traditional graduation requirements. The data also explains why football and drama were as important as science, and why the program was so student centered: why the youth selected the adults with whom to learn, selected their own advisors, designed their interest and need studies, scheduled their own time on a daily basis, participated in interdependent curriculum activities, spent many hours volunteering in the community, and went to Mexico for two months each year to study Spanish. They did not miss anything, for when they returned they continued their other individualized learning experiences. The Mexican exchange youth came to Mankato for a month. Sister school international programs have been part of good education for decades; the concept is not "reform."

One key to the Wilson success was student involvement in the process; faculty members were considered friends and helpers, usually on a first name basis. Youths and adults liked their environment; they tried to come to the program even when sick. They learned to live the adopted motto: "With freedom goes responsibility" – and with those, courtesy and commitment. Most current restructuring projects are national organization, community, administration, teacher involved, doing it for – rather than with – the students.

Implementing humane learning creates a need for year-round education. It has been unprofessional to close schools in July and August. Would the medical profession recommend closing the hospitals in the summer? Since 1968, year-round programs have flourished, proving how unnecessary and illogical the September to June calendar, yet most schools still perpetuate such a time frame. Lifestyles and societal conditions demand continuous learning opportunities. Conferences are not needed on the sense of being open year-round, as the philosophy is not restructuring, but only a confirmation of an educationally sound practice that should have been adopted long ago. William Wirt recognized this in 1904 when, as superintendent in Bluffton, Indiana, he implemented a rotating continuous calendar, based upon the historically famous "platoon system." It will soon be 2004.[32]

The great debates on choice and learning styles further validate the obsolescence of reform. The original concept of alternative was "alternatives," in the plural. Each district was to offer a wide range of options open to all students within the public school sector – from liberal to conservative. Had this been done on a national scale, there would be little controversy surrounding choice, private schools, business, segregation, religious issues, and vouchers. "Alternatives" was never intended as the now commonly used notion of an "alternative school" – usually for dropouts or "marginal" students – nor was it intended to be part of the desegregation efforts to overcome white flight from the inner cities, or a magnet traditional school recruiting students for one curriculum focus. The Southeast Alternatives Project in Minneapolis in the 60s/70s, where elementary students were in a cluster concept – a complete neighborhood choice of fundamental, continuous progress, open, and free school programs – proved the validity. In the beginning of educational alternatives nationally, in most good open schools, students chose their own teachers and advisors based upon six factors – perception, age, gender, interest, skill, and personality – long before the learning styles workshops became popular.[10, 42]

These programs realized the affective domain was by far the most important factor in school success, followed by the psychomotor. The least important proved to be the cognitive, especially reading and math at the primary level. If students were in gear in the affective and psychomotor, the cognitive was not a problem, if the experience was introduced at the proper time – the research on the "teachable moment." At Mankato Wilson, some children could read at age three; others were not in a structured reading program even at age nine. The early Greek culture acknowledged this factor, as the Athenian society focused upon physical and social maturation until age ten.[27] Now for many schools in America, the first priorities need to be breakfast and lunch, washers and dryers, and clean and warm clothing. The growing problems of homelessness and abused children reduce the cognitive imperative.

With personal and world economic wealth and power at the center of so many national, state, and local political education discussions, it is easy to overlook the fact that the failures in the savings and loan industry, the expensive political junkets, the construction of minimally safe cars, the polluted air and water, and the families in poverty are problems of the affective domain, not the cognitive and lower test scores than students in Japan. Toxic chemical dumping was orchestrated by college graduates. So, too, was the Nazi effort to exterminate millions in the gas chambers, in a nation even then recognized for its excellence in conventional core curriculum disciplines.

Many have long recognized that the ongoing election years rhetoric for more traditional requirements and higher standards is not the answer. Over 50 years ago, in 1938, the Education Policies Commission of the National Education Association stated: "In a democracy struggling against strangulation by a myriad of urgent, real human problems focusing on learning that the sum of the square of two numbers equals the sum of them squared plus twice the product, might be appropriate for some, but for the great majority of boys and girls, such learning is transitory, and of extremely little "value."[28] Yet in the 90s, schools remained trapped by new curriculum saviors as "the gospel" according to the current popular projects – and such verbiage as "Integrated learning." Futures learning should be much more eclectic in nature; good ideas should be taken from many sources and tailored to the individual, not the group.

The triangle used by YM/YWCAs denoting that the whole person is a composite of the spirit, mind, and body sets the stage for significant transitions. If the affective, cognitive, and psychomotor are interwoven on an interdependent basis, confluency evolves in the triangle, and former "academic" and "non-academic" disciplines become one. Knowledge is not segmented; it is interrelated. There is no core curriculum that makes sense for all children in the same age span. The cognitive push for reading and math in the young ages is contra-indicated for large numbers of youth. This is especially true for students with environmental illness, and perhaps those children of drug-addicted pregnancies.

As documented in *The Impossible Child* and *Is This Your Child*, a significant number of students suffer from chemical and food intolerances.[29] They are allergic to paint, perfume, and carpet fumes; to such common staples as milk, wheat, corn, oranges, and eggs; and to such factors as dust, grass, and mold. Many of the learning and behavior problems, as well as so many borderline special education students, are victims of reactions to foods, chemicals, and inhalants. Innovative leaders suggest that health and safety specifics are the only "must learn" core requirements; these, combined with the self-image affective domain curriculum components, can make a far greater difference in the lives of people. Reading and math are important in the society, but the cognitive areas cannot compare with first ensuring the human essentials.

Such philosophical, experiential, and research supported beliefs are why physical education should be the most important traditional curriculum component in the K-2 years, followed closely by complete programs in home economics, industrial technology, music, and art – gross and fine motor development. In 1991, the President's Council on Physical Fitness announced alarming "misfitness" among American youth. Yet this same cry arose in the 1950s when the Council was first established. In 1956, the Iowa, Oregon and Indiana studies, using the Kraus-Weber Test of Minimum Muscular Fitness, verified low scores at the elementary level, as did the Oregon secondary studies utilizing the Rogers Physical Fitness Index. Dr. H. Harrison Clarke of the University of Oregon further documented these results during a 15-year longitudinal study of child growth and development in the Medford, Oregon, schools (1957-1962).[30] Thirty years after the Oregon studies, few physical education programs have improved, yet models of how to achieve excellence in this field have been available since the establishment of Springfield College, Massachusetts, in 1885 – an institution designed to focus on this component of development.

In the current literature, for those preparing for restructuring, the recommendation is for strategic planning. Once again, the significant schools of the 60s followed a process of looking ahead without naming it. In 1966, when the World Future Society was formed, the purposes were to study the potential societal conditions, encourage long range planning, and create preferable futures.[31] The recent concepts of strategic planning, quality circles, cooperative learning, student styles, collaborative teaching, integrated curriculum, and authentic assessment, among others, paired with the renewed interest in non-grading and year-round education, are not well understood philosophically – only expediently – by the majority. They are not new, as there were many successful mirrors of these practices in the 60s/70s, based on experiences from the 30s. Further, strategic planning that does not adequately provide for discontinuities, does not guarantee success, as the Japanese learned when they lost the Battle of Midway, in spite of overwhelming odds; innovators have discovered that "good planning is often dumb luck," as realized by the American forces at Midway.

Why should "strategic planning" be needed to consider year-round eduction, almost a century later? Why should educators need to rediscover such "new" patterns, or finally realize that many of the delivery systems of the one-room schoolhouse were superior to most "modern" traditional segmented patterns. Even the current technological capabilities have not been well utilized. In 1968, Mankato Wilson had six year olds on the computer terminal. Yet, there existed in the early 90s elementary schools where students received no computer instruction, nor did the teacher integrate technology into the classroom curriculum. There are still many efficient schools; there are a number that are effective; there are only a few that are truly significant.

In 1973, a suburban Philadelphia high school principal who advocated significance was released.[33] He wanted to organize four optional schools-within-a-school, with multiple small satellites in two of them. One of the negative factors cited was his effort, without the support of the teacher union, to create a full-time position for an expert in technology to lead the development of a technological infusion into all the curriculum, with the very latest equipment, software, teacher training, and ongoing updating. It was to be an exemplary national model. Ironically, the 1993 Technology Master Plan for California Schools advocated much of what was proposed by this principal 20 years earlier. Futurists ask why educators and communities have been so reluctant to accept what has been known and encouraged by societal and educational change agents for several decades.

Exciting Designs
The Wilson Campus School, from 1968 to 1977, was considered as the most innovative experimental public school in the United States.[34,10] The staff did everything wrong, backward, and upside down, if judged by conventional wisdom, yet the program proved beyond a doubt that going far beyond traditional instructional patterns proved to be highly successful for those enrolled students. Their experiences confirmed that "if schools are to be significantly better, they must be significantly different." Wilson was not alone, but rather a contemporary of a number of other similar exciting research and development designs. These later 60s, earlier 70s programs, borrowed heavily from previous pioneers. The schools of the *Eight-Year Study* in the 1930s contributed – the Ohio State University Lab School being one – and from the same era, the history of the Gary, Indiana, district during the tenure of Superintendent William Wirt. Wilson also borrowed from the 1900s University of Chicago lab school, and the 1912 Newark, New Jersey; the 1925 Nashville, Tennessee; and the 1928 Aliquippa, Pennsylvania, year-round programs.

From the late 50s/early 60s, it adopted ideas from the non-graded elementary school programs in Milwaukee, and the non-graded high school at Melbourne, Florida. Much was adopted from Walker School, perhaps the most exciting elementary program in the United States during the early 60s, and from its companion secondary program in Tucson, Arizona, the Canyon del Oro Jr. Sr. High, where the staff co-developed with Brookhurst in Anaheim, the first national daily flexible scheduling processes in 1963. Wilson utilized ideas from Ridgewood High School in Norridge, Illinois, and Bishop Ryan High School in Omaha, perhaps two of the top five secondary schools in the United States in the early 60s devoted to innovation, change, and experimentation. The Nova Complex in Fort Lauderdale, Florida, added to the knowledge base.

Surprisingly, the most dramatic statewide effort from 1967-70 to change (restructure/reform three decades ago), was in, "of all places," South Dakota, where schools had been ranked near the bottom in many traditional evaluations related to money spent and the acceptance of innovations. The Title III consortium programs in Watertown, Huron, Brookings, Sisseton, and Waubey brought visitors from throughout the country,

239

especially to see the Lincoln Learning Laboratory in Watertown, and the nationally recognized individualized home economics curriculum at Brookings High School.[36]

The most exciting school district for change and innovation in the United States in the mid-60s was in University City, Missouri.[37] There an attempt was made to rapidly and significantly overhaul all K-12 schools, using curriculum reform – ITA reading, Piaget early childhood, interrelated teams, Unipacs, and the elimination of departmentalization in the secondary; daily and modular scheduling; revamping of all facilities, including tearing down 67 walls in 13 buildings between August-December, 1965; new resource media centers in every school; a national model for team teaching and schools-within-a-school; professional development center concepts; improved teacher education relationships with Washington University of St. Louis; and research projects to document the impact of such reforms in conjunction with the federally funded regional CEMREL Educational Laboratory in St. Louis.

Contemporary 60s/70s programs also included the efforts at the St. Paul Open School in Minnesota; the School of Tomorrow design in Glen Cove, New York; the Berkeley, Minneapolis, and Franklin Pierce (Tacoma) federally funded alternatives efforts; the Individually Prescribed Instruction (IPI) structure in Pittsburgh; the districtwide innovations in Cherry Creek, Colorado; the modular schedule models at numerous secondary schools, including one of the better overall efforts at Abington (PA) High; the K-12 locations identified by the Kettering Foundation as "programs worth visiting;" and later, such NASSP Model Schools Project sites as Bishop Carroll High School in Calgary and Wilde Lake in Columbia, Maryland.

At Mankato State, an undergraduate teacher education program was added to the Wilson Campus School. It was possible to earn a teaching certificate without taking college education classes, by interning at Wilson; thus this new Studios for Educational Alternatives (SEA) option gave direction to learning and teaching in an entirely different context. Attached to this effort was the first nationally accredited master degree program in Experiential Education – 48 quarter hours with no requirements – a design your own, do it your way high standards North Central Association accredited graduate degree. Classroom leaders were assisted to become facilitators and advisors, not "teachers," and to envision the potential of a transformation.

Though most innovations were lost during the political backlash campaigns of the late 70s and the 80s, the involved states, universities, communities, districts, and schools proved the value of immediately shifting away from conventional practices for many youth. Thirty years after these documented results, 60 years after the *Eight-Year Study*, and 90 years after the concept of year-round education, educators and politicians are calling for Plan 2000, restructuring, and reform, when all the evidence, techniques, and concepts were available decades ago.[38,39] Designing new learning systems for the future, not planning for revising old schooling practices, holds greater promise for beyond 2000.

<u>Realistic Leadership</u>
Major credit for past reform efforts must go to one of the truly great educators of this century, Dr. J. Lloyd Trump. In 1960, his book, *Images of the Future*, clarioned the need.[40] In the same year, the National Association for Secondary School Principals (NASSP) produced his film titled, *And No Bells Ring*, depicting how much better a high school could be without bells or chimes. Thirty years later, the hourly noise still dominated

most secondary campuses. Even a strong call from their own organization could not convince secondary leaders to do something as simple as turn the switch to off – not a monumental feat of restructuring – but terribly significant, in that if a faculty would not consider silencing the bells, how could it be expected that change of a substantive nature would ever occur in education.

Lloyd Trump, from his role as Associate Secretary of NASSP during much of the 1960 to 1980 era, traveled the country – lecturing, encouraging, calling for dramatically different formats – and directing the Danforth Foundation funded Model Schools Project to assist principals and staffs to become agents of change. Lloyd Trump catalogued his concepts in a landmark book, *A School For Everyone* – already forgotten by the majority of administrators.[41] He went far beyond calling for the "excitement" of core curriculum, rigor, homework, and a longer school day; he focused on the learning opportunities for individual students. Eugene Howard, one of the disciples of Dr. Trump, developed a pioneering model of the proposals at Ridgewood High in Norridge, Illinois, long before "restructuring" became a political football involving the White House, National Governors Association, American Federation of Teachers, National School Boards Association, and most of the other advocacy organizations.

Trump and Howard were not alone; many other visionaries joined the 60s/70s efforts with their own designs. They included Evelyn Carswell, principal at the famous Walker School in Tucson; Wayne Jennings, creator of the nationally recognized St. Paul Open School; Robert Finley, innovative superintendent at both Barrington, IL, and Glen Cove, N.Y.; Virginia Roth, principal of the Omaha non-scheduled Bishop Ryan High School; Ann Grooms, educational consultant pioneer of almost every reform of the 60s/70s; Glen Ovard, professor and designer of the first computerized daily demand schedule at Brigham Young University lab school; Dwight Allen, dean of the exciting graduate school of education at the University of Massachusetts; William Alexander, professor at the University of Florida, leader of efforts to reform the high school and, with Emmett Williams of Florida and a small national group, a catalyst for the invention of the middle school; Gardner Swensen, principal at Brookhurst Jr. High in Anaheim, and co-creator of daily flexible scheduling and the Unipac development; Mary Anne Raywid, professor at Hofstra University and spokesperson for alternatives – with a plural(s) – in education; Joe Nathan, educational consultant and champion of schools of choice; John Jenkins, principal of the model Wilde Lake High School in Columbia, Maryland; and David Beggs, professor at Indiana and early leader in structured flexible scheduling – all three decades before the heralded "Charter Schools" legislation.

This roll call of 60s/70s reformers further includes the wonderful William Van Til, whose precious book, *My Way of Looking at It*,[45] clearly stated the need for educational change, and historically preserved the work of the lab schools of the 30s; Robert Anderson and John Goodlad, who in 1959 in *The Non-Graded Elementary School*, documented the need to adopt multi-age grouping patterns; James Nickerson, Kent Alm, Merlin Duncan, and Brendan McDonald, four administrators who almost succeeded in overhauling an entire university of 14,000 at Mankato State; John Holt, Herbert Kohl, Jonathan Kozol, and George Dennison who represented the insights offered by the perceived "radicals" of the 60s; the many private school educators who continued the concepts of Maria Montessori, Rudolf Steiner, and A.S. Neil (*Summerhill*); and Don Glines who was the first person hired as a "vice-president for heresy" to create change in an entire school district.

History

The many leaders of educational innovations in the 60s tried to portray significantly better practices based upon the research available to them from the innovators of the 20s and 30s, and their own desire to invent better learning opportunities for youth and adults. Too often current politician educators have denied the existence of such inventions and have promoted reinvention of practices that will not make a positive difference (curriculum frameworks, more rigor, national examinations), rather than adopting promising practices (continuous learning, individualizing, affective domain) or overleaping these 30s and 60s concepts to focus on the potential created by the growing shifts in societal paradigms.

An early 90s effort of the Education Commission of the States included a national forum on the concept that "all kids can learn." Ironically, that perception was already a hallmark of the 30s and 60s reforms, and one of the reasons that futurists have pioneered interdependent learning and an end to segmented curriculum disciplines; it is why such schools as Mankato Wilson mainstreamed special education students in the 60s, and partially explains why most gifted students are bored with their classes.[43,93] Certainly late is better than never, but understanding that all students can learn is another illustration of old wine in a different wineskin – as is the sad new term, "inclusion education."

Most defenders of the status quo, or of a go-slow change process, cite community resistance. Advocates believe that "reshaping schooling" – as promoted by the Association of Supervision and Curriculum Development[44] – will be accepted by the voters; that by improving existing Chapter 1 programs, math curricula, textbooks, test scores, and discipline; and by lowering dropout rates and class size with increased financial support, educational problems will be solved for the near future 2000. Conversely, most societal and educational futurists promote rapid adoption of the better documented practices of the past now for the majority, while volunteers within a win/win philosophy, in experimental environments, invent the future. They believe educators have a responsibility to educate communities regarding the need to replace the structure of schooling.

Delightful Research
The major studies that so influenced Wilson are especially important to reemphasize when considering historical futures. In reviewing the lessons from the previous decades, the most significant of all overlooked research in education was the *Eight-Year Study*, launched in April, 1930, when 200 educators met in Washington, D.C.;[46] the implementation design began in the Fall, 1933, involving 30 of the best high schools and 300 of the best colleges. In 1936, the first 2,000 of the *Eight-Year* participants entered 179 colleges. Prior to the study, an evaluation indicated that "most graduates were not competent in the use of the English language; the majority seldom read and were unable to express themselves effectively in speech or writing. The teachers, as a whole, were not well equipped for their responsibilities. The principals and teachers worked hard, but had no real measure of whether they had met the objectives, affective needs, and interests of their students." Similar comments were made by critics of education in 1990 – 60 years later.

The participating sites utilized schools-within-schools; student-teacher advisor systems; student grouping on the basis of mutual interests; written reports of progress rather than traditional marking; team planning; independent study; learning how to learn; and interrelated curriculum – in science, it was difficult to recognize a course on physics or biology. There were few requirements; students spent much time in the community.

In 1940, when the *Eight-Year Study* evaluations were completed, the positive results were clear: graduates were not handicapped in their college work; major departure from traditionally required subjects did not lessen the readiness of the student; youth from the schools which deviated most from the traditional achieved distinctly higher results. The findings concluded that the strict requirement of certain subjects was no longer tenable; the assumptions of conventional college entrance criteria should be abandoned; students could be trusted with greater degrees of freedom; and the courses taken in high school had no relationship to success in college and later life. In spite of such evidence, 50 years later, few significant changes had occurred in most American high schools.

The faculty at Mankato Wilson (and the other 1960s leaders) knew they would be successful; the results of the *Eight-Year Study* and the multiple innovations of the 20s and 30s were conclusive.[47] The staff adopted many of the practices, and applied the concepts to the elementary level too. Ironically, another Wilson High – in Long Beach, California – during the 1940s had utilized some of the results – most notably a four-day week class attendance pattern; five days were not needed to "cover the book." Graduates were highly successful; the school was acclaimed as one of the best in the nation in 1947. As often happens, when principal Harry Moore retired, the incoming administration abandoned this exciting experiment. In the same district, in the 1930s, the Luther Burbank Elementary, with a grant from the Burbank Foundation, included gardening as a basic subject. Reduced time in the other "basics" did not handicap the students.

Further evidence was available. In one of the many studies supporting innovation, the American College Testing Service examined four factors: achievement in co-curricular activities; high grades in high school; high grades in college; and high scores on the American College Tests.[48] The only factor useful in predicting success in later life was achievement in co-curricular activities. The same proved true for the Scholastic Aptitude Tests.[49] In a related study, Project Talent interviewed 1,000 thirty year olds.[50] The conclusions of the interviews suggested that a conventional high school education – as a whole – "serves no useful purpose."

An international study of mathematics achievement concluded that students who began math at age eight rather than six caught up quickly, and had fewer negative attitudes toward math, self, and school.[51] The non-graded elementary, and the British Infant School, drew on the Plowden Report, which indicated that students who had part of their primary schooling in the bomb shelters in England during World War II did as well or better than students who had traditional lesson plans, books, and schoolrooms.[52,53] In a study of open schools versus conventional, in every area measured, the open school students did as well as the traditional.[54]

Further questions regarding the value of existing practices arose from a strike of Philadelphia teachers. Some schools were closed for eight weeks, while other comparable sites remained open. Those students who missed the two months did as well at the end of the year as those who had been in school.[55] The Goodlad study, *Behind Closed Doors*, found that classrooms were inadequately using agreed upon principles of learning.[56] Philip Jacob reported that there was no difference between graduates characterized as having a liberal education from liberal arts colleges, and those graduating from technical colleges.[57] In an affluent New York suburban district, the schools were given 35 percent more money each year for three years.[58] There was no difference in student achievement. Paulo Friere helped Brazilian peasant adults learn to read in 30 hours.[59] In a related report, reading was identified as a talent, as is music; the conclusion was that beginning reading should occur anywhere from ages three to 14, depending upon the individual.[60]

The Mankato Wilson program refused to require reading, instead permitting students to read when they were ready – usually some time between ages three and 10.[34] Seven hundred reading teachers in New Mexico confirmed from their classroom experiences that not all first graders should be in formal reading by interrupting the keynote speaker at their 1984 state conference with a rousing ovation when he stated that it is well known all six year olds should not be in reading, and especially from single series adopted textbook sets. Reading must be matched to the learning styles of the student – thus necessitating perhaps over 20 program approaches in a given school.

Fordham University experimented with secondary students. One group was allowed to finish grades 7-12 in four years; the other group took the conventional six years. Both groups were guaranteed admission to Fordham, regardless of the results. As might be guessed, the four year students did every bit as well as those who stayed for six; the two years skipped were the 7th and 8th grades. It has long been known that the traditional curriculum for those younger youth was highly irrelevant.

It is especially important to understand historical and current research in the face of changing demographics. California presents a striking example, where over 50 percent of the school youth are minority/majority representing 106 spoken languages; Limited-English-Proficient students approximate 25 percent of the enrollment. For ten years, the state gained 225,000 school-aged youth annually – the majority from lower income homes. Nationally, over 13 million youth live in poverty; high divorce rates and single parent households have compounded the problem.[87] The continuing unacceptable dropout numbers, and static low national test scores, only reinforce the claim that restructuring the existing system will not improve the conditions for most children from low socioeconomic households.[61] Education cannot make a major difference unless health and social services are interwoven with the money provided for such programs as Chapter 1 reading and mathematics supplementary support.[62] Add in the increasing percentage of drug-addicted births, and the task of overhauling schooling at times does seem impossible.[89] Futurists respond: "We must begin doing the impossible; the possible is no longer working."

It is good schools only teach reading, and not walking and talking, or the cost of remedial instruction might be prohibitive; brain-compatible learning validates that conventional schooling practices do not match the patterns identified by brain research.[63,88] Teacher education professors in general do not help, as it was concluded that the typical teacher graduate is expected to "learn what is taught from the books."[64] One of the most amazing education histories is that the Carnegie Unit, the base of high school credits for so long, originated from a Carnegie grant to investigate how to provide college professors a pension.[65] It is clear why educational futurists reject efforts to "restructure" such practices.

Enjoyable Change

One of the most delightful yet sad change stories was chronicled in the 1970 *Letter to a Teacher* by the Schoolboys of Barbiana, where the authors concluded that "school is a war against the poor."[66] It is a beautiful recounting of students who were failed in the structured Italian system. A priest, in very non-conventional settings, proceeded to help the schoolboys. To prove they did not major in "basket weaving," they then took the Italian state exams; all passed. Later they wrote to the education officials and asked: "Why could you not help us learn? Why did you fail us? Why did we have to be helped by a priest instead of teachers?" Why, knowing the experiences of these youth, do communities continue to find acceptable the number of current students who dropout and learn to loathe school? Sadly, of interest, in a survey of leading "intellectual citizens" which included such as Albert Einstein, the word most popular in describing their reactions to schools was "loathed."

Will truly innovative educators ever be allowed to develop an entire system – to create from scratch – or will the 1903 observation of William James prove to be correct: "The institutionizing on a large scale of any natural combination of need and motive always tends to run into technicality and to develop a tyrannical machine with unforeseen powers of exclusion and corruption."[67]

Numerous publications over the decades have clearly established principles for processing education reforms. In 1965, in *Change Process in the Public Schools*, Everett Rogers of Michigan State noted that innovative principals are "in tune with a different drummer; they march to a different beat."[68] Arthur Blumberg, professor at Syracuse, confirmed this difference in an evaluation of the personalities and styles of principals.[69] Such findings had been suggested by the *Eight-Year Study* and related research from the 30s. During the 60s era, the "Designing Education for the Future" series further delineated the knowledge; Volume III focused on *Planning and Effecting Needed Changes in Education*.[70] William Van Til reported the process through experiences of youth who were not excited about existing educational structures; he stated: "School was a place where you gave them back the facts they told you; school had nothing to do with living, thinking, feeling."[45] Ironically, some of the most successful experimental schools, such as Mankato Wilson, were the products of mandated, top down "voluntary change" – sometimes a necessary step in the creation of systems designed to address the deficiencies of tradition. The site was mandated for change, but voluntary in that teachers, parents, and students could request/receive transfers to other programs.

Matthew Miles, Columbia University; Egon Guba, Indiana University; Daniel Stufflebeam, Ohio State University; Warren Bennis, Cincinnati University; Gordon Lippitt, Michigan University; and LaVerne Cunningham, Ohio State, were among the many others who produced publications evaluating successful change processes. Don Glines, in the *NASSP Bulletin*, reviewed "Why Innovative Schools Do Not Remain Innovative."[71] In *The Predictable Failure of Educational Reform*, Seymour Sarason clarified the ineffectiveness of restructuring by identifying the unwillingness to focus on children rather than subject matter, and the inability to alter power relationships in most schools.[72] He suggested that people learn – they are not taught – and that most children already possess higher order critical thinking skills than given credit when entering schooling. Robert Everhart analyzed the effect of choice in a community from the viewpoint of an ethnographer.[73] The barriers inherent in promoting new directions were summarized in *Contributing to Educational Change*, edited by Phillip Jackson of the University of Chicago,[74] including explanation, speculation, and documentation as to why parents, communities, universities, administrators, unions, and teachers have been so reluctant to change, or to sustain the innovation once a program was established.

History

If educators possessed a win/win philosophy, change would be much easier. Illustrating from year-round education, if 51 percent voted for the September to June calendar, and 49 percent voted for year-round, that would be beautiful. Both would be offered. There would be voluntary choices, options, alternatives within the district, community, or state. But communities have followed a win/lose policy of uniformity and mandated for all programs. In this case, 51 percent voted for a nine-month calendar; therefore, everyone had to follow the "majority" who know best! This partially explains why voucher issues, proposals for schools of choice, and charter schools have surfaced on the agendas for education. Change process students suggest that these debates need not reach conflict, if decisions are made by judgment – by dialogic agreement whereby change is incorporated into human understanding; avoiding decisions by consensus or vote can assist in creating positive climates for learning.[16]

People know how to change; additional money is desirable but it is not the primary concern. Most of the truly innovative schools of the 60s operated on the same per pupil cost as the traditional.[10,37] More important is a clear statement of philosophy: "We are going to begin the transition away from schooling for those who are ready because" – followed by utilization of the documented success methods, and a commitment to risk; futures studies have determined that one must be disoriented before being oriented – must unlearn schooling before learning new systems. This was certainly true at Mankato Wilson, which was funded at the district per pupil ratio. Change occurred based on philosophy, not finance. Parents and students were given the option of transferring to a traditional school, or becoming part of essential experimental research. If restructuring must be the next step, rather than transformation, then it can occur, given good leadership.[42] For those who believe they need a cookbook recipe, an overflow of guides have been published.[75]

The many restructuring projects of the early 90s were well-intentioned good efforts, but they were not enough. As illustration, the Coalition for Essential Schools offers that one of their nine tenets is to "teach" students – rather than help them learn – and that academic rigor is best achieved by limiting the curriculum.[76] This narrowness would suggest, given past history, that the Ted Sizer led network has little chance of long term success on a national level. However, the Coalition, and The Next Century Schools Fund, provided by the RJR Nabisco Corporation; the California SB 1274 legislation to create "model" restructuring programs; the Blandin Foundation Center for Educational Reform at the University of Minnesota; the innovative projects by the W. P. Kellogg, Ford, and Danforth Foundations; the Washington Schools for the 21st Century Project; St. Paul Saturn and similar pilot programs in other districts; Project 2061 for the Advancement of Science; the Chrysler World of Work Program; the Holmes Group and Carnegie Foundation plans for teacher education; the Minnesota, California, Colorado, Georgia, New Mexico, Massachusetts, and Wisconsin Charter Schools legislation – the first seven in the nation; and numerous other proposed or implemented reform programs, have had value.

These sparks are creating brush fires, which, as societal conditions continue to erupt, could burst into transitioning bonfires and eventual transformation. Unfortunately, the analogy now appears closer to the completion of a newly designed car model. The individual parts may be improvements, but until the engine, chassis, fenders, wheels, and suspensions come together as one, the separate pieces do not make the existing autos much better. Like the remodeled older car, with the addition of one or two of the parts, the same school remains, but in a slightly modified version. The initial restructuring proposals were too limited in scope; they focused on schooling. Even the quantity was suspect. California has almost 8,000 public schools; 1,500 applied for state restructuring grants. Only 200 received planning funds; 130 were to be funded; what happened to the other 7,800? The lessons on innovative designs are there to be learned by those who are committed to inventing new learning delivery systems.

Preferable Futures

Mickey Mouse and Donald Duck represent the past industrial age era. Perhaps the most delightful of all Disney characters, Figment – that precious purple dragon – does represent hope for the future. Serving as the guide, with his friend Dreamfinder, for the *Journey Into Imagination*, Figment reminds all that the ability to learn to unlock imagination can create an exciting supportive world. Enjoyment of the present, and the creation of preferable futures – not just societal survival – are within the grasp of humankind.

Negative critics, reviewing the 1920s/30s and 1960s/70s, say the innovations did not work, that they were too "loose," and that they are past history – that the programs, processes, and people are not relevant for entering 2000 and beyond. Those "leaders" do not understand that the existing programs of the mid-90s were the same as they were in those "old days." Secondary schools still had period 1-2-3 schedules, ABC report cards, and required English, history, math, and science – and football teams and cheerleaders. The only thing that had changed was the addition of some technology, and students with drugs rather than gum. Elementary schools had self-contained classrooms, grades 4-5-6, and reading for all first graders. Ironically, rather than lack of structure, the fact was that the good innovative programs had more, for it was essential to create the desired flexibility, choices, and responsibility options.

The reforms of those earlier eras worked well where they were understood philosophically, the implementation methods were correct, and the research and evaluation supported the change. The blotched rejections occurred when change was tried without sound philosophy, commitment, and implementation techniques – and the opposition was politically astute.

Shining failures are reflected in the demise of such appropriate considerations as flexible scheduling, open pod classrooms, and team teaching. Ironically, though much of the blame for the illness of education is placed on the damage caused by prior innovation – progressives, open education, alternatives, free-schoolers, and radicals – only one percent of the schools nationally – and less than five percent in the "innovative states" – tried the major reforms. A prime illustration is Mankato, Minnesota, where Wilson became a national model for a "far-out" program, yet the other K-12 schools remained basically conventional. One of 13 is not a viable excuse for the supposed "downturn" in education. If there was one, it was created by continuation of traditional patterns in the face of changing conditions. The many promising practices – the 69 changes implemented at Mankato Wilson – were never given a chance as a whole program in the remaining schools. Innovators of the 60s now see this closed laboratory school as an obsolete model for the 21st Century. However, when described to most mid-90s educators, it still was considered "wildly radical;" statements were made that "teachers and parents would never accept such extremes." Yet Wilson borrowed from the 20s/30s, and from the one room country schoolhouses.

History

If schooling is ultimately to be eliminated, Buckminster Fuller outlined the process in *Critical Path*. He began: "We are at the dawning of a golden age – maybe."[77] His explanation communicated that the golden age would only arrive if people, as individuals, were willing to change their lifestyles, their priorities, their values, and their <u>institutions</u>. He could not envision a golden era if schooling remained a central focus of society. In a more radical manner, two decades earlier, neither could Ivan Illich.[85]

It has been the societal futurists, not educators, who have been leading the effort to transform, not restructure or reshape education. Willis Harman, in *An Incomplete Guide to the Future*,[78] noted such a need, as did Robert Theobald in both *Rapids of Change*, and *Turning the Century*.[16] Harold Shane, a longtime leader in school curriculum, in *Educating for a New Millennium*,[79] called for new forms, as did the contributors to *No Limits to Learning: Bridging the Human Gap*,[80] and Joel Barker through a videotape series on paradigm shifts.[81] Michael Marien, editor of *Future Survey*, has for 20 years charted the recommendations of the many advocates to design 21st Century learning, not reinvent 20th Century education.[82] Earl Joseph, editor of the Minnesota Futurist, years in advance outlined for educators the coming impact of smart machines on future learning systems, and the technological approaches that must be interwoven with the human aspects, self-esteem, and synergetic learning.[83,84,86,91,92]

In the literature, a number of concepts, hazy visions, and concrete proposals for the future have been advocated. They range from small jumps, as used in the automobile industry, where the new model is on the drawing board ten years in advance – and is produced and tested five years before it is presented to the public, to the quantum leap format used by NASA, where only selected individuals working as teams pioneer radical departures by flying an experimental rocket, rather than reinventing the single engine flying machine.

In summary, the often described but still one of the best yet future designs for education serves as review and illustration of the reality for transforming to learning. The proposed Minnesota Experimental City (MXC) was planned for a cross-section of 250,000 people; partly covered with a geodesic dome; no automobiles in the city; waterless toilets; village living centers; extensive shared open land; and the most advanced technological equipment. More important, it was to be a community with no schools. The city was to be the life-long living/learning laboratory. As envisioned by Ron Barnes and his educational design team, the MXC learning system would serve everyone, from birth to death. He described its basics in the *Phi Delta Kappa Fastback #9* in 1972 – over 20 years ago.[83]

An entry focal point was the DOR – disorientation, orientation, reorientation center. In creating change, the MCX process included the need to be disoriented before being oriented – to unlearn the old before learning the new. The LORIN computer network was planned to immediately access and match resources, both human and material. As part of the learning system, family life centers would focus on human services and information meetings; stimulus studios would provide a constantly changing array to extend learning perceptions; gaming studios would stimulate and design opportunities; project studios would offer work or life experiences; and community facilities utilization would enhance the concept that learning was a part of the culture, not separated from normal living, nor confined to special places or hours at a particular time in life. Much learning would occur at home and in the businesses, offices, and natural environments. It was, and still is, an exciting, potentially realistic proposal for the years ahead. The concepts can be adapted by current experimental project schools and learning centers, and eventually by newly constructed communities.

For those citizens and districts not yet ready to volunteer for a modified MXC environment, the beyond restructuring view can be the adoption of many of the formats from the research of the 30s and 60s, enhanced by the most recent knowledge and equipment from the current decade.[92] Though it is true that the innovations of the past will soon not be appropriate for the longer range future, for the immediate they hold answers to the necessary transitions during the remainder of the 90s. The task beyond for educators is to truly IMAGINEER – imagine, invent, and implement – learning opportunities that are not yet available – or not even envisioned. Imagineering is the key for a society that must change its institutions. Willie Wonka of *The Chocolate Factory* said it best: "We must create dreams out of realities, and realities out of dreams, for we are the dreamers of the dreams" – for the learning future of America.

Rewarding References

The histories, illustrations, research, statistics, ideas, visions related to "Creating Educational Futures" are well documented. There is fascinating information to support the need to eliminate such words as alternatives, restructuring, reform, and choice, and the efforts to reinvent the past. There are even more exciting possibilities advocated by societal futurists. The rewarding references selected are far from inclusive. There are literally hundreds of studies, books, articles, tapes, and printed speeches available to assist educators to quickly move through the remaining 90s, as a period of transition, toward leading a learning transformation early in the next century.

1	Jennings, Wayne and Nathan, Joe "Startling/Disturbing Research on School Program Effectiveness," *Phi Delta Kappan*, March, 1977

2	"Bush Education Plan," EDCAL, Association of California Administrators, Sacramento, April 22, 1991

3	Conley David "Restructuring Schools: Educators Adapt to a Changing World," *Trends and Issues #6*, ERIC Clearinghouse, University of Oregon, 1991

4	"Restructuring Schools: What's Really Happening," *Educational Leadership*, (entire volume) Association for Supervision and Curriculum Development, May, 1991

5	Lewis, Anne *Restructuring America's Schools*, American Association of School Administrators, Arlington, VA, 1989

6	*Today's Children, Tomorrow's Survival: A Call to Restructure Schools*, National Association of State Boards of Education, Alexandria, VA, 1990

7	Dewey, John *The School and Society*, University of Chicago Press, Chicago, 1900

8	Washburne, Carleton "A Program of Individualization," *24th Annual Yearbook: National Society for the Study of Education*, Public School Publishing, Bloomington, IL, 1925

9   Willis, Margaret *Guinea Pigs: 20 Years Later*, Ohio State University Press, Columbus, OH, 1961

10   Glines, Don *Educational Futures III: Change and Reality*, Anvil Press, Millville, MN, 1978 one of a series of five volumes, *Educational Futures I-V*, 1978-1980

11   Raywid, Mary Anne *The Case for Public Schools of Choice*, Phi Delta Kappa, Bloomington, IN, 1989

12   Nathan, Joe *Public Schools by Choice*, Institute for Teaching and Learning, St. Paul, 1989

13   Monroe, Paul *Source Book on the History of Education*, The Macmillan Co., New York, 1915

14   Miller, Ron *What Are Schools For?* Holistic Education Press, Brandon, VT, 1990

15   Coates, Joseph and Jarratt, Jennifer *What Futurists Believe*, World Future Society, Bethesda, MD, 1989

16   Theobald, Robert *Rapids of Change*, 1987, and *Turning the Century*, 1993, both Knowledge Systems Publishers, Indianapolis, IN

17   Brown, Lester *The State of the World*, Worldwatch Institute, Washington, DC, 1993

18   Banathy, Bela *Systems Design of Education: A Journey to Create the Future*, Educational Technology Publications, Englewood Cliffs, NJ, 1991

19   Fox, Matthew *Creation Spirituality*, Harper, San Francisco, 1991

20   Glines, Don "Can Schools of Today Survive Very Far Into the 21st Century," *NASSP Bulletin*, February, 1989

21   Goodlad, John and Anderson, Robert *The Non-Graded Elementary School*, Revised edition, Teachers College Press, New York, 1987

22   Williams, Emmett *The Emergent Middle School*, Holt, Rinehart and Winston, New York, 1967

23   Alexander, William *Innovations in Secondary Education*, 1970, and *The Exemplary Middle School*, 1981, both Holt, Rinehart and Winston, New York

24   Beane, James *A Middle School Curriculum: From Rhetoric to Reality*, National Middle Schools Association, Columbus, OH, 1990

25   Glines, Don "Implementing a Humane School," *Educational Leadership*, November, 1970

26   National Society for the Study of Education "Adopting the Schools to Individual

Differences," *24th Annual Yearbook*, Public School Publishing, Bloomington, IL, 1925

27   Monroe, Paul *Source Book on the History of Education for the Greek and Roman Period*, The Macmillan Co., New York, 1901

28   Educational Policies Commission *The Purpose of Education in an American Democracy*, National Education Association, Washington, DC, 1938

29   Rapp, Doris *The Impossible Child*, 1986, and *Is This Your Child*, 1992 Practical Allergy Research Foundation, Buffalo, NY

30   Clarke, Harrison and Clarke, David *Application of Measurement to Physical Education*, 6th edition, Prentice-Hall, Englewood Cliffs, NJ, 1987

31   *World Future Society*, 7910 Woodmont Avenue, Bethesda, MD 20814

32   Glines, Don and Bingle, James, *National Association for Year-Round Education: A Historical Perspective*, 3rd Edition, National Association for Year-Round Education, San Diego, 1993

33   Tucker, Judy "Futuristic Principal Seeks Humane Ideas," *The Evening Bulletin*, Philadelphia, September 14, 1973

34   Morton, John "Nothing is Too Far Out to Be Tried in the Wilson School," *The National Observer*, July 28, 1969

35   Long, Kathleen *Teacher Reflections on Individual School Restructuring: A Study of Alternatives in Public Education*, unpublished doctoral dissertation, College of Education, University of Oregon, 1992

36   O'Toole, Kathy "Old Methods; Old Taboos Vanish," *Watertown Public Opinion* (SD), March 4, 1968

37   Glines, Don "Changing a School," *Phi Delta Kappan*, December, 1966

38   Silberman, Charles *Crisis in the Classroom*, Random House, New York, 1970

39   Coombs, Philip *The World Educational Crisis: A Systems Analysis*, Oxford Press, New York, 1968

40   Trump, J. Lloyd *Images of the Future*, 1960, and *Guide to Better Schools: Focus on Change*, 1961, both Rand McNally, Chicago

41   Trump, J. Lloyd *A School for Everyone*, National Association for Secondary School Principals, Reston, VA, 1977

42   Fadiman, Dorothy *Why Do These Kids Love School*, videotape, Concentric Media, Menlo Park, CA, 1990

43   Slavin, Robert "Are Cooperative Learning and Untracking Harmful to the Gifted," *Educational Leadership*, March, 1991

44   "Breaking the Mold: Reshaping Schooling," San Francisco Conference, Association for Supervision and Curriculum Development, Alexandria, VA, 1991

45   Van Til, William *My Way of Looking at It*, Lake Lurie Press, Terre Haute, IN, 1983

46   Aikin, Wilford *Story of the Eight-Year Study*, Harper and Brothers, New York, 1942

47   Dewey, John *The Way Out of Educational Confusion*, Harvard University Press, Cambridge, MA, 1931

48   Hoyt, D. P. "Relationship Between College Grades and Adult Achievement: A Review of the Literature," *ACT Report No. 7*, American College Testing Service, Iowa City, IA, 1965

49   Wallach, Michael "Psychology of Talent and Graduate Education," presented for *Graduate Record Examinations Board* Conference, Montreal, 1972

50   "Project Talent," *The School Administrator*, American Association of School Administrators, Arlington, VA, February, 1976

51   Husen, Torsten *International Study of Achievement in Mathematics*, Vol. 2, Almquist and Wilsells, Uppsala, Sweden, 1967

52   Central Advisory Council for Education, *Children and Their Primary Schools*, Her Majesty's Stationery Office, London, 1967

53   Weber, Lillian *English Infant School and Informal Learning*, Prentice-Hall, Englewood Cliffs, NJ, 1971

54   Horowitz, Robert *Psychological Effects of Open Classroom Teaching and Review of Research*, University of North Dakota Press, Grand Forks, 1976

55   Lytle, James "The Effects of a Teacher Strike on Student Achievement," *Phi Delta Kappan*, December, 1973

56   Goodlad, John *Behind The Classroom Door*, Wadsworth, Belmont, CA, 1970

57   Jacob, Philip *Changing Values in College*, Harper and Brothers, New York, 1957

58   Martin, John et al *Free to Learn*, Prentice-Hall, Englewood Cliffs, NJ, 1972

59   Brown, Cynthia *Literacy in 30 Hours*, Expression Printers, Ltd., London, 1975

60   Postman, Neil "The Politics of Reading," *Harvard Educational Review*, May, 1970

61   Coleman, James, "The Children Have Outgrown the Schools," *Psychology Today*, February 1972

62   Knapp, Michael and Shields, Patrick, eds. *Better Schooling for the Children of Poverty: Alternatives to Conventional Wisdom*, National Society for the Study of Education, University of Chicago Press, 1991

63   Hart, Leslie *Human Brain, Human Learning*, Longview Press, New York, 1983

64   Taylor, Harold *The World as Teacher*, Doubleday, Garden City, NJ, 1969

65   Tompkins, Ellsworth and Gaumnitz, Walter "Carnegie Unit: Its Origin, Status, and Trends," *Education and Welfare Bulletin No. 7*, U.S. Government Printing Office, Washington, D.C., 1954

66   Schoolboys of Barbiana, *Letter to a Teacher*, Random House, New York, 1970

67   Cheney, Lynne, edt. *Tyrannical Machines*, National Endowment for the Humanities, Washington, DC, 1990

68   Rogers, Everett, et al *Change Process in the Public Schools*, Center for Advanced Study of Educational Administration, University of Oregon, Eugene, 1965

69   Blumberg, Arthur *The Effective Principal: Perspective on School Leadership*, Longwood/Allyn and Bacon, Rockleigh, NJ, 1980

70   Morphet, Edgar and Ryan, Charles, eds. *Planning and Effecting Needed Changes in Education*, Designing Education for the Future: An Eight State Project, Denver, CO, 1967

71   Glines, Don   "Why Innovative Schools Do Not Remain Innovative," *NASSP Bulletin*, February, 1973

72   Sarason, Seymour *The Predictable Failure of Educational Reform*, Jossey-Bass, San Francisco, 1990

73   Everhart, Robert *Practical Ideology and Symbolic Community: An Ethnography of Schools of Choice*, The Falmer Press, Philadelphia, 1988

74   Jackson, Phillip, edt. *Contributing to Educational Change*, McCutchan, Berkeley, CA, 1988

75   Hansen, John and Liftin, Elaine *School Restructuring: A Practitioners Guide*, Waterspun Publishing, Swampscott, MA, 1991

76   Sizer, Theodore *Coalition for Essential Schools Network*, School of Education, Brown University, Providence, RI, 02912

77   Fuller, Buckminster *Critical Path*, St. Martins Press, New York, 1981

78   Harman, Willis *An Incomplete Guide to the Future*, W. W. Norten, New York, 1979

79   Shane, Harold "Educating for a New Millennium," *Phi Delta Kappa*, Bloomington, IN, 1981

80   Botkin, James, edt. *No Limits to Learning: Bridging the Human Gap*, Pergamon Press, Elmsford, NY, 1979

81   Barker, Joel *Discovering the Future*, Charter House Learning Corporation, Burnsville, MN, 1990

82   Marien, Michael *Future Survey*, World Future Society, Bethesda, MD, 1993

83   Barnes, Ron "Learning Systems for the Future," *Phi Delta Kappa* (Fastback), Bloomington, IN, 1972

84   Ellul, Jacques *The Technological Bluff*, William Eerdmans, Grand Rapids, MI, 1990

85   Illich, Ivan *Deschooling Society*, Harper and Row, New York, 1971

86   Norris, Neal, edt. *Community College Futures*, New Forum Press, Stillwater, OK, 1989

87   Griffith, Jeanne et al "American Education: The Challenge of Change," *Bulletin 4*, Population Reference Bureau, Washington, DC, 1989

88   Caine, Renate and Caine, Geoffrey *Making Connections: Teaching and the Human Brain*, Association for Supervision and Curriculum Development, Alexandria, VA, 1991

89   Miles, Matthew and Seashore, Karen *Improving the Urban High School: What Works and Why*, Teachers College Press, New York, 1990

90   Pavan, Barbara "Analysis of Research on Nongraded Schools," *Elementary School Journal*, March, 1973

91   California Task Force *Toward a State of Esteem*, Department of Education, Sacramento, CA, 1990

92   Glines, Don and Long, Kathleen "Transitioning Toward Educational Futures," *Phi Delta Kappan*, March 1992

93   National Society for the Study of Education "On the Education of Gifted Children," *23rd Annual Yearbook*, Public School Publishing, Bloomington, IL, 1924

94   Anderson, Robert and Pavan, Barbara *Nongradedness: Helping it to Happen*, Technomic Publishing, Lancaster, PA, 1992

chapter twenty-eight

TEACHERS

Teaching and teacher education must change if communities are to develop their version of Wilson, and ultimately learning for the 21st Century. Institutions of education cannot continue to look like those seen today. They will be different in ways that will be startling, particularly considering their almost unchanging nature in the last century. Projections give hope that finally schools and colleges will change – that they will begin to move away from schooling toward learning.

The potential futures will affect all levels of learning from early childhood through adult. As a result, teacher education programs should prepare for coming transitions. Universities must both lead and follow the public and private school efforts; a new era of cooperation is required. At the same time, schools will need to rethink their programs to provide roles for the new generation of educators who will help mold improved learning delivery systems. There is ample evidence which supports the view that society and education should create different approaches. A surprisingly large number of books, articles, and reports are published each month providing data, resources, and challenges related to the years ahead; many of these are reviewed in *Future Survey*. Educators must analyze these interpretations and findings.

There is a need to help create preferable futures. People may not be content with current probable, or many of the possible, alternative futures. Creating a preferable future – imagining and inventing – is an essential task. Visionary futurism is a requirement if humankind is to move from the Industrial Age to the Compassionate Era (one of the approximate 80 names given to the emerging period).

For such transitions to occur, educators should first examine, as well as possible, the potential alternative futures. There are at least 64 global topics that need consideration: energy, food, population, ecology, values, cities, technology, oceans, space, pollution, poverty, despair, and lifestyles, to cite a few.

Second, the educational implications of these potential global conditions need analysis. Do they have general meaning for all schools and colleges, or are the global crises and opportunities of no real concern to the education systems of the future. Are these projections of little value in light of past and present educational and political climates, or are they of a high priority?

Third, community and professional educational leaders should ask: Do the global dilemmas and potential implications for education have significance for schools and colleges for practical, now-oriented programs within current budgets and political realities?

In addressing these three areas, it is important to begin with a search of the theoretical, the alternative possibilities for societal futures. The information technology systems explosion illustrates one of the global factors that will bring major changes in society and education in the next century. The implications for the field of education are staggering, yet exciting and challenging. They offer new potentials for learning for millions of people of all ages throughout the country.

The ecological conditions of the globe further indicate that changes in society are certain. Fish populations are but one small example; the depletion of ocean fish is a serious warning for humankind. The dramatic increase in world population – growing at approximately two percent per year – has led the United Nations Population Commission to forecast that world population will triple in just 70 years. Although some countries have reached zero population growth, others are exploding at a rate of 3.5 percent. The restrictions placed on the world food supply border on involuntary suicide; there is yet plenty of food, but the world economic and distribution systems will not permit distribution to the people who have the greatest need. Millions are starving; mega-famines may occur along with riots and wars over food and water.

It is essential for teachers, and especially for teacher educators, to realize that society is changing. Lifestyles – which do affect attitudes, values, and learning – are different. There are now more persons over 55 years of age than students in K-12 schools; they command enormous political clout. Four of five Americans are over 18; forty percent of all adults in the 20-24 age range are single. The impact on school and teacher education programs is enormous.

The most important area of study for teachers and teacher education is the global scene. It far outweighs core curriculum, authentic assessment, and standardized tests. According to *The Global Report to the President*, a bluntly worded document from 14 federal agencies, the assessment of possible world conditions in the 2000-2005 period is basically pessimistic– if conditions do not improve. Degradation of the ecological systems, rising populations, swarms of insects, denuded forests, world food shortages, skyrocketing oil prices, the have-have not gaps, and breeding grounds for wars are some of the concerns that support a pessimistic projection, if people/countries continue business as usual. An optimistic view is possible only if there are changes in values, priorities, and world conditions.

The implications of these global concerns for schools, educators, and education are monumental, if the views of most future writers are correct. Early recognition of this came in the 1974 book, *Learning for Tomorrow* (Toffler). One passage states: "American education is obsolete; it produces people to fit into a reasonably well-functioning industrial society and we no longer have one. The basic assumption draining American education, one both deceptive and dangerous, is that the future will be like the present. Schools are preparing people for a society that no longer exists. As society shifts away from the industrial model, schools will have to turn out a different kind of person. Schools now need to produce people who can cope with change."

There is mounting evidence to support the notion that current education systems are obsolete. Research indicates that humans are on the verge of breaking through the aging process. Present-day kindergarten children may have a potential life expectancy of 100 to 125 years. What do people who will be in their prime in the year 2050, assuming society makes it through the coming transitional decades, need to shape their futures? Is the current curriculum – history, mathematics, science, new versions of Dick and Jane, all taught as separate subjects, really appropriate for the transitioning years into a new century? The majority of futures writers have a clear answer: No. They illustrate that instant information retrieval not only ends jobs in the world of work, it ends subjects in the world of learning!

Yet, schools, colleges, and teacher education programs continue to fragment. Most secondary and university institutions have departments of English, science, mathematics. Teacher education "models" continue to have elementary and secondary departments, or divisions of curriculum, administration, and educational psychology. Elementary schools have not been much better. Instead of departments, one self-contained teacher has tried to handle 14 subjects in a compartmentalized approach — reading, 9:00-10:15; recess, 10:15-10:30; arithmetic, 10:30-11:20; lunch.

Consider curricula related to global survival: hunger, industrialization, pollution, resource depletion, war, and population. These six components of the whole could enhance the pessimistic view of the *Global 2000 Report*. Using hunger as an example, in the current school organization, who is going to cope with this priority topic? Which department should assume the responsibility: home economics, science, social studies, industrial arts, mathematics, English, or health? All of these subjects and teachers can address a part of the world dilemma, but not one of these separate entities is prepared to pull together the interdependent whole. Yet hunger is one of the components that may determine a positive or negative human future.

Efforts have been made over the years to change these conditions. T. H. Huxley, in 1880, proposed to the University of London the elimination of separated compartments of knowledge. Later, Aldous Huxley stated: "The trouble with all specialized knowledge is that it is an organized series of celibacies. The different subjects live in their monastic cells, apart from one another, and simply do not intermarry . . . The problem is to try to arrange marriages between these various subjects . . . and share the relationships between objective knowledge and subjective experience."

While this resistance continues, the electronics revolution rushes ahead. The potential technology exists to eliminate most current classrooms in the first decade of the new century, moving from a campus to a community-oriented learning system. A postliterate society is on the verge of arriving; reading will become a luxury, a leisure pastime, or a choice, but not an absolute essential.

Yet, the seventh grade programs in junior high and middle schools continue with the bleakness of 50 years past. Most still require English, history, science, math, and physical education, along with a semester of art and a semester of music. They have period 1, 2, 3 schedules; A, B, C report cards; tardies; notes from home; textbooks. Perhaps even worse is the fact that most colleges still prepare teachers for this antiquity; and administrators, who in spite of the goals professed in graduate courses, continue to perpetuate the system. Is it any wonder that *Learning for Tomorrow* labeled education obsolete? Harold Taylor had also recognized this even earlier when in 1969 he wrote *The World as Teacher*.

Ron Barnes, in *Tomorrow's Educator: An Alternative to Today's School Person*, listed his descriptors of a New Age educator — a person who thinks systematically; accepts and promotes diversity; demonstrates a holistic perspective toward life; strives for self-awareness; promotes interdependence; is comfortable with the unknown; considers human values of highest priority; is experimental; works toward changing schools; has a more open approach to knowledge; and is a true futurist.

Teachers

The Club of Rome, through its study, *No Limits to Learning: Bridging the Human Gap*, has shifted from previous emphasis on global resources to the human imperative. The view is that Spaceship Earth can only have a preferable future if people change. Therefore, the focus is on closing the gap between where persons find themselves in their old Industrial Age lifestyles and where they should be if they are to reach preferably into the next century. Futurists believe that institutions attempting to exist on outdated assumptions will soon discover they are trying to survive in a world that no longer exists.

The futures literature is clear: It is time for teachers and teacher education to develop new institutions. The call is to carefully and humanistically dismantle the old ones before they crumble and possible take society with them. How such efforts might be launched in the late 90s, given the reality of the current school climate, may be the most important immediate task for educational leaders.

One method could be to adopt the proposed Minnesota Experimental City (MXC) designed during the 70s by creative futurists. Although the Minnesota legislature put a hold on the project to the extent that it may never be built in that state, the concepts still have global significance. Recall that this truly experimental city of 250,000 people was to be built on 60,000 acres of virgin land, only 10,000 of which were to be cemented, partly covered with a Buckminster Fuller geodesic dome, no cars, waterless toilets, people movers, and the latest electronic systems. In regard to education, there were to be no schools, no superintendents, no teachers in the conventional terminology, no colleges, and certainly no schools of education. The city was designed as a living learning laboratory; everyone was to be a teacher, everyone a learner. Learning was to continue from birth to death – a true lifelong process.

Although such an approach is not completely possible in school communities now, many of the concepts are immediately transferable to present school and teacher education programs. They can be achieved carefully and humanistically, as recommended in the futures literature, and as modeled by the Wilson Campus School in an earlier era.

Consider the opportunities, not only for student learning and parent participation in the development of new approaches toward the future, but, in addition, the great potential for preservice and graduate professional education programs in the colleges. Professors at the institutions, working with their students, would have the opportunity to help design and implement learning systems designed for the 21st Century.

What would this group create to replace the current junior high if they could start all over again – as in the MXC? No traditions, no rituals – a new learning approach now at no additional cost – and without disrupting or eliminating the current conventional programs for the people who see those approaches as their preferred avenue to the future.

What would the MXC group possibility plan for the coming year? Perhaps student time in an "imagineering studio"; a Utopia project; a seminar on New Age values; a workshop on technological forecasting; a seminar on global survival; a "sociosphere station for human forecasting"; a writing lab creating a scenario; an action lab – working in a hospital for handicapped children; a war simulation experience; involvement in the disorientation, orientation, reorientation (DOR) program; a computer dialogue in the stimulus center; or a biomedical engineering laboratory experience.

Certainly such a modest start is not 21st Century in scope, but it is a break from existing programs toward the coming decades. Implemented at no additional cost, and providing the conventional options, the MXC portion eliminates period 1, 2, 3 schedules and more importantly, the departmentalized segmentation of knowledge. Curriculum becomes interdependent, and essential for the New Age. The focus becomes the human potential for caring and creating.

How are teachers prepared for such optional learning choices – for alternatives within the existing system? Part of the response is in the form of new professional preparation efforts. Current schools of education could organize into four centers. The Center for Contemporary Learning would continue to prepare teachers for what exists; that remains a viable choice. The Center for Transitional Options would prepare people for experiences in a team, flexible approach program. The Center for Community Opportunities would assist leadership toward the Parkway school-without-walls concepts. The Center for Alternative Futures would prepare new leaders for the development of their versions of the MXC education system in districts throughout each state.

Students and professors would "headquarter" in one of the four centers. However, they could cross-select work and approaches to provide for broad interdependent experiences. All the programs would focus to some extent on the future, with the alternative futures group the most heavily engaged. Key windows are essential for such diversified philosophies to succeed: win/win, options, and trust. "In order for me to win, you must win" is a priority belief, replacing the present win/lose, "in order for me to win, you must lose," syndrome. It is essential that options be provided for everyone. This can be accomplished through trust, which is a basis for Compassionate Era education. Each are regular, each are options. Choices can be provided in large programs of 6,000 or small ones of 100. The mechanics are available. The excitement, the challenge of possibly creating or inventing a learning system for the 21st Century, propels the experiment.

Teacher education programs can help teachers to not only design new approaches, but also, while the changes begin to occur, increase future studies in schools. One is by greater inclusion of futures topics or units within existing courses and curricula. A second is the offering of a course in the curriculum titled "Alternative Futures." At the elementary level, units during science and social studies might focus on cities of the future, oceans in the future, food for the future, the future of outer space, and saving water.

A third approach at the elementary level, a small beginning but one that holds great development for expansion without upsetting the apple cart or costing more money, is to help volunteer teachers create every Wednesday, from 1:00-2:30, a "Center for the Future." If that title frightens, call it science and social studies. Every Wednesday, the teacher in his or her own classroom for 90 minutes, tries new teaching/learning methods, new facility arrangements, and most important, new curriculum topics and person involvement.

Teachers

Purposely chosen and offered in a futures sense are learning activities related to the future of deserts, forests, water, population, food, families, transportation, cities, robots, energy, grasslands, wetlands, nutrition, conflict, peace, fish, technology, weather, oceans, space, and a multitude of other topics depending upon teacher interest, student interest, resources available, and current concerns in the local community. Little time is needed for preparation and little, if any, money is required. The idea is not dramatic; it is not always interdependent, but small steps can lead to the future. Immediately, U.S. history can be taught from the perspective of the year 2050. The future of economic systems, wars, racial conflicts, food shortages, energy, social systems, music, sports, religions, can be addressed. Past and present history is interrelated as appropriate, but the focus is on helping students create a preferable U.S. future, rather than on memorizing past events or learning outmoded formulas (algebra).

These few of the many possibilities provide credence to the statement that teachers, teacher education programs and school districts can create futures-oriented learning programs, approaches, and systems in the late 90s that lead to the next century and beyond, within existing budgets and political realities. What tremendous opportunities there are, not only for teacher education programs to support these efforts, but to lead in the encouragement and creative design of possibilities for the probable coming transformation.

Are these efforts really essential? Are not present-day educational programs preparing people for the future? The answer appears to be a resounding no, if the comments of most futurists have validity. Willis Harman, in *An Incomplete Guide to The Future*, signaled the need for new approaches in education. He lists the awesome powers facing people. Society now has, or soon will have, the power to change to an unlimited degree the characteristics of the physical environment of the biosphere; modify without limit the physical characteristics of individual human bodies by means of biological and genetic engineering; alter drastically the human social and psychological environment; annihilate large segments of the human race with weapons of mass destruction; and change significantly the world that is handed to the next generation.

It is time for school districts and teacher education programs to do more than talk. It is time for humans to help create preferable educational futures. This is no longer 21st Century theory; it is current reality.

A quotation from *Beyond Despair* may summarize the need for new directions:

> The future is ours for us to create. But creation requires knowledge, imagination, and perseverance. Will we generate these qualities in sufficient measures to change the world? If we fail to do so, the destruction of the human race is certain; if we should succeed, none of us has sufficient imagination to perceive the potentials of our future.

Wilson teaching and teacher education were an experiment to create the future, to eliminate schooling, and to assist in preparing for a different and better society.

STUDENTS

Twenty years after the participation of the Ohio State University Laboratory School in the famous *Eight-Year Study*, as chronicled in *Were We Guinea Pigs*?, Margaret Willis and a group of the former students documented their success in adult life in *Twenty Years Later: Guinea Pigs Revisited*. The results were significant. The youth from the "innovative" lab school were more successful when compared with their counterpart graduates from the "traditional" schools in all conventional measurements: number of professionals and college degrees; salaries achieved; position accomplishment; stability of marriage; and other similar factors.

Former Wilson staff and interested researchers plan a similar twenty-year study of the Mankato students. Graduates, as well as those who spent considerable time in the program (five years), will be surveyed; also included will be the reflections of parents. Previously, numerous effects on teachers and students were documented through a dissertation and a videotape by Dr. Kathleen Long. Another videotape, *Wilson Campus School Remembered*, by retired faculty at Mankato State, archived the reality of the program.

Fortunately, too, in small midwest communities such as Mankato, most families maintained their homes. Thus, informally there was already considerable known data on the outcomes for students and their parents, as interested staff continued visitation contacts with "Wilsonites," individually, and as a group through the occasional all-school Wilson reunions.

It is undeniable that, in general, an overwhelming majority of the students liked the school and have been successful to date in their adulthood. The "crazy" Wilson program did not deny them the opportunity to attend university, find employment, receive a scholarship, enjoy marriage, compete for salaries, and other evaluations sought by "traditionalists." The great percentage of parents continued to express their support; they were glad their children had the opportunity to enroll. By remaining in contact, many of the former faculty were able to personally document the outcomes achieved by those who participated in this major learning experiment in "some such place called Mankato."

Objective and subjective data was gathered related to Wilson students and their interface with the learning philosophy through over 30 master degree and education specialist theses and graduate class papers, a sampling of which are cited as partial evidence of student competencies and attitudes. However, the staff of Wilson knew before they began, that if they implemented the philosophy with humaneness, common sense, commitment, and attention to prior research, that Wilson youth should find success, not only when they attended the program, but throughout their adult years.

Prior to Wilson, the often cited famous *Eight-Year Study*, reported in a five volume series, involved students in high schools from September 1933 to June 1941; those who attended college were enrolled at that level between 1936 and 1943. Unfortunately, World War II drew attention away from the exciting results. Prior to the study, the situation of high school students from 1930 to 1932 was analyzed. Though summarized as part of "History," the preliminary report and eventual outcomes are repeated, as they are so important for research and evaluation in the late 90s, and the potential effect of new designs on students and programs:

1. Most high school graduates were not competent in the use of the English language; they seldom read; they were unable to express themselves effectively either in speech or writing.

2. There was little evidence of unity in the work of students in typical high school subjects; courses were added without concern for unity.

3. The absence of unity in the curriculum was matched by a lack of continuity.

4. Complacency characterized high school programs: the elementary schools had begun some reform, but the high schools remained traditional.

5. Teachers were cited as not being well equipped for their responsibilities; they lacked knowledge of the nature of youth.

6. Principals did not conceive their responsibility as democratic leadership; to the contrary, they viewed their role as being an autocratic good fellow.

7. Principals and teachers of this era worked hard and often sacrificed, but were without any comprehensive evaluation of the results of their efforts; they only knew the results of the marks they gave students, but not whether their cognitive and affective objectives had been met, or whether the students were really interested.

8. A high school diploma meant only that students had accumulated credits, but without a long range purpose.

9. The relations of schools and colleges were unsatisfactory to both parties.

In further reviewing the historical perspective of the 1930s, eleven years later, when the *Eight-Year Study* students had graduated from college, the following conclusions were drawn regarding those who were enrolled in the experimental programs in the 30 high schools and accepted by the 300 leading universities.

1. GRADUATES OF THE 30 SCHOOLS WERE NOT HANDICAPPED IN THEIR COLLEGE WORK.

2. DEPARTURES FROM THE PRESCRIBED PATTERNS OF SUBJECTS AND UNITS DID NOT LESSEN THE READINESS OF THE STUDENTS FOR THE RESPONSIBILITIES OF COLLEGE.

3. STUDENTS FROM THE PARTICIPATING SCHOOLS WHICH MADE THE MOST FUNDAMENTAL CURRICULUM REVISION ACHIEVED IN COLLEGE DISTINCTLY HIGHER STANDINGS THAN THOSE OF STUDENTS OF EQUAL ABILITY WITH WHOM THEY WERE COMPARED.

4. LIBERAL ARTS PREPARATION, WITH THE TRADITIONAL PRESCRIBED SUBJECTS, WAS NO LONGER TENABLE.

5. ASSUMPTIONS UPON WHICH SCHOOL AND COLLEGE RELATIONS HAD BEEN BASED IN THE PAST MUST BE ABANDONED.

6. SECONDARY SCHOOLS AND STUDENTS CAN BE TRUSTED WITH A GREATER MEASURE OF FREEDOM THAN COLLEGE REQUIREMENTS NOW PERMIT.

The *Eight-Year Study* provided an excellent base for the rash of new studies which descended upon education in the late 60s and early 70s; these were augmented by a search of past literature to discover other significant reports affecting students which might have been overlooked as conventional school practices became more and more unquestioned traditions.

The Ford Foundation conducted several investigations of the reform process. Among the reported findings were the following: instructional personnel must change themselves if they are to really effect change in educational programs; colleges and universities are seldom effective forces for improving schools; middle-sized projects are the most successful — but with large scale involvement; and small schools change faster than large schools. Additional studies from the University of Texas Research and Development Center concluded that students from open elementary schools face a smoother transition into traditional junior highs than students from conventional elementary programs, and that peer-rating techniques can be used in place of in-depth psychological evaluation to identify special needs of students. Evaluation of the Individually Prescribed Instruction (IPI) programs of the 60s and early 70s reported that the self-concept of pupils in IPI schools was significantly higher than for pupils in traditional schools: parents considered children more motivated and self-directed.

In 1968, Rollins reported findings that ability grouping locked in the pupil self-image and teacher expectancy levels, and built discrimination into the schools. Another related study placed 1,800 educable mentally retarded students in three different methods groups: heterogeneous, high achievers, and low achievers. There were no significant differences in achievement among the 1,800.

Several studies emerged during the early 70s related to attitudes. One at John Hopkins University determined that small mixed ethnic groups with incentives developed positive interdependence — that barriers were reduced. Another survey reported that positive or negative attitudes toward others are reflections of the attitudes one holds toward self — and that positive self-regard is necessary for intelligent behavior. A study of the attitudes of 3,000 urban teachers reported that if they considered their students below average that the motivation and aspiration of the students reflected the teacher attitude — they had below average motivation and aspiration.

A University of Nebraska study of students enrolled in high schools in five midwestern states reported that when students were asked if some teacher in their school really cared about them, one-third responded with a strong 'no'; one-third just said 'no'; and only one-third said 'I think so' or 'yes.' Another attitude study stated that during the school year, students in general undergo negative changes in attitudes toward themselves and toward others; positive attitude is partially regained over the summer; the negative attitude changes became worse in secondary schools and colleges, as contrasted with the elementary schools.

Barbara Pavan, while doing doctoral work at Harvard, reported in 1972 that studies of students contrasted for involvement in open or closed education concluded that the students in open education were doing significantly better. Ironically, many of the ideas of open education were advocated in an exciting book titled *The Ideal School: A Look Forward*, written in Pueblo, Colorado in 1901 by Preston W. Search. From 1907 to 1937, the Gary, Indiana, schools reported successful results with community education; before non-graded schools became popular in the U.S., Peter Petersen in Germany advocated the concept. Much of the "new" education is not new, but only revivals of good concepts suggested years earlier but never fully implemented.

Innovation studies continued in the early 70s. One reported that 85 percent of the reading difficulties in the U.S. were found among boys; most had female teachers. But in Japan, Germany, and in Jewish schools, where male teachers were in the majority, the largest group of non-readers were female. Another of the more interesting reports is the survey of WWII veterans who did not have the proper background for college: they had not graduated from high school, or had received unacceptable grades for college admission standards. They scored the highest identifiable group grade point average ever recorded in colleges. The two factors that made the difference were motivation and maturity.

A number of early 70s studies related to teacher education raised further questions regarding teacher training and certification. Popham reported in 1971 that students taught by teachers trained in teachers colleges do no better than those taught by laypersons (housewives, mechanics, electricians) with knowledge in those areas they taught. Moody, in the same year, found that children taught by inexperienced college students learned just as much as did students led by college-trained, experienced teachers. Moody and Bousell in 1972 reported that teaching practice effect was demonstrated using the same materials: the conclusion was that teacher preparation as provided by colleges of education does not result in increased student achievement; Bousell also reported that children taught by students who had completed student training and required methods and materials courses did not learn significantly more than children taught by college students who had not had this training.

Further, 1972 evaluation of Title I results in math and reading — an $800 million project — as reported by the U.S. Office of Education, presented the following conclusions: 17 percent of the students involved made more than normal progress; 13 percent made less than normal progress; 67 percent were apparently unaffected: there was no significant difference in their progress.

The Coleman Report, if valid, and that remains an "if," indicated that schools bring little influence on achievement independent of the socioeconomic background of the child; that a key to improvement seemed to lie in altering ways parents relate with the child; and that the least promising approach seemed to be in increasing school expenditure — there was little evidence of appreciable effect on achievement. The related and controversial Jencks Report indicated that school has little effect on income and economic success — that such items as personal characteristics play a greater role.

Whether changing schools does or does not help many of these and similar factors is still questionable. However, if change is of value, a major finding of the 34 million dollar

Ford Foundation study indicated that leadership is the single most important factor; the innovative leader gets the task accomplished.

A 1976 report to the National Institute of Education titled "Economy, Efficiency, and Equality: The Myths of Rural School and District Consolidation," published as a book in 1977 titled *Education in Rural America: A Reassessment of Conventional Wisdom*, seriously questions one of the most successfully implemented educational policies of the past 50 years: the consolidation of rural schools and school districts. It notes that the magnitude of savings in changing from a district of 0-300 to one of 301-2,499 is $2,100 per $100,000 of budget, but that is usually not enough to cover the diseconomics of transportation, nor enough to warrant the dislocation of large numbers of students. The report is full of interesting data, most all of which questions much of the past consolidation. It does close with three important observations for anyone interested in research and change: (1) small schools deserve more attention; (2) alternatives to consolidation and reorganization should be seriously considered; and, (3) research to demonstrate the value of proposed reforms should be scrutinized carefully.

Reports may be questioned as to validity and reliability, but the evidence is that they are probably more right than wrong. They may not present overwhelming proof of a given aspect of change, but they do reinforce the fact that educators are sure of very little in education – that there are only TENTATIVE TRUTHS. As a result there is great need for further research, evaluation, analysis, and experimentation. New efforts are necessary, as well as reexamination of existing data, information, opinions, and proposed reforms – as they affect students.

As late as 1962, Scott Foresman was publishing their "new basic readers," a modification of a program copyrighted in 1921. One title was SALLY, DICK, AND JANE. The first pages showed white, blue-eyed, blonde and brown haired children in suburbia, and of course, the wagon, the famous dog Spot, and the cat Puff, with the captions: "Go, go, go; Go, Dick, go." Is this what is desired by the "back-to-basics" advocates? From such primers developed the bluebirds, the greenbirds, and the redbirds, the latter of whom became the "remedial readers." It is hard to believe, with all the crises of the approaching decades, that not long ago, "Run, Spot, run" dominated the American scene. Such an approach was defended because "thousands of children learned to read" from primers that said: "Oh, Sally, Sally." Most people forgot to mention all those who did not learn to read, or read well, or who developed confused or warped senses of values from these and the "Think and Do" workbooks, or similar versions from other publishing companies. Perhaps the new century is finally the time to examine cherished educational practices.

One of the longtime critics of present forms of evaluation in most conventional schools was J. Lloyd Trump. His paper, "Evaluating Pupil Progress in Team Teaching (or in any class, for that matter)," and his book *A School for Everyone*, recorded not only his criticism, but constructive suggestions for improvement. He proposed a reexamination of the evaluation of several factors, including the following: quality of teaching; conditions of learning; quality of pupil learning; and improvements, not standard measurement. Trump stated: "The most basic proposal is that evaluation be considered an integral part of the teaching-learning process. Most evaluating should be done by the pupils with procedures that enable individuals to judge for themselves what they have learned and what they need to do next to achieve what they have not yet attained."

Students

Learning goals for, and evaluation by, students is not difficult to envision, given professional assistance. In *Learning for Mastery*, Benjamin Bloom stated: "We are expressing the view that, given sufficient time (and appropriate help), 95 percent of the students can learn a subject up to a high level of mastery. We are convinced that the grade of A as an index of mastery of a subject can, under appropriate conditions, be achieved by up to 95 percent of the students in a class. In general, we find a zero or slightly negative relationship between final grades and the amount of time spent on homework."

A 20-year longitudinal study of more than 150 New York City public school children, reported in the book, *Yesterday's Children*, concluded that success or failure in traditional schools is well-indicated by age nine. "Reading levels and behavioral problems that will influence a person as an adult are established by the end of the third grade." Experiments at Wilson found that when students are allowed to select the adult persons with whom they wish to study, they seek a warm, open person to whom they relate; then they determine what would be interesting, valuable, and fun to learn. As an illustration, perhaps "social studies" was heavily enrolled with students – what would appear as the most popular subject in school. "Science" might be almost empty of students: seemingly very few liked it. But it was discovered that if those popular social studies teachers were placed in science, and the science teachers were placed in social studies, suddenly the enrollment figures switched; most students left social studies and went to science; even if the teachers did not know as much about the subject, the students devised topics to study with them; the students sought people over content. This further validated that **the most important ingredient in the entire open school movement was not facilities, equipment, flexible scheduling, curriculum revision, more money, or nongrading, but the trust and responsibility established between warm, open, humane persons who became concerned about each other and the world in which they lived**. This factor alone can set the tone for a complete revamping of the accepted traditions of assigning teachers, rooms, content, and subjects in the schools of the United States.

The importance of this human relationship was again portrayed in a sad study by Dr. Herbert Harari, a psychology professor at California State University in San Diego. He found that names such as Sanford, Hubert, Melody, Otto, and Ralph were "loser's names," and that youngsters so named consistently got poorer grades than others because teachers discriminated against them. As part of the study, two popular names, David and Michael, and two unpopular names, Hubert and Elmer, were placed on four compositions written by fourth and fifth graders. Each was graded by 80 teachers and student teachers. Then the names were switched on the compositions and resubmitted to the teachers, but so that they did not grade the same paper twice. Compositions bearing the names David and Michael averaged a letter grade higher than when submitted by Elmer or Hubert. The most experienced teachers showed the greatest bias in their grading – they had previously learned that Hubert and Elmer were losers.

Though there is much exciting and significant research, most has gone largely unnoticed, or even if considered, has not been adopted to the extent that it has made much difference in the way schools are organized or in their approaches to learning. It is clear, as an illustration, that more money should be spent on the first three years (k-2) than any other three years in the current "schooling" process. **Yet, "decades later," it is difficult to find a district which spends more on primary age children than on secondary students.**

Students

The good acceptable evidence has not had an immediate wide impact on truly improving student learning. Wilson staff were determined not only to prevent this from happening in their Mankato site, but more, to add to the growing body of literature which confirmed there are alternatives to the conventual methods used in most schools. The theses cited multiply the evidence related to student outcomes when variations from the traditional are created. They further document what happened to youth who attended the "develop-your-own-recipe" program at Wilson.

THESIS ABSTRACTS

#1. A COMPARATIVE STUDY OF STUDENT ATTITUDES TOWARDS PHYSICAL EDUCATION IN OPEN, ELECTIVE-REQUIRED, AND TRADITIONAL PHYSICAL EDUCATION PROGRAMS, by John R. Eggers

Purpose: This study was designed to measure student attitudes towards physical education in open, elective-required, and traditional physical educational programs.

Findings: At the .01 level of significance, the students in the open program had a more favorable attitude towards physical education than the students in the traditional and elective-required programs. No significant difference was found among the students in the elective-required and traditional programs.

#2. IMPLEMENTING CONCEPTS OF CHILD DEVELOPMENT INTO A PRE-SCHOOL THROUGH SECONDARY CURRICULUM IN AN OPEN CAMPUS SCHOOL ENVIRONMENT, by Joan M. Barker

Purposes:
1. To consider the need for child development to be taught in the primary and secondary schools.
2. To report the method of implementing concepts of child development into a primary and secondary open-campus school system.
3. To evaluate filing materials to supplement the implementation of the program.
4. To draw conclusions and recommendations for the future of this program.

Findings:
1. The results of the 1969-70 program at Wilson demonstrated the need for child development education in primary and secondary schools.
2. The program was taught through the home economics and early childhood centers using preschool children to provide basic laboratory experiences in child development concepts.
3. A filing system was developed on child development concepts as well as a table of criteria for evaluating materials.
4. It was recommended that teachers of this program should ideally be college majors in child development rather than home economics, psychology, sociology, or elementary.

#3. THE PRESENT AND POTENTIAL USE OF CAI IN MATHEMATICS AT WILSON CAMPUS SCHOOL, by John W. Bull

Purpose: The purpose of this literature review was to determine the advantages, problems, and feasibility of CAI (Computer Assisted Instruction) for use in the Wilson Campus School.

Findings:
1. CAI is helping reform curriculum in the United States.
2. CAI needs to be developed in the areas of tutoring and dialogue forms of math.
3. CAI is causing educators to explore and try to determine how people learn and retain information.
4. Mathematics teachers have been made aware of order in presentation of basic math. Math is the cognitive subject easiest to program for CAI.
5. CAI is not an education cure-all. It is a viable aid to teaching and instruction.
6. CAI is creating jobs not available before 1945.
7. Wilson Campus School, because of its individualized approach, could make use of CAI.
8. Wilson Campus School could receive funds (i.e., USOE) to help implement the use of CAI.

#4. INDIVIDUALIZED INSTRUCTION OF HIGH SCHOOL ENGLISH, by Marianne Erdal

Purpose: The purpose of this study was to determine, through a review of literature, the significance of individualized instruction in the teaching of senior high school English. It was developed in part on the basis of personal experience in teaching senior high English in traditional high schools – the most recent having been Mankato High – and in an innovative-type, specifically Wilson Campus School. The attitudes of students and teachers in both styles of schools were considered in the study.

Findings: Instructional materials, the arrangement of a learning atmosphere, provisions for individual differences in English curriculum and the development of the Learning Activity Package are some of the needs for the development of a program centered on individual learning concepts. The provision for individual differences in English curriculum is influenced by the quality of instructional and administrative leadership; a school which is planned, constructed, and staffed for individualization can better achieve its purpose for students.

#5. DEVELOPMENT OF A FAMILY LIFE EDUCATION CURRICULUM FOR PRIMARY-AGE STUDENTS, by Cathy Glovka

Purpose: To create an experiment to develop a curriculum in family life education at the primary school level. The basic philosophy of home economics was utilized in construction, including study of the family life cycle, personality development, and interrelationships of family members.

Findings: Journal observations indicate enthusiasm on the part of students about activities relating to family life. Elementary students displayed a willingness to talk about their own families while showing an understanding of family interrelationships. Recommendations include formation of gender heterogeneous family life classes, integration of the family concept into the curriculum at all levels, utilization of the home economics instructor as a curriculum consultant, and parental input into the program assessment.

#6. A STUDY OF STUDENT ATTITUDES AND ACHIEVEMENT BEFORE AND AFTER THE IMPLEMENTATION OF THE HIGH SCHOOL GEOGRAPHY PROJECT AT WILSON CAMPUS SCHOOL, by Larry William Herke

Purposes:
1. To determine the attitudes of 20 high school students toward geography before implementing the HSGP materials.
2. To determine the attitudes of the same 20 high school students toward geography after implementing the HSGP materials.
3. To discover the changes of attitude found after completing the implementation of HSGP materials with the 20 high school students while using the chi-square test and the summary of percentages formula.
4. To determine the mastery of HSGP information by the 20 high school students before implementing the HSGP materials.
5. To determine the mastery of HSGP information by the 20 high school students after implementing the HSGP materials.
6. To discover the changes found in the mastery of HSGP information after completing the implementation of the HSGP materials with the 20 high school students while using the t-test.

Findings:
1. Nine of the 30 opinions surveyed revealed meaningful (20 percent gains in agreement) or significant (at the.05 confidence level) positive changes in attitude. The nine statements were:

   (a) Geography has taught me how to think.
   (b) Most of my time in geography has been spent locating cities, countries, crops, mountains, lakes, oceans, and deserts.
   (c) Geography places more emphasis on "where" than on "why."
   (d) One of the most important things I can learn from geography is to be able to decide where to locate things.
   (e) One of the most important things I can learn from geography is to explain why things are located where they are.
   (f) The study of geography has helped me to realize that answers to problems are often tentative and not final.
   (g) If I wanted to solve a problem, it would be more worthwhile to collect all the facts concerning the problem than to investigate why people disagree on the proper solution to the problem.
   (h) I can read geographic information and form definite opinions.
   (i) Most questions concerning geography have one correct answer.

2. The achievement test results revealed significant cognitive gains when the t-test was applied at the .05 confidence level.

#7. A PLAN FOR AN EXPANDED TYPEWRITING CURRICULUM, by Susan Hjermstad

Purpose: The purpose of this paper was to show the usefulness of introducing typewriting to (1) students in the kindergarten through junior high levels; (2) physically handicapped children; (3) visually handicapped children; and, (4) slow learners.

Findings: The writer concluded that typewriting should be expanded to include all students in the school from the kindergarten to the senior high to the disadvantaged student. This can be implemented in a traditional program, but ideally would be used in an "open" school. The typewriter has proven useful in the development of reading, spelling, arithmetic, and handwriting in the elementary grades. There is also a vocational and academic need for the junior high as well as for the disadvantaged student.

#8. A STUDY OF GROWTH OF HEALTHY SELF-CONCEPTS AMONG STUDENTS AT THE WILSON CAMPUS SCHOOL, by Raymond Lewis Holden

Purpose: What happens to student self-concept as a result of attending Wilson Campus School?

Findings: A perusal of the interview responses makes it quite obvious that there is a strong trend toward positive self-image growth in the Wilson Campus School environment.

#9. THE READING POTENTIAL OF SELECTED THREE, FOUR, AND FIVE YEAR OLD CHILDREN IN A WILSON CAMPUS SCHOOL SETTING, by Helen Ann Holmes

Purpose: The purpose of this study was to determine the reading potential of selected three, four, and five year old children in a Wilson Campus School setting.

Findings: This study revealed that individual children ranging from three, four, and five can be taught to read. The study further revealed a need for evaluation of the current available reading systems as they relate to the teaching of reading to the young child.

#10. THE IMPACT OF PREKINDERGARTEN ATTENDANCE UPON COGNITIVE, SOCIAL-EMOTIONAL AND PSYCHOMOTOR PERFORMANCE IN KINDERGARTEN, by Darlene J. Janovy

Purpose: What is the relationship between group prekindergarten experience and kindergarten performance in the cognitive, social-emotional and psychomotor domain?

Findings: Prekindergarten experience is associated with higher ratings in all domains, and these associations are statistically reliable at or beyond the .05 level of confidence. According to the contingency coefficients, socioeconomic status appears to be the most powerful predictor of high ratings in the cognitive domains. The strong relationship may be the result of variation in teacher expectations for children from high versus lower socioeconomic groups.

#11. PSYCHOMOTOR DEVELOPMENT IN INDUSTRIAL ARTS AT THE ELEMENTARY SCHOOL LEVEL, by Thomas J. Jeffrey

Purpose: The purpose of this study was to determine whether an industrial arts program would significantly enhance the psychomotor skills of elementary school children. Specific attention was given to (1) control precision; (2) rate control; (3) manual dexterity; (4) finger dexterity; and, (5) arm-hand steadiness.

Findings: The data collected for Test 1, Hand-Sawing – Control Precision Test, indicated that no significant difference existed between the control and experimental groups. The data collected for Test 2, Scroll-Sawing – Rate Control Test, indicated a significant difference did exist between the control and experimental groups. The data collected for Test 3, Hammering – Manual Dexterity Test, indicated that a significant difference existed between the control and experimental groups. The data collected for Test 4, Nut and Bolt – Finger Dexterity, indicated that no significant difference existed between the control and experimental groups. The data collected for Test 5, Hand Steadiness Counter, Arm-Hand Steadiness Test, indicated that a significant difference existed between the control and experimental groups. The data collected for this study indicated that elementary school children who are involved in an industrial arts curriculum will achieve a significantly higher level of psychomotor development at the culmination of an industrial arts program than those students who are not involved in an industrial arts program.

#12.   GUIDELINES FOR THE DESIGN OF AN INDIVIDUALIZED TYPEWRITING CURRICULUM IN A NONGRADED SCHOOL, by Martha Johnson

Purpose: The purpose was to delineate the guidelines and learning activities developed during the 1969-70 school year at Wilson Campus School, to enable future professionals to add continuity, test models, and build a relevant typewriting curriculum in a nongraded, individualized school.

Findings: The basic design for individual differences, goal setting, and evaluation devices in a nongraded typewriting curriculum includes student contracts, student assignment sheets, individual business conferences, flexible goals, three minute typewriting timings and individual progress charts. An immediately available collection of supplementary drills and exercises for developing speed, accuracy, and control in typewriting is also a necessary part of the individualized nongraded curriculum.

#13.   THE IMPORTANCE OF TEACHING A FOREIGN LANGUAGE IN THE PRIMARY GRADES, by Olga Frances Navarette Jondahl

Purpose: This study was designed to investigate the importance of teaching a foreign language in the primary grades. The study cites reasons an elementary age child is more apt to learn a foreign language than an older student.

Findings:
1. Research has established that the young possess a definite ability to absorb languages.
2. A strong factor for having foreign language in the elementary school is that a child is apt to learn more quickly through lack of inhibitions.
3. Neurologists emphasize that childhood is the ideal period for acquiring a native or near native pronunciation.
4. A young child is more willing to learn about others with different customs and cultures.
5. The most effective techniques used in foreign language programs today are the audio-lingual and audio-visual methods.
6. There is a need to establish a continual language program through the 12th grade.

#14.   THE DEVELOPMENT OF MEDIA MATERIALS FOR INSTRUCTION IN PHYSICAL EDUCATION, by Cheryl Lynn Kalakian

Purpose: The purpose of this study was to determine the feasibility of creating teacher-made media materials in physical education. It was demonstrated that they may be used for both individualized and self-paced instruction and are produced inexpensively.

#15. A COMPARISON OF COLLEGE GRADES BETWEEN MATCHED STUDENTS FROM GRADED AND NONGRADED HIGH SCHOOLS, by Allen P. Larson, Master of Arts in Teaching

Purpose: Is there a significant difference in grades in selected college classes between students graduating from a nongraded school and a graded school when both groups are matched on certain achievement influencing criteria?

Findings:
1. There was a significant difference in combined college grades between 1970-71 Wilson Campus and Mankato High School graduates. This difference favored Wilson Campus School.
2. Wilson Campus School students earned significantly higher grades than Mankato High School students in the area of natural science. Wilson Campus students also achieved higher average grades in each of the five general education categories although these results were not statistically significant.
3. There was no significant difference between Wilson Campus students and Mankato High students in any of the individual classes investigated. However, Wilson Campus students averaged higher grades in all subjects except English 1023; Art 1004 and 1603; and English 1113, 1123, and 1133.
4. No cause and effect conclusions can be drawn from this study.

#16. THE OVERALL EDUCATIONAL ENVIRONMENT, WITH PARTICULAR EMPHASIS ON 'FINE ARTS THROUGH SOUND' CAN EFFECTIVELY MEET THE NEEDS OF ITS CONSUMERS BY DEMONSTRATING THAT FLEXIBILITY IN THE PROCESS OF EDUCATION IS OF PARAMOUNT IMPORTANCE, by Denis A. Luber.

Purpose: Societal educational structures and systems are finding increasing difficulty in meeting the needs of its consumers. The rapid development and "stirrings" in the technological, sociological, and philosophical areas are demanding that schools reexamine their methods and goals. The author first examined this problem in a general sense and secondly through the specific discipline of 'fine arts through sound.'

Findings: The results of this study showed that educational systems and methods are slowly changing. The critical need today is for broad-minded educational leaders to foster a climate of constructive criticism and creative enthusiasm in tackling these situations. An examination of the specific area of 'fine arts through sound' revealed a need for a more comprehensive and interdisciplinary mode of operation. Societal educational needs in the near and distant future can be met through creative systems analysis.

#17. A COMPARISON OF ACT SCORES BETWEEN MATCHED STUDENTS IN TRADITIONAL AND EXPERIMENTAL SCHOOL SYSTEMS, by Timothy J. O'Connell

Purpose: To determine if there is a significant difference in achievement as measured by the scores on the ACT tests between graded and nongraded schools when groups of students representing both school systems are evenly matched using relevant achievement-influencing criteria, for ACT scores are required by many midwest colleges.

Findings:
1. There is no significant difference in ACT scores between matched pairs of students from Wilson Campus School and Mankato High School.
2. Apparent differences in achievement between Wilson Campus School and Mankato High School are likely due to differences in IQ and parental occupation rather than type of school attended.
3. Some differences may exist between Wilson Campus School students and Mankato High School students who did not take the ACT tests. Those students were not compared in this study.
4. There may be other outcomes caused by these contrasting school systems other than that measured by the ACT test.

#18.   A COMPARISON ANALYSIS OF THE THEATER CURRICULUM IN SCHOOL DISTRICT 77 AND WILSON CAMPUS SCHOOL, by Marcia Olauson

Purpose: The purpose of this study was to present a comparative analysis between the theater curricula in Independent School District 77 and Wilson Campus School.

Findings: In the Independent School District 77, none of the elementary schools have a specific children theater or creative dramatics program for children and none of the teachers is required to have special dramatics training. It is felt by the district that creative dramatics can be most effective when it is integrated into the study of the subject matter; i.e., literature, social studies, oral composition. In the junior and senior high schools, theatrical activities were more formally analyzed and provided for in the curriculum.

At Wilson Campus School, theatrical activities are available at any time for students k-12. Since there is no curriculum guide for the students, theatrical expression is designed by them to meet their needs. A list of such activities is included at the end of this study.

#19.   A STUDY OF AN INDIVIDUALIZED HOME ECONOMICS PROGRAM FOR ELEMENTARY AGE STUDENTS AT WILSON CAMPUS SCHOOL, by Carloyn Schommer

Purpose: The purpose of this study was to gain an insight of the concepts of home economics education and to develop an individualized learning unit in foods to incorporate into the Wilson Campus School home economics program.

Findings: Current literature indicates that little research has been conducted in the pursuit of elementary home economics, and little has been done to promote this area. Wilson Campus School has been encouraged to continue to research the value of elementary home economics in the psychomotor domain. Valid curriculum programs should be developed for those teachers who wish to experiment with home economics and psychomotor skills.

#20.   THE DEVELOPMENT OF A PHYSICAL EDUCATION CURRICULUM IN AN INDIVIDUALIZED SCHOOL SYSTEM, by Mark H. Schuck

Purpose: The purpose of this paper was to make recommendations for devising an individualized physical education curriculum. The primary purpose was to show a probable procedure for changing from the "traditional" to a more individualized curriculum, including changes in scheduling, content offerings, methodology of teaching, and materials used.

Findings:
1. It is the personal belief of the author that physical education of today must take on a wider scope of activities to meet the personal needs of all students.
2. With the help of a flexible schedule, a broadening effect on both materials and activities in the curriculum will accrue.
3. There must be individual diagnosis and prescription by the teacher and student. The goals and behavioral objectives must be determined with the student.

#21. EXAMINATION OF THE CHILD-PET RELATIONSHIP WITH SELECTED STUDENTS, by Sally Sherwin

Purpose: To examine characteristics of elementary children who consistently demonstrated affection for pets at Wilson Campus School and compare the findings with a random sample of students who did not consistently demonstrate affection for pets.

Findings: The two groups of subjects examined in this study did not vary significantly from each other. It is likely that other variables, other than the 20 examined, influence students. A possible relationship exists between the gender of the child and his or her involvement with pets.

#22. A COMPARISON OF RESPONSES FROM MANKATO HIGH STUDENTS AND WILSON HIGH STUDENTS TO SELECTED ATTITUDES STATEMENTS CONCERNING SCHOOL, by Stephen J. Sontag

Purpose: Is there a determinable difference in attitudes of Mankato High students and Wilson High students toward school?

Findings: The responses to eight of the ten attitude statements given to a sample of Mankato High School and Wilson High students showed that a statistically significant difference in attitude does exist between the two schools as measured by the questionnaire. The two statements, which show no difference in response, were "I dislike school because I don't get along with some teachers," and "I enjoy school because I can be with my friends."

#23 A DEVELOPMENTAL NEEDS PHYSICAL EDUCATION PROGRAM, by William A. Tartaglia

Purpose: To present examples of the necessary components that will enable a program to be individualized to meet the needs of students.

Findings: Students were able to progress through the program at their own rate of development. Students were able to experience activities that fit their own interests, needs, and capabilities as they grew and developed. When students have freedom of choice in activities, guidance and counseling become a vital necessity for the success of the program.

#24.   CIGARETTE SMOKING AND HEARING ACUITY, by Peter B. Toews

Purpose: The purpose of this study was to examine from an educational perspective the effects of smoking on hearing acuity.

Findings: Hearing disorders are grouped into two categories: conductive and sensori-neural.

1.   Conductive hearing loss is caused because sound waves are not transmitted effectively to the inner ear because of some mechanical interference in the functioning of the external canal, the eardrum, the ossicular chain, the middle ear cavity, the oval window, or the Eustachian tube. Heavy smokers seem to have a greater chance of having hearing loss. It was projected that tobacco smoke produces damage in the Eustachian tube and thus affects hearing.
2.   In sensori-neural hearing loss, sound is conducted properly to the fluid of the inner ear, but it does not reach the brain properly and therefore cannot be analyzed or perceived normally. In sensorineural hearing loss (a) nicotine produces vasospasm of varying degrees and duration in small caliber blood vessels including that of the internal ear; (b) this vasoconstriction can and does produce, in a number of people, lesions in the internal ear.

There is sufficient evidence available to discuss the potential of hearing loss as a result of smoking in the educational programs advising people as to the hazards of smoking and to suggest further scientific inquiry in this regard.

#25.   THE RELATIONSHIP OF AFFECTIVE TEACHER CHARACTERISTICS TO THE FREQUENCY OF ADVISOR SELECTION AT WILSON CAMPUS SCHOOL, by Lorna M. Wing

Purpose: Do faculty members who were chosen more frequently as advisors differ in genuineness, warmth, and empathy from faculty members who were chosen less frequently as advisors when rated by their students on the Truax Relationship Questionnaire?

Findings: The results of this study showed that teachers who were selected more frequently as advisors were rated significantly higher at the .05 level in the areas of genuineness, empathy, and warmth than those teachers who were selected less frequently as advisors. When these affective qualities are assessed by students, they do choose those teachers as advisors who emit high levels of these qualities.

#26.   AN INVESTIGATION OF STUDENT ATTITUDES TOWARD THE INNOVATIVE MATHEMATICS PROGRAM OF WILSON CAMPUS SCHOOL, by Marven H. Wolthuis

Purpose: The purpose of this study was to investigate the attitudes of students concerning the innovative changes that had taken place in the education philosophy at Wilson during the 1968-69 school year.

<u>Findings</u>: As shown by the data, 86 percent indicated their preference for the new approach. There was a favorable reaction to self-pacing and setting their own goals; the majority of those questioned felt they had gained a sense of responsibility. The researcher feels further studies and projects are needed to gain truly conclusive results.

These few samplings of a cross-section of "studies," "reports," "research" at Wilson indicate that though the school did not give traditional grades, grade-point-averages, or test results, that the faculty was extremely concerned with the effect of their efforts on the students and wanted to ensure that they were helping, not harming the youth. Thus between 1968 and 1977, more research and accountability efforts occurred at Wilson than in any other school in Minnesota.

References Cited

Amidon, Edmund *Interaction Analysis: Theory, Research, Application* Addison-Wesley, Reading, Massachusetts, 1967

Bloom, Benjamin S. *Human Characteristics and School Learning* McGraw-Hill, New York, 1976

Class of 1938, Ohio State Laboratory School *Were We Guinea Pigs?* Henry Holt and Co., New York, 1938

Houts, Paul, ed. *The Myth of Measurability* Hart Publishing Co., Inc., New York, 1977

Hoyt, D.P. "Relationship Between College Grades and Adult Achievement: A Review of the Literature" *ACT Research Report #7*, Iowa City, 1965

Long, Kathleen *Teacher Reflections on Individual School Restructuring: Alternatives in Public Education*, unpublished doctoral dissertation. University of Oregon, Eugene, 1992

Patterns in ESEA Title I Reading Achievement Educational Policy Research Center, Syracuse University, Syracuse, New York, 1976

Perrone, Vito "The Abuses of Standardized Testing" (Fastback) *Phi Delta Kappa*, Bloomington, Indiana, 1976

Summary of Research on Open Education Educational Research Service, 1815 N. Ft. Myer Drive, Arlington, Virginia, 1975

Summary of Research on Prekindergarten Program Educational Research Service, 1815 N. Ft. Myer Drive, Arlington, Virginia, 1975

Willis, Margaret *Twenty Years Later: Guinea Pigs Revisited* Ohio State University Press, Columbus, 1961

Wilson Campus School Remembered, 50-minute videotape, College of Education, Mankato State University, Minnesota, 1993

SPECIAL ATTENTION

Eight-Year Study Progressive Education Association: Commission on Relations of Schools and Colleges, published as Adventure in American Education Series, Harper and Brothers, New York, 1942 (Now out of print.)

Volume I: *The Story of the Eight Year Study* – with conclusions and recommendations by Wilford M. Aikin

Volume II: *Exploring the Curriculum* – the work of the 30 schools from the viewpoint of curriculum consultants, by H.H. Giles, S.P. McCutchen, and A.M. Zechiel

Volume III: *Appraising and Recording Student Progress* – evaluation, records, and reports on the 30 schools, by Eugene R. Smith, Ralph W. Tyler, and the evaluation staff

Volume IV: *Did They Succeed in College* – the follow-up study of the graduates in the 30 schools, by Dean Chamberlin, Enid Chamberlin, Neal Drought, and William Scott

Volume V: *Thirty Schools Tell Their Story* – each school writes of its participation in the *Eight-Year Study*

SPECIAL ARTICLES

Jennings, Wayne "Startling Delightful Research," *KAPPAN*, March 1977, (Phi Delta Kappa, Eighth and Union, Bloomington, Indiana)

"Special Research Bibliography" by Wayne Jennings from the above March 1977 *KAPPAN* article; reprinted by permission of the author

Central Advisory Council for Education *Children and Their Primary Schools*, two volumes. Her Majesty's Stationery Office, London, 1967

Coleman, James S., et al. "Equality of Educational Opportunity," Superintendent of Public Documents, Washington, D.C., 1967

Gartner, Alan; Kohler, Mary; Riesman, Frank *Children Teach Children* Harper and Row, New York, 1971

Goodlad, John I. *Behind the Classroom Door* Wadsworth, Belmont, California, 1970

Horwitz, Robert A. *Psychological Effects of Open Classroom Teaching on Primary School Children: A Review of the Research* University of North Dakota Press, 1976

Husen, Torsten *International Study of Achievement in Mathematics*, Vol. 2. Almquist and Wilsells, Uppsala, Sweden, 1967

Neale, D.C.; Gill, N.; Tismer, W. "Relationship Between Attitudes Toward School Subjects and School Achievement," *Journal of Educational Research*, Vol. 63, 1970

Neale, D.C., and Proshek, J.M. "School Related Attitudes of Culturally Disadvantaged Elementary School Children," *Journal of Educational Psychology*, Vol. 58, 1967

Tompkins, Ellsworth, and Gaumnitz, Walter "Carnegie Unit: Its Origin, Status, and Trends" *Education and Welfare Bulletin No. 7*, U.S. Government Printing Office, Washington, D.C., 1954

chapter thirty

RETROSPECT

Teacher Reflections on Individual School Restructuring: Alternatives in Public Education is a doctoral dissertation completed at the University of Oregon in 1992 by Kathleen Long. Its major focus is a documentation of the Mankato Wilson School, confirming that it really existed, was successful, and actually implemented all 69 advertised changes. The study especially focused on the transition of the teaching staff from working in a traditional school to a completely open-ended program. A number of her conclusions are reflected in support of the Wilson concepts as a transition toward the eventual transformation of education.

Dr. Long found that the Wilson philosophy believed in providing alternatives in content and methodology designed to meet individual needs through student-centered learning. This meant new interpretations of time, personal relationships, space, knowledge, and decision-making; the power to create, name, and decide was diffused among students, teachers, and administrators. She also documented that Wilson viewed the affective, psychomotor, and cognitive as interdependent, but emphasized the affective, psychomotor, creativity and learning styles as the keys to cognitive growth. This enhanced motivation, and coupled with student selection of teachers and the development of their own studies, made a significant difference at Wilson.

The dissertation, was planned as a book (Long, *Mankato Wilson School: Reflections on Restructuring)*, cited numerous other findings. Teachers were treated as professionals and had the same optional attendance, freedom, responsibility, individualization, and self-selection policies as the students. Person-centered relationships emerged: they were more reciprocal than hierarchical, reflecting on the understanding of the interdependence of the participants.

Concrete physical alterations in the structure occurred too. Walls were removed and doorways created to connect what were once individual classrooms. Curriculum, too, was restructured. The lines between what had previously been considered discrete subject areas were blurred as teachers teamed across disciplines. The non-graded structure allowed students to progress at their own pace. The open curriculum concept helped staff realize even more the developmental nature of learning and the paramount importance of continuous progress and individualization.

Dr. Long stated that the Wilson environment extended into the community and the larger world. Integrated course work and site-based learning experiences provided direct evidence that learning is an integral part of life, not something that occurs within the space and time designated for certain activities by the school. Before the changes, staff had not realized how much their thinking and actions were actually tied to the traditional classrooms.

In the "new Wilson," students focused on topics according to their individual development and interest, and attended school more often because attendance was their choice. There were few restrictions on staff or students for taking time for personal matters. Hours were allocated for affective development, as reflected through the Advisor System – a demanding process, but an overwhelmingly successful committment.

Because teachers had the opportunity to evolve intimate relationships with their students, they felt they were far more effective educators.

The most far reaching change made at Wilson, according to the Long study, was in the redistribution of power. When the students were allowed to decide on their advisors and teachers, they, in essence, defined who were and were not the teachers and advisors among the faculty. When afforded the privilege of deciding what content to study, they defined to a large extent the curriculum. Faculty members became friends and helpers; they were viewed as human, approachable, and trustworthy. Faculty felt it was much more important to know why a student was performing in a given manner than to be concerned over what the student was doing.

Dr. Long also cited that the open philosophy was one of the reasons Wilson was successful with troubled or marginalized students. The school took in more than its share of non-traditional students, for the personal, individualized nature of the program made it easier to meet their needs. The advisor/advisee relationship and personalized curriculum content were key components. The non-judgmental assessment techniques enhanced the likelihood of individual student success, including the most "advantaged."

At Wilson, groups were not mandated or formed by artificial mechanisms. Instead, they most often formed through common interests. The collaboration which was promoted among both students and staff created a different atmosphere. Cheating was impossible, as students were encouraged to help each other learn; there were no grades, curves, or class ranks to score high or to keep others beneath them. Individual and group community service was a large part of the humaneness in the curriculum.

The study further determined that experiential learning provided the students an immediate way of knowing. They participated widely in "doing" activities, including the exchange program with youth in Mexico. Students set their own goals and evaluated their own progress in collaboration with their advisors; they learned to monitor their own development. Students were also invited to evaluate the teachers. Since they were not separated by grade, age, or ability levels, they taught one another.

An important aspect of the Wilson philosophy was summarized by the phrase, "With freedom goes responsibility." Faculty found this of great benefit, for they could shift from being ogres to helpers; they were no longer adversaries. Students realized they were responsible for any subsequent "ignorance." The inclusion of the students in the decision-making processes of curriculum and instruction kept the staff on their toes; the students had power, for they could chose not to select a teacher or class. Wilson provided a safe but responsive environment for students to test limits, and worked to meet student needs without creating self-centeredness.

The results of the investigation also reflected that fewer instances of student resistance and negative behavior surfaced at Wilson. Discipline was handled differently. It became less the domain of an authority figure and more that of individual and group student responsibility. Positive means were sought to modify annoying behavior. Antagonisms between students and teachers melted away, as they were not forced to confront each other, as through the power of choice, students aligned themselves in situations where they could cope or excel. Wilson was focused on building from student successes; remedial courses and retention were not used as representing the traditional concept of failure.

Further, Wilson attested to the long held notion that too often schooling interferes with learning. By removing traditional barriers and creating space for new forms to emerge, the students and faculty were able to revitalize educational opportunities. Students were able to actually practice democratic principles. They were asked to accept responsibility and develop self-control. They were able to be creative, committed, and caring, and could design their own processes. They were encouraged to create their own boundaries. By allowing such autonomy, the Wilson format provides significant messages for those who want to go beyond re-conceptualizing schooling and instead envision new learning systems.

The dissertation by Kathleen Long, available from the library at the University of Oregon, triggered another documentary of Wilson. From recovered slides and film clips, former staff created a 50-minute videotape depicting the program. It further confirmed that Wilson existed and was successful in all it claimed. The narrative clearly illustrated the personalized, non-graded, choice oriented plan implemented. Titled "Mankato Wilson Campus School Remembered," it is available from the College of Education, Mankato State University, Minnesota. As a bonus, the second part of the tape contains an original 30-minute 1972 explanation for visitors of the rationale for change by the then director of the Campus School. A shorter 15-minute tape, *The Wilson Experience*, by Dr. Long is available from Performance Learning Systems, Nevada City, California. These tapes not only archive the past, but more importantly offer a prototype that schools of the late 90s can use to restructure their designs immediately, as a transition toward the transformation of learning which is essential as society moves into the first two decades of the new century.

PART V

SUMMARIZING EXPERIENCE

chapter thirty-one

REMEMBERED

From the Author – In Review of Chapters 1-30

Historical perspective is crucial for those envisioning preferable futures.   The story of Wilson and prior efforts to change was written because my professional and personal concerns are with the present and future – with the societal conditions which are and will even more, affect education.   My focus is on learning systems for the 21st Century, and a time when schooling and schools will be eliminated.   I am not interested in restructuring or reforming schools which already should not exist; instead the need is to begin with a new mission – the creation of an educational space capsule to Mars, but while it is being developed, continue to experiment in the Discovery.   I no longer want to try to improve educational Being 777s or Saab 340s, and certainly do not want to fly in covered wagons (graded schools, ability grouping, ABC report cards, period 1-2-3 schedules, self-contained classrooms).

For those not yet ready to design the capsule to Mars, or even experience the Discovery – for those who cannot accept a complete transformation of learning – there is a dramatic need for transitional steps and suggestions.   The described Mankato State University Wilson Campus School "model," from the 1968-1977 era, can help fill that gap. True, the facility closed; however, its philosophy, concepts, practices, successes, and documented research provide dreams for existing programs, as educators consider their personal visions of learning in the decade following 2000. Wilson today is perhaps even more valid to study than in the 60s and 70s, for it can cause reflection on what was, what might have been, and what could be coming beyond most current limited goals of school reform.   If technology can launch a one year voyage to Mars, then in the first two decades, certainly in the next 20 years, communities can prepare for a society without schooling.

The past as future – a Camelot remembered from 1968-1977 – can create new directions for transitioning learning toward the 21st Century and beyond. But, 30 years ago, what led to Wilson, a school focused on tomorrow, and why is it necessary to begin again?   Why should current educators once more take arms against the famous "windmills?" What antecedent factors still spark a fire in me toward yet continuing to try to eliminate the 7th grade – and all grades for that matter – but especially the 7th – in the belief that no child should ever be mandated, without choice, into the programs required of most middle and junior high schoolers closing out the 90s. Such a conviction causes a momentary pause to relate experiences, dreams, and realities of the past 30 years, before proceeding with summarizing the prior pages covering Wilson, the Minnesota Experimental City, and the possibilities these remembered perspectives offer for the future.

Personal Reflections

My own visions began with the concept of educational alternatives. I was solidly committed to the notion in the 1958-1960 period, the result of reflecting on the outcomes of the *Eight-Year Study* of the 1930s; through observing the efforts in the late 50s to implement such changes as the non-graded schools, including reading *The Nongraded Elementary School* (1959); visiting the Eugene Howard directed famous Ridgewood High School in Norridge, Illinois; and mentoring from J. Lloyd Trump, one of the truly great educators of this century. My first opportunity to implement the school-of-choice concept came in Tucson, Arizona, in 1963, when students were given the option of attending the traditional junior/senior highs, or the new ones planned for innovations. The Canyon del Oro Secondary and the Lulu Walker Elementary Schools in the Amphitheater District were two of the first three in the U.S. to implement daily demand flexible scheduling – before the Stanford, inflexible flexible patterns – through the leadership of superintendent Marion Donaldson and principals Evelyn Carswell, Bob Dunsheath, and the author.

In my own schooling I had been fortunate to graduate from a four-day week high school with a revolving schedule, and from an elementary program where gardening was considered a basic skill. At the college level, a religion course and book, *The Legacy of the Liberal Spirit* with and by Fred Bratton, and the Springfield philosophy, added to the mix. Thus the seeds of discontent with traditional schooling may have been sown well before embarking upon a professional career.

As a young teacher, following time in the army, though successful, I knew something was wrong. Either I did not belong in education, or the "schooling" I was charged with did not make much sense for the majority of even middle class white students, let alone Hispanics in the eastern zone of Los Angeles. Spending four years overseas after my doctorate, while moving into administration, gave me the opportunity to reflect and experiment. Upon my return, I was fortunate to help lead the Amphitheater efforts in Tucson. I then fully realized how badly needed was the elimination of required traditional schooling. My career thus unfolded as an educational futurist and specialist for implementation of new ideas.

In 1965, I was hired as a "Vice-President for Heresy" – a full-time districtwide change agent in University City, Missouri. There we overhauled total schools, created schools-within-schools, developed programs-within-schools, teaming, forms of open enrollment, and total curriculum reform. In 1967, as the "change agent" for South Dakota, we resurrected excitement in that state, the most recognized of which was the Lincoln Learning Laboratory in Watertown (the Disneyland of South Dakota by student definition). It was a K-6 completely open, optional school of choice for all students, regardless of past school performance – thereby ensuring a cross-section of "gifted" and "at-risk" youth.

In 1968 I was offered the privilege of directing the transformation of the Wilson Campus School from a traditional college laboratory to an alternatives program which became recognized as the most experimental public school of choice in America – one open on a voluntary basis to all students in Mankato, regardless of ethnicity, gender, school achievement, or past behavior – again ensuring "A through F" youth, football players, scientists, poets, and preschoolers. We participated in the World Future Society and the Eight-State Designing Education for the Future Project in the 60s; we did not wait for the 90s, or some politically motivated "America 2000 Plan."

These fortunate experiences led to being asked to deliver over 900 addresses on alternative futures in education; the writing of twelve books; and the publication of over 120 articles on change, innovation, alternatives, and year-round education. Citing these personal memories is not intended as egotistical, or to indicate that my perceptions outlined in this book are the only "correct ones;" instead the intent is to convey an ongoing commitment to options, and to set the stage for reviewing comments and recommendations presented regarding the past, present, and future.

<u>Philosophical Perspectives</u>

Oversimplifying, part of our efforts as the "innovators" of the late 50s/early 60s resulted in trying to "sell everyone" on a conversion to the then "new education." One expressed motto in those days stated: "If schools are to be significantly better, they must be significantly different." The Lloyd Trump books, *Images of the Future* and *A School for Everyone*, also reflected this direction. The concepts involved team teaching, flexible scheduling, non-gradedness, the elimination of ABC report cards and self-contained classrooms, student centered learning, reducing the inequities of the American society, individualized learning, personalized curriculum, advisor systems, open-pod facilities, acoustical flooring (carpets), futures oriented concerns with the global dilemmas, person centers for the difficult behavior personalities, and over 60 other similar listed "changes." It was felt then that most all students would benefit from such "improvements," – now – meeting their existing needs and preferences.

Two factors intervened: (1) the innovators found they could not convert entire systems, or the nation, or sometimes even single schools, at that moment in history, without knockdown battles – few of which were successful. As a result, less than five percent of the schools in the nation actually changed to these ideals; and (2) the innovators soon discovered that not all youth, at that moment in their development, most benefitted from one status quo being replaced by another. For numerous reasons, many students and families still needed the traditions of the old system.

The notion of choices and options, though always in the rhetoric, emerged as the primary response to address these two realities. The leaders during the late 60s began to promote methods of implementing alternatives; lists, such as "36 Ways to Futurize Learning," surfaced. The original intent involved programs for everyone within the public school system – choices from "liberal" to "conservative." Title III school innovations, paired schools, open pod facilities, open education, small liberal arts academies, interest programs within large high schools, and multiple variations within districts became commonplace in the showcase communities and the literature – remembering that these were always that small minority. It was, however, a start, and illustrated that the workshop theory could become site reality.

The important historical pattern here to be highlighted was the notion of <u>alternatives</u> – the plural. Every program was a regular program for the student who selected it; every program was an alternative. <u>There was to be no "regular education," and no "alternative education."</u> There was no intent for remedial, at-risk, teen-age pregnant minors, gifted, and dropout prevention labels. There were only to be designs for individuals – for John, Mary, Juan, Wong, Clarissa. The concept was that of educational options for all; the offerings were not to be restricted to small non-comprehensive programs for students unhappy with the traditional norms and structure – though escaping the conventional was a key. Individual schools could develop their own pattern of what they perceived as best fitting their situation. The philosophy involved self-directed learning. Unfortunately, such beautiful beliefs were not accepted by the majority. As the late 70s turned to the early 80s, alternatives were being eliminated in favor of uniformity; opponents painted misperceptions of them as the 60s: "hippies," free-schools, and Summerhill (student governed resident learning) – untruthful political rhetoric.

Remembered

To survive, to keep the ideals alive, and to function as they believed they could best contribute to facilitating learning for their students, committed teachers accepted whatever they could bargain. Magnet schools became popular, for originally they focused on a curriculum area; it was later that they grew as a means of addressing segregation patterns. Programs expanded for "non-regular" students – those not making it in the conventional setting. The greatest deviation, though, that led to alternative education, rather than the plural, "alternatives," came through accepting the concept of "at-risk" students. To the great credit of those in alternatives, they saw a crisis. Here were 30 percent of the students receiving Ds and Fs; many were dropping out. To meet their needs, to develop student-centered learning, these teachers and innovators established multiple varieties of programs to provide for the "out-of-sync" youth. Unfortunately, such approaches led to the notion that alternative education was for the students who did not function properly in conventional classrooms; thus regular and alternative became, to the general public, the "good" and the "bad" – or the conforming and the non-conforming. They could not understand student-centered social justice approaches to eliminate the inequities of the content, teacher-centered, uniform world of the conventional – geared toward the historical past. Thus enters the importance of the Mankato Wilson School, and the transitions leading toward a transformation in the early 21st Century – from the "second wave" concept of schooling to new patterns of learning for the "third wave."

Revisiting Educational Reform

The past four decades, educational alternatives, year-round education (YRE), and "futuristic" proposals have existed in varieties of communities, and in many curriculum, site, and philosophical formats. Schools-within-schools; programs-within-schools; magnets; schools-without-walls; storefront and continuation centers; mandated designs to save space; voluntary continuous learning plans; university laboratory; experimental; and holistic schools represent the many implementations. The public offerings have been supplemented by a wide spectrum of private and secular models: Montessori, Waldorf, community-based and independent schools, Catholic, and other denominational preferences, and "home schooling." Most of the public K-12 choices have been small, ranging in size from 50 to 250, except for some urban programs over 500 at the high school level. Though growing numbers of communities have considered YRE for potential educational, lifestyle, and employment pattern benefits, and as a choice of calendars, the great majority originally began the programs to alleviate overcrowding where money was not available for new buildings – especially in the larger districts.

The majority of laboratory schools have focused on improving the existing conventional model of education – self-contained elementary, and period 1-2-3 scheduled secondary forms. Typically, they have enrolled from 300-500; some state university campuses have even charged tuition, creating, in effect, a publicly supported private school. Their value has been in assisting traditional teacher education through observation, participation, and student teaching patterns. Few have been true research and development laboratories, experimental in nature and futuristic in design. Most have seldom seriously challenged the status quo, beyond writing new curriculum projects, or trying one deviation at a time, such as team teaching or non-graded classrooms. Three exciting exceptions during the 20th Century were: the University of Chicago school in the early 1900s; the Ohio State program in the 1930s; and the Mankato State design of the late 60s/early 70s. Perhaps the best combination of a truly non-graded, public educational alternative, year-round education, and college laboratory devoted to experimentation, research, and developing patterns toward the future, was the Wilson Campus School at Mankato State University from 1968 to 1977. We resurrected and then far went beyond the famous *Eight-Year Study* of 1932-1940.

Two of the significant Mankato factors were its size, and its holistic – or "comprehensive" – offerings. Wilson wanted to enroll enough students to reach a critical mass – to be large enough to provide most all programs, or to arrange for community and global resources, to meet the needs of each individual student. Its 600 K-12 youth (200 elementary, 200 middle, and 200 high school), when mixed in a non-graded format, created the staffing to additionally include pre-birth and pre-school programs, and master degree and senior citizen components – and to be continuously open 12 months through a Personalized Continuous Year Calendar. Unlike most alternatives, Wilson maintained – here using traditional vocabulary – competitive sports (reaching the state finals in basketball), cheerleaders, dances, drama, music, art, industrial technology, home economics, advanced foreign language/science/math – and special education, early childhood, and all-day food service. Its facilities were adequate to accommodate such offerings year-round, and were supplemented by the school-in-the-community concept, utilizing many learning sites in Mankato, in Minnesota, in the other states – and even internationally – especially in Mexico. Large conventional schools automatically have had these options, though they have been seldom used or made available to the majority.

The current limited educational choices – magnet, alternative, continuation, gifted, and programs-within-a-school – generally do not offer such comprehensiveness. During the essential learning transitions leading into the 21st Century, those with experience from the 60s/70s believe there should be more "Wilson-style" sites available throughout the United States. The existing small alternatives patterns lose many students who would prefer to transfer from the conventional nine-month school, but they do not, for they still want football, advanced Spanish, college mathematics, auto shop, band, early childhood centers, and conventional playgrounds – but in non-traditional forms. From the lessons of the past, the message for educational change agents is clear: if the innovators are to overcome the barriers now faced, they must, in addition to the small, focused programs, provide the availability of holistic/comprehensive year-round settings that cater to the broader segment of families. The often perceived negative connotations of alternatives – at-risk or gifted – will not vanish until a broader cross-section of students is enrolled. Most current choices are good to outstanding for the volunteering individuals, but "traditionalists" most often yet equate the banner with unsuccessful, – or conversely, very talented – students. Matriculating the football, chemist, and band populations not only provides options for them, but illustrates that year-round alternatives are for all youth. Wilson represented one lesson from the past, suggesting how to accomplish a broader environment for those who would desire such a flexible continuous learning setting.

Peeking at the Future

Beyond the Mankato program, a look at the future is essential, for when considering the early 21st Century probabilities and possibilities, Wilson is immediately obsolescent. It, though, is still valuable as one acceptable, documented, and researched design for transitioning 2000. The future must bring opportunities to the student, and not continue to rely primarily on people arriving at a designated site. Schooling must be eliminated; education must be year-round, continuous learning.

Reviewing again the design for the Minnesota Experimental City (MXC), where in the early 70s a community of 250,000 was planned with no schools, does illustrate the potential of what lies ahead. Though never constructed, the concepts for the MXC learning system are valid, and can be adapted as part of continuous innovation. The components were based upon the assumptions developed by Dr. Ronald Barnes and the education design team for the MXC: 1) Learning is life; we never stop learning; 2) Learning occurs everywhere; 3) People can learn on their own; 4) Everyone is important, regardless of how much they know; 5) Authority is shared by all; 6) Education is a lifelong process of learning, and should be tailored to meet the needs of the individual; and 7) People will form positive social networks on their own without formal schooling.

The delivery of learning opportunities was planned conceptually through a variety of avenues, none of which were a school or site where students were transported each day. The design included multiple forms: 1) Existing facilities, including homes, businesses, public buildings – an updated vision of schools-without-walls; 2) Beginning Life Centers, offering an environment promoting creative experiences for young children, and for parents and older students the opportunity to learn of the needs of the young; 3) Stimulus Centers, offering films, tapes, sounds, smells – a constantly changing array of stimuli to bombard, provoke, and extend learners; 4) Gaming Centers, for learning to occur through educational games, simulated design, and techniques to address the complex realities in a simpler fashion; 5) Project Centers, for working on activities, as in making a movie, building a boat, designing a new vehicle; 6) Learner Banks, for loaning or using tools, materials, and equipment needed by the learners; and 7) Family Life Centers, for families to learn together; for seminars, meetings, tutoring, community discussions; social and health services; and playing fields and equipment. The entire system was linked through the LORIN (Learning Objectives Retrieval Information Network) – a sophisticated computer-based plan to connect learners with facilitators. Everyone was to be a teacher; everyone was to be a learner; the city was conceived as a lifelong learning living center.

As an education transition to eventual MXC concept systems, needed are more holistic, research oriented settings. Wilson was recognized in numerous international and national journal and media outlets as the most experimental public school in America during its era. It was and has been the focus of over 1,000 workshops, speeches, and evaluation studies. Visitors came from many corners of the world. Its recognition served the alternatives and year-round movements well, for it proved successful for a broad cross-section of Mankato, Minnesota, students. Unfortunately, the State Legislature closed all laboratory schools in 1977, more the result of the politics of the president and chancellor levels than the financial shortfalls of the existing state budget. In program and research evaluations, the Legislature praised the contributions of the Wilson staff and students toward the improvement of education in Minnesota.

It is time to resurrect new 2000 versions of Wilson – programs that are recognized, not for "gifted" or "at-risk" youth – or for "academics or test scores" – but for potentially all students and programs. Experimentation is essential, while expanding the breadth, depth, and acceptance of the philosophy of learning choices for everyone. Lessons learned since the inception of Wilson as one style of option can provide a springboard for imagineering life-long, living-learning systems for the future.

Wilson: Past as Present

Wilson was unique among year-round alternatives in that it was one of the few to maintain a "total program." Though small in size, and funded at no additional costs to the Mankato District, Wilson offered more available curriculum experiences than any other school in Minnesota – regardless of size or budgets. One student in nine years studied the History of Ireland without ever worrying about whether a teacher could be assigned or the class would be canceled if 25 did not register. It housed the teacher education option: SEA – the Studios for Educational Alternatives – and the master degree in Experiential Education – both of which allowed future and continuing teachers to avoid the conventional education classes. Wilson students could begin at pre-birth and complete an M.S. degree under one roof – and then continue there as a teacher/facilitator, community volunteer, or learner – and eventually become involved as participants in a program for golden-agers. Wilson was the beginning of turning formal lifelong learning from theory to reality.

The concepts were not unlike those in many experiments of its era. The difference was in their implementation in a larger, more comprehensive program catering to a broader cross-section of students. The "new" Wilson was created overnight. Prior to July of 1968, the school operated as a good conventional campus laboratory program with the usual waiting list – catering primarily to the demands of the college of education faculty; it was used, in cooperation with the university, as a neighborhood district public school. Thus there was little choice for students, except for high schoolers who could request the big conventional site to play at a higher level of competition, or enroll in a special curriculum program.

As the new director, I arrived during the summer of '68' with a mandate to turn it into the most experimental, alternative, up-side-down school in America. In two months the total "revolution" was underway, having completely dismantled tradition with an existing staff – many of whom did not want to see the "old" campus school program "destroyed." Wilson never claimed to be perfect; it had its share of problems. It was not a finished model with all the answers, but it did portray the tremendous need for changing outmoded schooling at a rapid, dramatic pace, challenging thinking, and offering stimulating ideas. It succeeded in creating discussion on the future of learning, while providing a significantly different program for those who volunteered to participate in the search for a transformation.

Wilson made 69 "changes" immediately. The most important was the aspect of human relations. Students selected their own facilitators and advisors; later surveys and interviews determined that consciously and subconsciously, the advisors were chosen on the basis of six factors: personality, perception, age, gender, interest, skill. The students found the adult they most loved and asked that person to serve as their confidante. No student was ever assigned to a teacher or advisor; no teacher was ever assigned to a student. As a result, all courses and requirements were eliminated. Curriculum became what the students wanted to study at that moment in time, with the persons they most wanted to share their learning.

Remembered

The affective domain was the key, followed by the psychomotor. The cognitive came third. Confluence was sought and generally achieved, but the priority was always the affective. Creativity was addressed, as a large number of the dropouts in many schools are those who score highest on "creativity tests." Learning styles were a prime consideration. Students selected staff who were more rigid or more flexible depending upon their relationships and current perceived needs in given areas. Kindergartners had the same choices; they were given more assistance by advisors, teachers, aides, and parents, but otherwise were relatively self-directing.

Curriculum was personalized and then individualized. Some three year olds were reading "3rd grade" level; some "3rd graders" were not reading and were not in remedial classes; maturation/motivation needed the right blends. If they had not started, or were moving at their own pace, they could not be "behind" or "below grade level." Five phase learning opportunities were stressed: individual instruction/discussion; independent study; open labs; small groups (with and without staff); and voluntary common thread large groups. Continuous progress was featured. Students paced at their own rate; some completed two or three years of college level math while in high school; others were content with minimal experiences in math. Curriculum was interdependent for the majority of the student learning activities; traditional departments and self-contained rooms were eliminated.

Wilson was open year-round; staff believed that learning alternatives should not be "closed" in the summer. Students could vacation whenever they desired for as long as they wanted, within the parameters of working toward the 170-day state requirement. Because the curriculum was individualized, they did not miss anything when they were away. Families of construction workers in the states like Minnesota need to vacation in January, not July; Dad cannot take time off during the June-July-August period. Staff and students can indicate ahead selected times to ensure a match of faculty, student needs, and budget. Attendance was optional year-round; all students, K-12, had the privilege of open campus. Food was served all day in the student center, as "lunch periods" were considered unacceptable for positive learning environments. The student mix in each center was non-graded; "kindergartners" and "seniors" had the same/similar programs, philosophies, facilities, and instructors. They were separated only when desired; age levels often shared activities and helped each other.

One of the attractions to visitors was how Wilson went from a traditional schedule — to a daily smorgasbord schedule where every student and teacher had a different time allotment every day — to a non-scheduled environment. It was not hard to accomplish in a school of 600 once curriculum and instruction were individualized and students learned to be self-directing. A major key to the success of Wilson was responsibility; staff accepted that it was not taught, but was to be given, learned, and accepted. The school slogan stated: "With freedom goes responsibility and courtesy." In a big school, house plans allow for the same non-schedule potentials.

There were no A, B, C report cards; no class rank lists; no traditional transcripts. Students completed goal sheets with their selected staff; some worked with only 2-3-4 faculty at one time, while others were engaged with 12-14. There were no graduation requirements; students left when ready with approval of their advisors, parents, and a review committee, though a great majority received their diplomas after the conventional 13 years. They stayed because they liked it, for financial or home reasons, their age, or involvement with sports and friends, but they could, and many did, graduate early. Others took a furlough and later returned to graduate at an older age.

The physical environment was changed: arches were cut through walls, or they were removed, or new ones were constructed; moveable air partitions were installed. The school interior was painted interesting colors and part of the facility was carpeted. The two gymnasiums and hallways were in constant use, as students moved on their own schedules. The Beginning Life Center focused on three through six year olds who could stay there all or part of the day, but who also could participate throughout the building – which almost all did. Parents returned in the evening as part of the lighted school pilot; special education students were completely mainstreamed as early as 1968. Community service and volunteering were critical components. Wilson people were "everywhere," but were especially involved in the senior citizens home and the state mental health hospital – as aides, friends, and learners.

A highlight experience for most students was the Mexican exchange with Centro Escolar in Puebla. Participating Wilson youth spent four to twelve weeks in Mexico, increasing their fluency in Spanish and learning the culture. The Mexican youth reciprocated by coming to Mankato two to four weeks each year. Lasting relationships were common, as students and parents have continued to exchange visits years after graduation and the closure of Wilson.

There were no eligibility rules for sports; students played as long as they were enrolled. There were no sets of textbooks, rows of desks facing the chalkboard, bells, notes from home, hall passes or study halls – all common in the Midwest in the Wilson era – and certainly no self-contained classrooms. Student teachers and master degree interns learned to "teach" – facilitate learning – by teaching at Wilson; they could be exempted from all the traditional college of education classes and still receive their degree and credential. Wilson was a special environment for those who chose to attend; it was unique among the educational alternatives of the 60s and 70s.

Personalized Continuous Year

The calendar at Wilson was simple. In theory the school was open 365 days a year, 24 hours each day. In facility/staff reality, it was somewhere between 225-240 days, the result of the faculty contracts with the college and the usual budget restraints. The mechanics were a simple formula: students "owed" the school 170 days (Minnesota requirement for financial support), minus illness and special consideration absences. They could attend any 170 of the 240 days the facility was open – or all 240 – or gain "credit" through approved off-campus ventures: rappelling in Colorado: French in Quebec: Sioux cultures at Pine Ridge.

With the curriculum completely personalized and individualized, students had flexibility. Staff had the same optional attendance choices. There was no coverage problem, as faculty worked in teams of teachers with whatever combination of aids, volunteers, and student interns was available at a given moment or budget year. If 600 students were enrolled, it was assumed that perhaps 500 would attend each day, and that three to five teachers might be absent. Therefore, balance was not a problem. Families/students/staff could vacation whenever they desired year-round – for a day, week, month, months – or even furlough for a year.

They did not even have to request permission – except for long periods (as furloughs). Most students informed their teachers and/or advisor, but if Dad could take two days off during hunting season, or had an opportunity to take the family on a business trip, or if Mom was ill and needed care, or if she just wanted them to go to "grandmothers," that was great. Staff had the same options. The year-round calendar schedules were completely <u>voluntary</u>. Wilson did not believe in the rigid <u>mandated</u> "vacation days" in the different single and multiple track plans – such as in the 60-20.

For schools overcrowded – where they must relieve <u>space</u> and be more accountable to parents/community/state – the Personalized Continuous Year was designed for implementation on a mandatory-with-options plan. Assuming 600 students in a school built for 450, families and staff request by 1st, 2nd, and 3rd choice the weeks they prefer their vacation days. They are told that most (exceptions are possible) must take some time off in the "winter" and be in school sometime during the "summer". The scheduling process assigns people according to their selections to ensure that 450 students and appropriate staff are in the building, and 150 youth and perhaps five faculty are on vacation for that week/month. Individual variations are permissible, as it does not actually matter whether the count is 140 or 160 youth, and four or seven teachers out, as long as an approximate balance is maintained.

Subject/grade level "matches" are not a problem, for all staff teach K-12 students; they function in 2nd or 3rd "subjects" as part of the interrelated curriculum, and work as members of teams. The only key is to ensure that at least one teacher who knows "science" well, and at least one who can 'hug' "kindergarten" children are in the building. The mandatory-with-options system is not theory – it works – and is not time consuming after the first year when the mechanical "bugs" are eliminated. The personalized YRE calendar is an exciting transition toward the future.

The "mechanics" which made Wilson a success – the 69 advertised changes – involved a glossary of concepts including personalized learning, individualized instruction, integrated curriculum, ad hoc student small groups, teacher small groups, team teaching and planning, differentiated staffing, non-graded age mixes, peer/cross age tutoring, independent study, open laboratory, occasional common thread large voluntary groupings, interrelated technology, non-scheduling, folders and portfolios, advisor and teacher selection, goal sheets, non-competitive testing as needed or desired, reference rather than textbooks, mini-vans rather than buses, no required courses, interdependent learning combinations, community volunteering, all day food service, optional attendance, open campus, no A, B, C report cards, responsibility and courtesy, and Imagineering.

The Wilson program exemplified the pioneering spirit of the early inventors. The Wright Brothers are but one example; they changed transportation and revolutionized the world. They were bicycle shop proprietors without a high school diploma. Certainly educators, with college degrees one hundred years later, can do more than restructure existing schooling.

Summary
        Wilson was not alone in being "special," nor was the format a program to adopt en masse by everyone, but it did assist many others in their beginning. It contributed richly to the history of yesterday, yet still has significance for today and tomorrow. For the former, it pleads for more year-round alternatives that are holistic, self-contained, and reach a wider cross-section of youth. For the latter, it clearly stands as a reminder that if the new learning concepts are to flourish in the years ahead, leaders must experiment. They must truly envision, continue greater efforts to explain the need for more choices for students, and unify their voices for multiple options. James Moffett in *The Universal Schoolhouse: Spiritual Awakening Through Education* (1994) confirmed this requirement, and the potential that does exist for those who are willing to quest. From a societal view, Duane Elgin, in *Awakening Earth* (1993) reflects the same message.

        Noble efforts over the past 40 years to create new approaches to learning have been witnessed. During the 60s in such diverse communities as Cambridge, MA; St. Paul and Minneapolis; Seattle and Portland; Berkeley; Ithaca, N.Y.; Grand Rapids, MI; Harlem, N.Y.; Denver; Louisville; Los Angeles; Las Vegas; University City, MO; Tucson; Ft. Lauderdale; Chicago; and Philadelphia – the listing could go on for several paragraphs – efforts were made which attest to the commitment visionaries in specific eras have had in their convictions to overcome the rigid traditional system of uniform schooling. Before these 60s versions were spotlighted, exciting programs occurred in such as Bluffton, IN (1900s); Gary, IN (1910s); Winnetka, IL and Nashville, TN (1920s); and the famous *Eight-Year Study* locations (1930s). A number of university laboratory schools of this century – Chicago, Ohio State, Northern Colorado, Florida, UCLA, Brigham Young, Indiana State, and Mankato State, as a sampling – contributed to the attempts to pilot new directions for education. Involved were many alternatives leaders as Nate Blackman at Chicago Metro, and Leonard Solo in Cambridge.

        But these are all part of the past, of which Wilson served as one historical portrait; it would be facing massive change, were it still open. The task now is to learn from this link to the past, and examine the present, but of greatest priority, is the creation of new futures for learning beyond 2000. There are lessons for the years ahead from the 1968-77 experiences of the Mankato Wilson Campus School, and the proposed Minnesota Experimental City.

BIBLIOGRAPHY

BIBLIOGRAPHY

There are many outstanding books, experimentation reports, and research studies which support the philosophy and program at Wilson. Section One following contains a small sampling of those completed predominately in the 1960 to early 1980s era – the period within which Wilson prospered. These focus on educational change.

Section Two identifies a brief sampling of the publications – several historically from prior decades, but most from the early 80s into the 90s focusing on societal and educational futures – which document the need to go beyond redesigning schooling, and instead, create the new learning systems that Wilson was advocating. **The Mankato School destroyed the myths that educators must follow tradition: rigid schedules, required classes, report cards, assigned teachers, standardized tests, self-contained classrooms, separate subjects and courses, and the multitude of other conventions.**

Wilson proved that the rituals of schooling could be abandoned, and that educators could address different approaches. **More importantly, the Wilson experiment confirmed that communities could Imagineer — that they could imagine, invent, and implement — a better future for learning.**

Section One

Aikin, Wilford *Story of the Eight-Year Study*, Harper and Brothers, New York, 1942

Alexander, William *The High School of the Future: A Memorial to Kimball Wiles*, Charles Merrill, Columbus, OH, 1969; *Innovations in Secondary Education*, 1970; and *The Exemplary Middle School*, 1981, both Holt, Rinehart and Winston, New York

Amidon, Edmund *Improving Teaching: The Analysis of Classroom Verbal Interaction*, Holt, Rinehart and Winston, New York, 1966

Anderson, Robert H. *Opting for Openness*, National Association of Elementary School Principals, Arlington, VA, 1973

Beggs, David *Flexible Scheduling*, 1965; and Team Teaching, 1964, both Indiana University Press, Bloomington, IN

Bellanca, James, and Sidney Simon *Degrading the Grading Myths: A Primer of Alternatives to Grades and Marks*, Association for Supervision and Curriculum Development, Arlington, VA, 1977

Benjamin, Harold *The Saber-Tooth Curriculum*, McGraw Hill, New York, 1939

Bloom, Benjamin *Stability and Change in Human Characteristics*, Wiley and Sons, New York,
1964

Blumberg, Arthur *The Effective Principal; Perspectives on School Leadership*, Longwood Division, Allyn and Bacon, Rockleigh, NJ, 1980

Bibliography

Bremer, Ann, and John Bremer *The School Without Walls: Philadelphia's Parkway Program*, Holt, Rinehart, and Winston, New York, 1971

Brown, B. Frank, (Commission on the Reform of Secondary Education), *The Reform of Secondary Education*, McGraw-Hill, New York, 1973

Combs, Arthur *Myths in Education: Beliefs that Hinder Progress and their Alternatives*, Allyn and Bacon, Boston, MA, 1979

Coombs, Philip *The World Educational Crisis: A System Analysis*, Oxford University Press, New York, 1968

Davis, Harold *How to Organize an Effective Team Teaching Program*, Prentice-Hall, Englewood Cliffs, NJ, 1966

Dennison, George *The Lives of Children*, Random House, New York, 1969

Downing, John *To Be Or Not To Be*, Pittman Publishing, New York, 1962

Duffy, Frank *Ungrading the Elementary School*, Parker Publishing, West Nyack, NY, 1966

Eight-Year Study, Progressive Education Association: Commission on Relations of Schools and Colleges, published as *Adventure in American Education Series*, Harper and Brothers, New York, 1942

Fantini, Mario *Public Schools of Choice: A Plan for the Reform of American Education*, Simon and Schuster, New York, 1973

Featherstone, Joseph *Schools Where Children Learn*, Liveright, New York, 1971

Freire, Paulo *The Pedagogy of the Oppressed*, Herder and Herder, New York, 1970; and *Education for Critical Consciousness*, Seabury Press, New York, 1973

Friedenberg, Edgar *The Vanishing Adolescent*, Beacon Press, Boston, MA, 1960

Frymier, Jack *A School for Tomorrow*, McCutchan Publishing, Berkeley, 1973

Gage, Ned *Teacher Effectiveness and Teacher Education*, Pacific Books, Palo Alto, CA, 1971

Gardner, John *Self-Renewal: The Individual and the Innovative Society*, Harper and Row, New York, 1964

Glasser, William *Schools Without Failure*, Harper and Row, New York, 1969

Glatthorn, Allan *Alternatives in Education: Schools and Programs*, Harper and Row, New York, 1975

Bibliography

Glines, Don *Creating Humane Schools* (1970); *Implementing Different and Better Schools* (1969), Campus Publishers, D. M. Printing Co., Mankato, MN; *Educational Futures I: Imagining and Inventing; Educational Futures II: Options and Alternatives; Educational Futures III: Change and Reality; Educational Futures IV: Updating and Overleaping; Educational Futures V: Foresighting and Creating*, Anvil Press, Millville, MN, 1978-1980

Goodlad, John, and Robert Anderson *Non-Graded Elementary School*, Harcourt, Brace, World, New York, 1959

Goodlad, John *Behind the Classroom Door*, Charles Jones Co, Worthington, OH, 1971

Goodman, Paul *Compulsory Mis-Education*, Vintage Books, New York, NY, 1962

Greenleaf, Robert *Servant Leadership*, Paulist Press, New York, 1977

Gross, Beatrice, and Ronald Gross, eds. *Radical School Reform*, Simon and Schuster, New York, 1969

Guba, Egon, and Yvonna Lincoln *Effective Evaluation*, Jossey-Bass, San Francisco, 1981

Havelock, Ronald *The Change Agent's Guide to Innovation in Education*, Educational Technology Publications, Englewood Cliffs, NJ, 1973

Hentoff, Nat *Our Children Are Dying*, Viking Press, New York, 1966

Herndon, James *The Way It Spozed To Be*, Simon and Schuster, New York, 1968

Holt, John *How Children Fail*, Pittman Publishing Co., New York, 1965

Howard, Eugene *School Discipline Desk Book*, Parker, West Nyack, NY, 1978

Illich, Ivan *De-Schooling Society*, Harper and Row, New York, 1971

Jenkins, John, and Edward Buffie *Curriculum Development in Nongraded Schools*, Indiana University Press, Bloomington, IN, 1972

Jennings, Wayne "Startling Delightful Research," *Kappan*, March 1977

Joseph, Stephen M., ed. *The Me Nobody Knows: Children's Voices from the Ghetto*, Avon Books, New York, 1969

Kimbrough, Ralph B. *Politics, Power, Polls, and School Elections*, McCutchan Publishing, Berkeley, 1971

Kohl, Herbert *The Open Classroom*, Random House, New York, 1969

Kozol, Jonathan *Death at an Early Age: The Destruction of the Hearts and Minds of Negro Children in the Boston Public Schools*, Bantam Books, New York, 1968

Bibliography

Lurie, Ellen *How to Change Schools: A Handbook for Parents*, Random House, New York, 1971

Martin, John Henry, and Charles Harrison *Free to Learn: Unlocking and Ungrading American Education*, Prentice-Hall, Englewood Cliffs, NJ, 1972

Miles, Matthew *Innovation in Education*, Teachers College Press, Columbia University, New York, 1964

Miller, Richard *Perspectives on Educational Change*, Appleton-Century-Crofts, New York, 1967

Mintz, Jerry, Edt. *Alternative Schools Handbook*, MacMillan, Solomon Press, New York, 1994

Morphet, Edgar, Edt. *Planning and Effecting Needed Changes in Education*, Designing Education for the Future, Council of State School Chiefs, Denver, 1967

Napier, Rod *Wad-Ja-Get?*, Hart Publishing, New York, 1971

National School Boards Association *Alternative Education*, Arlington, VA, 1976

Neill, A. S. *Summerhill*, 1960; and *Freedom, Not License*, 1966, both Hart, New York

Ovard, Glen Change and the *Secondary School Administrator*, MacMillan, New York, 1968

Piaget, Jean *To Understand is to Invent: The Future of Education*, Viking Press, New York, 1974

Postman, Neil, and Charles Weingartner *Teaching as a Subversive Activity*, Delacorte Press, New York, 1968

Rasberry, Salli, and Robert Greenway *Rasberry Exercises*, Freestone Publishing Company, Freestone, CA, 1971

Reimer, Everett *School is Dead*, Doubleday, New York, 1971

Rogers, Carl *Freedom to Learn*, Charles Merrill Publishers, Columbus, OH, 1969

Rogers, Everett *Diffusion of Innovation*, Free Press, New York, 1962

Rosenthal, Robert *Pygmalion in the Classroom*, Holt, Rinehart and Winston, New York, 1968

Rubin, Louis *Curriculum Handbook: Administration and Theory*, Allyn and Bacon, Boston, MA, 1974

Russell, James *Change and Challenge in American Education*, Houghton Mifflin, Boston, MA, 1965

Bibliography

Saxe, Arthur *Schools Don't Change*, Philosophical Library, New York, 1967

Schoolboys of Barbiana *Letter to a Teacher*, Random House, New York, 1970

Seldin, Clement *Schools-Within-Schools: An Answer to the Public School Dilemma*, Blythe-Pennington LTD, Croton-On-Hudson, New York, 1978

Silberman, Charles *Crisis in the Classroom*, Random House, New York, 1970

Solo, Len *Alternative, Innovative and Traditional Schools: Some Personal Views*, University Press of America, Lanham, MD, 1980

Stufflebeam, Daniel, et al. *Educational Evaluation and Decision Making*, Peacock Publishers, Itasca, IL, 1971

Summary of Research on Open Education, Educational Research Service, Arlington, VA, 1975

Taylor, Harold *How to Change Colleges: Notes on Radical Reform*, Holt, Rinehart and Winston, New York, 1971

Thelan, Herbert A. *Education and the Human Quest*, University of Chicago Press, Chicago, 1972

Thomas, George Isaiah *Administrator's Guide to the Year-Round School*, Parker Publishing, West Nyack, NY, 1973

Torrance, E. Paul *Encouraging Creativity in the Classroom*, Wm. G. Brown Publishers, Dubuque, IA, 1972

Trump, J. Lloyd *A School for Everyone*, National Association Secondary School Principals, Reston, VA, 1977; and *Guide to Better Schools: Focus on Change*, Rand McNally, Chicago, 1961

Van Til, William, ed. *Curriculum: Quest for Relevance*, Houghton Mifflin, Boston, 1971; and *My Way of Looking at It*, Lake Lure Press, Box 316, Terre Haute, IN, 1983

Veatch, Jeannette *How to Teach Reading with Children's Books*, Teachers College Press, Columbia University, New York, 1964

Washburne, Paul *Winnetka - The History and Significance of an Educational Experiment*, Prentice-Hall, Englewood Cliffs, NJ, 1963

Weber, Lillian *English Infant School and Informal Learning*, Prentice-Hall, Englewood Cliffs, NJ, 1971

Weinstock, Ruth, ed. *Alternative Schools: Pioneering Districts Create Options for Students*, National School Public Relations Association, Arlington, VA, 1973

Bibliography

Weisgerber, Robert A., ed. *Developmental Efforts in Individualized Learning*, Peacock Publishers, Itasca, IL, 1971

Wiles, Kimball *The Changing Curriculum of the American High School*, Prentice-Hall, Englewood Cliffs, NJ, 1963

Williams, Emmett *The Emergent Middle School*, Holt, Rinehart and Winston, New York, 1967

Willis, Margaret *Guinea Pigs: 20 Years Later*, Ohio State University Press, Columbus, OH, 1961

Wirt, William *The Great Lockout in America's Citizenship Plants*, Horace Mann School Student Publishing, Gary, IN, 1937

York, Jean *Team Teaching* (A series of seven booklets on teaming aspects) The Leslie Press, Dallas, 1971

Section Two

Anderson, Robert and Barbara Pavan *Nongradedness: Helping It To Happen*, Technomic, Lancaster, PA, 1992

Barker, Joel *Future Edge: Discovering the New Paradigms*, Morrow, New York, 1992

Barnes, Ronald *Tomorrows Educator: An Alternative to Today's School Person*, Transitions, Inc. Prescott, AZ, 1977

Barney, Gerald, Edt. *Global 2000 Report to the President: Entering the 21st Century*, Pergamon Press, Elmsford, N.Y., 1980

Botkin, James *No Limits to Learning: Bridging the Human Gap*, Pergamon Press, Elmsford, NY, 1979

Boulding, Elise *The Underside of History: A View of Woman Through Time*, Westview Press, Boulder, 1976

Boulding, Kenneth E. *The Meaning of the Twentieth Century: The Great Transition*, Harper, New York, 1964

Bouvier, Leon *How Many Americans?* Sierra Books, San Francisco, 1994

Brown, Lester, et al. *Saving the Planet: How to Shape an Environmentally Global Economy*, W.W. Norten, New York, 1991; *Vital Signs: Trends Shaping the Future*, Worldwatch Institute, Washington DC, 1993; and *State of the World*, W.W. Norton, New York, 1994

Bundy, Robert, ed. *Images of the Future: The Twenty-First Century and Beyond*, Prometheus, New York, 1976

Bibliography

Caine, Geoffrey, et al. *Mindshifts: A Workbook on Brain Based Learning*, Association Supervision Curriculum Development, Alexandria, VA, 1991

Capra, Fritijof *The Turning Point: Science, Society, and the Rising Culture*, Simon and Schuster, New York, 1982

Cetron, Marvin et al. *Crystal Globe: The Haves and Have-Nots of the New World Order*, 1991, and *American Renaissance*, 2nd ed. 1994, both St. Martins Press, New York

Clarke, Arthur C. *Profiles of the Future: An Inquiry into the Limits of the Possible*, Holt, Rinehart and Winston, New York, 1984

Cohen, Ronald *Children of the Mill: Schooling and Society in Gary, Indiana*, Indiana University Press, Bloomington, 1990

Combs, Arthur *The Schools We Need: New Assumptions For Educational Reform*, University Press of America, Lanham, MD, 1991

Didsbury, Howard, Ed. *The Years Ahead: Perils, Problems, and Promises*, World Future Society, Bethesda, MD, 1993

Drucker, Peter F. *The Age of Discontinuity: Guidelines to Our Changing Society*, Harper, New York, 1969

Ehrlich, Paul and Ornstein, Robert, *New World New Mind*, Knowledge Systems, Indianapolis, 1991

Elgin, Duane *Awakening Earth: Exploring the Evolution of Human Culture and Consciousness*, William Morrow, New York, 1993

Elkins, David *Ties that Stress: Family Balance*, Harvard Press, Cambridge, 1994

Everhart, Robert *The Public Monopoly: A Critical Analysis of Education*, Ballinger Books, Cambridge, MA, 1982

Fadiman, Dorothy *Why Do These Kids Love School* (videotape), Concentric Media, 1070 Colby Ave., Menlo Park, CA, 1991

Ferguson, Marilyn *The Acquarian Conspiracy: Personal and Social Transformations in the 1980s*, J.P. Tarcher, Los Angeles, 1980

Ferkiss, Victor C. *The Future of Technological Civilization*, George Braziller, New York, 1974

Fisher, Jeffrey *RX2000: Breakthroughs in Health, Medicine, and Longevity*, Simon and Schuster, New York, 1992

Fuller, R. Buckminster *Critical Path*, St Martin's Press, New York, 1981

Bibliography

Fuller, R. Buckminster *Grandfather of the Future*, (video cassette), World Future Society, Bethesda, Maryland, 1990

Gang, Philip, et al. *Conscious Education*, Daqaz Press, Chamslee, GA, 1993

Gardner, Howard *Frames of Mind: The Theory of Multiple Intelligences*, Basic Books, NY, 1983

Goodlad, John *A Place Called School*, McGraw-Hill, New York, 1983

Greenberg, Daniel *Free At Last: The Sudbury Valley School* 2nd edt., Sudbury Valley Press, Framingham, MA, 1991

Harman, Willis W. *An Incomplete Guide to the Future*, W.W. Norton, New York, 1979

Harrington, Michael *The Politics at God's Funeral: The Spiritual Crisis of Western Civilization*, Holt, Rinehart and Winston, New York, 1983

Hart, Leslie *Human Brain and Human Learning*, Revised, Books for Educators, Tacoma, WA, 1990

Hawken, Paul, James Ogilvy, and Peter Schwartz *Seven Tomorrows: Toward a Voluntary History*, Bantam, New York, 1982

Heilbroner, Robert L. *An Inquiry Into the Human Prospect*, W.W. Norton, New York, 1974

Helmer, Olaf *Looking Forward: A Guide to Futures Research*, Sage Publications, Beverly Hills, 1983

Henderson, Hazel *Paradigms in Progress: Life Beyond Economics*, Knowledge Systems, Indianapolis, 1991

Houston, Jean *Life-Force: The Psycho-Historical Recovery of Self*, Delacorte Press, New York, 1981

Huxley, Aldous *The Human Situation*, Harper and Row, New York, 1977

Jantsch, Erich *The Self-Organizing Universe*, Pergamon Press, New York, 1980

Joyce, Bruce *The Structure of Educational Change*, Longman, New York, 1983

Kidder, Rushworth *Shared Values For a Troubled World*, Jossey-Bass, San Francisco, 1994

Kozol, Jonathan *Savage Inequities: Children in America's Schools*, Crown Publishers, New York, 1991

Land, George and Jarman, Beth *Breakpoint and Beyond*, Harper Collins, Mew York, 1992

Bibliography

Lane, John and Edgar, Epps, eds. *Restructuring the Schools: Problems and Prospects*, McCutchan Publishing Co. Berkeley, 1992

Laszlo, Ervin *The Choice*, Tarcher/Putnam, New York, 1994

Long, Kathleen *Teacher Reflections on Individual School Restructuring: Alternatives in Public Education* (Dissertation), University of Oregon, Eugene, 1992

Marien, Michael *Future Survey* (Monthly and annual journal reviews of futures related books and articles), World Future Society, Bethesda, MD., 1993

Markley, O.W., and Willis W. Harman *Changing Images of Man*, Pergamon Press, New York, 1982

Masuda, Yoneji *The Information Society as Post-Industrial Society*, World Future Society, Bethesda, 1981

McHale, John *The Future of the Future*, George Braziller, New York, 1969

Meadows, Donella, et al. *Beyond the Limits: Confronting Global Collapse*, Envisioning a Sustainable Future, Chelsea Green Publishers, Boston, 1992

Michael, Donald N. *On Learning to Plan and Planning to Learn: The Social Psychology of Changing Toward Future-Responsive Societal Learning*, Jossey-Bass, San Francisco, 1973

Miller, Ron *What Are Schools For?* 2nd edition, Holistic Education Press, Brandon, VT, 1992

Moffett, James *The Universal Schoolhouse: Spiritual Awakening Through Education*, Jossey-Bass, San Francisco, 1994

Moorcroft, Shelia, Edt. *Visions for the 21st Century*, Adamantine Press, London, 1992

Mumford, Lewis *The Transformations of Man*, Harper, New York, 1956

Myers, Norman *Ultimate Security: The Environmental Basis of Political Stability*, W. W. Norten, New York, 1993

Nanus, Burt *Visionary Leadership*, Jossey-Bass, San Francisco, 1992

Nathan, Joe *Free to Teach*, 2nd edition, Pilgrim Press, New York, 1991

O'Neill, Gerard *2081: A Hopeful View of the Human Future*, Simon and Schuster, New York, 1981

Pignatelli, Frank and Pflaum, Susanne, edts. *Celebrating Diverse Voices & Progressive Education and Equity*, Bank Street College of Education, New York, 1993

Postman, Neil *The Surrender of Culture to Technology*, Alfred Knopf, New York, 1993

302

Bibliography

Sarason, Seymour *The Predictable Failure of Educational Reform*, Jossey-Bass, San Francisco, 1990

Satin, Mark *New Options for America*, California State University Press, Fresno, 1991

Scales, Peter *Windows of Opportunity: Middle School Teacher Preparation*, Center for Adolescence, University of North Carolina, Chapel Hill, 1992

Schell, Jonathan *The Fate of the Earth*, Knopf, New York, 1982

Schiller, Sherry *Dispelling Megatrend Myths*, Schiller Center, Alexandria, 1994

Schmookler, Andrew *Sowings and Reapings*, Knowledge Systems, Indianapolis, 1989

Shane, Harold G. *The Educational Significance of Future, 1973*; and "Educating for a New Millennium," 1981, *Phi Delta Kappa*, Bloomington, IN

Smith, Frank *Insult to Intelligence*, Arbor House, NY, 1986

Sloan, Douglas *Insight — Imagination*, Teachers College Press, New York, 1983

Teilhard de Chardin, Pierre *The Future of Man*, Harper, New York, 1964

Theobald, Robert *The Rapids of Change*, 1986; and *Turning the Century*, 1993, both, Knowledge Systems, Indianapolis

Thompson William Irwin *Darkness and Scattered Light: Speculations on the Future*, Anchor, New York, 1977

Toffler, Alvin, ed. *Learning for Tomorrow; The Role of the Future in Education*, Vintage, New York, 1974; and *The Third Wave*, Bantam, New York, 1981

Tough, Allen *Crucial Questions about the Future*, University Press of America, Lanhem, MD, 1991

Wagar, Warren *The Next Three Centuries*, Adamantine Press, London, 1992

Wilson Campus School Remembered, College of Education, Mankato State University, MN, 1992; *The Wilson Experience*, Performance Learning Systems, Nevada City, CA, 1994 (videos)

Wirth, Arthur *Education and Work for the Year 2000*, Jossey-Bass, San Francisco, 1992

Wood, George *Schools That Work: Teaching for Democracy*, E.P. Dutton, New York, 1992

RESOURCES

Center for Advanced Reform in Education, Rockhurst College, 1100 Rockhurst Road, Kansas City, MD, 64110

Center for Plain Living, P.O. Box 200, Burton, OH, 44021

City Innovation, 4900 IDS Tower, Minneapolis, MN, 55402

Commission on Restructuring, NASSP, 1904 Association Dr., Reston, VA, 22091

Community Learning Centers, 2550 University Ave. W., St. Paul, MN, 55114

Education Futurists Network, 5300 Glen Haven, Soquel, CA, 95073

Educators in Private Practice, N7425 Switzke, Watertown, WI, 53064

Envisioning Your Future, 3024 Sunnyside Rd., Bemidji, MN, 56601

Growing Without Schooling, 2269 Massachusetts, Cambridge, MA, 02140

Institute for Alternative Futures, 106 Alfred, Alexandria, VA, 22314

Learning Alternatives Network, 417 Roslyn Road, Roslyn Heights, NY, 11577

National Society for Experiential Learning, 3509 Haworth, Raleigh, NC, 27609

National Society for Study of Education, 5835 Kimbark, Chicago, IL, 60637

Performance Learning Systems, 224 Church Street, Nevada City, CA, 95959

Population Reference Bureau, 777-14th Street, N.W., Washington, D.C.

Resource Center for Redesigning Education, P.O. Box 818, Shelburne, VT, 05482

School Climate Association, 1922 S. Magnolia, Denver, CO, 80224

Self-Esteem Group, 6035 Bristol Parkway, Culver City, CA, 90230

Tranet Alternative Networks, Box 567, Rangeley, ME, 04970

World Council Institute, 777 United Nations Plaza, NY, 10017

World Future Society, 7910 Woodmont Ave., Suite 450, Bethesda, MD, 20814

Worldwatch Institute, 1776 Massachusetts Avenue, N.W., Washington, D.C., 20036

INDEX

INDEX

PERSONS

See also Historical References pp 249-254 and 276-277, as well as the Bibliography p 294 ff.

INDEX

TOPICS

ABOUT THE AUTHOR

Don Glines, Director of Educational Futures Projects, and a member of the World Future Society since 1968, has presented over 900 addresses and workshops on the future of education, innovation and change, educational alternatives, continuous year-round learning, and designs for the 21st Century.

He was the originator of the famous Wilson Campus School program as the research and development arm of the College of Education at Mankato, Minnesota, State University. While serving there as director of Wilson, and as co-director and professor of the Center for Alternatives and Experiential Learning, he was recognized by the National Observer as "one of the foremost apostles of educational innovation." The Wilson program was reported to be "probably the most innovative public school in America."

Dr. Glines has written 14 books on futures, change, year-round education, and alternatives; published 115 articles in such journals as *Education Leadership*, *Kappan*, *NASSP Bulletin*, *Thrust*, and *Instructor*; consulted with over 500 school districts in 53 states and countries; and appeared on numerous television and radio talk shows related to the future of education. He was probably the first person ever hired by a school district as a full-time consultant for innovation. In December, 1966, the *Phi Delta Kappan* referenced him as a "vice-president for heresy."

His passion has been that of a win-win philosophy of choice. He has long advocated the elimination of the 7th grade — the level, curriculum, structure, requirements, and organization, all of which he has stated are out of sync with the developmental ages of those youth. He was one of the prime movers in the creation of the true middle school plan, and in 1965 keynoted for 3,000 junior high principals the session on "The Future of the Middle School." His belief has been that if schools are to be significantly better, they must be significantly different. Toward that end, he consulted for the proposed Minnesota Experimental City (MXC) plan, a community of 250,000 persons with no schools, as schooling was to be replaced by learning.

In *Creating Educational Futures: Continuous Mankato Wilson Alternatives*, Don Glines has combined his knowledge of innovation and research from the 1900s to 1930s; the experimental programs of the 1960s and 1970s; and the designs and implementation processes at the Mankato Wilson School, with the societal and educational potentials for learning beyond 2000 — including such dreams as the MXC. It is a visionary manuscript — weaving the past with the future — while offering successful methods from a practicing educator and career change agent.

Dr. Glines completed his B.S. at Springfield College, Massachusetts, and his M.S. and Ph.D. degrees at the University of Oregon. He has worked in California, Oregon, Missouri, Colorado, South Dakota, Minnesota, Pennsylvania, New Hampshire, Spain, Taiwan, Germany, and Haiti. His experiences have led to citations in over ten honorary publications, including *Who's Who in American Education*, *Outstanding Educators of America*, and the *Futures Research Directory*. He was one of four in the nation selected in 1982 to receive the initial Year-Round Education Four Seasons Hall of Fame Award. A long held commitment has been assisting with the essential transformation from schooling to learning — designing new concepts for the next century.